Rocky Neck Art Colony
1850–1950

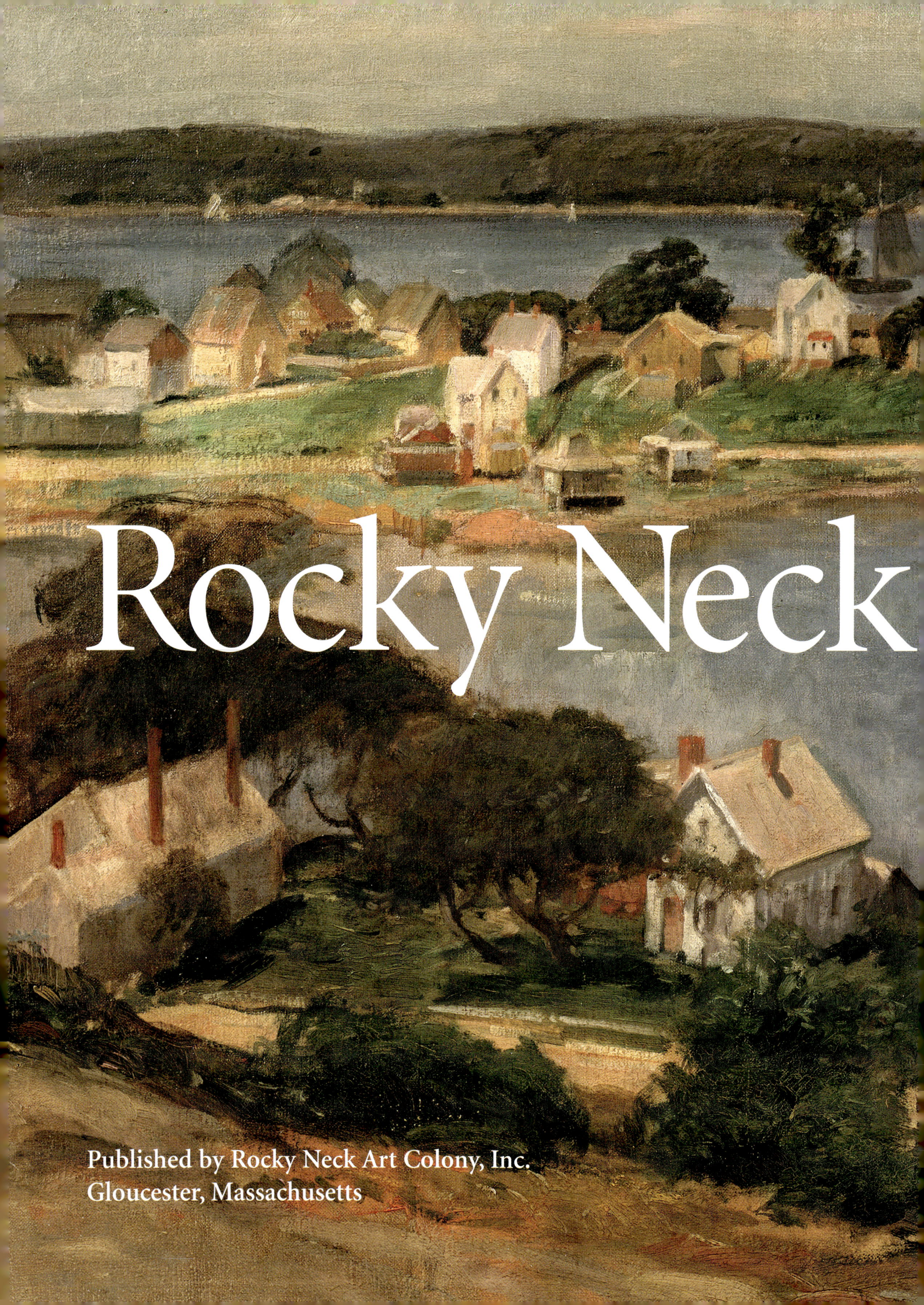

Rocky Neck

Published by Rocky Neck Art Colony, Inc.
Gloucester, Massachusetts

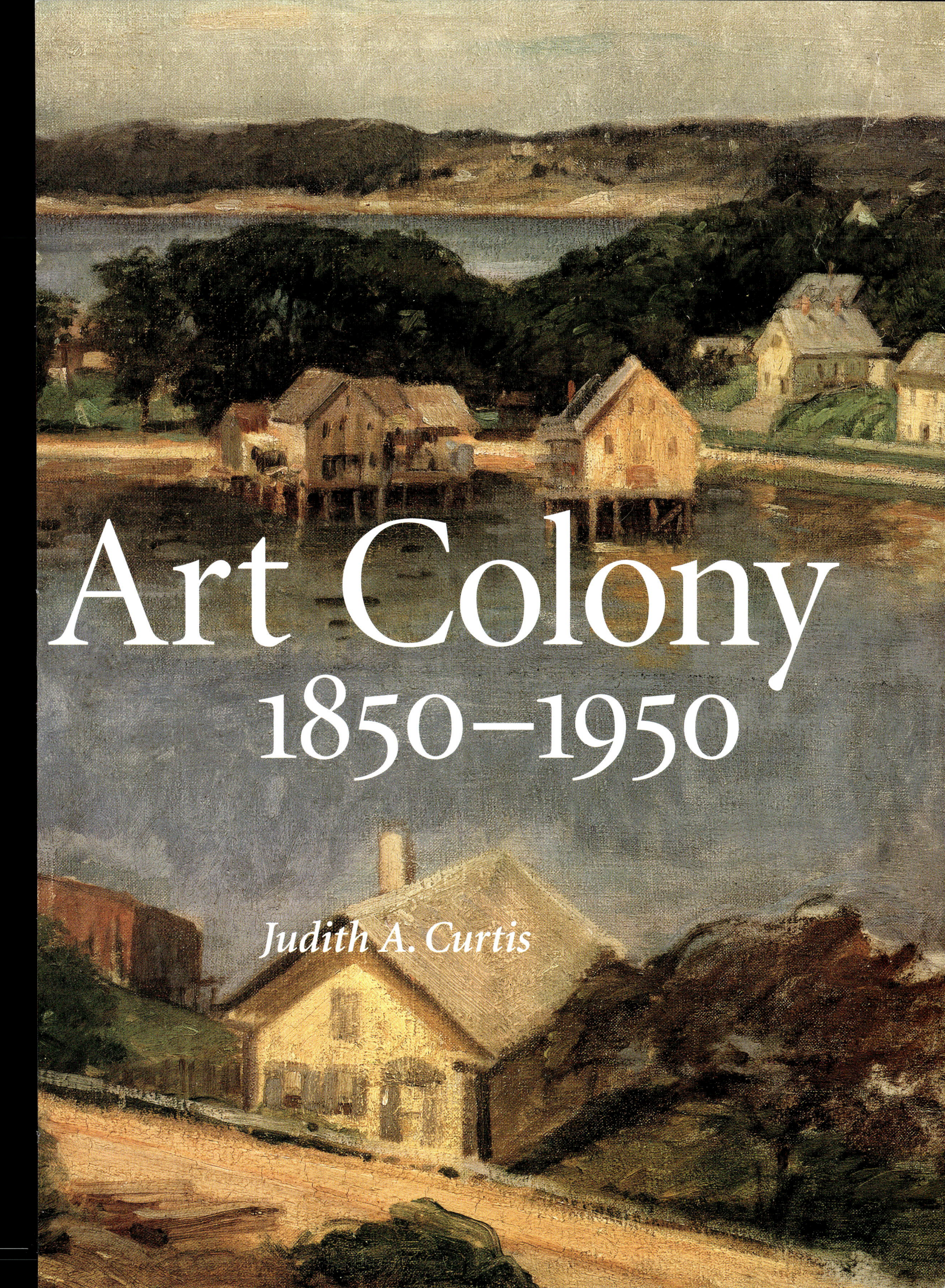

Art Colony 1850–1950

Judith A. Curtis

Published by Rocky Neck Art Colony, Inc.
PO Box 60, Gloucester, MA 01931

ISBN-13: 978-0-9794505-0-1

Design and production by Stephen Bridges, bridgesdesign@comcast.net
Typeset in Adobe Minion
Printed in China by Regent Publishing Services Limited, Hong Kong

Distributed to the book and gift markets by Commonwealth Editions
Beverly, Massachusetts 01915
Visit www.commonwealtheditions.com

Jacket illustration (front)
Willard LeRoy Metcalf
Gloucester Harbor, 1895
Oil on canvas, 26⅛ x 29¼ in.
Mead Art Museum, Amherst College,
Amherst, Massachusetts (ACP.1932.16)
Gift of George D. Pratt, class of 1893

Jacket illustration (back)
Joseph Rodefer DeCamp, N.A.
Seascape, 1891
Oil on canvas, 25 x 30 in.
Farnsworth Art Museum,
Rockland, Maine
Museum purchase, 1944 (44.409)
Photo: Melville D. McLean

Title pages 2-3 (detail)
Frank Duveneck, N.A.
Smith Cove from Banner Hill, c. 1905
Oil on canvas, 25 x 36 in.
Private collection
Photo courtesy of Owen Gallery,
New York

Contents

Dedication

This book is dedicated to Helen Wessel, and the memory of her dear husband, Robert Wessel, with grateful thanks from the Rocky Neck Art Colony for making this historical book project possible.

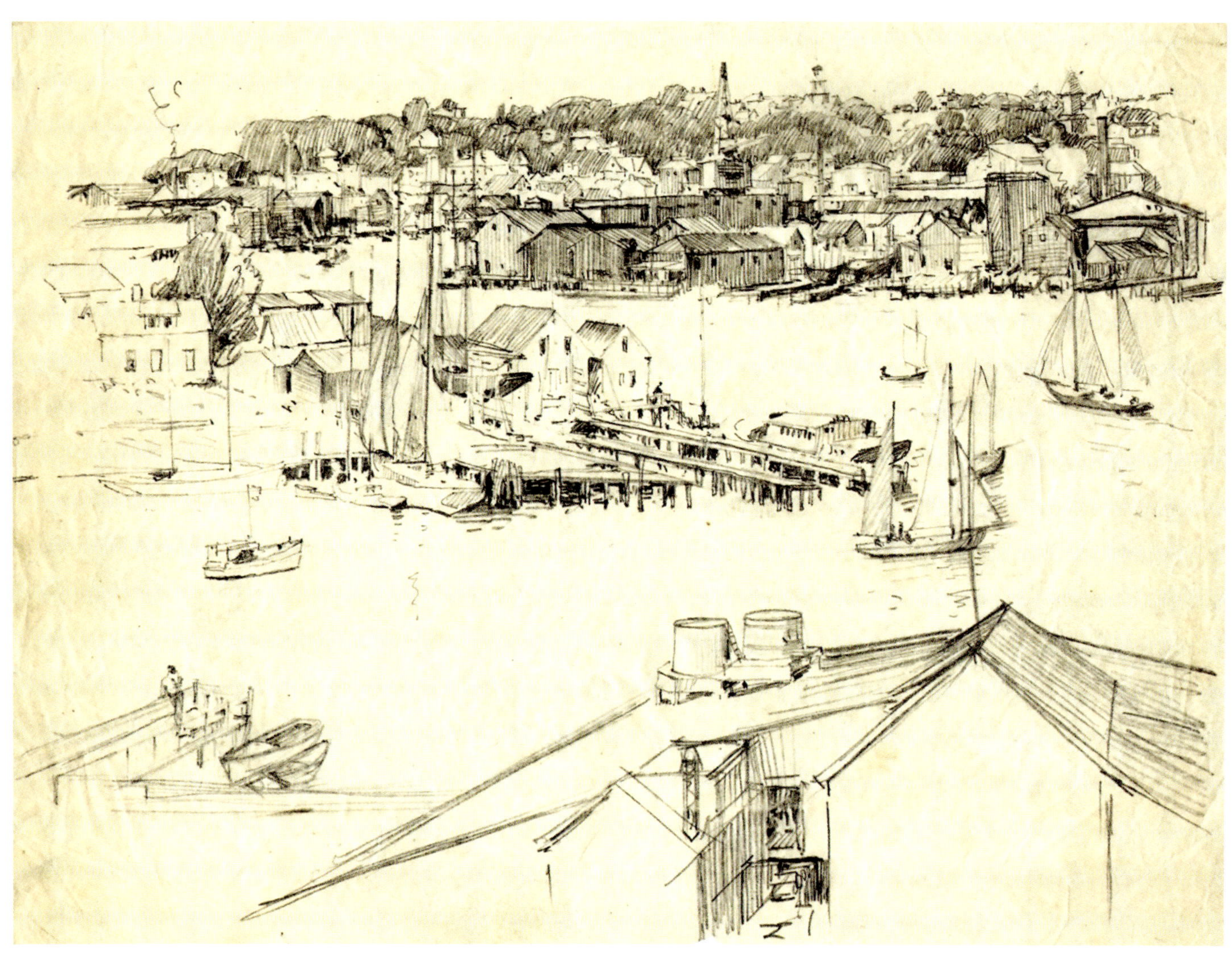

Herman H. Wessel
Drawing A
Pencil on paper, 8½ x 11 in.
Collection of Wessel House Archives, Cincinnati, Ohio

Preface

When the Rocky Neck Art Colony Historical Book Project was first conceived several years ago by Helen Wessel and then RNAC president Martha Ingalls, the intention was to perpetuate in prose and painting something of the history and ambiance of the area, and to discern what drew so many artists to this Avalon, which ultimately became a cradle of painters, poets and visionaries. Rocky Neck, in Gloucester Harbor, Massachusetts, has played a vital role in the nation's art history since the mid-1800s. For more than a century—beginning with marine artist Fitz Henry Lane—this bustling seaport, the oldest working harbor in the nation, has nurtured and inspired the artistic. With Cape Ann's unique luminescent glow and rugged topography, Rocky Neck offered everything the plein air painter could want. In addition, the dichotomy between the hardy fishermen and the genteel summer visitors resulted in the artists banding together to form their own sense of community, and so was born the art colony at Rocky Neck.

This small spit of land—a virtual island in the beginning when locals had to wait for low tide before they could cross Peter Mud's Neck—has been accessible to all since the raising of the causeway a century and a half ago. And it was that very accessibility to a sparsely populated area (there were fewer than one hundred and fifty inhabitants living among the sheep pastures in 1859) that lured the creative soul to admire and recreate its simple beauty, in an atmosphere thick with the essence of fish and salt and the sweet heady smell of clethra drifting across the moorland. The arrival of the electric trolley in the late 1890s, dropping its passengers at the junction of Wonson Street and Rocky Neck Avenue, made the art colony ever more accessible and, for a while, brought the world to the doors of the Rocky Neck artists. And because so many of those artists came from Boston, New York, Cincinnati and Europe—beginning with Homer's first visit in 1873, the coming of Frank Duveneck and his coterie, plus the arrival of John Sloan, Stuart Davis and the New York contingent—Rocky Neck evolved into a microcosm of American art that has never been surpassed.

It is, of course, impossible to include everyone who contributed to the artistic atmosphere of Rocky Neck over the years; however, I have tried to include a cross-section from some of the best-known names in American art to lesser known, but no less talented, artists such as Agnes Richmond, Alice Schille, and Herman and Bessie Wessel. No slight is intended to those artists not included in this book. The intention was not to write a definitive history of Rocky Neck, but to paint a picture of the characters and their traditions of excellence that created the colony in the beginning. These traditions are most ably carried on today by the present members of the Rocky Neck Art Colony.

Acknowledgments

I would like to extend my grateful thanks to all those who have helped during the writing of this book. Special thanks go to my husband, David, my sons, Noah and Sam, and my mother-in-law, Winifred J. Curtis, all of whom were a constant source of encouragement and support during the more stressful moments of bringing this project to fruition.

I would also like to thank the following museums, galleries, organizations, private collectors, and other individuals for their generous support when I was researching information and seeking reproductions. Most especially I would like to thank Helen Wessel and the Wessel Foundation without whose munificence none of this would have been possible.

E. Bonnie Akerley; Art Resource; Dr. and Mrs. Joel E. Berenson; Blue Heron Gallery; Westin Boer; Boston Art Club; Stephen Bridges; Brooklyn Museum; Bryan Memorial Gallery; Cape Ann Historical Association; Charles G. Martignette Collection of American Illustration Art; Cincinnati Art Galleries; Cincinnati Art Museum; Comenos Fine Arts; The Crane Collection; Winifred J. Curtis; Farnsworth Art Museum; Ann Fisk; Florence Griswold Museum; James B. Hand Fine Art; Harry Haworth of Dancing Shadow Fine Art Photography; High Museum of Art; Hollis Taggart Galleries; Martha J. Ingalls; Jack Kane; Roger King Gallery of Fine Art; Kenton County Public Library, KY; Keny Galleries; Knoke Fine Arts; Ann Lainhart; Lepore Fine Arts; Ward Mann; Walter Manninen; Marilyn Pink Fine Art; Mead Art Museum; MME Gallery, NY; Mosher Gallery; John Mullen; Amanda Nash; Mr. and Mrs. Tom Nicholas; Norton Museum of Art; Thomas O'Keefe III; Owen Gallery; Margaret L. Pearson; Pennsylvania Academy of the Fine Arts; Pierce Galleries; Dr. Matthew Panagiotu; Mr. and Mrs. Sam Robbins; Rockport Art Association; Carl and Carol Samson; Robert N. Shapiro; Spanierman Gallery, LLC; Michael Storella; Ted Tysver; Terra Foundation for American Art; Mr. and Mrs. William H. Trayes; Tibor de Nagy Gallery; Vose Galleries; Washington County Museum of Fine Arts; Helen Wessel; Peter Williams.

Judith A. Curtis
Gloucester, Massachusetts
August 2007

George H. Story, A.N.A. (1835-1923)
Meadow at East Gloucester, 1887
Watercolor, 12 x 18 in.
Cape Ann Historical Association,
Gloucester, Massachusetts

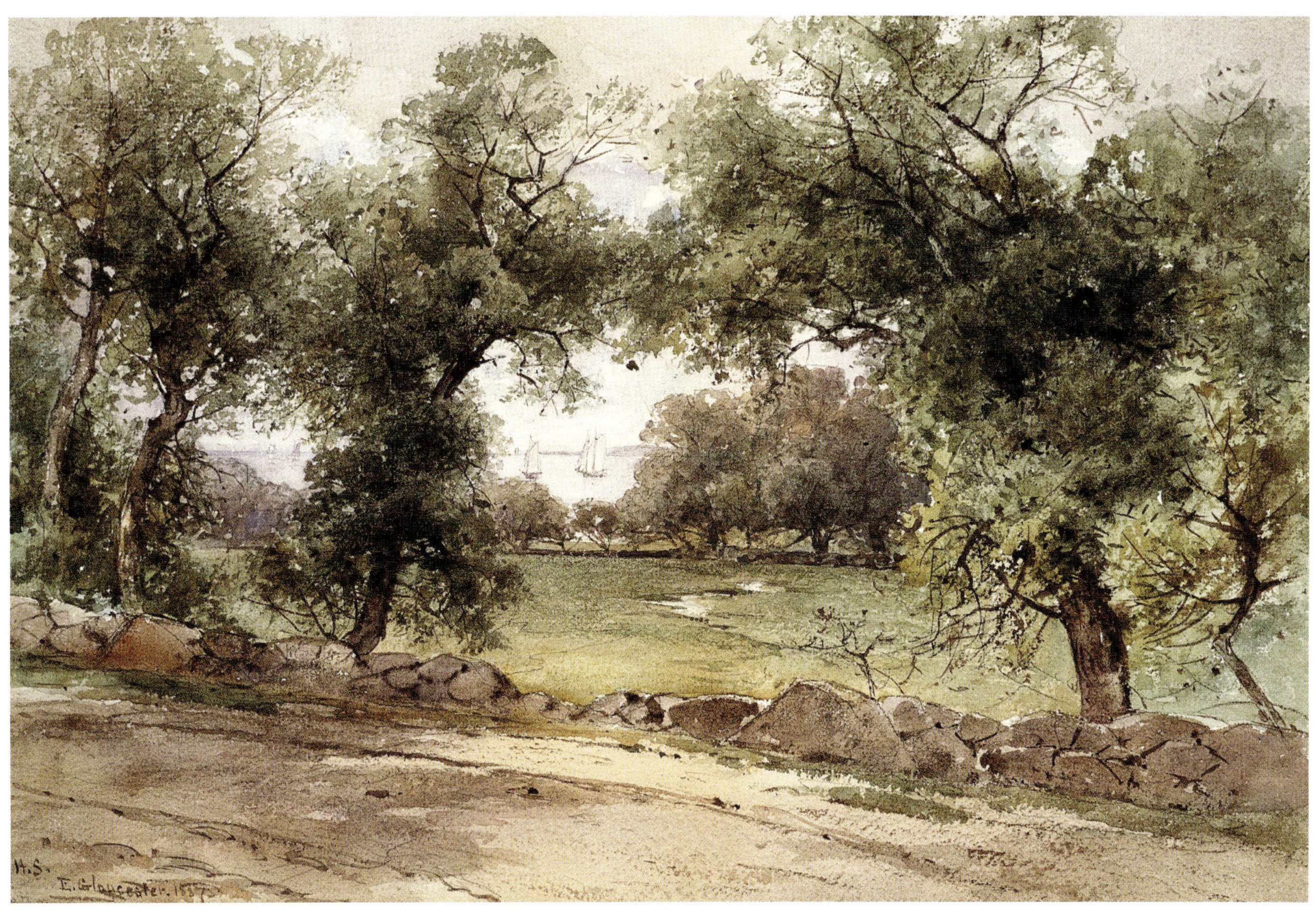

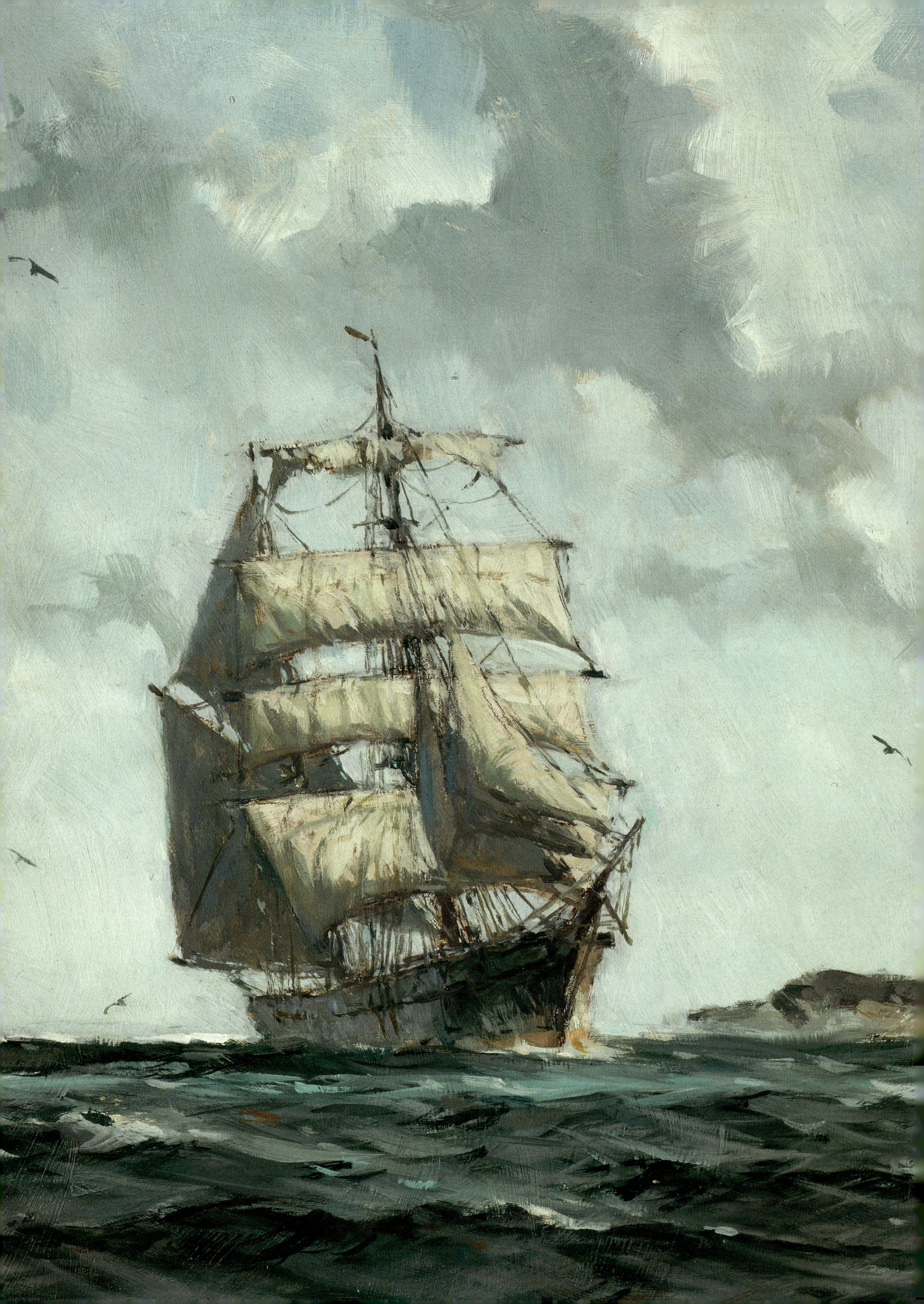

The Art Colony at Rocky Neck

"Our whole life is given to looking at little things.
We refuse to see broadly, to grasp a whole."

—William Morris Hunt, *On Painting and Drawing*

Rocky Neck—a small spit of land jutting into Gloucester's inner harbor on Cape Ann, Massachusetts—has a singular position in the annals of American art. Few other regions can boast such a rich and eclectic complement of artists, whether homegrown or just passing through, as can this small yet enticing peninsula. So, what is Rocky Neck's secret? Is it something in the water, or in the air? Regardless, Rocky Neck's popularity with the American artist can only be described as an enduring attraction between the creatively inclined and creation itself, for the fundamental nature emanating from this Avalon goes far beyond mere ambiance.

Rocky Neck, or Peter Mud's Neck as it was called in the 1600s, is practically an island. In the beginning, it was joined to the world by stepping-stones at low tide, but now travelers find it more convenient to use the Causeway, which was raised a century and a half ago to make the passage across more convenient. Cape Ann itself is an island, a granite gem surrounded by water—its umbilical cord sliced through at the Cut, the canal at the entrance to the Cape—separated from the mainland like a headstrong child distancing itself from its mother. Only the Blynman Drawbridge and the advent of the railroad in 1847 kept Cape Ann connected to the rest of America until the middle of the twentieth century when a state highway and the A. Piatt Andrew Bridge were constructed to span the Annisquam River.

Since its settlement, Cape Ann, "a microcosm fighting to remain unspoiled,"[1] has clung to the rugged individuality that first proclaimed it. Dubbed Cap aux Trois Îsles[2] by French explorer Samuel de Champlain, and later Tragabigzanda by English adventurer John Smith, the land received its final appellation in 1624 when Prince Charles—later Charles I of England—peremptorily named the cape after his mother, Queen Ann. There have been suggestions that Cape Ann may be the location of fabled Vinland, the lost colony of the Vikings, which Thorwald was seeking when he apparently met an untimely death in a skirmish with unfriendly locals.[3]

Whether Thorwald was truly here is immaterial. This stuff of myth and legend—it does not take an enormous leap of faith to imagine Thorwald striding hereabouts among the oaks and vines—instills this glacial outcropping with an air of mystery; thus, the essence of inspiration stirs the imagination and augments the cape's enduring appeal.

For almost two centuries now Cape Ann has inspired countless artists, sculptors, writers and musicians. Some were born here; others visited and then remained, while still more migrated here every summer from diverse parts. Fitz Henry Lane—formerly known as Fitz Hugh Lane—is considered the first and foremost Gloucester artist. Native born in 1804, Lane made a successful career for himself as a lithographer in

Detail
Gordon Grant
Return to Port, c. 1940s
Oil on panel, 12 x 16 in.
Collection of Tom and Gloria Nicholas

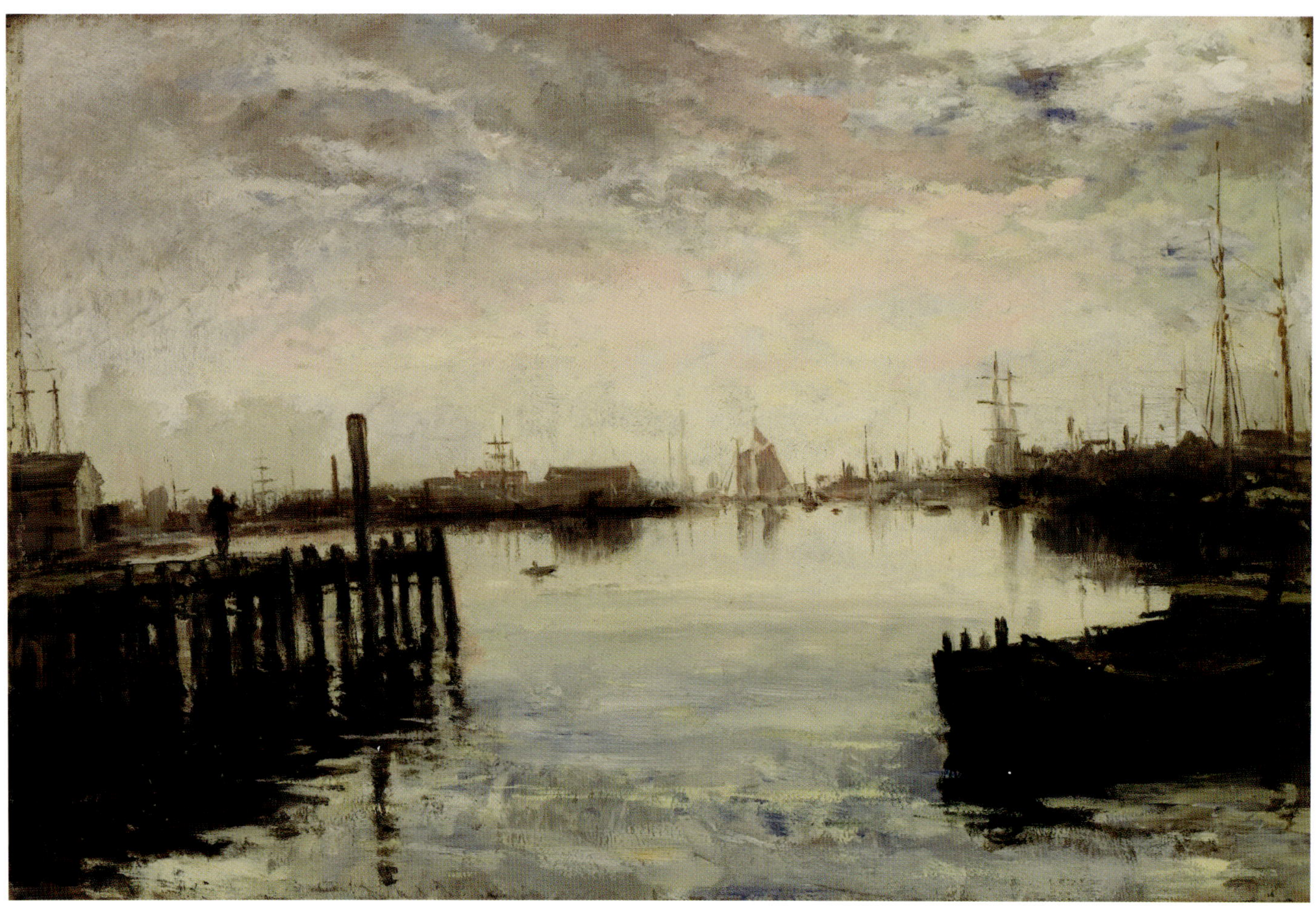

William Morris Hunt
Gloucester Harbor, 1877
Oil on panel, 21¼ x 31 in.
Brown-Corbin Fine Art, Lincoln, Massachusetts
Photo: Kwesi Arthur

Boston, but returned to his home town to devote himself to painting, and so began the romanticizing of Gloucester Harbor in stunning canvases of luminescent light evocative of the Hudson River School. Today, we are grateful to Lane, and those who followed—such as Winslow Homer, Stephen Parrish, A. W. Buhler and Walter L. Dean—for leaving us not only eloquent works of art, but also a painterly record of the past.

Lane, who died in 1865, is credited with only one serious student during his lifetime, and it was Barbizon painter William Morris Hunt who first introduced the area to a wider artistic audience in the mid-1870s, when he set up a studio in Magnolia, just across the harbor from Rocky Neck yet still within the purview of Gloucester. Hunt (1824-1879), a great innovator and an admirer of Millet and Corot, favored the realistic depiction of landscape en plein air. He was a well-respected teacher, and one of his most promising students, Elizabeth Boott, later married Frank Duveneck, the German-American painter who at the turn of the century became a major influence in establishing the art colony at Rocky Neck in East Gloucester.

During the mid-1870s, however, artists were still something of a rarity among the regular population. Hunt came to Cape Ann seeking suitable landscape compositions and found not only uncorrupted views, but a rare quality of light and atmosphere that bathed the area in a pure glow. Hunt's contribution to American art included a vital infusion of French aestheticism coupled with an appreciation of the sweeping nature of the American landscape. During his time here, Hunt discovered the fleeting moments of flawless luminosity that make Cape Ann unique. On one occasion, he was euphoric enough to announce "I believe that I have painted a picture with light in it!"[4]

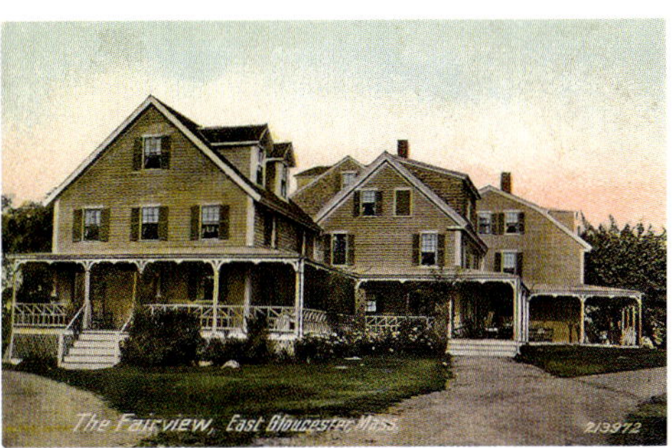

Fairview Inn
Postcard by The Leighton & Valentine Co., New York City, c. 1912
Private collection

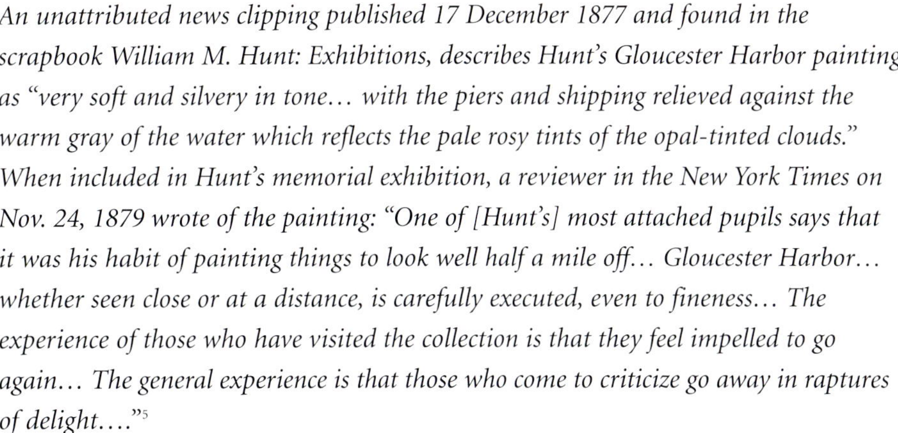

An unattributed news clipping published 17 December 1877 and found in the scrapbook William M. Hunt: Exhibitions, describes Hunt's Gloucester Harbor painting as "very soft and silvery in tone... with the piers and shipping relieved against the warm gray of the water which reflects the pale rosy tints of the opal-tinted clouds." When included in Hunt's memorial exhibition, a reviewer in the New York Times on Nov. 24, 1879 wrote of the painting: "One of [Hunt's] most attached pupils says that it was his habit of painting things to look well half a mile off... Gloucester Harbor... whether seen close or at a distance, is carefully executed, even to fineness... The experience of those who have visited the collection is that they feel impelled to go again... The general experience is that those who come to criticize go away in raptures of delight...."[5]

Hunt's arrival on the cape was not universally acclaimed among the local fishing worthies, who were uncertain of what to make of this bohemian character. This may have been exacerbated by his penchant for wearing signs saying, "I can't talk," and "I can't hear," to discourage spectators. Fortunately, a Gloucester lady of some refinement who owned property in the area, assured them Hunt was a notable artist and his coming would only strengthen the reputation of the area.[6] Hunt, however, was drowned two years later in a tragic accident on Appledore, one of the Isles of Shoals, and without its charismatic leader, the art colony at Magnolia drifted apart, in much the same way as Hunt's beloved studio, affectionately named "The Hulk."

If Magnolia viewed Hunt with initial trepidation, the port of Gloucester—perhaps because of its own cosmopolitan makeup—positively embraced the arrival of transient summer visitors. Visitors provided not only an influx of wealth into the city's economy, but also offered an endless topic of conversation among the locals who were, for the most part, of European heritage and temperament, with an Old World appreciation for the arts. Rudyard Kipling found the ethnicity of Gloucester an ideal background for his celebrated seafaring novel, *Captains Courageous,* published in 1897. He made several brief visits to Gloucester between 1894 and 1896, collecting color for his novel, and generally favored East Gloucester's Fairview Inn with his presence.

The Fairview Inn was always in demand by summer visitors, but the Beachcroft, the Hawthorne, the Harbor View and the Rockaway were also popular. These were idyllic days, fanned by gentle sea breezes. During Kipling's visits, "he would gather [the children] on the piazza on a warm afternoon, under the shade of an ancient apple tree, and recount to them many a ballad and tale which held the little ones entranced. There must be a number... who, as children, came under the master storyteller's spell in those days spent on the East Gloucester moor land."[7] One can imagine the artists doing much the same thing, congregating on the porch after supper to swap stories and discuss the idiosyncrasies of the art world.

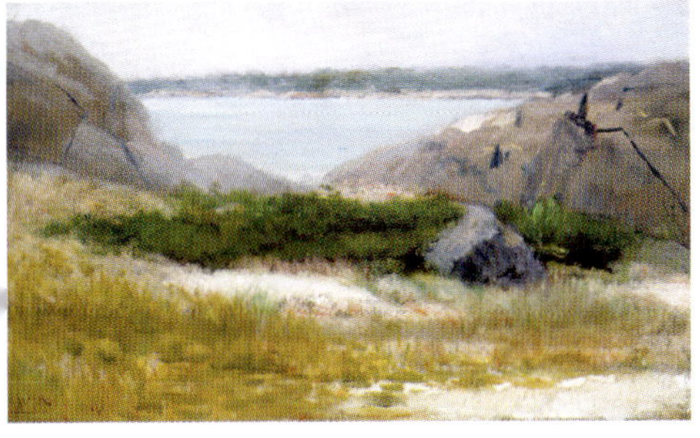

Helen Mary Knowlton
Rockbound Coast
Oil on canvas, 12 x 20 in.
Vose Galleries, Boston

Due to a dearth of gallery space in Gloucester in the late 1800s, hotels would often host exhibitions of their patrons' work. On one occasion, after Hunt's favorite student, Helen Mary Knowlton, was taken ill, the artists of the fledgling East Gloucester colony rallied to help arrange an auction of her paintings at the Hawthorne Inn to help pay her medical bills.[8] This support for a needy colleague—a tangible expression of genuine camaraderie in the colony—typifies the congeniality and affection that most of the artists had for one another.

East Gloucester had much to offer visiting artists from the tranquil ambiance of a warm summer day to the fury of the ocean boiling over in the turmoil of a raging nor'easter. These rampaging seas were beloved by marine painters such as Frederick Waugh and Winslow Homer.

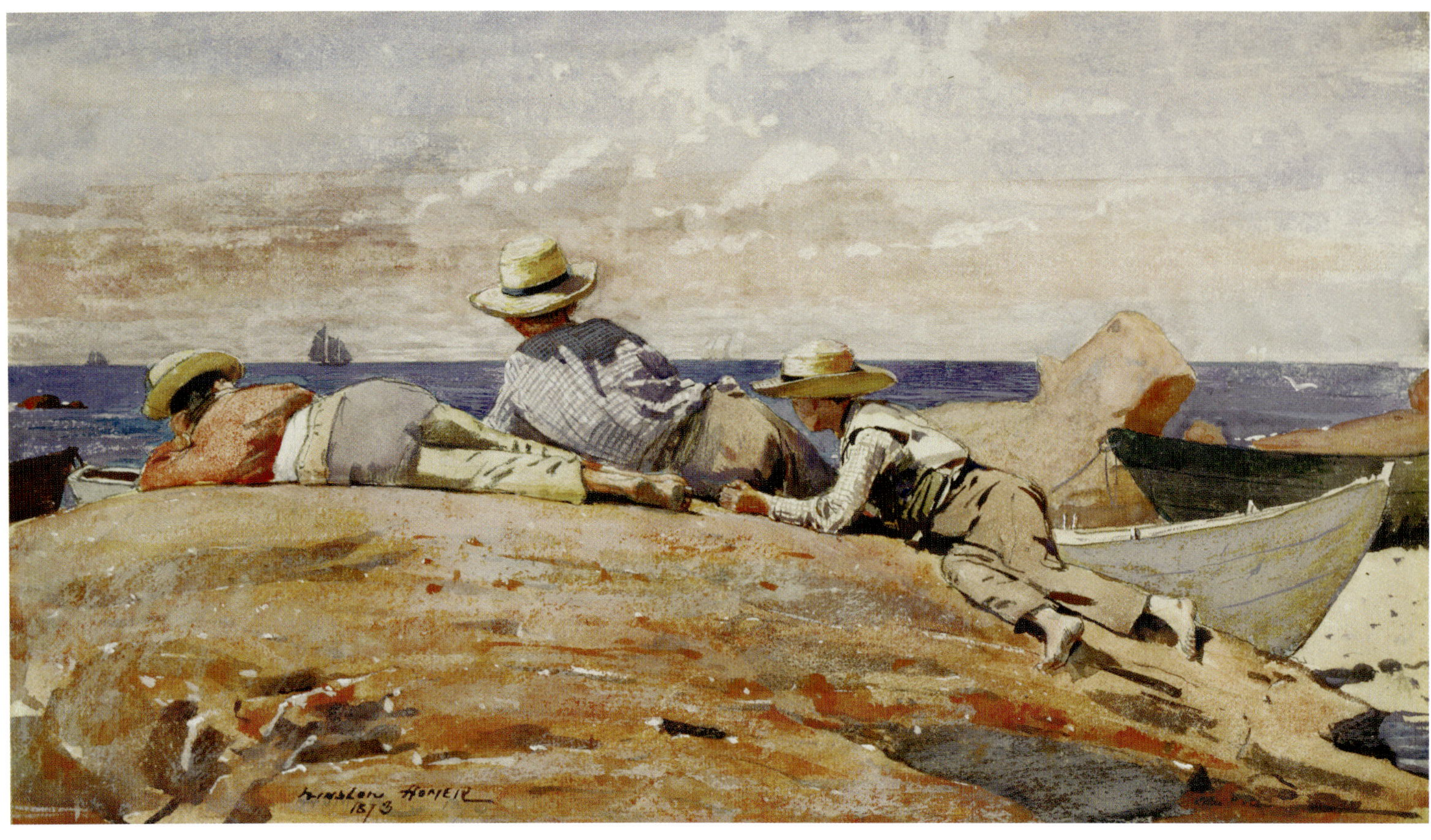

Winslow Homer
Three Boys on the Seashore, 1873
Gouache and watercolor on paper mounted on board, 8⅝ x 13⅝ in.
Daniel J. Terra Collection (1999.75)
Terra Foundation for American Art, Chicago
Photo: Terra Foundation for American Art, Chicago / Art Resource, NY

Winslow Homer, N.A., A.W.S. (1836–1910)

Winslow Homer came to Gloucester in June 1873 when he was already celebrated for his prowess as an illustrator. Mention of his visit was made in the Cape Ann Advertiser on August 22 of that year: "Winslow Homer, the artist, has been summering at the Atlantic House. Several bright sea-side sketches in Harper's Weekly will prove that he has not been idle."[9] Homer had, in fact, executed a whole series of watercolors during his two-month stay, a series that depicts his first serious use of the medium. It was also on this first visit to Gloucester that the world of children, idling or at play, became a focal point of his work. Discovering a successful bond between theme and medium, Homer went on to perfect this combination over the years and he is now considered to be America's premier watercolorist.

Whether Homer chose to depict childhood as a conscious sop to his own longings —he remained unmarried and childless throughout his career—or whether he saw it as a commercially viable theme for a nation emerging, shaken, from the Civil War and anxious to return to the idyllic days of a more rustic era, is uncertain. However, we do know that he developed, over a half dozen years, a unique watercolor manner that has never been equaled. *Three Boys on the Seashore,* painted in 1873 during Homer's first visit to Gloucester, is executed with a warm palette of strong color and fluid brushstrokes. Although at this point in his career, Homer was better known for his oil paintings and illustrations, he took to the subtler medium of watercolor without hesitation. Painting in natural light, Homer utilized the possibilities of the medium by employing opaque color and gouache rather than attempting the subtleties of a transparent wash. Prime color notes and elegant draftsmanship characterize Homer's watercolors, enabling him to capture both atmosphere and movement.

At nineteen, Homer was apprenticed to a Boston lithographer, and at twenty-one, he set up as an independent illustrator in his own studio. For one who had little artistic training, Homer combined inherent ability and a desire to create to become one of America's best-loved artists. His only concession to formal study was his attendance, for a month, of Saturday night classes with French artist Frédérick Rondel at New York's National Academy of Design.[10] While this lack of academic art training allowed Homer a certain freedom of vision to portray life with simple veracity, it also brought some disparagement from the critics. In 1875, Henry James, Jr., who was offended by Homer's unsophisticated manner, wrote, "Before Mr. Homer's little barefoot urchins and little girls in calico sunbonnets... the whole effort of the critic is instinctively to contract himself up, as it were, so that he can creep into the problem and examine it humbly and patiently, if a trifle wonderingly."[11]

In the face of such disparagement, it is perhaps not surprising that the artist became more reclusive. When Homer returned to Gloucester in 1880, for his second and last visit to Gloucester, he chose to stay with the lighthouse keeper on Ten Pound Island in the middle of Gloucester Harbor, rather than downtown at the Atlantic House. However, regardless of the reasons for his seclusion, Homer found much to interest him from his new vantage point, which gave him a broader perspective of the harbor than he had observed on his first visit. Gloucester was an ever-burgeoning seaport in the late 1800s, and with its warm clear light, as well as the constant movement of ships, Homer found much to stimulate his interest. He was friendly with local fishermen, whom he found less judgmental than art critics, and spent the summer capturing the comings and goings of Gloucester's fishing fleet. Although work from this visit is perhaps more brooding than his 1873 series, Homer did much to popularize Gloucester in the eyes of the American public who, lured by the romanticism of sailing ships, began coming to Cape Ann to see it for themselves as did artists such as Walter L. Dean, Gordon Grant, and A. W. Buhler.

A. W. Buhler (1853-1920)

Augustus Waldeck Buhler had a long and successful association with the East Gloucester art colony. Born in New York City, Buhler began his art training in Worcester, Massachusetts, after his family moved there when he was twelve. He moved to Boston in 1879, after his marriage to Mary Endlich, and began studying with Tommasso Juglaris at the Boston Art Club. In the mid-1800s, he summered in Annisquam, on the north-

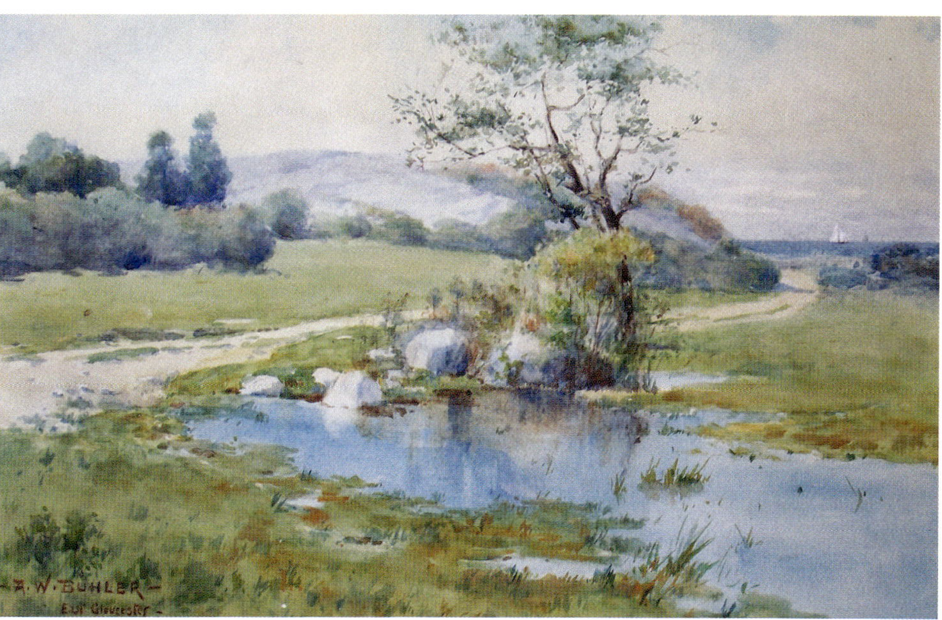

Augustus W. Buhler
Landscape, East Gloucester
Watercolor, 11¾ x 19½ in.
Private collection

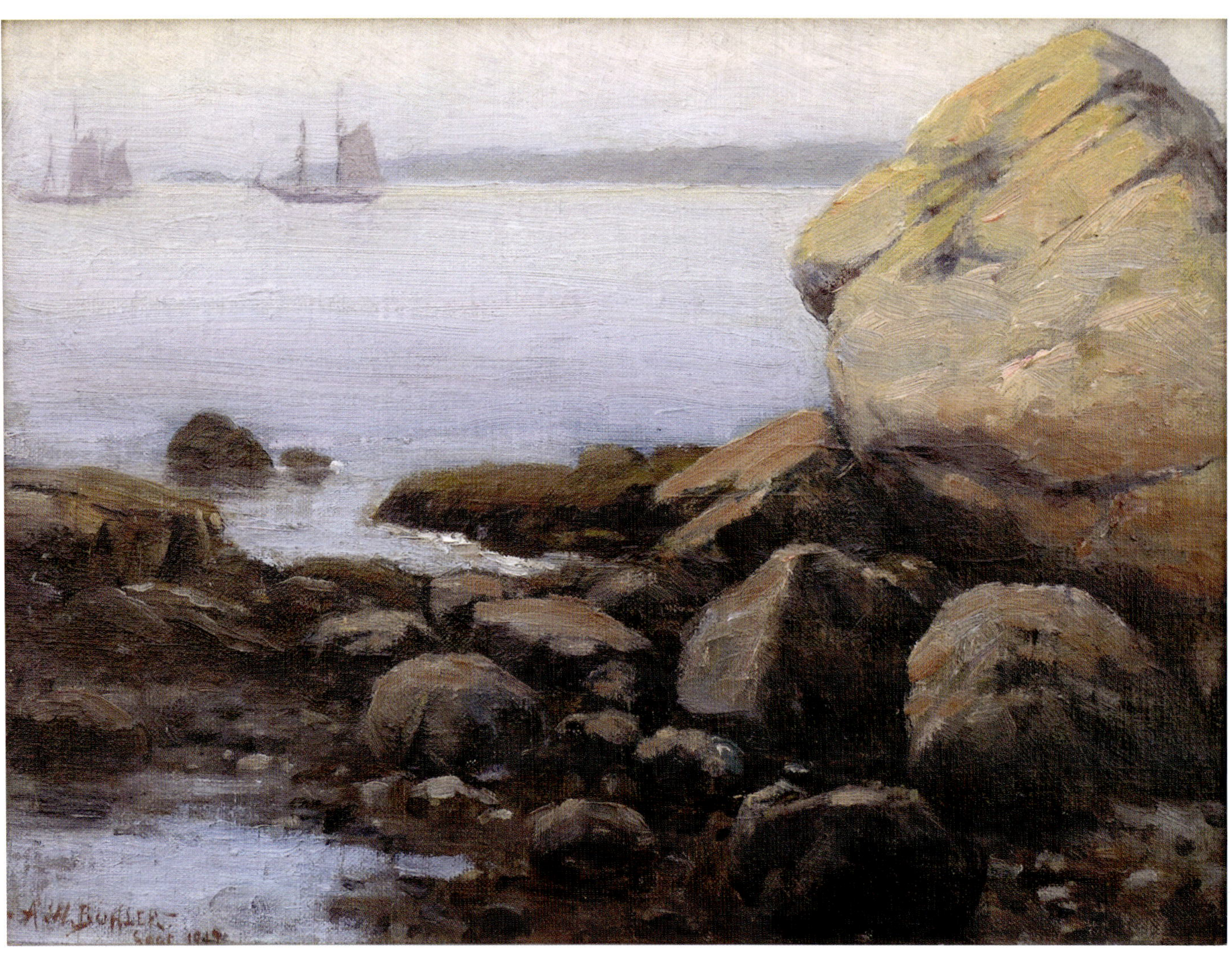

Augustus W. Buhler
Norman's Woe from Wonson's Cove, East Gloucester, Sept. 1917
Oil on canvas board, 9 x 12 in.
James B. Hand Fine Art, Gloucester, Massachusetts

west side of Cape Ann, before moving to Europe in 1888 to continue his art education. Buhler spent two years studying at the Ecole des Beaux Arts and the Académie Julian in Paris, while in the summer he painted in Etamples, France, and Dordrecht, Holland. By 1901 he was back in America opening a studio in Boston, and fast becoming an artist of repute, "particularly noted for his successful sea and coast pictures in which he introduces the hardy and rugged fishermen… in their picturesque clothing."[12] Buhler also moved his summer location from Annisquam to Rocky Neck, "setting up a studio in a sail loft on Charlie Fred Wonson's wharf."[13] According to his daughter, Dorothy, Buhler made the move because he wanted to be among the Gloucester fishermen, watching their weather-beaten faces as they mended their nets and baited their hand lines. He painted his famous "Man at the Wheel" in 1901, which was eventually sold to Gorton's of Gloucester in 1904, becoming not only the trademark insignia of the company, but a symbol of the heroic Gloucester fisherman recognizable around the world. The Buhlers often lodged at the Hawthorne Inn in East Gloucester, as well as at the Pilgrim House. In 1914, the Hawthorne Inn hosted an exhibition of Buhler's paintings featuring scenes of streams, salt marshes and dunes as well as his trademark marine scenes of fishermen and dories.

Buhler realized he was recording a swiftly disappearing era. He once told a reporter, "These people of New England stock will in the next generation be superceded by other races, mostly Greeks, Italians, and Portuguese. Very few of the young men of New England stock are engaged in the fisheries, preferring other vocations. This picture is a record of vanishing days."[14] Today we are fortunate to have Buhler's painterly record of the hardy Gloucester fisherman who regularly risked his life to put food on American tables. A.W. Buhler passed away on April 18, 1920.

Other well-known artists painting in East Gloucester during the early days of the Rocky Neck colony were George Wainwright Harvey, George L. Noyes and Gordon Grant, all notable not only for their individual talent, but also for their depiction of Gloucester at the turn of the twentieth century.

Fitz Henry Lane (1804-1865)

Born in Gloucester on December 19, 1804, Fitz Henry Lane was christened Nathaniel Rogers Lane, but disliked the name enough to petition the General Court of the Commonwealth of Massachusetts for permission to change it to Fitz Henry Lane on December 26, 1831. Permission was granted on March 13, 1832. The confusion over his name came about early in the twentieth century when Lane's reputation had slipped into obscurity. Dealers faced with signatures such as F.H.L., F.H. Lane and Fitz H. Lane apparently selected a name at random to fit the initial, and advertisements exist from 1938 offering work by Fitzhugh Lane.[15]

After suffering a form of paralysis as an infant, possibly from eating Jimsonweed, as there was no outbreak of polio in Gloucester at the time[16], Lane was restricted by his resulting disability from joining in the activities of his friends. Instead he pursued the more solitary pastimes of painting and drawing. As a young man, Lane tried his hand at making shoes for a living, "but… seeing that he could draw better than he could make shoes, he went to Boston and took lessons in drawing and painting and became a marine artist."[17] This abbreviated version—from the artist's nephew, Edward—of the route Lane took to become America's best known nineteenth century marine painter, belies the hard work and training Lane went through to polish his natural skills and artistic vision. In 1832, when he was 28 years old, he apprenticed as a lithographer at Pendleton's in Boston, a firm already noted for excellence in this exacting medium. Lane quickly established a reputation for himself, prompting the editor of the *Gloucester Telegraph* to announce, "[Mr. Lane] will someday become a distinguished artist."[18] Lane later became a partner in the lithography firm of Lane and Scott before

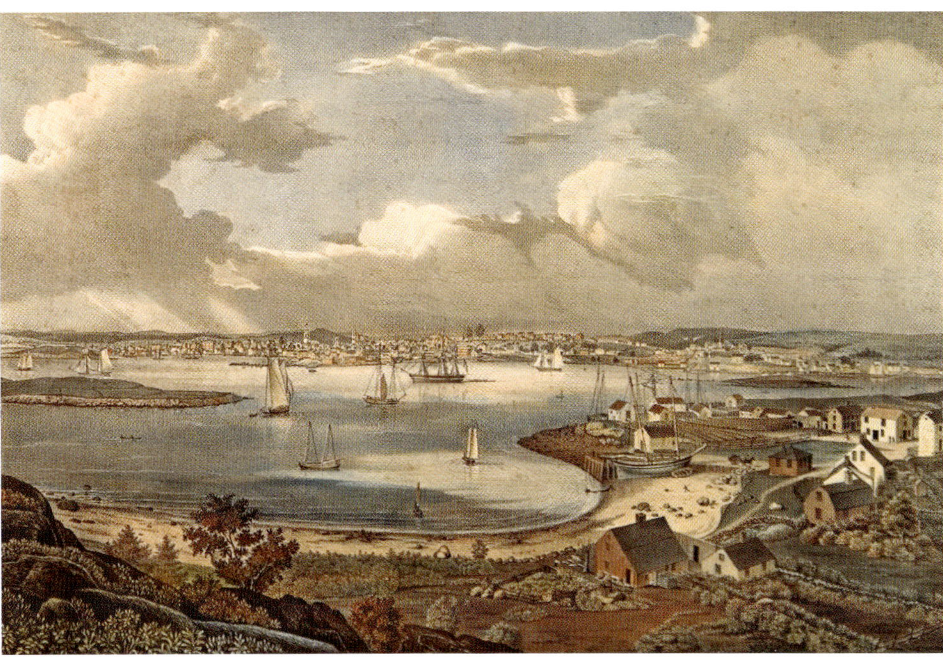

Fitz Henry Lane
View of the Town of Gloucester, Mass.
1836, signed, 12¾ x 19¾ in.
Drawn from nature and on Stone by F. H. Lane Pendleton Lithography, Boston
Collection of Mr. and Mrs. William H. Trayes
Photo: Dancing Shadow Photography

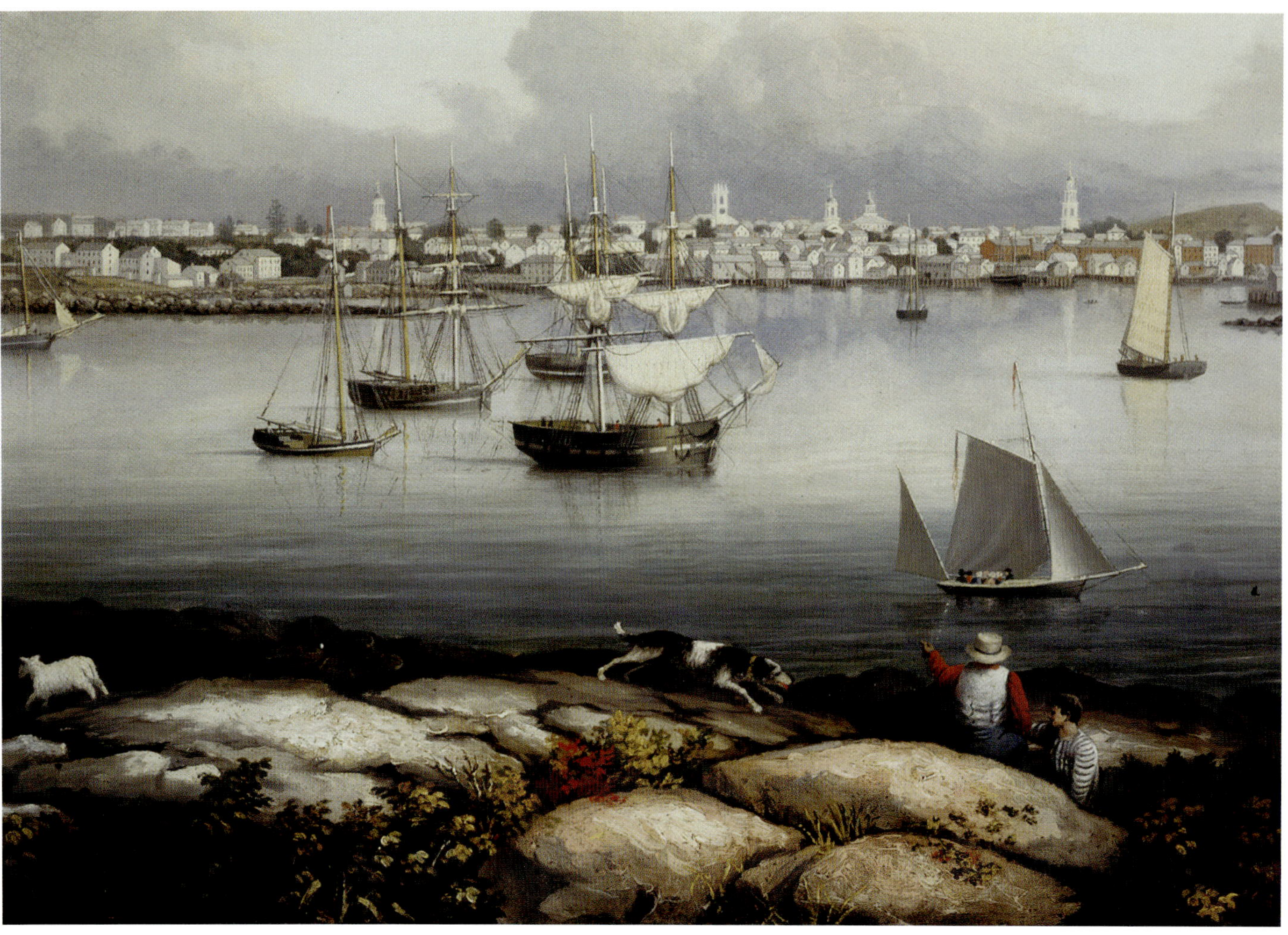

Fitz Henry Lane
Gloucester Harbor from Rocky Neck,
1844 (detail)
Oil on canvas, 29½ x 41½ in.
Cape Ann Historical Association,
Gloucester, Massachusetts
Gift of Jane Parker Stacy
(1289-1)

returning to Gloucester, in 1848, to concentrate on marine painting.

Fitz Henry Lane was Cape Ann's first native son to become a nationally known painter, recording the era and mood of nineteenth century Gloucester in richly detailed, atmospheric canvases that still resonate with the viewer today. Because of his physical disadvantage, Lane rarely traveled far afield and was content to find subject matter within a stone's throw of his home, a gabled granite edifice, designed by Lane and raised upon Duncan's Point. It provided a sweeping view of Rocky Neck on the opposite side of Gloucester's Inner Harbor. Physically, Lane was small and slight of build, and contemporaries thought him "nervous, quick and dyspeptic."[19] He was fortunate, however, to have a good friend in Joseph L. Stevens, Jr., a local Gloucester man who not only assisted Lane on his painting excursions, but also acted as his sales agent. The two made regular trips on a charter boat, cruising the New England coast as far as Penobscot Bay, Mount Desert and the surrounding islands, as well as Castine and Portland.

The fact that Lane never trained abroad in the European manner suggests that what we see in his work is a very personal vision of nature. His earliest oils and watercolors are tightly drawn, which may be due to the influence of Robert Salmon—an English marine painter active in Boston during the 1830s and '40s—or perhaps Lane's own lithographic training influenced him to record every small detail. He had an excellent sense of design, often composing the dark and dominating aspect of a ship's hull against the more simplistic and flatly painted architecture of the wharf. He also favored a muted, tonal palette to reflect the nature of the land and coastline that inspired him.

In later years, Lane's work shows a more mature and relaxed hand that concentrates

Fitz Henry Lane
On the Wharves, Gloucester Harbor,
1847
Oil on panel, 9¾ x 14½ in.
Cape Ann Historical Association,
Gloucester, Massachusetts
Gift of George O. and Jane Parker Stacy
(1289-2)

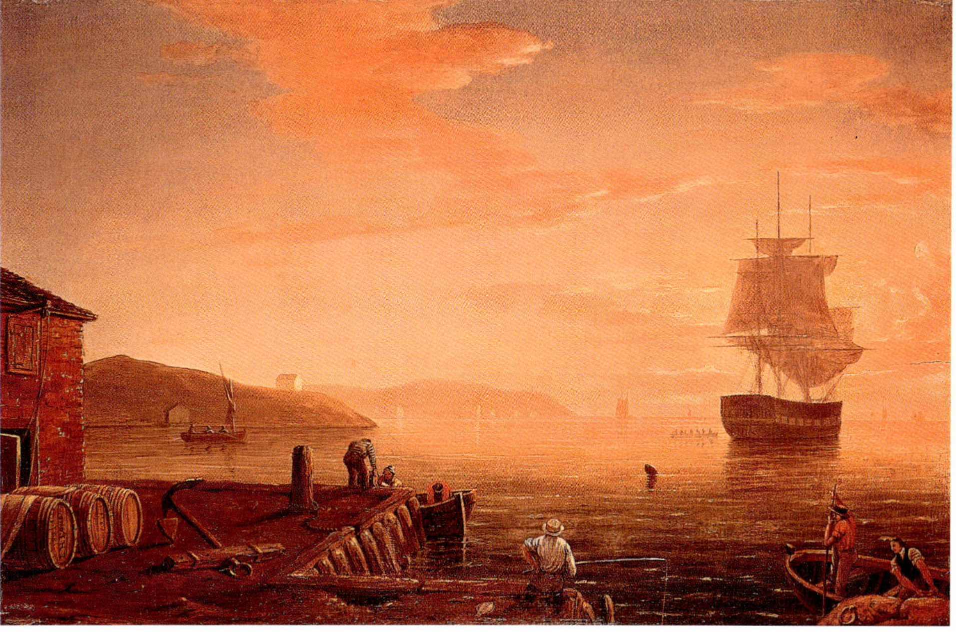

less on every nautical line and emphasizes instead the essence of luminosity and atmosphere. Although his late works are often classed as the epitome of Transcendentalism, Lane's ethereal skies may owe more to a sense of romanticism welling up at the end of a life that had been sadly austere. These late compositions are interesting for Lane's stylistic approach to design—generally two-thirds sky to one-third land—with the nature of the foreground stiff and somewhat mannered in contrast to the sublime effect of his rich and atmospheric skies. His aerial perspective is exemplary. That Lane was something of a romantic and a visionary is confirmed by his reaction to a dream he experienced in his last years. "Sometime last fall while lying in bed asleep, a richly furnished room was presented to my imagination. Upon the wall my attention was attracted to a picture which I have endeavored to reproduce. The dream was very vivid and on awakening I retained it in memory for a long time. The effect was so beautiful in the dream that I determined to attempt its reproduction…. The drawing is very correct, but the effect falls far short of what I saw, and it would be impossible to convey to canvas such gorgeous and brilliant coloring as was presented to me."[20] He died August 14, 1865, after a short illness, and the *Boston Daily Evening Transcript* (Aug. 16, 1865) announced, "[Fitz H. Lane] has left behind him a name synonymous with all that is excellent in art and lovely in character. No man was more heartily admired in the town where he has resided so many years, and no death can be more lamented."

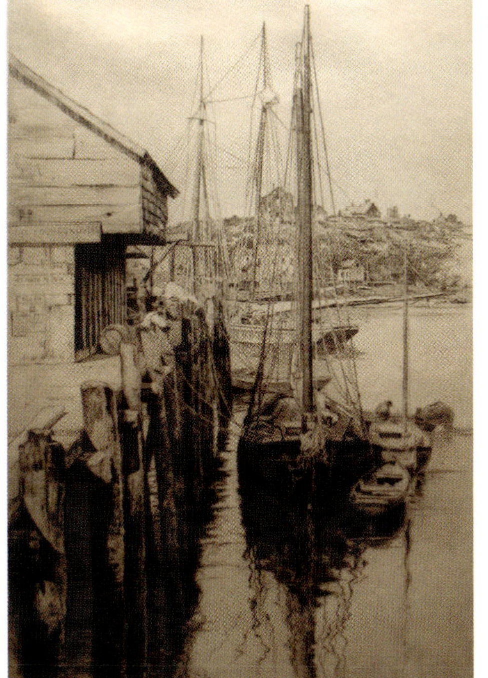

Stephen Parrish
Rocky Neck, 1880
Etching, 18 x 12 in.
Collection of E. Bonnie Akerley

Stephen Parrish (1846-1931)

Although the art of Stephen Parrish is somewhat eclipsed today by the more familiar work of his son Fred, better known as Maxfield, the elder Parrish nevertheless deserves his place in the annals of American fine art.

Born in Philadelphia in 1846, Stephen Parrish was brought up in the sober atmosphere of a Quaker household. Although familial legend holds that Stephen had to sneak up to the attic to indulge his artistic skills, the indications are that his parents turned a blind eye to this errant pastime. As a young man, Parrish followed a mercantile career and pursued painting merely for his own pleasure. However his interest in art led him to make an extended visit to the Paris Exposition of 1867, financed in part with a loan of $1,000 from his parents,[21] indicating a certain tolerance if not encouragement of this

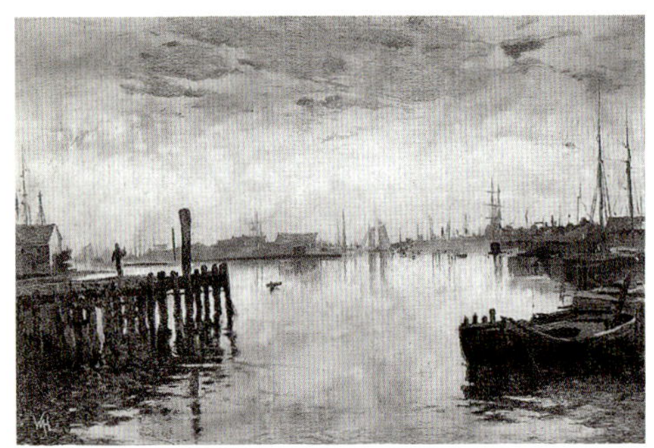

Stephen Parrish
Head of Harbor (after W. M. Hunt)
1880
Etching, 14 x 21 in.
Cape Ann Historical Association,
Gloucester, Massachusetts

interest. The Exposition made a big impression on Parrish, then barely 20 years old. He wrote in his diary, "I never knew before that men could do some things which this day I have seen and wondered at. I never knew that the art of painting was such a vast and splendid profession. There are some effects produced on canvas which I never conceived the possibility of before...."[22]

Back in Philadelphia, Parrish returned to his business as a coal dealer with Brittain and Parrish. He married Elizabeth Bancroft in 1869 and, in 1870, shortly after the birth of their son, Frederick, Parrish gave up the coal business and invested in a stationery store. In 1877, however, despite having a wife and child to support, Parrish gave up the stationery store to become an artist. This was a daring decision considering he had no formal training in the arts. Nevertheless he was ready to take the leap having come to the realization he had spent "thirteen years of his best life in business to wake up in middle life to the consciousness that there was something better in him."[23] Although sales were sparse in the beginning (in 1879, he sold only seven of thirty-three paintings[24]), Parrish remained optimistic. In an effort to add to his repertoire, he took etching lessons from Philadelphia artist Peter Moran. He quickly became skilled in the technique, rising to become one of America's preeminent etchers.

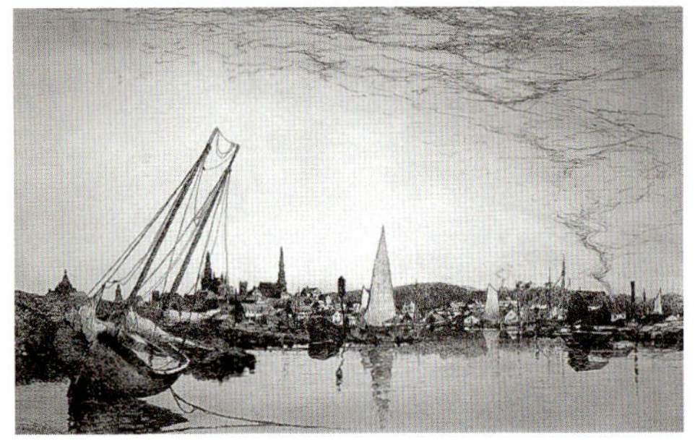

Stephen Parrish
Evening, Gloucester Harbor
Etching, 8 7/16 x 13 7/8 in.
Cape Ann Historical Association,
Gloucester, Massachusetts

As his work gained in popularity, Parrish began traveling farther afield, searching along the New England coast and New Brunswick, Canada, for suitable compositions. In 1881, *Century Magazine* published an article, "Around Cape Ann, Annisquam to Marblehead," featuring nine illustrations by Parrish, seven of which were done on Cape Ann. The variety of these illustrations—from East Gloucester and Rocky Neck, to Annisquam and Bay View—demonstrates the eclectic nature of Parrish's composition and subject matter. Such work drew warm praise from the critics. "Mr. Stephen Parrish," said M. G. van Rensselaer, "whom I should put... in the very first rank of our... etchers, and who is the most popular of them all... is especially associated with seaboard scenes. Our ragged fisher-villages, with their rocky foundations and primitive vessels, have found in him a first and most clear-voiced interpreter."[25] In those days, Parrish liked to stay at the Fairview Inn in East Gloucester, where his visit was reported in the August 19, 1881 edition of the *Cape Ann Weekly Advertiser:* "Stephen Parrish, a

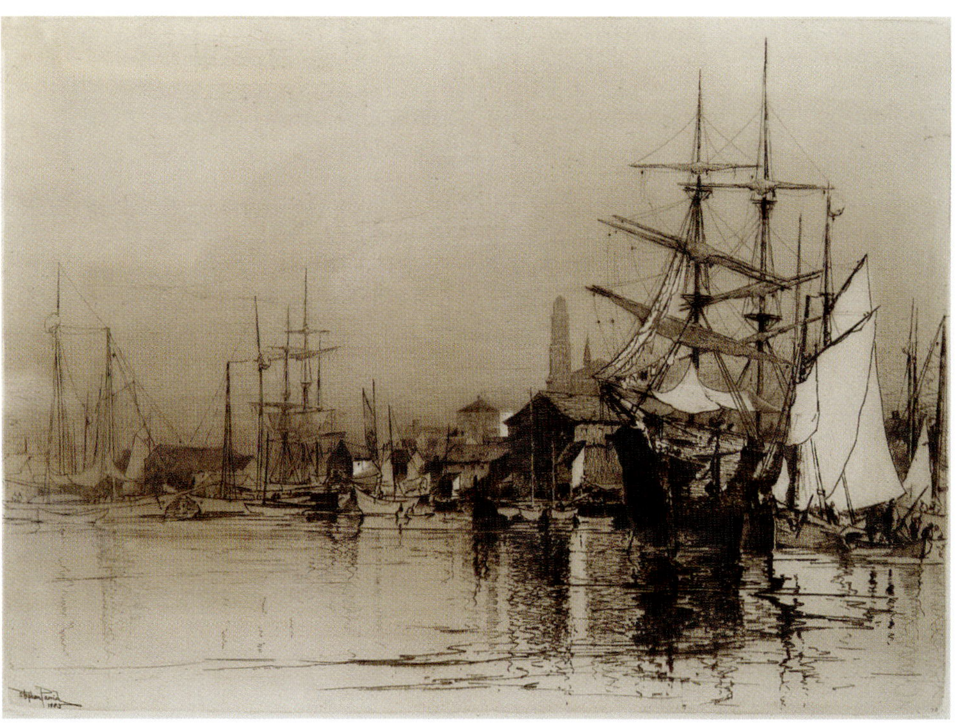

Stephen Parrish
Gloucester Harbor
Etching, 11 x 18 in.
Mosher Gallery, Rockport,
Massachusetts

New York [sic] artist has been spending a few weeks at Mrs. Renton's at East Gloucester, and has made some admirable etchings of Cape Ann scenery."[26]

In the summer of 1884, Parrish took his wife and son to Europe for a visit lasting almost two years and encompassing northern Italy, France and England. Returning to America in 1886, Parrish continued producing both sensitively rendered and soundly composed works utilizing both plate and paint for his medium of choice. He returned to Cape Ann in 1892 and 1893 in the company of his son, and the two of them spent hours painting the local shoreline and landscape. Parrish had much advice to offer about the artistic process, not least of which was the principle, "getting the darks and lights right was far more important than the color."[27] As this is a prerequisite of the impressionist way of seeing, one can only admire Stephen Parrish, the unschooled en plein air painter, as a man some years ahead of his time.

Perhaps the last word on Parrish, the man, should be left to portraitist Cecilia Beaux, who occupied the next-door studio to Parrish in Philadelphia, "Mr. Parrish was a charming man," she wrote in her memoir, *Background with Figures*, "and his talent was the expression of his exquisite perception of quality in things seen. He was by heredity a Friend (in Philadelphia 'Quakers' are the Society of Friends), and all their long exercised repression of beauty, as seen by the artist in Nature, had struggled for expression in him and triumphed."[28]

Walter L. Dean (1854-1912)

Although born in Lowell, Massachusetts, raised in Boston and trained in Europe, Walter Lofthouse Dean considered Gloucester his homeport. Dean was as passionate a sailor as he was an artist. He was never happy far from the ocean and so gravitated toward marine painting. Cape Ann, with its glorious coastline and charming harbors, suited him perfectly and he spent the latter part of his life in East Gloucester.

Dean's family moved to Boston while he was still quite young. The family had no artistic or nautical aspirations, but Dean exhibited an early affinity with the ocean and haunted the Boston waterfront at every opportunity. His parents encouraged this interest by presenting him, on his fifteenth birthday, with his own Hereshoff catboat. He quickly became an adept sailor and won several harbor races and regattas.

Dean attended the Boston Free Evening Drawing School for a time, and then enrolled at the Massachusetts Institute of Technology to study architecture. This did not last long, however, and he gave up MIT in favor of the Massachusetts Normal Art School. He found this more satisfying and crammed the four-year course into three. After graduation, he spent two terms as a drawing instructor at the Boston Free Evening School. He then went to Purdue University in Lafayette, Indiana, and spent two years there, as an art instructor, before returning to the New England coast to pursue marine painting, which he now realized was his true vocation. In 1882, after receiving advice to visit the French academies, Dean set out for Paris, enrolling at the Académie Julian and studying under Boulanger and Lefèbvre. Later he trained with landscapist Achile Oudinot who not only instructed Dean in the refinements of art, but also inspired the young American to express a more personal viewpoint.

Before he returned to the United States, Dean worked his way along the coast of Brittany, Belgium, Holland, Italy and England filling sketchbooks and oil panels with myriad views. This sojourn made a great impression on Dean. Later in life, he was still painting scenes of Scheveningen and the Dutch shore from memory. On his return to Boston in 1885, Dean bought an old yacht named *Undine*, which he fitted out as a

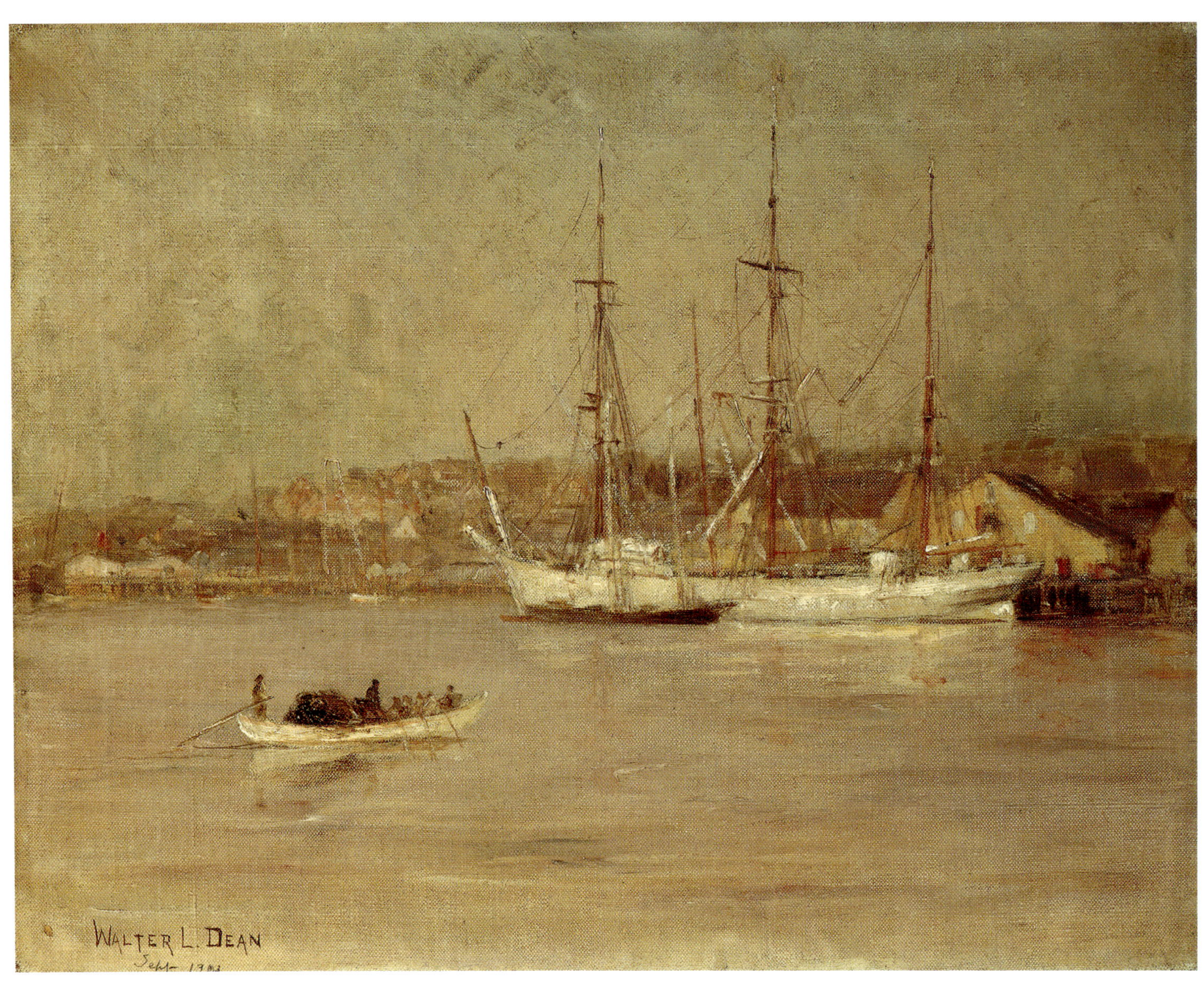

Walter L. Dean
The White Bark
Oil on canvas, 14 x 18 in.
(exhibited at the Detroit Museum of Art, 1906)
Collection of Tom and Gloria Nicholas

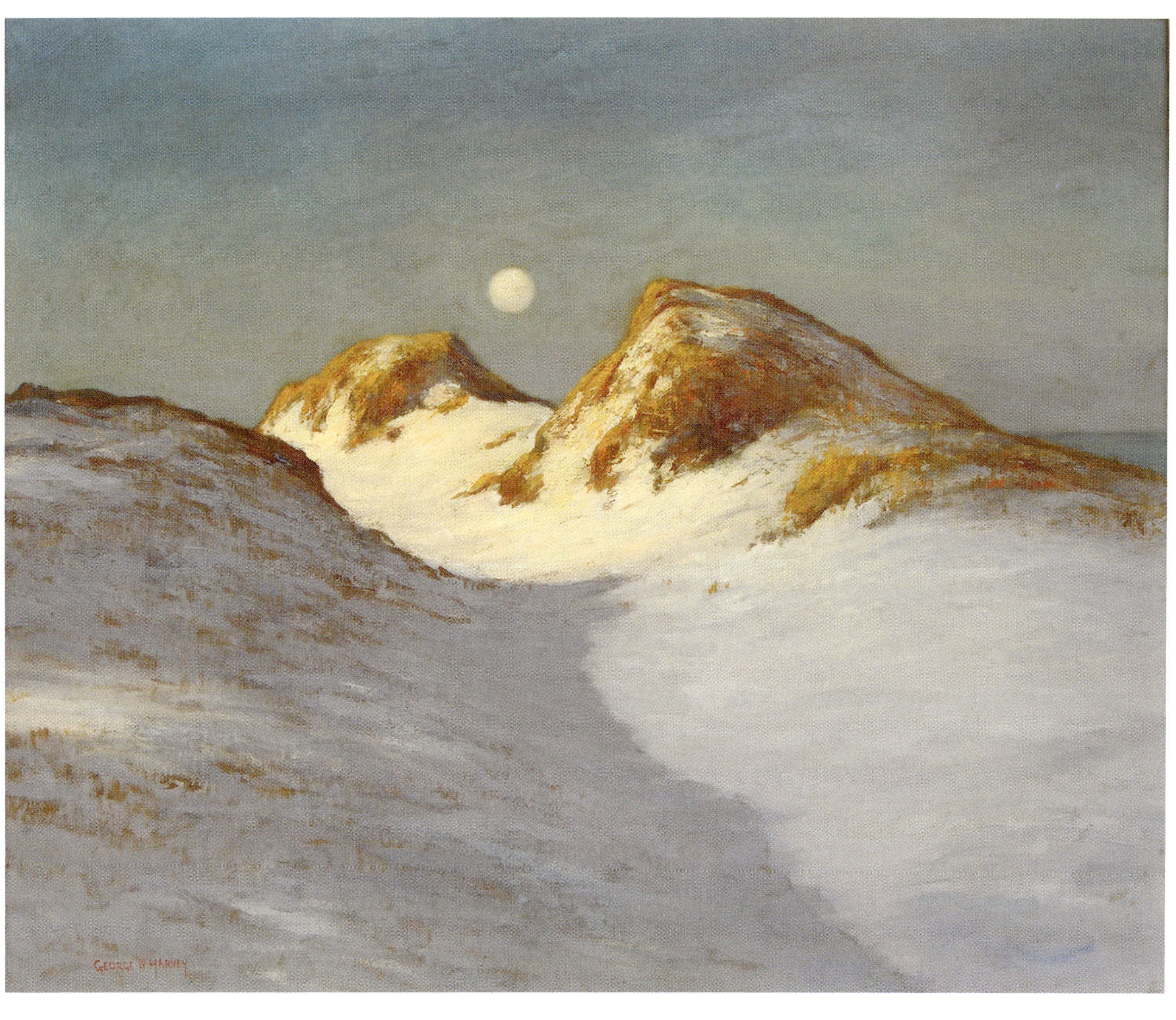

George Wainwright Harvey
Autumn Moon, c. 1900
Oil on canvas, 20 x 24 in.
The Crane Collection, Manchester, Massachusetts

floating studio and used on a four-month voyage along the New England coast. He particularly enjoyed painting late day and early morning effects, when the light suggested a soft and subtle palette. On arrival in Gloucester, Dean anchored the *Undine* for an extended visit. He had visited the port on previous occasions, the first time during a school vacation when he had shipped out on the *Annie C. Friend* to haul mackerel nets off the Grand Banks. This time Dean concentrated on painting and finished a dozen canvases including *Cape Ann Sand Dunes, Bass Rocks,* and *Home Port, Gloucester.* Before leaving, Dean held informal exhibitions of his work on the wharves where he moored and painted.

With the onset of winter, and the *Undine* in dry-dock, Dean shipped out as an able seaman on the barkentine *Christian Redman* to familiarize himself with the accoutrements of a 3-masted square-rigger. He knew it was vital for a marine artist to be au courant with the technicalities of the métier he portrayed. As Dean became known as a master marine artist, art critics hailed his work. None was more appreciated than his masterpiece *The White Squadron,* which he painted after many hours spent sailing around and scrutinizing the U. S. Atlantic Fleet in Boston. This heroic sized painting, which measures 75 x 81 inches unframed, shows five white cruisers—the flagship *Chicago* most prominent—laying at anchor, peaceful and serene as the artist perceives them through a veil of atmosphere, with a slight breeze suggested by ripples in the water. In 1893 the painting was selected as one of a handful to be shown at the Columbian World's Fair in Chicago. Dean personally installed the enormous canvas and renamed it *Peace,* believing that the tranquil mood suggested safety through strength rather than preparation for war. The painting was subsequently loaned to and finally purchased by the Office of Naval Affairs in Washington.

Although Dean considered Gloucester to be home, and in the late 1890s maintained a summer studio on the harbor, he still enjoyed taking voyages farther afield. In 1902-03 he spent time cruising the coast of Puerto Rico. Elected vice-president of the Boston Art Club at the turn of the century, Dean suddenly decided to leave Boston and bought a home on East Main Street in Gloucester. Now living permanently in his favorite location, Dean spent the last years of his life recording the atmosphere and character of Gloucester's waterfront and coves. He proclaimed the glorious views of Rocky Neck in Cape Ann's rarefied light long before it became fashionable to do so. When he died in his East Gloucester home on March 13, 1912, the art world lost one of its finest practitioners of marine art.

In a eulogy for Dean, the *Boston Post* said, "Mr. Dean… since he has reached the maturity of his genius, has been regarded as the foremost marine painter in America… He was a lover of the sea in all its moods and not only portrayed its magic but interpreted its mystery… there is made upon the beholder an impression of the certainty of the artist's knowledge of every rope, every spar, and every sail he paints."[29]

George W. Harvey (1855-1930)

Gloucester native George W. Harvey brought to his work a knowledge of light and atmosphere garnered from a lifetime of living beside the ocean, observing the vagaries of the weather and the subtleties of the season; a prime requisite for the plein air painter.

George Wainwright Harvey was born January 13, 1855, the son of a local sea captain. He grew up in East Gloucester and apart from a brief flirtation with fishing in the Bay of Fundy when he was eleven, during which time he was mostly seasick, Harvey expressed no inclination to follow in his father's footsteps. Initially self-taught, it is not recorded when Harvey first began experimenting with paint, but by 1875 his talent was recognized and reported in the *Cape Ann Weekly Advertiser:* "[W. H. Weisman, a Philadelphia artist vacationing at… Roger's Farm, East Gloucester] has for one of his pupils Mr. George Harvey, of this city, and… informs us that he gives promise of making a fine artist, having a natural genius and an ardent love for it."[30]

In his early work Harvey found inspiration in the genre of ship and sea surrounding him and from Gloucester's other native son, Fitz Henry Lane. Lane, however, remained a luminist throughout, whereas Harvey, particularly after his exposure to European art, grew to be more representational in both genre and light, and was never afraid to experiment when seeking an effect.

Harvey married photographer Martha Hale Rogers in 1884. Shortly after that, the couple set off on an extended tour of Europe. They visited England, France and Italy, but it was Holland where they lingered, particularly around Scheveningen and Katwijk, where Harvey made the acquaintance of Adolphe Artz, president of the Dutch Society of Artists. Harvey was made an honorary member of the DSA during his stay, and the work he did upon his return to the United States in December 1886 shows the distinct influence of the Dutch style and their interpretation of light.

Despite a lack of formal art training, Harvey was much sought after during his lifetime and was a frequent contributor to galleries as far afield as Chicago, as well as those closer to home, such as the Boston Art Club, the Gloucester Society of Artists and the North Shore Arts Association. He also showed extensively at The Chase Gallery in Boston, with an exhibition of watercolors of the North Shore in December 1884, followed by an exhibition of Dutch sketches on his return in 1886, and an exhibition of European and Cape Ann watercolors in December 1887.

Although best known for his oils, watercolors and line drawings, Harvey was also an accomplished etcher and wood engraver. "In the field of etchings George W. Harvey is without peer," reported one critic, reviewing a summer exhibition at the Gloucester Society of Artists. "His group on display at the exhibition is a fine expression of the man who so nobly enriched the entire field of art with his splendid work."[31] Initially, Harvey's Cape Ann etchings were pleasing but on the small side because he began with only a small press. Eventually, however, Gloucester notable Roger Babson made the artist a gift of a larger press and thereafter Harvey's etchings grew in both size and artistry.

For one who learned his craft from observation and, to some extent, trial and error, George Harvey carved out a successful career that was comparable to that of many art school-trained painters. He was a keen observer of humanity, as well as of nature, and possessed a fisherman's knowledge of atmosphere and weather. This enabled him to paint rich and emotive canvases. Harvey also excelled in design, and often created his focal point by flattening and subduing his background in order to bring his subject to the fore. Some of his early work has an almost illustrative finish that is quite refined, yet with a thoughtfulness of expression that lifts it beyond commercialism. While he enjoyed experimenting with different effects, Harvey's style, for the most part, reflects the influence of the Dutch school that he so admired.

George Harvey passed away on June 8, 1930, leaving a fine body of work that exemplifies Gloucester's abundant history in fishing and the arts. It was left to Harvey's lifelong friend, H. W. Abbott, to speak of this when he said at Harvey's committal service, "Fifty years ago when Edward Susbee was the eccentric art critic of the *Boston Transcript* George W. Harvey was discovered at Annisquam, painting with a sympathetic brush, the calm quiet sea-and-water scapes of Cape Ann draped with wisps of fog resembling Spanish Moss. Like Corot and Boudin, he loved the limpid greys and greens so often seen in our marshes and beaches that lent themselves to his interpretive brush. His canvases always expressed his extremely sensitive and affectionate character, so rare and little appreciated in this go-getting age of ours."[32]

Frederick Judd Waugh, N. A. (1861-1940)

Frederick Judd Waugh, preeminent marine painter of the twentieth century, was born in Bordentown, New Jersey, on September 13, 1861, the son of portrait painter Samuel Bell Waugh and his second wife, Eliza, a miniaturist. As a youth, Waugh took more interest in nature than academics. Encouraged by his father, Waugh enrolled at the Pennsylvania Academy of the Fine Arts in 1880, working under Thomas Eakins, a family friend, and his assistant, Thomas Anshutz. Waugh's early works suggest a natural talent, but his draftsmanship was too clean and hard-edged for Eakins, who believed pupils should concentrate on body mass, rather than outline. Eakins' advice was succinct. "Freddy, get more dirt into it."[33]

In 1883, Waugh left the Pennsylvania Academy and enrolled at the Académie Julian in Paris, receiving instruction from William Bouguereau and Tony Robert-Fleury. However, after summering in Grez-sur-Loing with Birge Harrison, Robert Louis Stevenson and Thomas Anshutz, Waugh took their advice, and gave up school in favor of working directly from nature. He returned to Philadelphia in 1885 after the sudden death of his father and for the next few years supported himself with portrait commissions and commercial work. He also painted landscapes and genre, which he exhibited at the Pennsylvania Academy.

Frederick Judd Waugh
Surf at Bass Rocks
Oil on canvas, 14 x 20 in.
Mosher Gallery, Rockport, Massachusetts

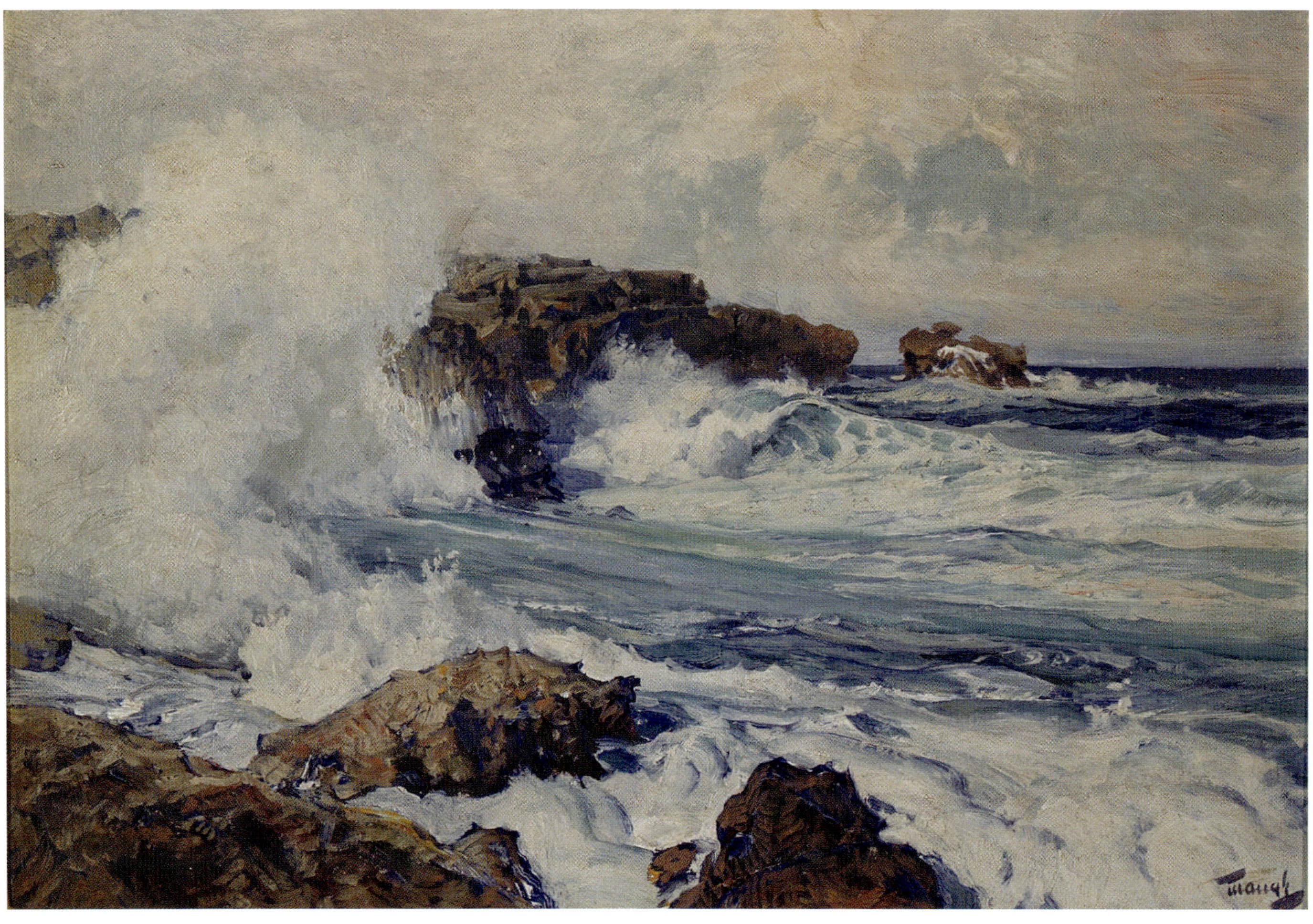

Frederick Judd Waugh
The Cove
Oil on canvas, 25 x 30 in.
Roger King Fine Art, Newport, Rhode Island

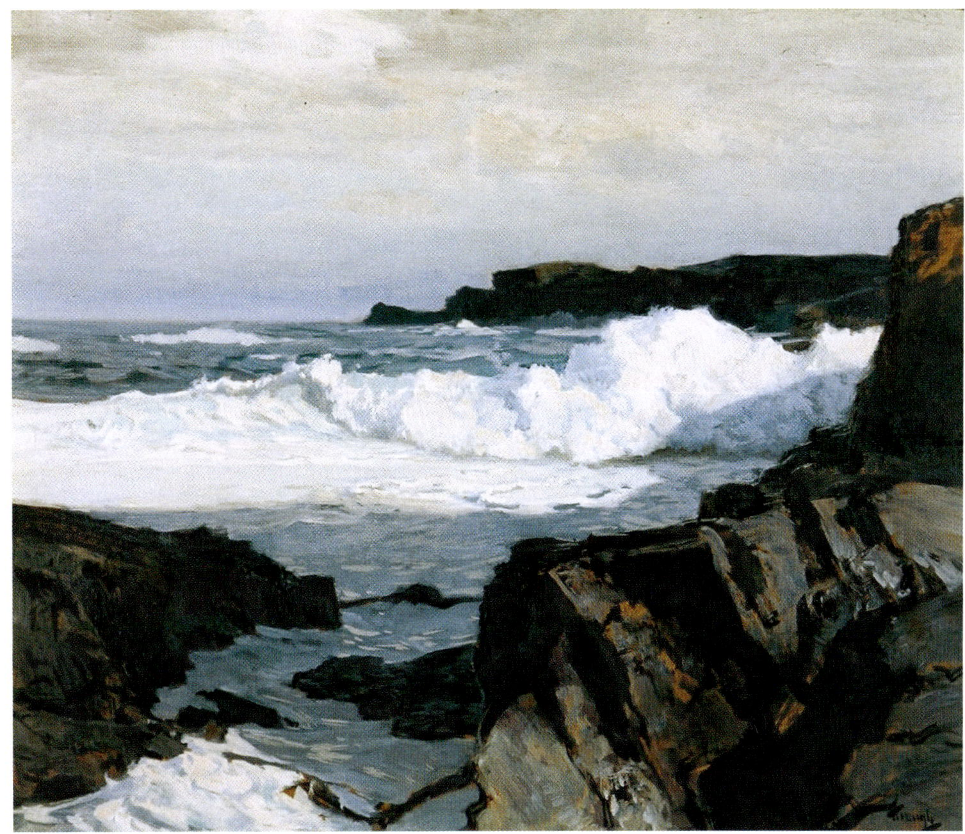

In 1892, Waugh married his long-time sweetheart, Clara Eugenie Bunn, and the couple settled in Paris. Waugh exhibited in the Salon of 1893, and at Easter of the same year, donated *Consider the Lilies*, a large religious canvas of Christ attended by angels, to the Episcopal Chapel of St. Luke in Paris. The canvas was intended for the World's Fair in Chicago until Waugh discovered it exceeded the size limitations. His donation was providential, however, because the rector of St. Luke's took a personal interest in Waugh and financed the couple's vacation to the island of Sark, in the English Channel.

Although the Waughs planned to spend only one month on Sark, they fell in love with the island and stayed two years. The dramatic coastline and the proximity of the sea made a huge impression on Waugh and, after spending months observing wave form and movement, he began painting the kind of works for which he is so well known today. "To paint the sea, you must love it," Waugh explained, "and to love it, you must know the sea."[34] He studied the ocean for hours at a time, observing and memorizing the complexity of wave structure, the effect of light shining through air-filled water, and the ensuing rhythm of foam patterns.

The Waughs returned to America in 1907 and settled briefly in Montclair, New Jersey. Within two years, Waugh was elected an associate member of the National Academy of Design, becoming a full Academician in 1911. The family regularly summered in Maine, on Bailey Island and Monhegan. However, in 1910, Waugh sought a change from the somber tones of the Maine coast and, at the suggestion of a friend, came to Cape Ann to revitalize his energies.

The local color of Gloucester Harbor, coupled with the intense Cape Ann light, inspired Waugh and he spent hours painting from a rowboat in the harbor. He developed a thicker impasto technique and a more vibrant palette to capture the brilliant effect of light and atmosphere. Although Waugh did not often paint ships, preferring to focus on the sea alone, the proximity of working schooners, the light shining through their drying sails and reflecting in the water beside dark hulls, inspired him to break with routine and paint the teeming harbor life.

"The sea itself is very subtle in color and ever changing," Waugh explained. "You must learn by heart these subtleties, if you want to do well."[35] Here then is the secret of Waugh's immense success as a sea painter: constant observation, deliberation and then application. "And I have also found that my best results are attained by impasto, thick painting, shadows and all… until the surface is very painty. And all this paint is put on as unmixed as possible, the long flexible round brushes I use dragged through several tints… and left upon the canvas…. There is no other way to reach a positive vibration, but to vibrate your color actually."[36]

Although Waugh enjoyed the immediacy of the ocean, particularly around Gloucester's backshore, he regretted the lack of surf and action during the summer months. So even though he became a long time member of the North Shore Arts Association in the '20s, Waugh did not return to Cape Ann after 1910.

In later life, Waugh regretted being considered only a sea painter, and would have welcomed appreciation for his still life, portraiture and murals. "[Marines] are my bread and butter," he said, "but I wish I could interest someone in something different."[37] He suffered from ill health in his last year, making it difficult to paint, and died September 10, 1940.

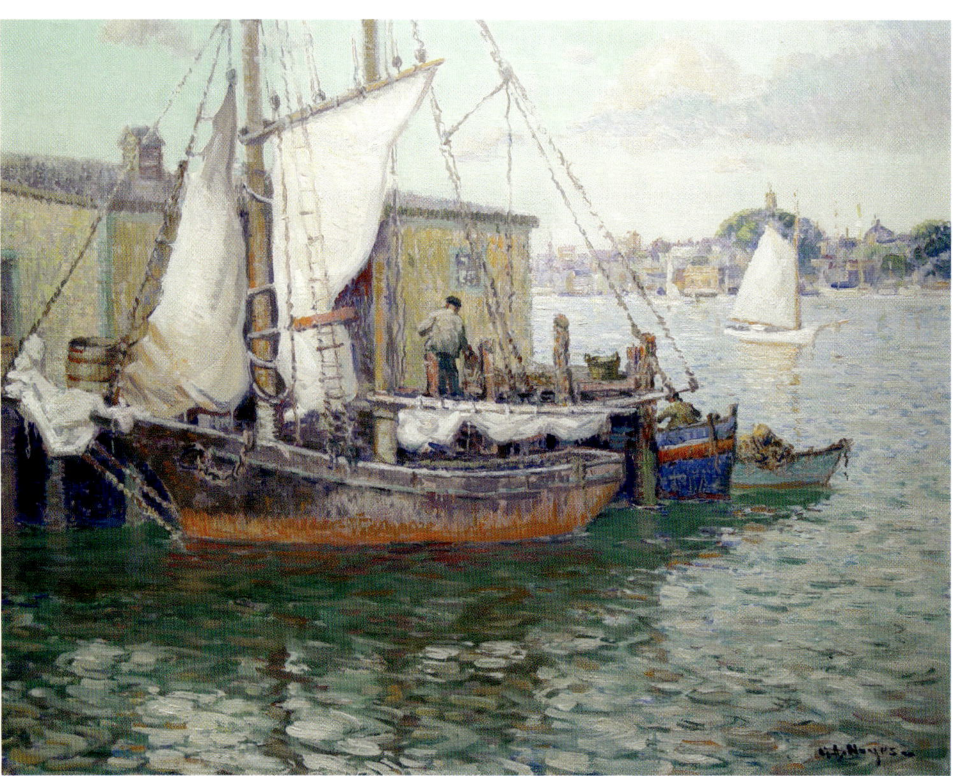

George L. Noyes
Gloucester Harbor
Oil on canvas, 25 x 30 in.
Blue Heron Fine Art, Cohasset, Massachusetts

George L. Noyes (1864-1954)

George Loftus Noyes has a reputation as one of America's foremost plein air practitioners despite losing the bulk of his oeuvre not once but twice in his career. Noyes was born October 26, 1864, the middle son of American-born parents living in Bothway, Ontario, Canada. Less than a decade later, the widowed Lima Noyes was managing a boarding house in East Cambridge, Massachusetts. Although money was scarce, George's mother encouraged him to pursue an art career and, as early as 1885, George was listed in the Cambridge City Directory as a decorator. While having no formal art school training, other than classes from George Bartlett, an English artist living in

George L. Noyes
Opalescent Fog, Gloucester, Mass.
Oil on canvas, 17½ x 22 in.
Private collection

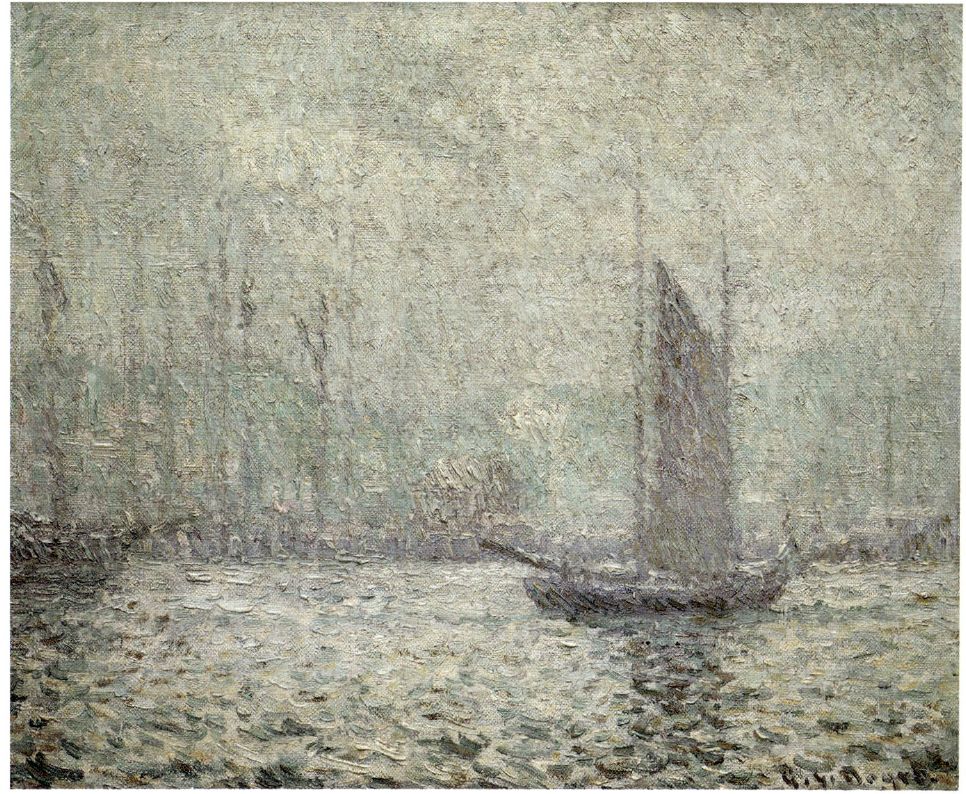

Boston, Noyes capitalized on a youthful talent for painting flowers and still life subjects and obtained a position with the New England Glass Company of Cambridge, painting designs on their products. Unfortunately, the company folded in 1888, and the following year Noyes left for France where he studied in the ateliers of Gustav Courtois and Joseph-Paul Blanc of the Académie Colarossi.

Noyes found Paris a congenial city, and by 1891 had made the acquaintance of several other Bostonian artists, among them Maurice and Charles Prendergast and H. Dudley Murphy. All of these shared with Noyes a mutual regard for design and craftsmanship in art. At the close of the school year, Noyes visited Brittany and discovered a penchant for painting en plein air. Early the following year he ventured further afield with a painting trip to Algiers. When his canvas *Sous les palmiers au vieux Biskra* was accepted into the Paris Salon, it was a clear signal to Noyes that his professional career had begun. He returned to America late in 1892 after summering in Venice, and settled in Malden, Massachusetts. He showed in the Boston Art Club's 47th Annual Exhibition and followed this with an exhibition of Algerian and Italian paintings at his School Street studio in January 1893.

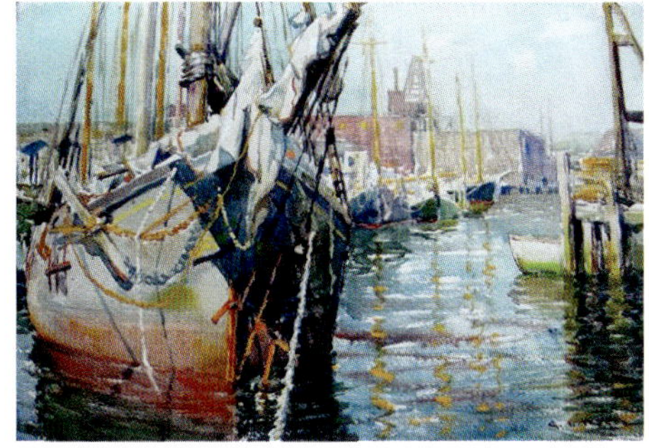

George L. Noyes
Gloucester Harbor
Watercolor, 15¼ x 22¼ in.
Lepore Fine Arts, Newburyport, Massachusetts

In 1897, Noyes, in the capacity of companion and assistant, accompanied an elderly Frederic Edwin Church on the first of two visits to Mexico. The two artists painted side by side in Cuernavara for three and a half months, during which time Noyes was fortunate to share Church's observations on painting in general and the poetry of nature in particular. As a result, Noyes's style lost some of its decorative aspect, and matured to a more naturalist view.

These artistic wanderings appealed to Noyes, who loved nothing more than discovering the perfect painting location, one unspoiled by man and his improvements. He did not, however, discover Cape Ann until the summer of 1900 when he rented a small studio in Annisquam. It was near the summer home of Henry Soule, a Boston businessman whom he'd met in Mexico. A mutual love of music brought Noyes into contact with Soule's sister-in-law, Mabel Winifred Hall, and the two of them were married in the summer of 1903.

The beginning of the twentieth century was an important time for Noyes. His paintings drew enthusiastic approval from the art critics: "Mr. Noyes in the past few years has developed rapidly as a colorist and his landscapes… grow more and more remarkable for their luminosity and radiance."[38] He also instructed a plein air summer school where many of the students were directed to him by Boston painter, Eric Pape. One of these was a young N. C. Wyeth. Wyeth was so impressed by Noyes that he returned to him in 1921, telling a friend, "I am arranging to study… with George Noyes. His color knowledge is superb and I think he will give me much help at this juncture."[39]

After his marriage to Mabel, Noyes took up a teaching post at Stanford University, and for the next three years, they lived in California and returned to Gloucester for summers. Disaster struck Noyes for the first time in 1906 when the great San Francisco earthquake robbed the artist of "practically all that he had in the world."[40] The couple returned to Boston, where Noyes joined the teaching staff at the Pape School on Boylston Street, and continued to summer on Cape Ann.

At this point in his career, Noyes was using a pigment-loaded brush and working alla prima, using the strength of his values to define the object, and broad brushstrokes to capture mood and movement. Over the next decade, however, he began experimenting with the broken color method, juxtaposing one value beside another to create color vibration. One uninformed critic complained, "his canvases at close view look as if the whole contents of his paint tubes had been squeezed out upon it in little ridges and daubs. It is only when one stands at proper distance… that this mingled chaos of color becomes perfect drawing and exquisite atmosphere and coloring."[41]

During the '20s, Noyes kept close ties with Gloucester, often staying at the Harbor View or the Rockaway, and interspersing these visits with painting trips to Europe. He exhibited at the Gallery-on-the-Moors in East Gloucester in 1918, and was an early member of the North Shore Arts Association. Noyes also held weekly exhibitions at the Green Studio on the grounds of the Harbor View, where his canvases brought critical acclaim from the summer colonists. In later years, Noyes moved to Braden, Vermont, where in 1939, disaster struck Noyes for the second time when a devastating barn fire destroyed the greater part of his life's work. No longer able to paint, George Noyes died in the Monadnock Community Hospital, Peterborough, New Hampshire, on September 10, 1954.

Gordon Grant, N.A., A.W.S. (1875-1962)

In an era far removed from the romance of clipper ships and square-riggers, the name Gordon Grant still resonates on Cape Ann as one of the most prolific and adept marine artists of the last century. Grant's affinity for the sea began soon after as he was born, on June 7, 1875, in the bustling west coast seaport of San Francisco. No doubt, his passion for drawing was fully satiated in the rich and eclectic milieu that made San Francisco so popular before the great earthquake of 1906. When he was only twelve, however, Grant's Scottish parents put him aboard *City of Madras*, a square-rigged Glasgow wheat ship, and returned him to their homeland to finish his education.[42] The journey, south around Cape Horn and then northeast across the Atlantic, took four months and, during that time, Grant learned not only to love the ocean, but also to respect its unpredictable moods. He also grew to appreciate the tall ships and the men

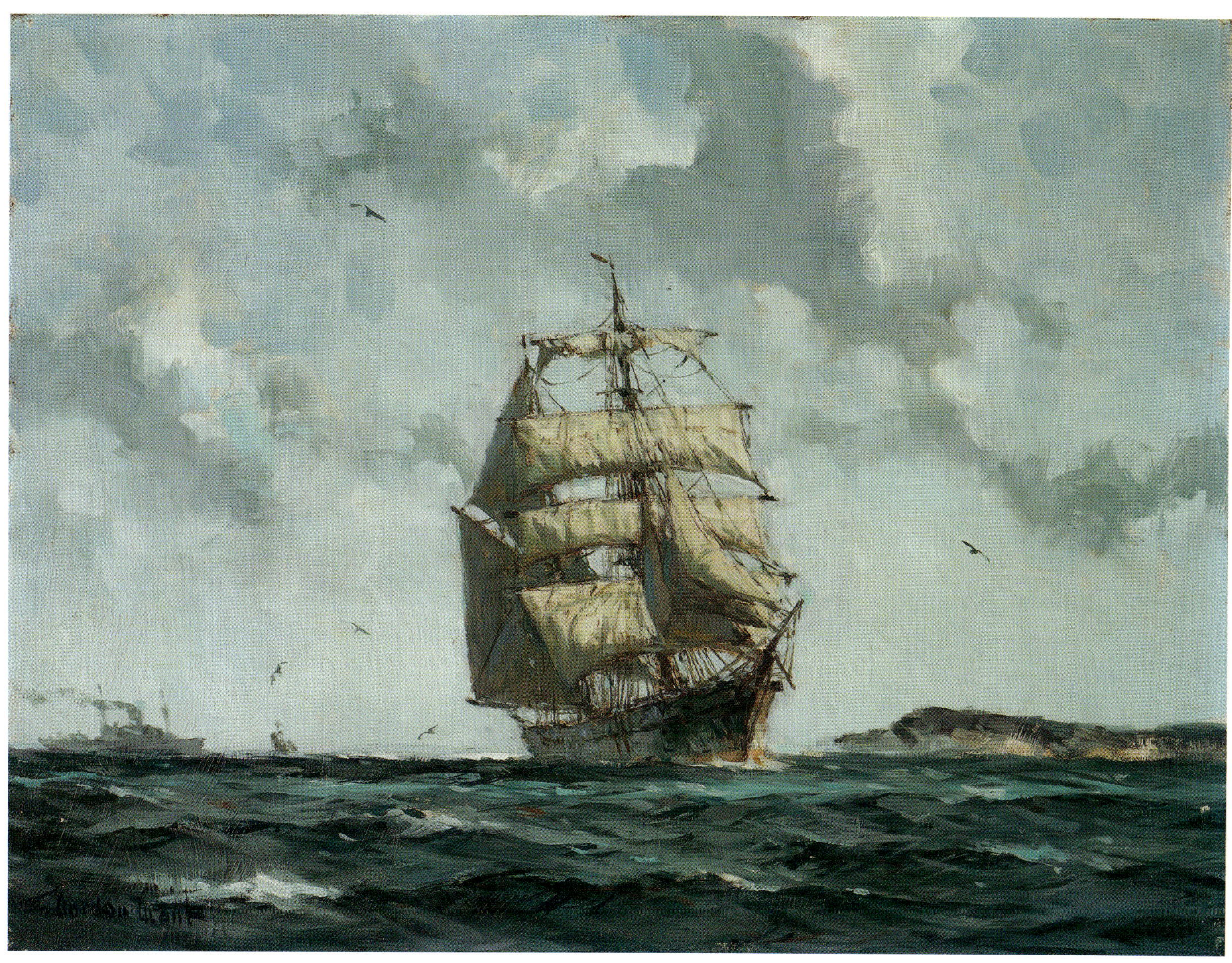

Gordon Grant
Return to Port, c. 1940s
Oil on panel, 12 x 16 in.
Collection of Tom and Gloria Nicholas

who plied the deep-water trade routes.

At the age of eighteen, having graduated from Fife Academy in Scotland, Grant moved to London, where he studied for two or three years, attending both Heatherly and Lambeth Art Schools. Details of his early life and artistic education are sketchy, but it would appear that by 1895 Grant was back in San Francisco working as a staff artist for the *San Francisco Examiner* and possibly the *Chronicle.*

Like many of the seaman he painted over the years, Grant had a touch of the wanderlust himself. In 1896, he was on the east coast, working for the *Sunday World* and the *Journal* in New York. Illustrators were much in demand at the turn of the century for both newspapers and magazines and Grant's reputation quickly built to an impressive level. In 1899 he became a combat artist for *Harper's Weekly* covering the Boer War in South Africa where, he later related, "Winston Churchill also served as a correspondent for a London paper."[43] Between 1901 and 1909, Grant worked as a staff artist for *Puck* contributing general illustrations. Apart from special assignments, he remained in New York for some time, possibly because it provided the most lucrative market for his work, and then in 1907, he joined the 7th Regiment of New York's National Guard. In 1916, Grant served on the Mexican border but, because of a foot disability, could not join his regiment when it was ordered overseas for World War I. He served instead as a captain in Washington.[44]

Regardless of where he worked, Grant never lost his affinity for the ocean, and soon became known as a specialist in marine genre, especially after his 1925 voyage to

Gordon Grant
Fish Stories
Watercolor, 14 x 20 in.
Mosher Gallery, Rockport, Massachusetts

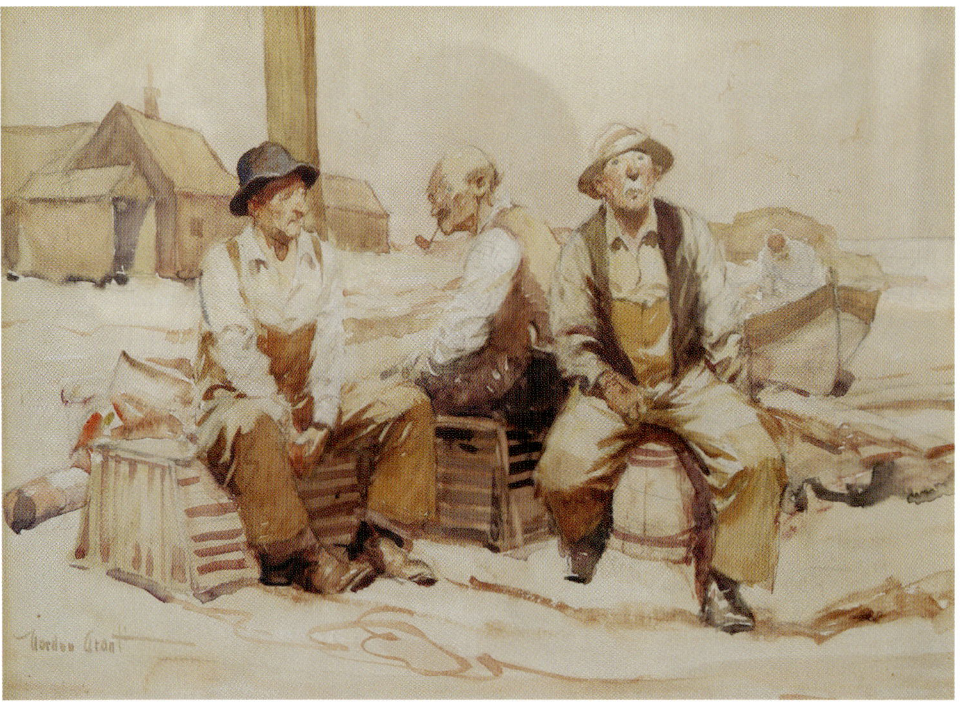

Chignik, on the Aleutian peninsula, aboard the salmon packer fleet windjammer, *Star of Alaska*. He made dozens of sketches during the trip, recording every detail of the workaday lives of the crew, and its complement of characters. He eventually collected these sketches in a book entitled *Sail Ho!*, dedicated, "To the unknown sailor:—the A. B.—the man before the mast—but for whose fortitude and labour the great ships would never have reached their perfection…."[45]

Aside from his illustrative work, Grant also became adept at oil and watercolor painting, lithography and etching. As a lithographer, he had the unusual habit of creating imprints in both the original state and then as a mirror image. One of his best-known prints is a portrait of the *USS Constitution*, Old Ironsides, which he originally created to help raise funds for the preservation of the historic vessel. Grant was also instrumental in founding the Ship Model Society and the Marine Museum of the City of New York.

Grant kept a summer studio on Rocky Neck and vacationed there with his wife for many years. Wade Hampton de Fontaine, art director of *Yachting* magazine, became a personal friend of the artist and was intrigued at the simplicity of Grant's sketching equipment: "a sketch pad of smooth paper… a lead holder in which a Negro lead (either black or brown) was inserted, a pen knife, and a backless stool…. With a single pencil he could get every tone he wanted, from the most delicate gray to the darkest tone."[46]

Grant also had a keen eye for composition and would often adapt a scene, moving or enlarging various elements to improve the overall design. His greatest ability, however, was the unique vision that allowed him to spontaneously capture the character of the men and women whom he met on his travels and whose faces and figures filled his sketchbooks, providing a wealth of material for his later studio works. A National Academician, with work hanging in the White House, Grant was well respected by his peers as an artist who knew and loved his subject. His ability to celebrate and record the great traditions of the age of sail not only left us with many fine images, but also provided a visual history of an era that is now long gone.

Notes

1 Kenney, Herbert A., *Cape Ann, Cape America* (Philadelphia: J. B. Lippincott, 1971), p. 17.

2 Connolly, J. B., *The Port of Gloucester* (New York: Doubleday, 1940), p. 1.

3 Gloucester Archives, Peterson File 'Early Explorations,' *Gloucester Daily Times*, July 9, 1982, *Summer Sun*, August 11, 1989, and July 2, 1993, October 16, 1997; quoted in Ray, Mary, ed. Sarah V. Dunlap and Gloucester Archives Committee, *Gloucester, Massachusetts: Historical Time Line, 1000-1999*, © 2002, p. 1.

4 Knowlton, Helen Mary, *Art-Life of William Morris Hunt*, 1899.

5 Brown-Corbin Fine Art, advertisement in *The Magazine Antiques*, 2007.

6 O'Gorman, James F., *This Other Gloucester* (Gloucester: Ten Pound Island, 1990) p. 60.

7 McAveeney, David C., *Kipling in Gloucester, The Writing of Captains Courageous* (Gloucester: Curious Traveller, 1966), p. 43.

8 Boer Notes: Harbor View Hotel, Roster Notes (TT).

9 Quoted in Atkinson, D. Scott et al, *Winslow Homer in Gloucester*, exhibition catalogue, Terra Museum of American Art (Chicago: Terra Foundation for the Arts, 1990), p. 7.

10 Cox, Kenyon, *What is Painting? "Winslow Homer" & Other Essays* (New York: W. W. Norton, 1988), p. 13.

11 James, Jr., Henry, "On Some Pictures Lately Exhibited," *The Galaxy*, 20:1 (July 1875): 90, quoted in Atkinson, et al, *Winslow Homer in Gloucester*, p. 47.

12 "Augustus Waldeck Buhler," *Maine in America*, Farnsworth Art Museum. Available at www.farnsworthmuseum.org/collections/downloads/Maine_in_America6.pdf, February 8, 2007.

13 "Buhler painted fishermen," *Gloucester Daily Times*, August 27, 1969, newspaper clipping, Buhler Papers, Cape Ann Historical Association (hereinafter referred to as CAHA).

14 "Augustus Waldeck Buhler," Farnsworth Art Museum.

15 Craig, James A., *Fitz H. Lane, An Artist's Voyage through Nineteenth-Century America* (Charleston, SC: History Press, 2006), p. 166.

16 Ibid., p. 18.

17 Wilmerding, John, *Fitz Hugh Lane 1803-1865 American Marine Painter* (Salem, MA: Essex Institute, 1964), p.11.

18 *Gloucester Telegraph*, November 16, 1836, quoted in Wilmerding, John, *Fitz Hugh Lane 1803-1865 American Marine Painter*, p. 12.

19 Wilmerding, John, p. 20.

20 Craig, James A., p. 119.

21 Parrish, Jr., Maxfield, *Stephen Parrish (1846-1938)* exhibition catalogue (Boston: Vose Galleries, 1982), p. 4.

22 Ibid., p. 8.

23 Archives of American Art, Smithsonian Institute, Washington, D. C., Sylvester Rosa Koehler papers, Microfilm reel D189, frames 274-275, letter from Parrish to Koehler, 4 March 1887. Quoted by Rona Schneider in *Stephen Parrish*, CAHA exhibition catalogue, October 1985, p. 8.

24 Ibid., p. 6.

25 Van Rensselaer, M. G. "American Etchers," *Century Magazine*, vol. 3, (n.s.), no. 4 (February 1883), p. 495. Quoted by Rona Schneider, p. 17.

26 Handwritten note, Stephen Parrish Papers, CAHA.

27 Parrish, Jr., Maxfield, p. 10.

28 Beaux, Cecilia, *Background with Figures* (New York: Houghton Mifflin, 1930), p. 94.

29 Kristiansen, Rolf H., and John J. Leahy, *Rediscovering Some New England Artists 1875-1900* (Dedham, MA: Gardner-O'Brien, 1987), p. 199.

30 *Cape Ann Weekly Advertiser*, August 6, 1875, p. 2.

31 *Cape Ann Shore*, July 12, 1930. Quoted in Usher, Donald K., *Gloucester's Own George and Martha*, exhibition catalogue, Annisquam Historical Society, March 28, 1981.

32 George W. Harvey Papers, Rockport Art Association Archives.

33 Havens, George R., *Frederick J. Waugh: American Marine Painter* (Orono, ME: University of Maine Press, 1969), p. 12.

34 Ibid., p. 209.

35 Ibid., p. 205.

36 Ibid., p. 207.

37 Ibid., p. 187.

38 "Fifty Fine Art Works," *Boston Sunday Post*, December 15, 1901, p. 3.

39 N. C. Wyeth to Sidney M. Chase, June 30, 1921, quoted in *The Wyeths, the Letters of N. C. Wyeth, 1905-1945*, ed., Betsy James Wyeth (Boston: Gambit, 1971), p. 678.

40 *Boston Daily Advertiser* (Dec. 7, 1906)

41 "Small Pictures in Variety Seen in Boston Shows," unidentified newspaper clipping. Quoted in Jarzombek, Nancy Allyn, "Paintings of George L. Noyes," *American Art Review*, April 2001, p. 119.

42 Cooper, Anice Page, *About Artists* (New York: Doubleday, 1926). Quoted in "Down To The Sea In Prints," Kraeft, June and Norman, exhibition catalogue, September 1987 (June 1 Gallery, Bethlehem, CT).

43 De Fontaine-Wade H., and Norman Kent *Gordon Grant Sketchbook* (New York: Watson-Guptill, 1960), p. 4.

44 Unattributed biographical information, Gordon Grant Papers, Rockport Art Association Archive.

45 Grant, Gordon, *Sail Ho! Windjammer Sketches Alow and Aloft* (New York: William Farquhar Payson n.d.)

46 De Fontaine-Wade, H., and Norman Kent, p.1.

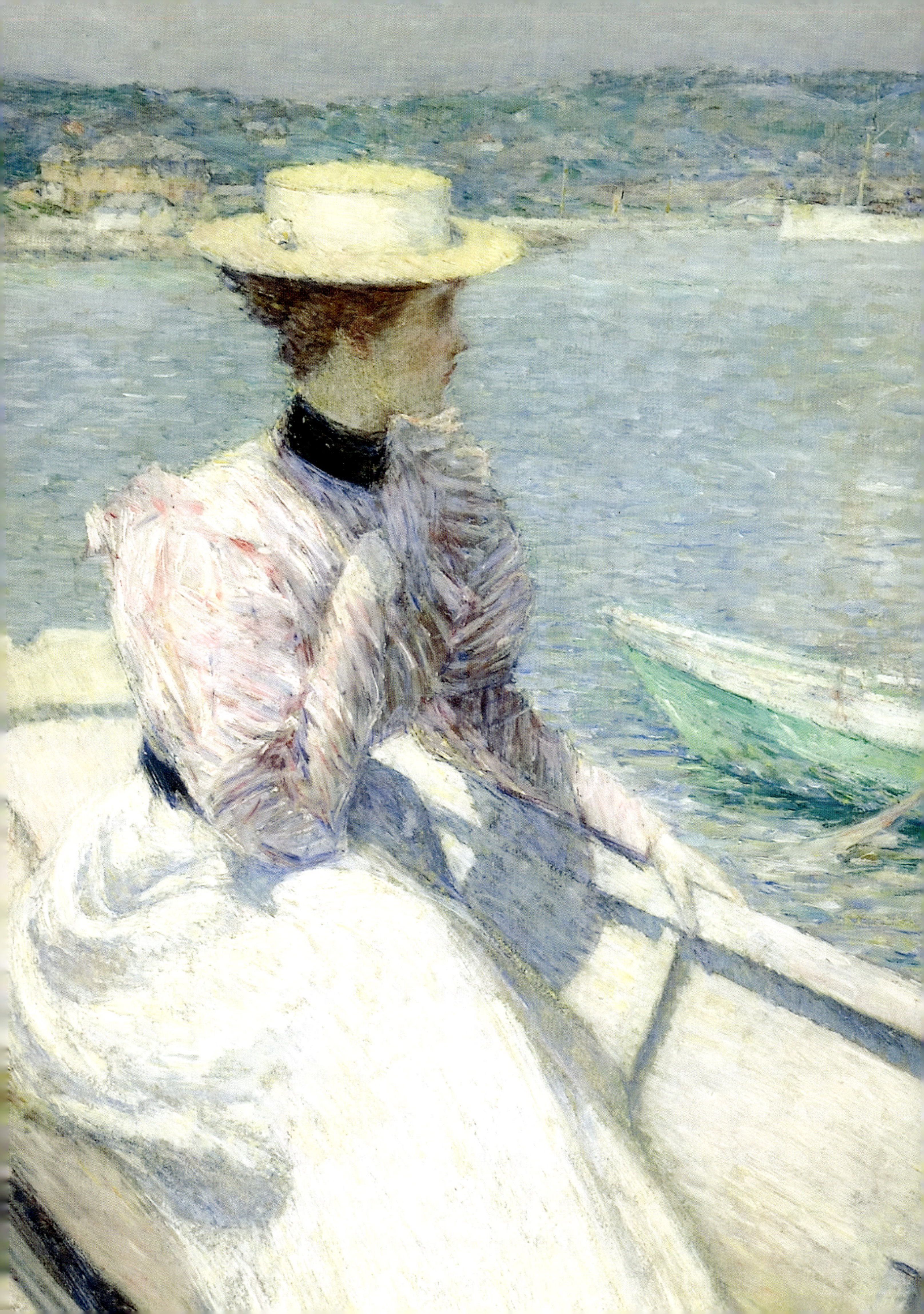

Duveneck and His Coterie

"The uninhabited moors were covered with wild roses and sweet smelling bay and when the harbor was filled with masts as thick as the forest... the great men of American art painted there—Metcalf, the great Duveneck, Hassam...."

— Alice Judson[1]

Of the many eminent artists who painted in and around East Gloucester during the last century and a half, none were greater or better loved by his contemporaries than Frank Duveneck—painter, sculptor, etcher and teacher. During a long and exemplary career, Duveneck not only carried his own art to distinguished heights—culminating in the presentation of a specially struck gold medal from an international jury of his peers at the 1915 Panama-Pacific Exhibition in San Francisco—but also raised countless students to the pinnacle of artistic excellence, including Boston portrait painter Joseph DeCamp, the avant-garde John Twachtman and Cincinnati's Herman and Bessie Wessel. John Singer Sargent called Duveneck "the greatest talent of the brush of this generation,"[2] and even Robert Henri, notable for his Ashcan School sensibilities, admitted, "Duveneck is a great master; no student of painting if he were awake could go through that [exhibition at the Cincinnati Art Museum] and not be inspired to develop for himself a technique of corresponding dignity. He is an extremely sensitive painter, a great draughtsman and every stroke of his brush manifests a consciousness of life, an intense conception of nature. His pictures are replete with life; no drawing of dead matter but rather a great refinement is evinced. A brush stroke which to the ordinary eye might seen [sic] crude or hasty is in his work the very perfect measure."[3]

Nonetheless, Duveneck—admired by his peers and revered by his students—dedicated so much of his time to teaching that he was less well known among the upper echelon of society. He was well aware that the "grand salon" portrait commissions of the New York bluebloods and Boston Brahmins would go to the more popular society painters, such as John Singer Sargent and William Merritt Chase. In 1904, after the Harcourt Street Studios fire destroyed much of Joseph DeCamp's landscape work, DeCamp, one of Duveneck's most accomplished students, turned to portraiture to support his family. He, in turn, was followed by his pupil, the inimitable William McGregor Paxton, whose small intimate portrait of his wife, Elizabeth Okie Paxton, reveals the refinement of his artistic lineage. The Paxtons were regular visitors to East Gloucester at the turn of the twentieth century when they maintained a summer studio on Rocky Neck and stayed at the Harbor View Hotel. They were artist members of the North Shore Arts Association and regular exhibitors during the 1920s.

For his own part, Duveneck did not aspire to move in society circles to garner commissions. He was far more interested in executing a good painting than in worrying about his social standing, much to the consternation of his father-in-law, Francis Boott, and his wife's literary acquaintance, Henry James. Both Boott and James, expatriate Americans, felt perfectly at home in the sophisticated milieu of nineteenth-century Europe, while Duveneck—as his detractors liked to describe him—was an

Detail
Childe Hassam
The White Dory, 1895
Oil on canvas, 26 x 21 in.
Private collection

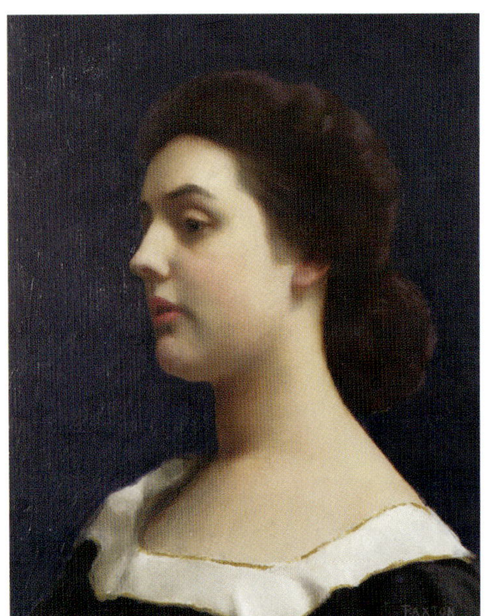

William Paxton
Elizabeth
Oil on canvas, 20 x 16 in.
Mosher Gallery, Rockport, Massachusetts

impecunious and itinerant artist of German-American Catholic stock from Covington, Kentucky. However, it was perhaps his stolid pioneering childhood on the frontier that gave Frank Duveneck the proper foundation on which to build a career. As a youngster he received his earliest art training with two German painters commissioned to decorate the mission church at Covington's Benedictine monastery. As an alter boy, Duveneck was already familiar with the dignity of his religion and the color and ceremony of Communion, and when the local priest recommended the boy to Schmidt and Lamprecht, the German painters, Duveneck's stepfather readily agreed to Frank's apprenticeship. This early training was in the manner of Renaissance schooling. "He was instructed in many crafts," says Josephine Whitney Duveneck, his daughter-in-law and biographer. "He carved wood, modeled figures, designed friezes, gilded surfaces, leaded glass panes and painted frescoes, thereby developing a facility of hand which characterized his later achievements."[4] Lamprecht, in particular, was a demanding master. As a product of the Munich Academy, Lamprecht set high standards for himself and those that worked with him. "Every morning before breakfast," reports Josephine, "[Lamprecht] made Frank draw two or three eyes until he found out how to do it with skill and dispatch."[5] Duveneck made good use of this skill throughout his career, for the eyes in his portraits often appear to reflect the soul of the sitter. Duveneck stayed with Lamprecht for some years, executing murals and church decoration from Louisville to Pittsburgh, Quebec, and Newark, New Jersey. When the job finally came to an end, one of the Church Fathers in Newark wrote to Duveneck Senior, suggesting Frank be sent to Munich to train as a religious painter. Although Frank's stepfather was not enamored of the idea, Frank's mother, Catherine Siemers Duveneck—who had worked in the home of artist James Beard after she was orphaned on the American frontier at the age of 13—believed that the profession of artist was an honorable one. Eventually her husband agreed that Frank could go to Munich once he reached the age of 21.

Consequently, in November 1869, Frank Duveneck began studying art in Munich. However, instead of aligning himself with a strictly religious painting education, Duveneck chose to enroll at the Munich Royal Academy where he sought a more secular approach to painting. He was totally unprepared for such basic work as drawing from the cast, but proved to be a quick learner and managed to redeem himself before they could reject him from the class. He went on to become one of the Academy's most apt pupils although even then he was more interested in achieving a particular effect and having done so, "the finishing of the picture was of no consequence," according to Josephine Duveneck. "Many of his pictures show a carefully painted head with the background and appurtenances scribbled in almost at random."[6]

An admirer of the Dutch and Flemish school, especially Rembrandt, Hals and the Spanish court painter, Velasquez, Duveneck emulated Hals's lively and spontaneous brushwork in the broad areas, while laying in the subject more in the manner of Velasquez, losing the edges of the model in shadow and modeling the features with passionate strokes. In a letter to a friend dated June 27, 1879, seven years before their marriage, Elizabeth Boott described Herr Professor Duveneck's working methods in enthusiastic detail:

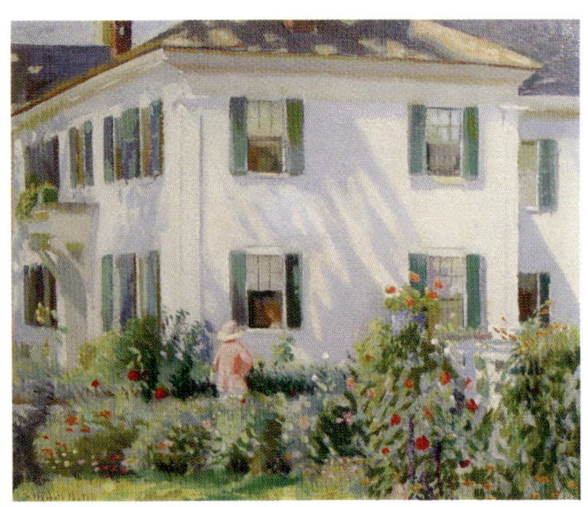

Elizabeth Paxton
Agnes Scott's Garden, Dedham, c. 1925
Oil on board, 14¾ x 18 in.
Private collection
Photo courtesy of Comenos Fine Arts, Boston

> *He sketched a head for me today. It is wonderful to see him sling the paint. He prefers a very smooth canvas as he uses his paint very oily, draws the thing in almost entirely with the brush in black with perhaps a little vermilion mixed. The shadows deeply and strongly in black, the hair and background all painted in together. With a large flat brush he lays on the flesh color, modeling it like clay, after the fashion of Mr. Hunt,*

gets the color very strong so that in the finishing it may not appear weak when the thing is fully modeled; uses more burnt siena [sic] than red in the flesh; this with yellow ochre and white makes a good mellow tone and a little red afterwards tells hugely. He even uses cadmium and all strong colors. The black makes a charming grey when the flesh tints meet it; he uses no blue, black seems to answer all the purpose. I think this school uses in painting black too much, but Duveneck loves brilliant color so much that one does not mind it. The dragging of dry color so much done in the French school, he does not seem to practice at all. Everything is moist, he paints in a puddle in fact, as one guesses from the look of his things. When he has carried a sketch as far as he thinks necessary and got it all in as a picture in a sort of splash of color and the values all connect, he lets it dry, then scrapes it down with a cuttle fish and finishes piece by piece, keeping the unfinished part in its primitive freshness always in his eye so as not to lose the breadth of the idea.... He is very nice, genial, simple, and friendly and ready to talk by the hour and tell all he knows.[7]

This willingness to share knowledge, and his unaffected midwestern manner, made Duveneck a perfect teacher. He was, according to Lizzie, "the frankest, kindest-hearted of mortals and the least likely to make his way in the world,"[8] and yet his students and friends loved him for his expansive and generous nature. It was perhaps a combination of this indolent attitude coupled with a peripatetic creative muse that gave Duveneck so much trouble in the latter part of his career. As Josephine Duveneck explains, "the pull between the artist and teacher kept him in a continuous state of indecision."

Duveneck began his first serious teaching when he returned to Cincinnati in 1873, conducting night classes at the Ohio Mechanics' Institute and teaching at the McMicken School of Design (later renamed the Art Academy of Cincinnati). Kenyon Cox was among his first pupils, as well as Joseph DeCamp and a young "Johnnie" Twachtman. Although Duveneck achieved some celebrity on the East Coast—after exhibiting several works with the Boston Art Club at the personal invitation of William Morris Hunt—he had no desire to become a Boston Brahmin society painter and resolved to return to Munich. When he left Cincinnati, several of his Cincinnati pupils went with him, including DeCamp, Twachtman and Theodore Wendel. Although Duveneck was only a few years older than most of his students, they deferred to him as "the old man," which of course made them "the boys." And the "Duveneck Boys" they remained as they followed him to the Royal Academy in Munich where he was Resident Artist, "leading a jolly life together, sharing each others' triumphs and defeats... living from day to day with a rich exuberant joy in life."[9] When Duveneck left the Academy to begin his own school, the boys went too, joining him in a move to Polling, Germany, and later to Florence and Venice.

Duveneck cut a larger than life figure. "Physically," one student recalled, "he was a big man, not much above average height, but massively broad-shouldered, deep-chested and robust.... the lordly lionesque head, with its thick carelessly tossed sandy-gray hair, the broadly blocked virile face, with its flowing moustache, full lips, determined jaw, and moody reflective eyes.... His bearing was quiet and unaffected, but a kind of sovereign dignity, suggestive of an inner consciousness of his powers and position, gave him an imposing presence."[10] Few have inspired such devotion in their students and acquaintances. Duveneck was no rigid academician, despite his years at Munich's Royal Academy. Instead, he straddled the line between the aesthetic of American realism and European impressionism to create a singular style that encouraged numerous young hopefuls to study with him and adopt "the high ideals of art and life he implanted."[11]

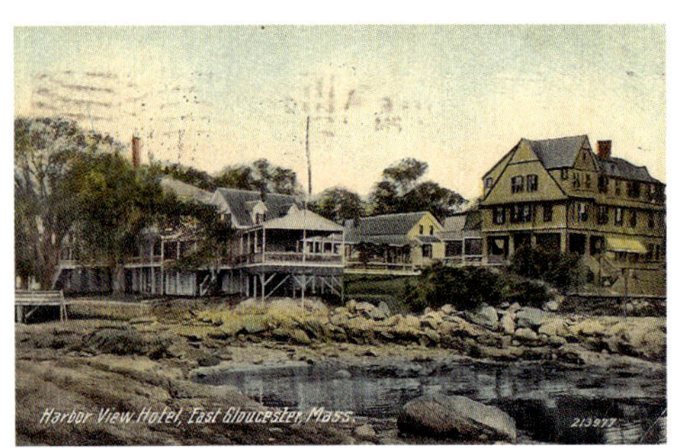

Harbor View Hotel, East Gloucester, Mass.
Postcard, c. 1912
Private collection

Throughout his career, Duveneck proved a charismatic character, not only attracting students of the caliber of DeCamp, Twachtman, Wendel, Julius Rolshoven and the Wessels, but also retaining them as close friends long after they had reached professional status themselves.

In 1888, in the wake of his wife's tragic death from pneumonia, Duveneck left Paris, where they had been living, and returned to the United States. He and Lizzie had been married for only two years, and their infant son, Francis B. Duveneck was suddenly motherless. Devastated, Duveneck brought his son to Cambridge, Massachusetts, to be raised by his late wife's Lyman relatives, and spent the rest of his life in a nomadic milieu of painting, teaching and traveling between Cincinnati, Europe and the fishing port of Gloucester, which because of its proximity to Cambridge proved an ideal location to spend the summers with his son.

Experts disagree on Duveneck's first visit to Gloucester. Suggestions have been made that he was here as early as 1881,[12] (Lizzie Boott studied with Hunt in Annisquam in 1874 and was obviously cognizant with the area) while other authorities say 1892,[13] and still others opt for 1890.[14] It is possible that Duveneck was in Gloucester in 1890, teaching summer classes. It would certainly have given him an opportunity to be near his young son after more than a year's separation. However, all agree that Duveneck summered at the Harbor View Hotel on Rocky Neck in 1892 and the following year he rented the Niles' Farm, just beyond the Rocky Neck causeway, where his five-year-old son and nurse joined him for the summer. Over a span of two and a half decades, Duveneck visited Rocky Neck some fifteen times and despite those who would label him lazy, indifferent, or still devastated by the loss of his wife, he still managed to paint 150 to 200 paintings that were eventually inherited by his son, who retained the majority of them in the family as treasured heirlooms. Duveneck himself chose to maintain a low profile, and gathered many of what he considered his best paintings to be given to the Cincinnati Art Museum for their permanent collection. Neither of these

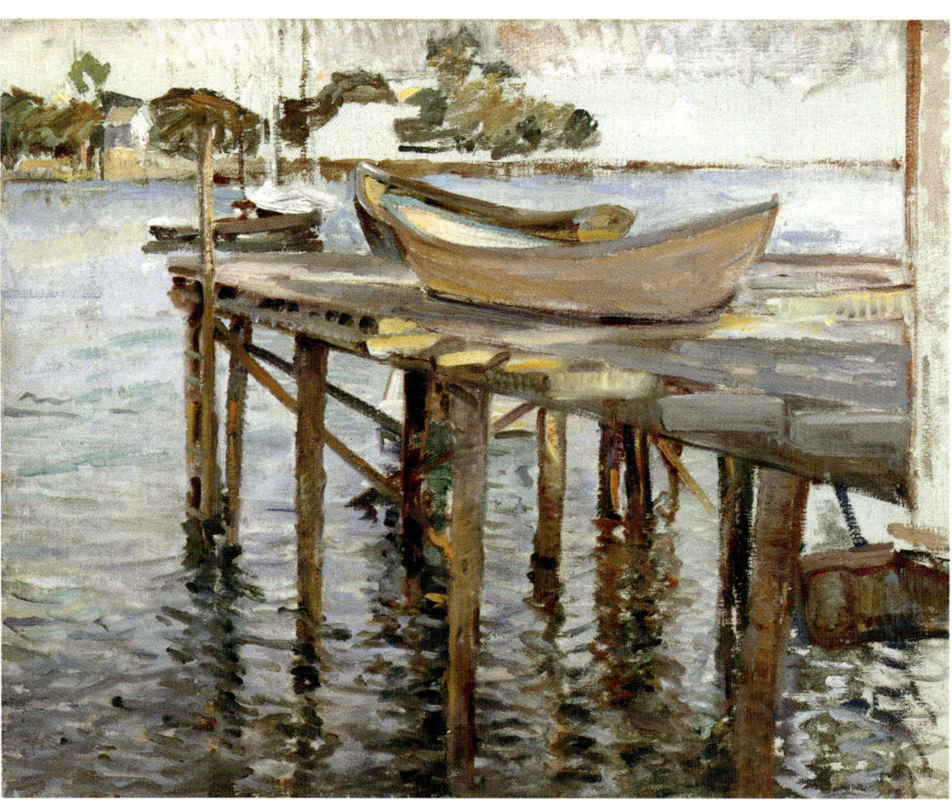

Frank Duveneck, N.A.
Smith Cove, Gloucester, Mass.
Oil on canvas, $20\frac{7}{8}$ x $25\frac{1}{16}$ in.
Farnsworth Art Museum, Rockland, Maine (75.1963)
Gift of Miss Dorothy Buhler, 1975
Photo: Steve Morrison

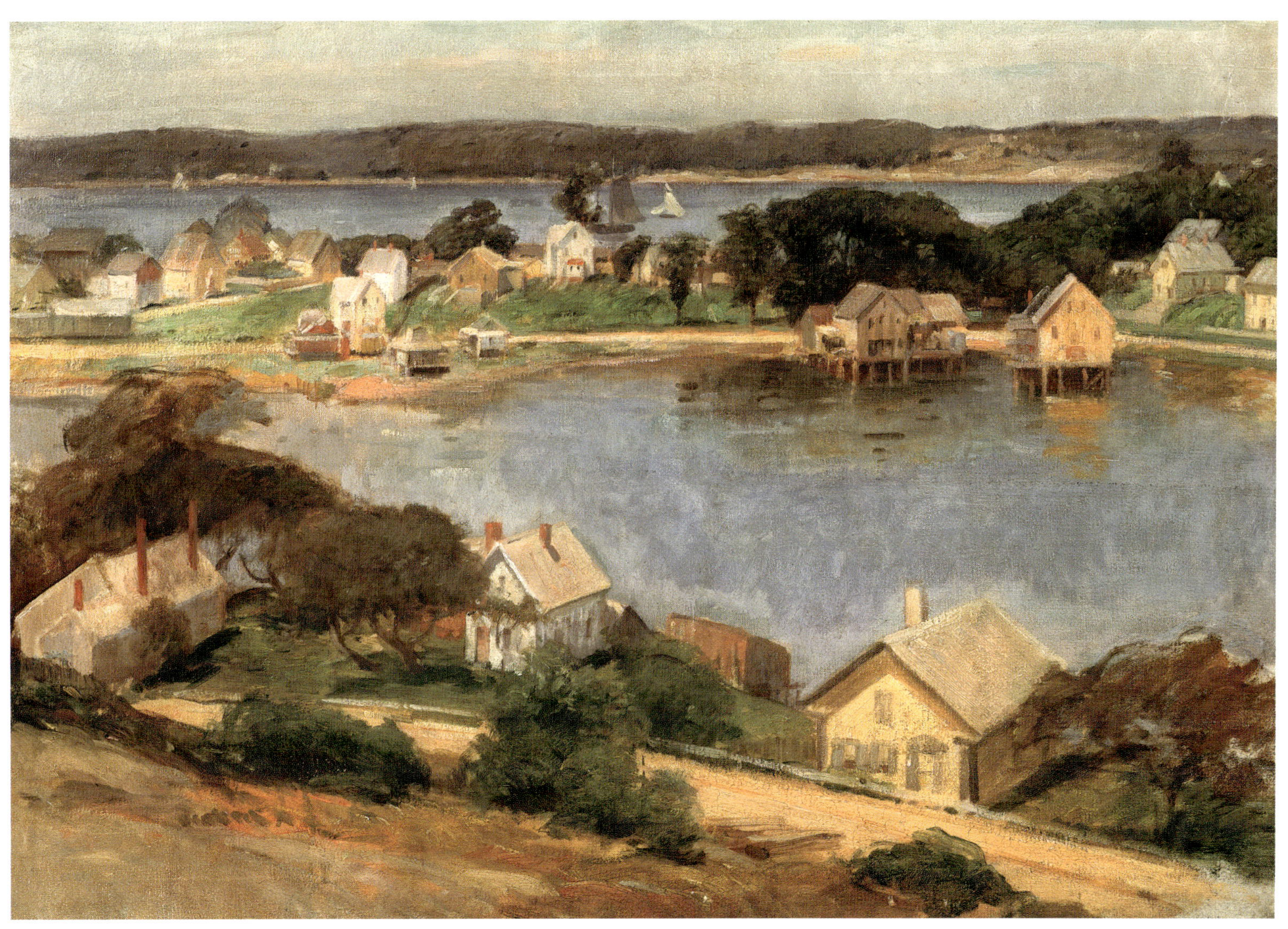

Frank Duveneck, N.A.
Smith Cove from Banner Hill, c. 1905
Oil on canvas, 25 x 36 in.
Private collection
Photo courtesy of Owen Gallery, New York

actions helped promote his recognition in the larger art world and yet that never appears to have been in the foremost of Duveneck's mind.

While painting in Gloucester, Duveneck chose to experiment with styles and techniques—color theories and light effects—that enabled him to paint in a higher key than before. He maintained a studio on Rocky Neck as well as Bass Rocks specifically to observe the effects of morning and afternoon light. Over the years, he was joined by several of "the boys," including Joseph DeCamp, who brought his wife and children; John Twachtman, who also came with family, and Theodore Wendel, who might well have painted side-by-side with Duveneck on Banner Hill. Cincinnati painters Herman Wessel and Bessie Hoover also visited regularly and were married at Duveneck's cottage during the summer of 1917. The Harbor View and the Rockaway were popular venues for the painter, both of which offered studio amenities for their artistic guests. In 1900, a note in the local newspaper announced,

> *East Gloucester… Delightful Entertainment and Exhibit at Hotel Rockaway… During the season such prominent artists as Duveneck, DeCamp, Churchill, Hazard, Pond, Potthast, Adams Case, Twachtman, Corwin, A. C. Fauley, L. S. Fauley, Katherine T. Farrell, Walter Clark and his son Eliot Clark, have arrived at the Rockaway, and in their coming the art of Massachusetts, Chicago, New York, Philadelphia, and the West have united in happy congeniality and the universal love of Gloucester and its never-*

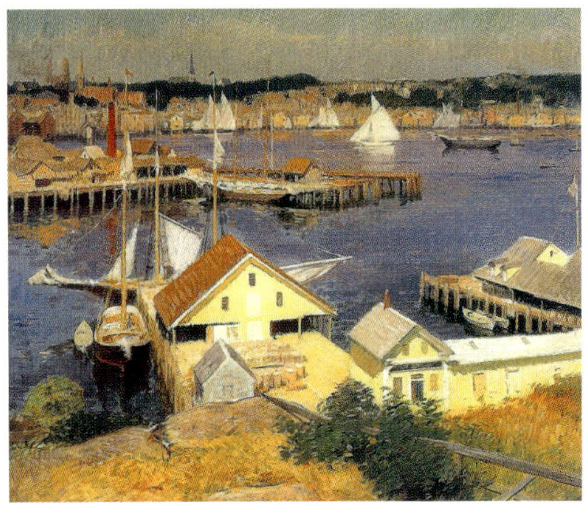

Frank Duveneck, N.A.
The Yellow Pier Shed, c. 1905
Oil on canvas, 36 x 40 in.
Private collection
Photo courtesy of Owen Gallery, New York

ending charms for the artist.

Mr. Duveneck's reputation as an artist and sculptor is too well known to need comment and his presence alone made all happy.

Mr. Twachtman is a New Yorker, a pupil of Duveneck and an instructor in the Art League and Cooper Institute of New York. His group of very small pictures which he termed 'postage stamps' were marked $100 each. Mr. Twachtman is a modern impressionist.

Mr. Corwin, who also exhibited some much admired pictures is an instructor in the Chicago art Institute and a pupil of Duveneck.

Mr. DeCamp who is termed one of the strongest painters of 'the new' is a pupil of Duveneck. Mr. Pond is a pupil of DeCamp.

Potthast, who exhibited some of his Adirondack sketches, was a winner of the $500 prize at the New York academy. He also won a reputation for his fine figure work.

Mr. Walter Dean joined the exhibitors and sent several of his fine marines to add to this charming exhibit. All the other artists added bits of seashore, country and harbor, conceptions which can only give to Gloucester and her right as a beautiful scenic spot.[15]

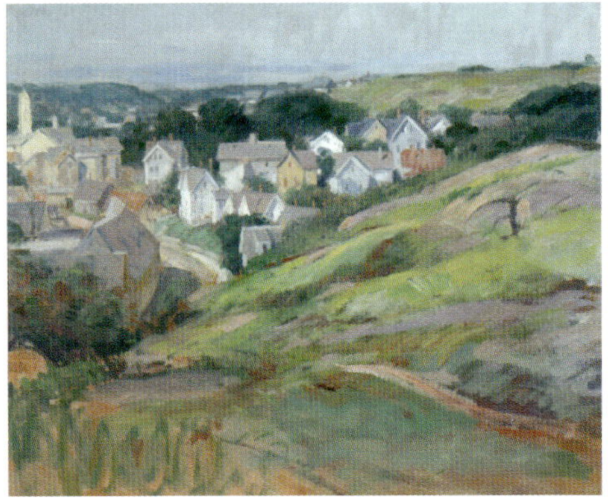

Frank Duveneck, N.A.
View from Hill, East Gloucester
Oil on canvas, 21 x 26 in.
Courtesy of the Kenton County Public Library, Covington, Kentucky

It is interesting to note that the critics and writers of the day considered Duveneck and his coterie to be "modern impressionists." Duveneck himself has been described as "Cezannesque,"[16] and yet in retrospect, Duveneck's abilities far outstrip soubriquets that pigeonhole the artist. His Gloucester work especially, as we can see from *The Yellow Pier Shed*, is much lighter in palette than his earlier Munich style, while the brushwork is flatter and more controlled in execution; small planes afford crisper handling of the paint.

Duveneck was often considered something of an experimenter in terms of chiaroscuro and color theory, and his painting sojourns in Gloucester produced

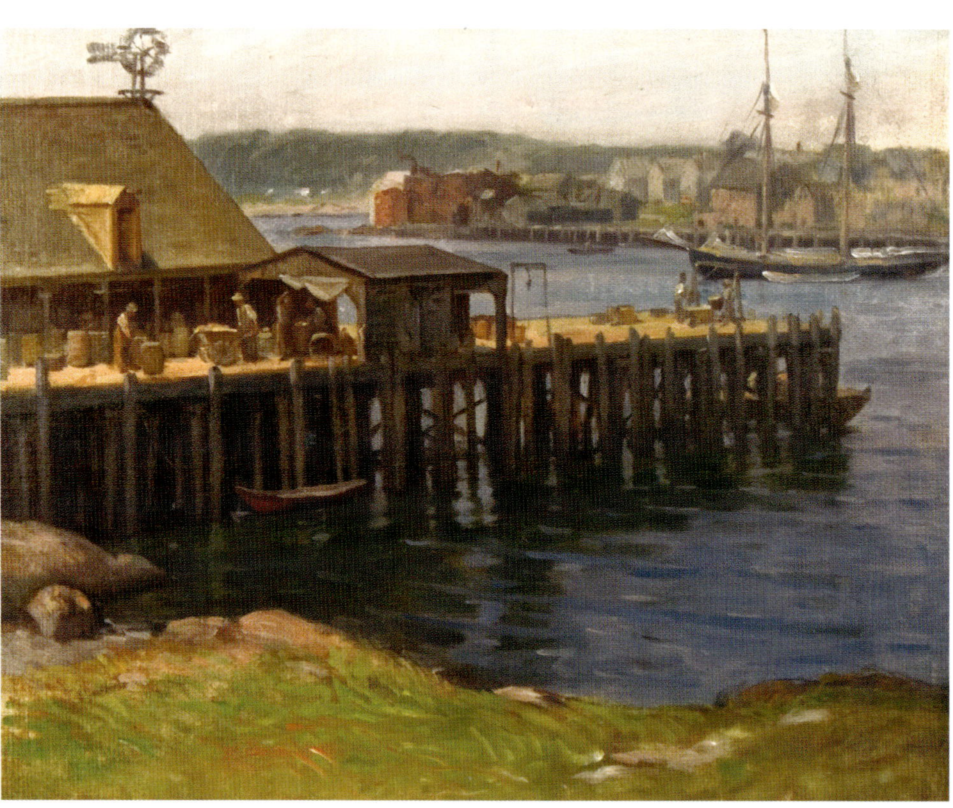

Frank Duveneck, N.A.
Dock Workers, Gloucester, 1910
Oil on canvas, 24 x 30 in.
Private collection

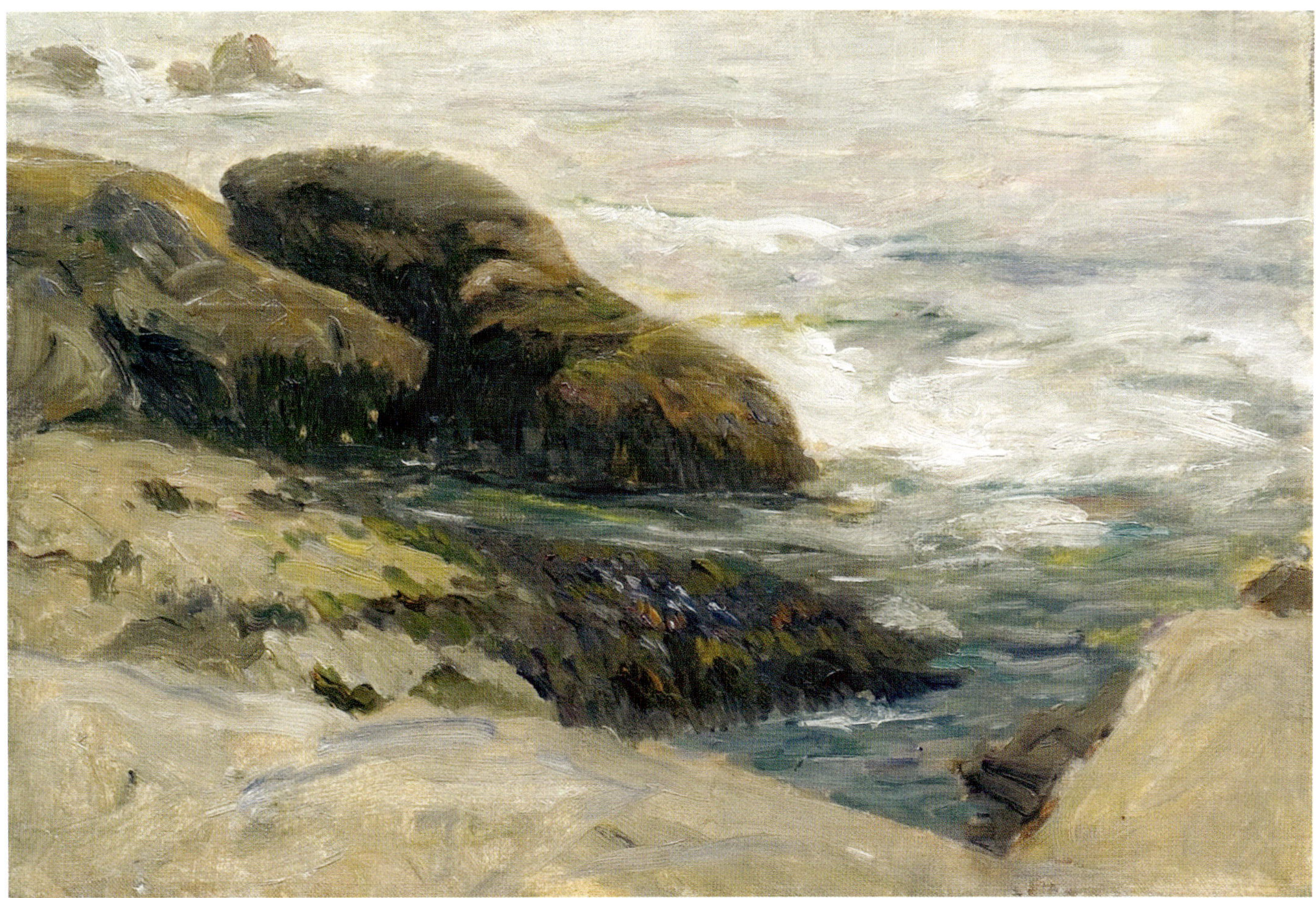

Frank Duveneck, N.A.
Rocky Coast, c. 1916
Oil on canvas, 12 x 18 in.
Private collection
Photo courtesy of Owen Gallery, New York

numerous alla prima works, including *Rocky Coast*, an intimate study of Bass Rocks, *View from Hill, East Gloucester*, and *Dock Workers*, all of which have the exuberant quality of a painter enjoying his work. Some detractors have suggested Duveneck lost his impetus to paint after the death of his wife in 1888. However, considering the amount of teaching he undertook, it is hardly surprising that on reaching Gloucester, Duveneck chose to relax and spend time with his son, and his own siblings, who often took the opportunity to visit with him in Gloucester. Consequently, his painting schedule was generally unhurried and executed more for enjoyment than to produce an inventory of work. "The boys" often encouraged him to join them at the easel, although it is perhaps telling that when someone inquired about Duveneck's preferred materials, his friend Clement Barnhorn responded, "Usually someone else's!" Nevertheless, "the Old Man" did not like to disappoint his students and once, while painting in Gloucester, when he was offered a large sum of money for a canvas right off the easel, Duveneck gently turned the offer down saying, "I have to take it back to show my boys I've been working." He did not care for "the rush of American life," and once confided that he felt "he had no right to shut himself up in a studio, and painting did not seem enough of an occupation, but [in Florence] one could be more idle and paint as and when one chose."[17] Gloucester, however, seemed to have much the same effect on Duveneck as the idyllic days of Florence, and he relished the opportunity to indulge himself in painting because he chose to and not because he had to.

John H. Twachtman (1853-1902)

According to his friend, artist J. Alden Weir, John Twachtman "was in advance of his age… he lived ahead of his epoch,"[18] while his colleague, Thomas Dewing, of the Ten American Painters, thought Twachtman a "most modern spirit… too modern, probably, to be fully recognized or appreciated at present, but his place will be recognized in the future, and he will one day be a 'classic'…."[19] Prophetic words because today Twachtman is applauded for his experimental ways and artistic foresight.

Poet, lyricist and dreamer, John Henry Twachtman progressed through several styles during a checkered career that saw him admired as a teacher at the Art Students' League in New York, and yet dismissed by an art-buying public that did not always grasp his modern impressionist style. An introspective soul, Twachtman appears to have been more concerned with the metaphysical approach rather than the purely pictorial and was often frustrated by a lack of appreciation for his extremely sophisticated landscapes. These paintings were executed with a subtlety of hand and palette that were admired by his peers but judged less favorably by critics and the public. Painter and critic Eliot Clark, who was in residence at the Hotel Rockaway on Rocky Neck in 1900 during Twachtman's first summer season, straddled a thin line between these two ways of thinking, describing Twachtman's work as "uneven" and "uncontrolled,"[20] and also as "an experiment… venturing into new realms of consciousness… and it is precisely this quickened spirit that the painter has so successfully imparted to the spectator."[21] We may conjecture that the writer was commenting on the ethereal effect seeping into Twachtman's painting, imbuing it with a transcendental quality that elevated the viewer as much as the artist.

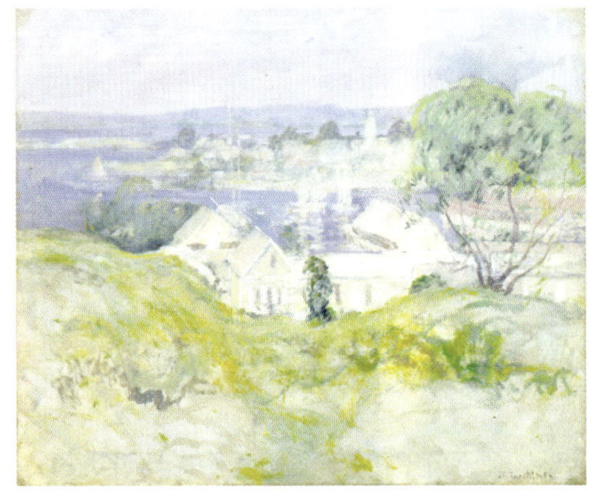

John Henry Twachtman
Gloucester, c. 1898-1902
Oil on canvas, 25 x 30 in.
The Florence Griswold Museum,
Old Lyme, Connecticut
Gift of the Hartford Steam Boiler
Inspection and Insurance Company

A Cincinnatian by birth, Twachtman began his artistic career painting floral designs on window shades for a local firm for which his father worked. During that same time Twachtman was studying at the Ohio Mechanics Institute in the evenings. In 1874, he began studying under Frank Duveneck at the McMicken School of Design in Cincinnati, and the following year accompanied Duveneck to Munich, enrolling at the Royal Academy in the fall of 1875. Thus, the dark palette and the unvarnished truth of the Munich school characterize Twachtman's first artistic period. However, although the dark values and spirited brushwork may have worked well for the figure painter, Twachtman was more interested in portraying landscape and representing the pure elements of nature. When Duveneck broke from the Royal Academy to form his own atelier, Twachtman and the rest of the "Duveneck Boys" moved with him, first to Polling, and then Florence and Venice. Here they met the ineffable expatriate American James McNeill Whistler and Twachtman became fascinated with the Whistlereque as well as the Japanese woodblock aesthetic, both of which would influence the artist for the rest of his career. In 1881, while on a European honeymoon with his bride, the former Martha Scudder, a fellow painter and etcher, Twachtman met Anton Mauve in Holland. Mauve was a plein air painter of the Dutch school whose technique also informed Twachtman's later style. These separate influences, combined with his studies at the Académie Julian in Paris, persuaded Twachtman to abandon the heavy tactile attributes of Munich and fully embrace the tenets of impressionism. Over the next decade, Twachtman fully utilized the brighter palette of the Impressionists, as well as their more fluid approach to form, to create lyrical works that in 1891 critics hailed as "delicate trifles"[22]

Yet, despite his expertise and innovative style, or perhaps because of it, Twachtman

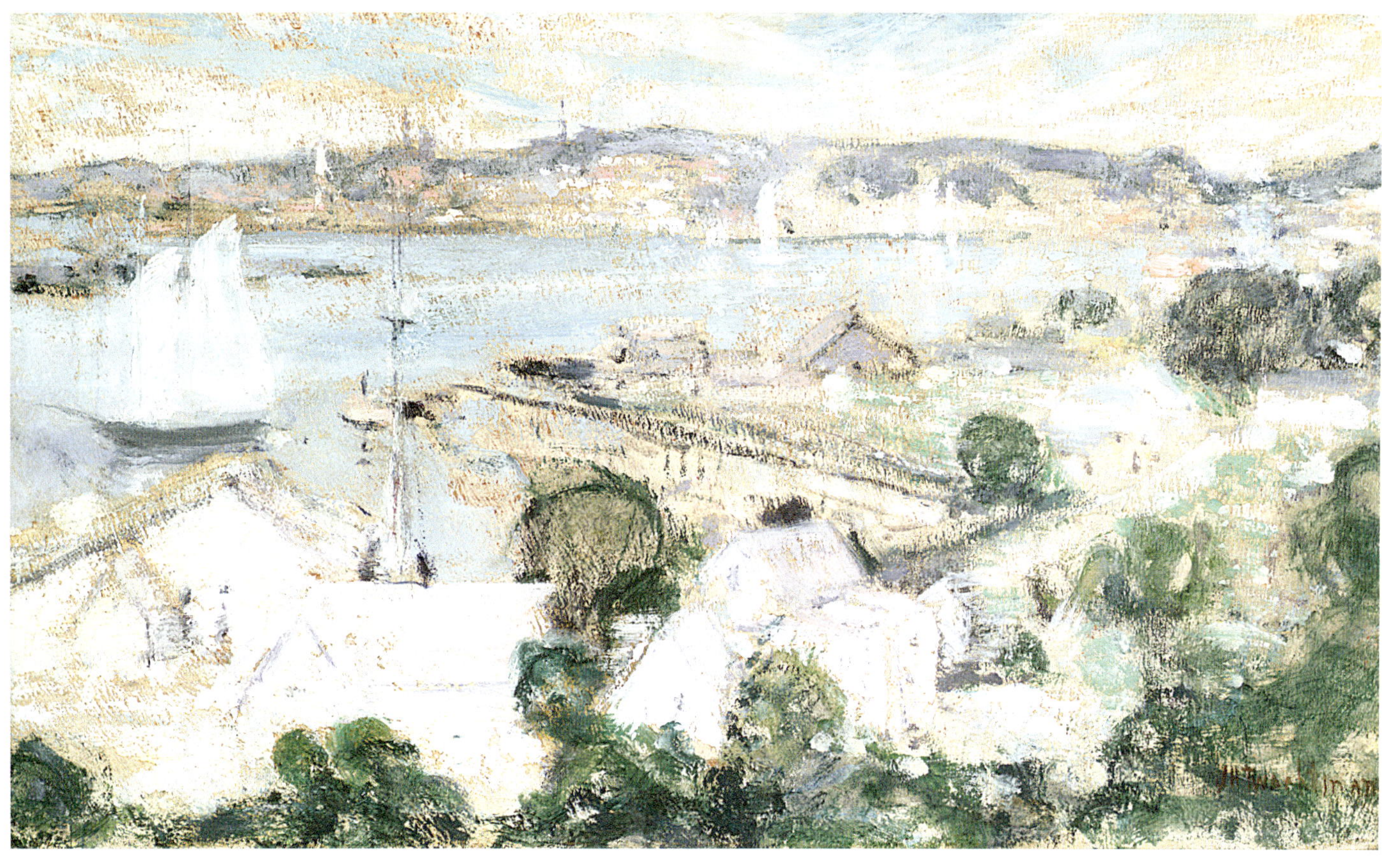

John Henry Twachtman
Gloucester Harbor, c. 1900
Oil on panel, 13¼ x 22¼ in.
Spanierman Gallery, LLC, New York

struggled throughout his career to justify his artistic viewpoint and earn a living to support his family without prostituting his talents. Twachtman turned to teaching and illustrating to supplement his income, and was so successful that within a short time he was able to purchase seventeen acres of land outside of Greenwich, Connecticut, on which to build a house and garden à la Monet at Giverny. He spent much of his time painting on his own property and some of his most notable works come from this era. However, he was still a restless soul at heart, and liked to isolate himself to pursue his own thoughts. Gloucester at the turn of the nineteenth century could hardly be described as isolated and Rocky Neck was full of artists painting en plein air, nonetheless Twachtman chose to visit in 1900, and made himself at home at the Rockaway, together again with his friends Joseph DeCamp and the ebullient Duveneck.

Perhaps it is just as well that no one knew how little time was left to Twachtman. The artists enjoyed their days, painting around the docks or from up on Banner Hill with Rocky Neck and the harbor spread below, and at night would gather to enjoy each other's company. Their comings and goings were duly noted in the newspaper: "East Gloucester… Mr. Twachtman and family of New York who have been stopping at the Pilgrim House awaiting an available cottage for their occupancy, have secured apartments in the 'Amenity cottage' the new Rockaway annex, for the season. Mr. Twachtman is a New York artist and decorator."[23] A week later, on June 12, the *Gloucester Daily Times* reported the artist's wife and eldest son had arrived to join the family. On August 17, 1900, under "Rockaway Hotel Notes," the *Times* announced, "The artists at the hotel are making a continuous exhibit of their pictures in the parlor and there are large numbers of visitor to view the work daily which is said to be the strongest from an artistic standpoint ever exhibited here." Less than a month later, the Rockaway was in the news again. "East Gloucester… The large numbers of artists

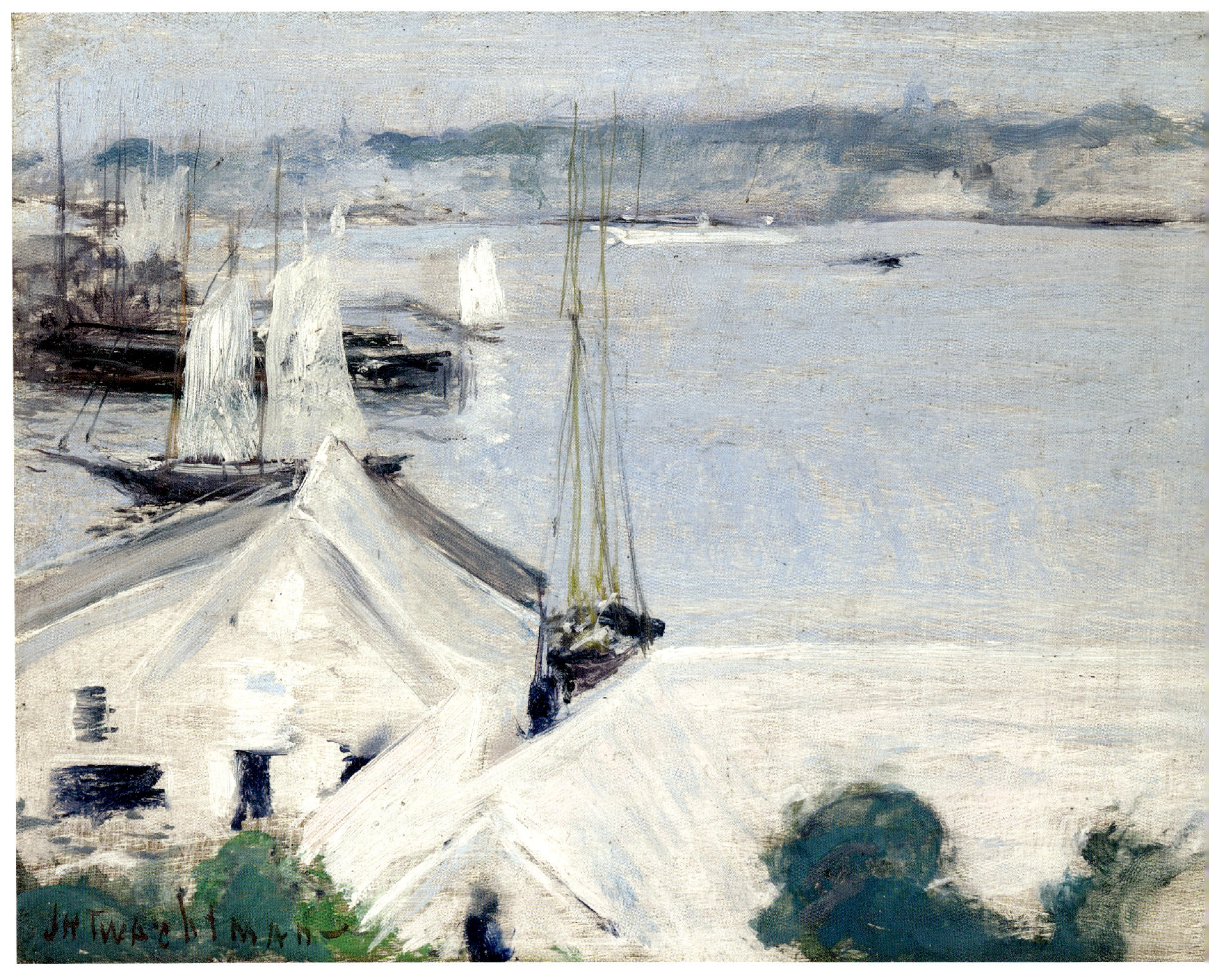

John Henry Twachtman
Boats at Anchor, c. 1900
Oil on panel, 7½ x 9⅝ in.
Spanierman Gallery, LLC, New York

congregated at the Rockaway, the equally large number of art students who have been under study here and the artist guests at the Hawthorne Inn, has seemed to renew the artistic atmosphere of by-gone seasons."[24] Twachtman remained on Rocky Neck until well into September, the *Times* reporting, "Mr. J. H. Twachtman's family have joined him at the Rockaway, among them his eldest son who won the Yale College scholarship of $2000 for future study abroad."[25] The hotel closed for the season shortly after.

No doubt Twachtman spent some time in Gloucester the following summer. Although he is not mentioned by name, his students certainly made their presence known with this note in the *Gloucester Daily Times* on August 20, 1901: "East Gloucester… The members of the Art Students League of New York, who are making the Rockaway their summer home were the prime movers in one of the prettiest and jolliest costume dances ever given in the summer colony at the Rockaway last evening… The veranda of the art students' cottage were also covered with jack-o'lanterns."[26]

While painting in Gloucester, Twachtman switched between the earthier toned palette of his dock scenes, suggesting a more grounded reality, and the other-worldly plane of his Banner Hill paintings, which are executed in a much higher key and with the chalkier finish of thinly applied paint, as if the effort of its application was almost too much for the artist. Even the contrasting notes are kept as bright as possible. *Gloucester Harbor* ca. 1900 is particularly representative of these almost ethereal works of Twachtman's with their high key tonality and freedom of application that suggests a fervent alla prima execution with emphasis on the spatial perspective and the feeling of light hitting the object, rather than accurate rendering of the form itself. One can readily appreciate the weightlessness of the artist's heart and soul in this quintessential view from Banner Hill.

Twachtman's Gloucester paintings are the culmination of his life's work. Nowhere in his oeuvre are the European influences of Mauve and Whistler, plus the simplicity of the Japanese woodcut ethic, more apparent than in the plein air paintings executed during the short time Twachtman spent on Rocky Neck. No matter whether painting big or small—*Boats at Anchor* ca. 1900 is what Twachtman referred to as a "postage stamp" size and was likely painted on one of the cigar box tops he often utilized—the artist always came up with a singular and lyrical viewpoint. He was never afraid to tackle a difficult composition and often went out of his way to discover an unusual perspective that captured the essence of the moment.

Twachtman's small two-room studio with its porch overhanging the waters of Wonson's Cove, across from Rocky Neck, was a well-known gathering point for his comrades. Although the studio withstood the natural elements for decades, it was no match for the whims of man and was demolished in the latter years of the twentieth century to make way for newer housing. Nonetheless, when Twachtman arrived on Rocky Neck for the summer of 1902, the ethics of progress could not have been farther from his mind. On June 24, 1902, the *Gloucester Daily Times* reported, "Mr. J. H. Twachtman, an annual artist guest, and a prominent instructor in the New York Art Students' League, will have a summer class here in conjunction with Mr. Joseph DeCamp, his collaborator in New York. Mr. Twachtman is at the Harbor View."[27] Who could have known that less than two months later, the *Times* would be reporting much sadder news:

> *GREAT ARTIST DEAD. John H. Twachtman Passed Away at the Addison Gilbert Hospital. John H. Twachtman, one of the greatest painters of the present period, died in Gloucester this morning.*
>
> *Mr. Twachtman and his daughter, Miss Margery, have been guests of the Harbor View Hotel for some time. A few days ago, he was taken ill and Dr. Knowles considered the case a critical one.*
>
> *Mr. Twachtman married Miss Scudder of Cincinnati. Four children survive him. The other members of the artist's family are in Paris.*[28]

Twachtman's sudden passing from a brain aneurysm cast a pall over the colony, particularly among those artists who knew him well. DeCamp in particular felt the loss of his friend deeply. Although he returned to Rocky Neck the following year, he found the memories too painful to bear and was unable to visit Rocky Neck again. It was a double blow for the colony to lose two such talented artists.

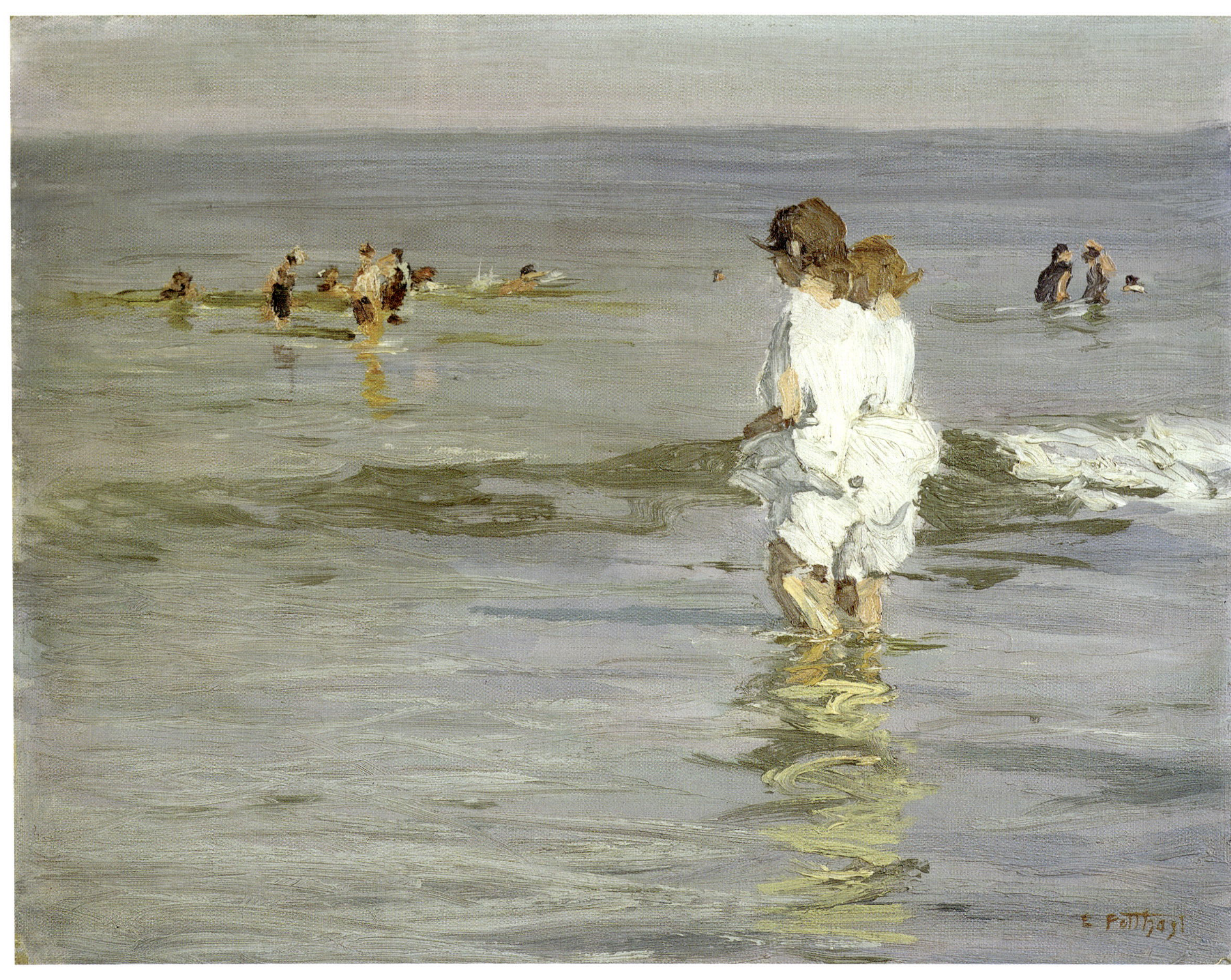

Edward Potthast
Chums
Oil on canvas board, 12 x 16 in.
Private collection
Photo courtesy of Keny Galleries, Columbus, Ohio

Edward Potthast, N.A. (1857-1927)

Edward Henry Potthast, like many of his colleagues in the art colony at Rocky Neck, hailed from Cincinnati and studied with Frank Duveneck. Potthast also studied at the Royal Academy in Munich, adopting their darker tones but after a short time at the Académie Julian studying with Boulanger and Lefèbvre, his palette became lighter as he experimented with the juxtaposition of complementary color notes to create high key vibration. While in Paris in 1887, Potthast adjusted his palette further, as well as his brushwork to assimilate the Impressionist ideal of scumbled edges and broken color. Potthast became adept in various media, including succulent oils, fresh and spontaneous watercolors, graphite and crayon. After returning to Cincinnati, he became known for light-drenched canvases normally the forte of the Barbizon School and the French Impressionists, and he was the only American artist to be included in the Light Pictures exhibition hosted by the Cincinnati Art Museum in 1894. Potthast, according to his friend Henry Farny, was his own worst critic: "If the man was not so infernally modest and allowed me to send some of his stuff to the World's Fair you would have heard a good deal more about him by this time. But no, he said they were only 'sketches' and I couldn't get the idiot to let them go."[29] In 1896, Potthast followed his friend John Twachtman to Manhattan, possibly because it offered him the opportunity to supplement his income in the lucrative illustration market created by such well-known magazines as *Scribner's, Harper's* and *Century Magazine*. Three years later, in 1899, Potthast received the Thomas B. Clarke Prize for figure painting at the National Academy's annual exhibition and he was subsequently elected an associate member, becoming a full Academician in 1906.

In the meantime, Potthast increased his reputation as a painter of light with works such as *Chums* executed during one of his summer visits to the seashore. Here, Potthast's restrained tonality and the subtle nuances of light and atmosphere capture a fleeting moment of two friends wading in a tranquil ocean. It is reported that Potthast first visited Cape Ann in 1896, perhaps at the behest of his numerous colleagues. The records show Potthast was one of the participants in the Hotel Rockaway's summer exhibition in 1900 in the company of his friends, Twachtman, DeCamp, and Duveneck. Potthast was a regular visitor to the Gloucester seashore for the next 25 years, where he regularly switched between a tonal palette to capture the laziness and haziness of a hot summer's day at the beach, and the vibrancy of his bolder palette utilizing strong contrasting colors to achieve a more flamboyant effect.

Edward Potthast
Gloucester Harbor
Oil on canvas, 30¼ x 40¼ in.
Collection of Dr. and Mrs. Joel E. Berenson

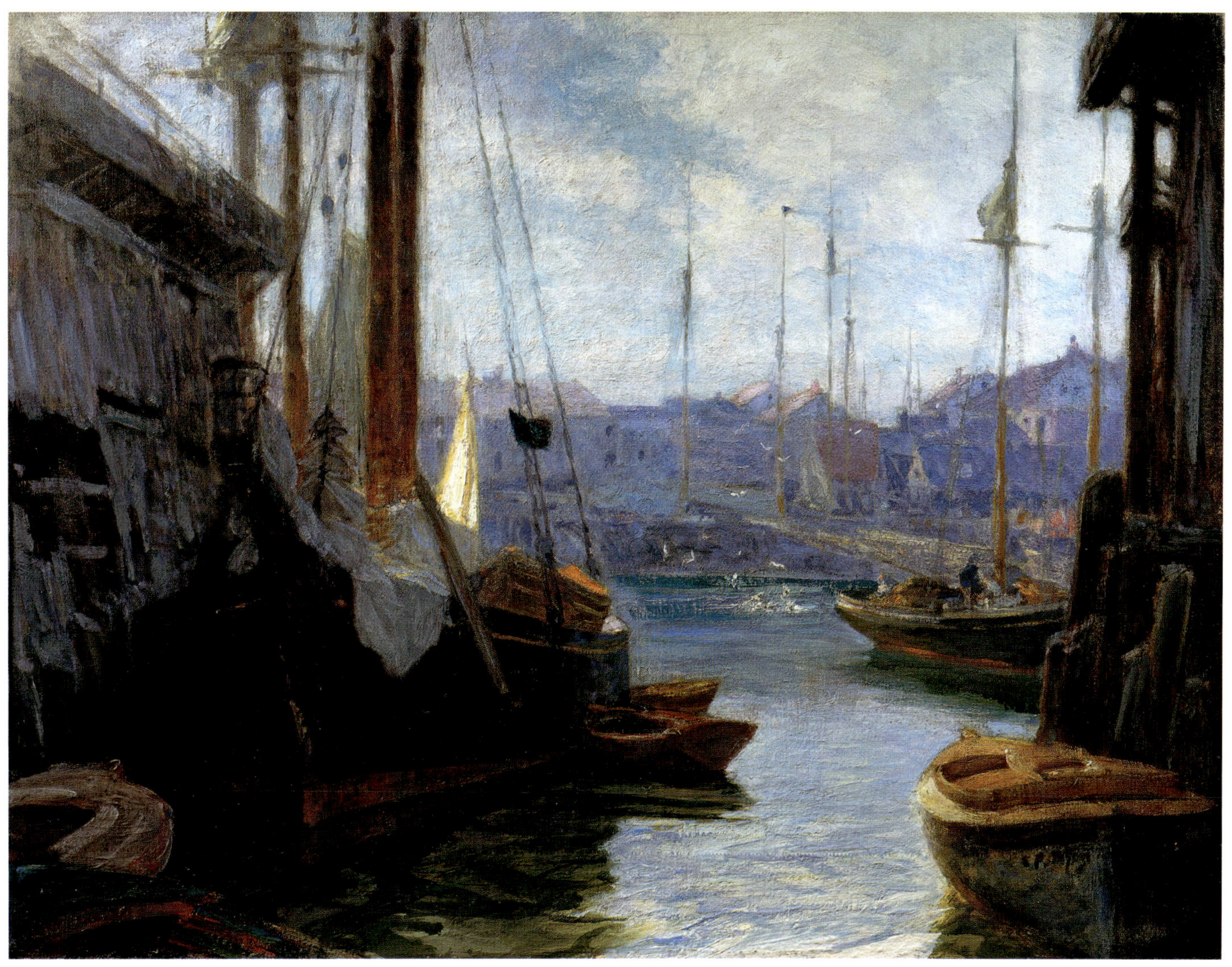

John Cook (1870-1936)

Although John Cook is today best known for his charming watercolors of Gloucester Harbor, which every visitor to the cape had to acquire before returning home, he was also capable of larger impressionistic works that captured the many moods of Gloucester. As a year-round resident, Cook observed and then portrayed myriad facets of the city, including the harsher days of winter when delivery men with wagons had to rely on real horsepower to get through the snow-clogged streets. Despite the tonal simplicity with values keyed close together for a cool effect, Cook still manages to find color in the snow squall and accumulated drifts to create atmosphere and light in the brumal air. Cook, like Fitz Henry Lane and W. Lester Stevens, was a Cape Ann native. At the tender age of eight he came across William Morris Hunt's sketching class at work, which, he claimed, inspired him to become an artist himself. Cook studied with Joseph DeCamp in Boston, and also E. L. Major, both of who were Rocky Neck regulars at the turn of the twentieth century. Although Cook did not travel far afield to paint, finding an abundance of coastal views, landscapes and marine themes in and around Rocky Neck, his name was well known throughout New England. As an active member of both the Gloucester Society of Artists and the North Shore Arts Association, John Cook did much to promote, and sometimes romanticize, Gloucester's image as a scenic yet dichotomous fishing port.

John Cook
Boats at Dock, Gloucester Harbor
Watercolor, 8½ x 11½ in.
Private collection

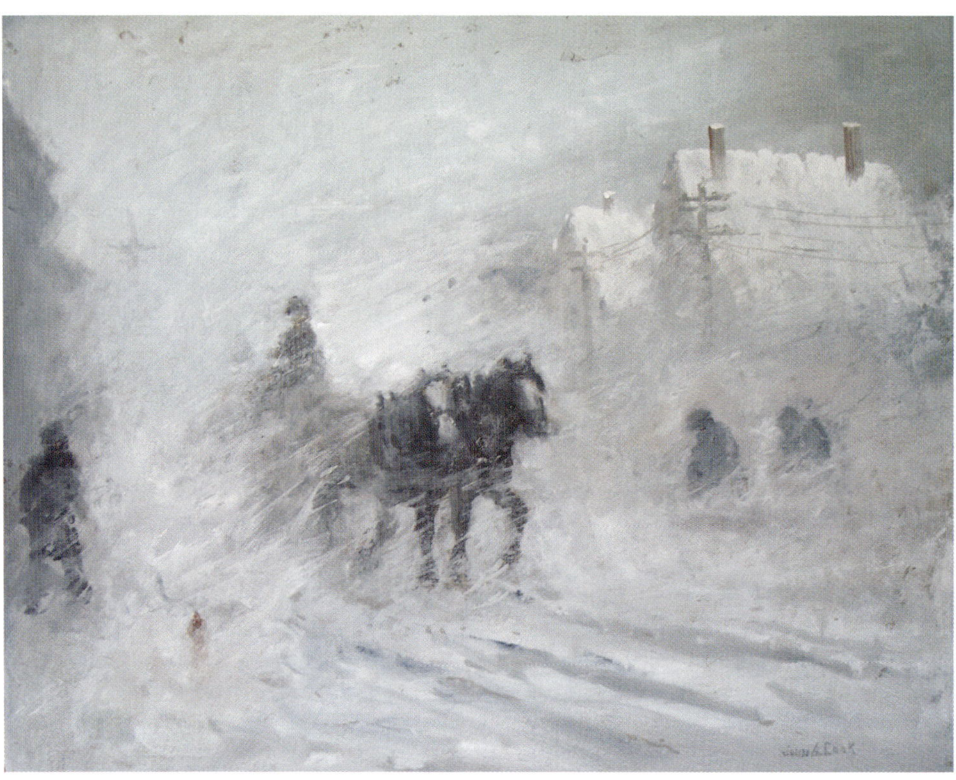

John Cook
Snowstorm, East Gloucester
Gouache, 15 x 19½ in.
Private collection

Joseph R. DeCamp, N.A. (1858-1923)

On July 7, 1890, the *Gloucester Daily Times* announced, "Mr. DeCamp, the artist, is here [in Annisquam] with a class of nine lady pupils." Noteworthy as this may have been, it was not the first time Joseph DeCamp had visited Cape Ann, nor would it be the last. DeCamp first arrived in the summer of 1886, searching for inspiration to lift him from the artistic doldrums he'd foundered in since returning to Cincinnati from Europe three years earlier. Trained in the Munich school under Frank Duveneck, DeCamp's work

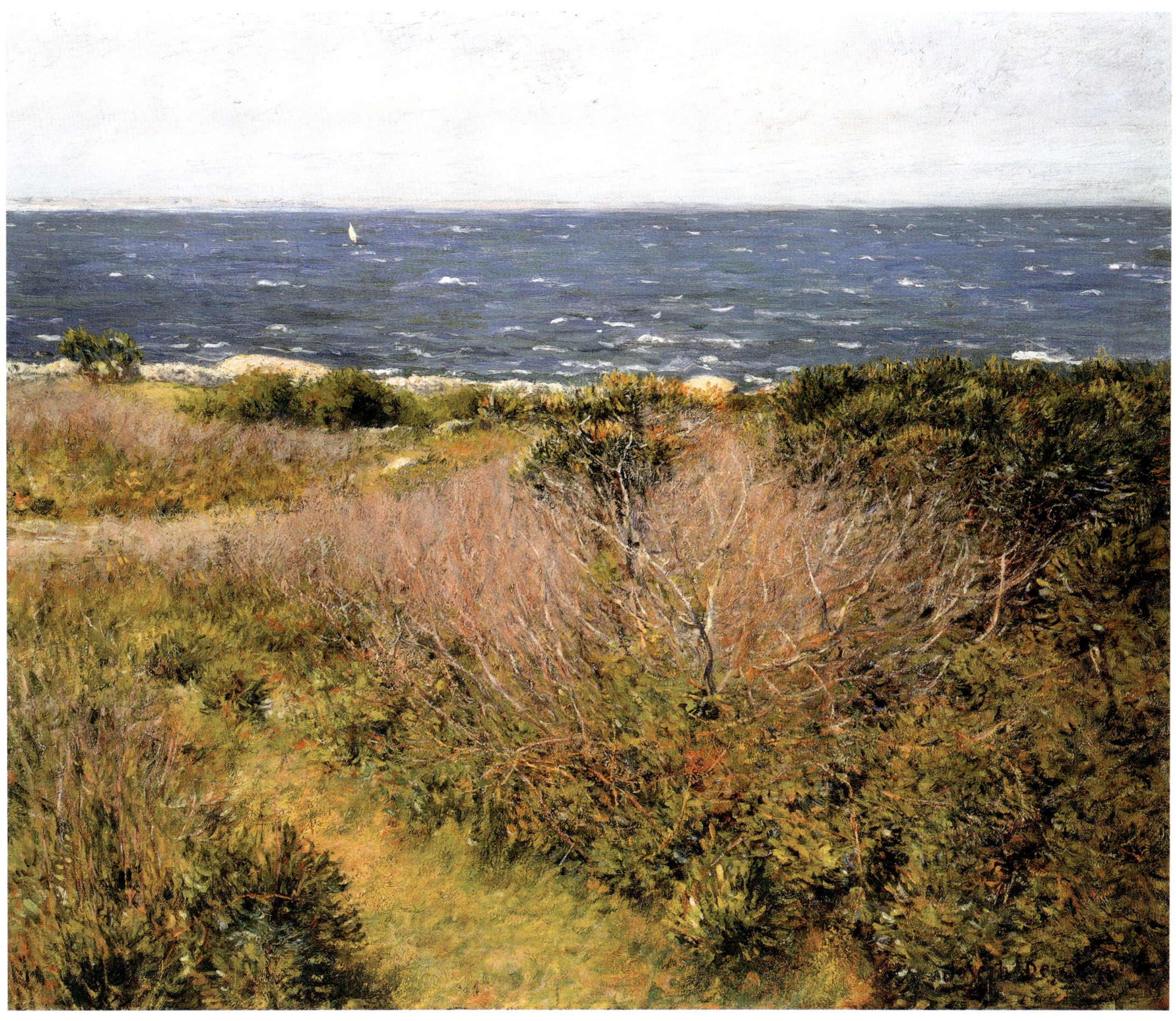

Joseph Rodefer DeCamp
Seascape, 1891
Oil on canvas, 25 x 30 in.
Farnsworth Art Museum, Rockland, Maine (44.409)
Museum purchase, 1944
Photo: Melville D. McLean

tended towards dark tonality and strong characterization, imbued with heavy impasto. While favorably reviewed by local art critics, it did not appeal to the buying public.

Joseph Rodefer DeCamp was born in Cincinnati on November 5, 1858, and educated in the city's school system. As a fifteen-year-old high school student, he attended night classes at the School of Art and Design, McMicken College, studying draftsmanship under Thomas S. Noble. He also studied briefly with Frank Duveneck, who blended his Munich school training with a sense of bold realism. DeCamp studied a further three years at McMicken before heading for Europe and the Royal Academy at Munich where Frank Duveneck had recently been appointed to the faculty. DeCamp studied one season with Wilhelm von Diez and then left to join Duveneck who had recently resigned from the Academy to start his own school. Summers were spent in Polling, near Munich, and winters in Florence and Venice, where James McNeill Whistler joined the "Duveneck Boys," and encouraged them in etching.

In 1883 DeCamp's limited finances precipitated a return home, where he and others, including John Twachtman and Theodore Wendel, organized an exhibition of works at the Closson Gallery in Cincinnati. DeCamp showed several European paintings that the art critic of the *Commercial Gazette* called "airy and light," and which suggested the artist's "fondness for... gay colors and bright water...."[30] These were in marked contrast to his rather austere portraits, executed with the somber Munich school palette. Disillusioned with the unenthusiastic response, DeCamp left Cincinnati and taught briefly at Cleveland Art Academy before heading east to teach at Wellesley College, near Boston. In 1885 DeCamp joined the faculty at the School of the Museum of Fine Arts in Boston.

While perusing the Boston galleries DeCamp became aware of exciting new works by William Lamb Picknell and Hugh Bolton Jones, French-trained artists working in Annisquam on Cape Ann. Impressed by the genre, DeCamp went to Annisquam in the summer of 1886 and the landscapes he produced there show an appealing change in mood and palette.

DeCamp taught at the Museum School for four years before moving on to the Cowles Art School, which had a more informal atmosphere. In 1889, he became acquainted with Dennis Miller Bunker with whom he shared a studio in Boston, and began adopting some of Bunker's new techniques. Bunker had learned these the year before after visiting John Singer Sargent in Calcot, England; they included looser brushwork and a more vibrant palette. DeCamp's paintings from this era—he spent four summers in Annisquam—abound with richly colored foliage and radiant luminosity. During this period, DeCamp also instructed outdoor landscape painting in Annisquam, his most notable group of students being the ladies of Philadelphia's Lavender Club in 1890 and '91.

Although DeCamp's early plein air work was pure landscape, after his marriage to Edith Baker, a former pupil, she and their children, Sally, Ted, Lydia and Pauline, began to figure prominently in his compositions. Art critic Royal Cortissoz suggested DeCamp was "[I]n the Monet advance,"[31] but while DeCamp may have embraced a high key Impressionist palette, he never sacrificed his ability to draw and design for the sake of a fleeting effect of light.

Eventually, DeCamp made East Gloucester's Rocky Neck his base. *The Little Hotel* was painted from the lawn of his cottage in 1903, while *Mrs. Ernest Major*, seated on a

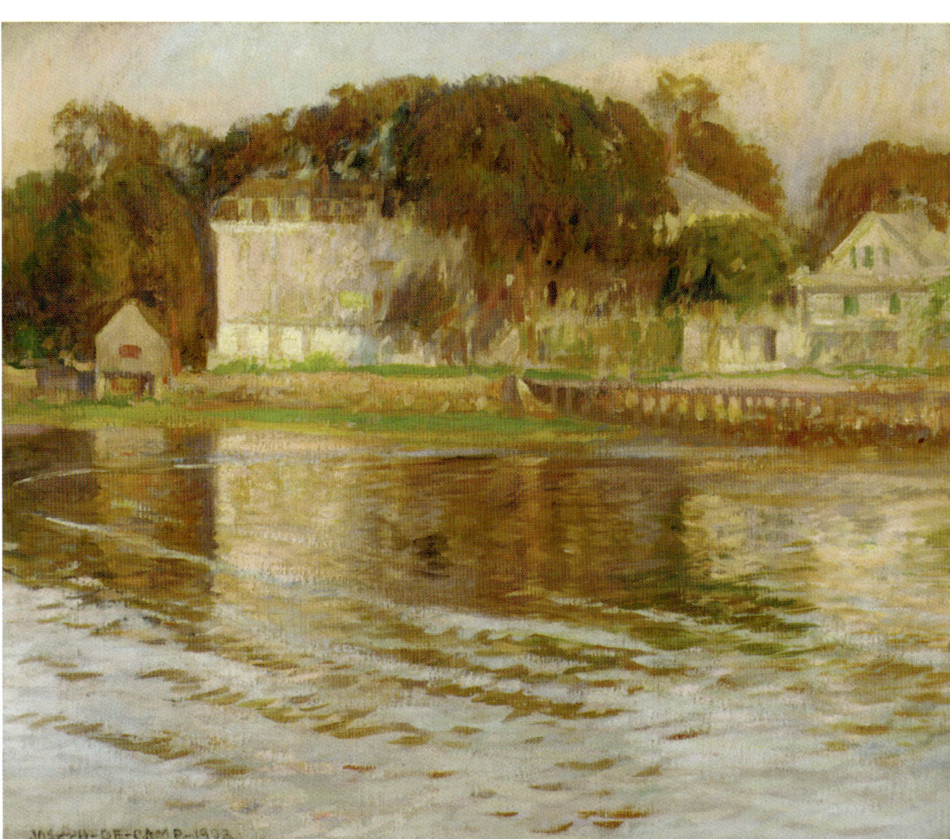

Joseph Rodefer DeCamp
The Little Hotel, 1903
Oil on canvas, 20 x 24 1/16 in.
Pennsylvania Academy of the Fine Arts, Philadelphia (1904.2)
Joseph E. Temple Fund

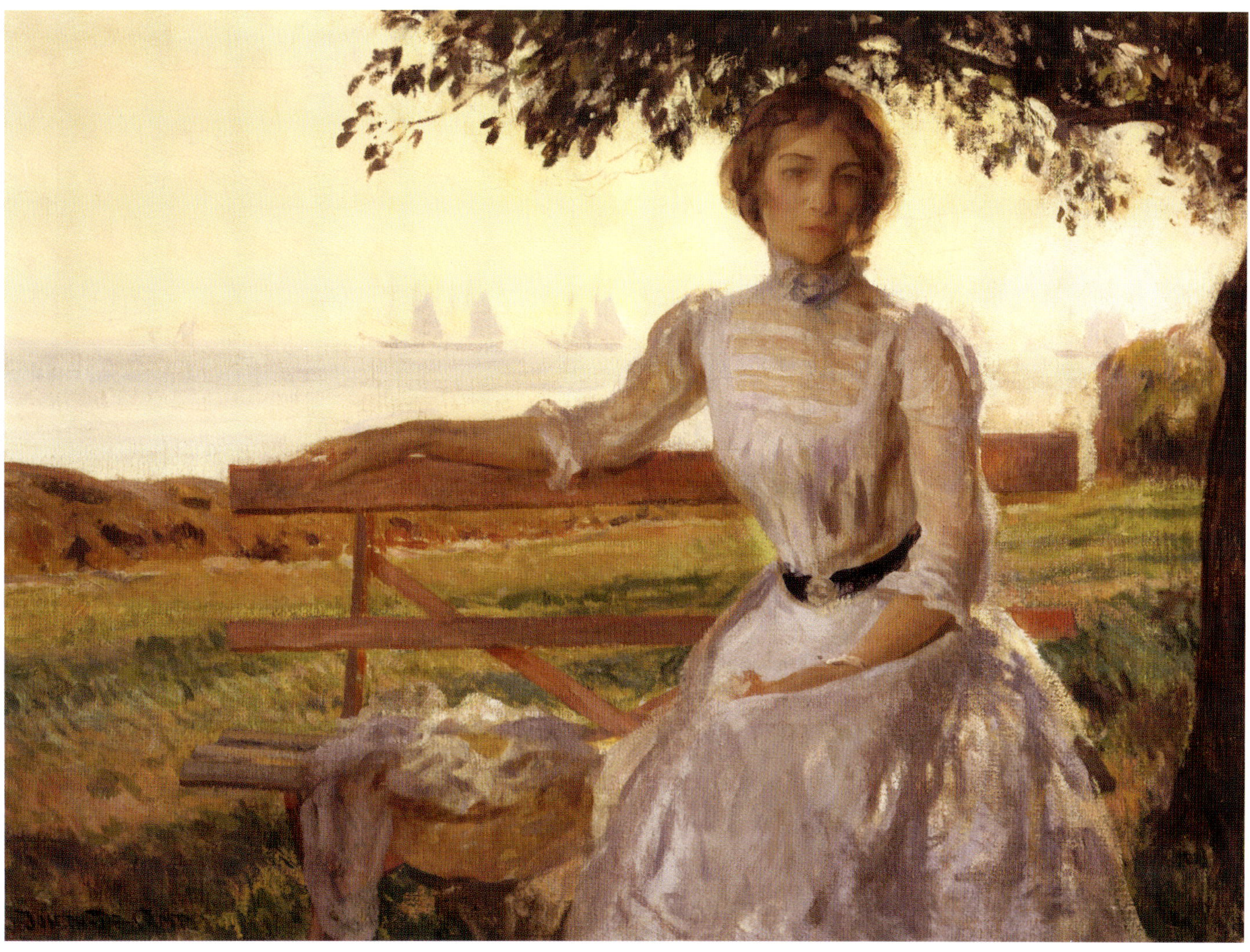

Joseph Rodefer DeCamp
Mrs. Ernest Major, 1902-03
Oil on canvas, 22¼ x 30¼ in.
Cincinnati Art Museum, Cincinnati, Ohio (2003.57)
Gift of the Procter & Gamble Company

bench against the backdrop of Wonson's Cove, was painted the previous year. Regrettably, much of DeCamp's accumulated work was destroyed in a fire at his Boston studio in 1904. Focusing on portraiture to sustain the immediate needs his family, DeCamp gave up plein air landscape for a number of years. In addition, the death of his good friend John Twachtman in 1902 made Gloucester a bittersweet experience for DeCamp and he found himself unable to return to a setting that held so many memories for him.

Joseph DeCamp, one of the Ten American Painters, died on February 11, 1923, in Boca Raton, Florida, while recuperating from a major operation. Writing to his friend, Joseph H. Gest, director of the Cincinnati Art Academy, shortly before he died, DeCamp said, "I am being sent… to Florida, in the hopes that a trip to a warmer climate will hasten my full recovery…. The various blood transfusions, as yet have shown no Cubist tendency."[32]

At the end of the nineteenth century, Rocky Neck played host to some of the best-known names in American art. Frank Duveneck, his friends and students—and eventually their students—comprised a coterie embracing the strongest practitioners of the plastic arts rivaling, if not surpassing, any of the French art colonies of the day. Gloucester's unique light, strong, rich and bathing the area in a rosy radiant glow, combined with a distinctive topography of rough moorland with granite crags and elevations where an artist could set up high above the harbor for aerial and linear perspective. This offered a rare chance for the American painter to work en plein air, with a wide range of subject matter in every direction. It was only to be expected that a more cohesive colony than before would spring up around these men and women as still more arrived, and often settled, into the bohemian venue offered by East Gloucester.

By the time Duveneck passed away in 1919, Rocky Neck had become the hub of a larger outlying area stretching a mile in each direction, encompassing within its environs a unique enclave that mirrored the greater happenings of the art world with its European 'isms,' and innovations. The great traditions of camaraderie and excellence promulgated by Duveneck and his colleagues continued through the trials of the Depression and other crisis perpetrated by man. There are many who would consider art a saving grace. As the surviving members of the Duveneck class pledged at a memorial to their friend and mentor in 1919, "We… are possessed of a treasure even richer, the inspiration of his character, of his vigorous and tender personality, of the high ideals of art and of life he implanted. Great teacher, most kindly and just of critics, dear friend, he has been to us like a father to his children… Be it therefore resolved: That we, his students, are united by the privilege of association with the master, the great teacher of his day. That we shall cherish the nobility of his ideals, striving not only to live up to the best in ourselves as he would have us do, but to keep alive and pass on to those with whom we may be associated, the teachings and ideals of one who has been an inspiration, not only in art, but in life itself."[33]

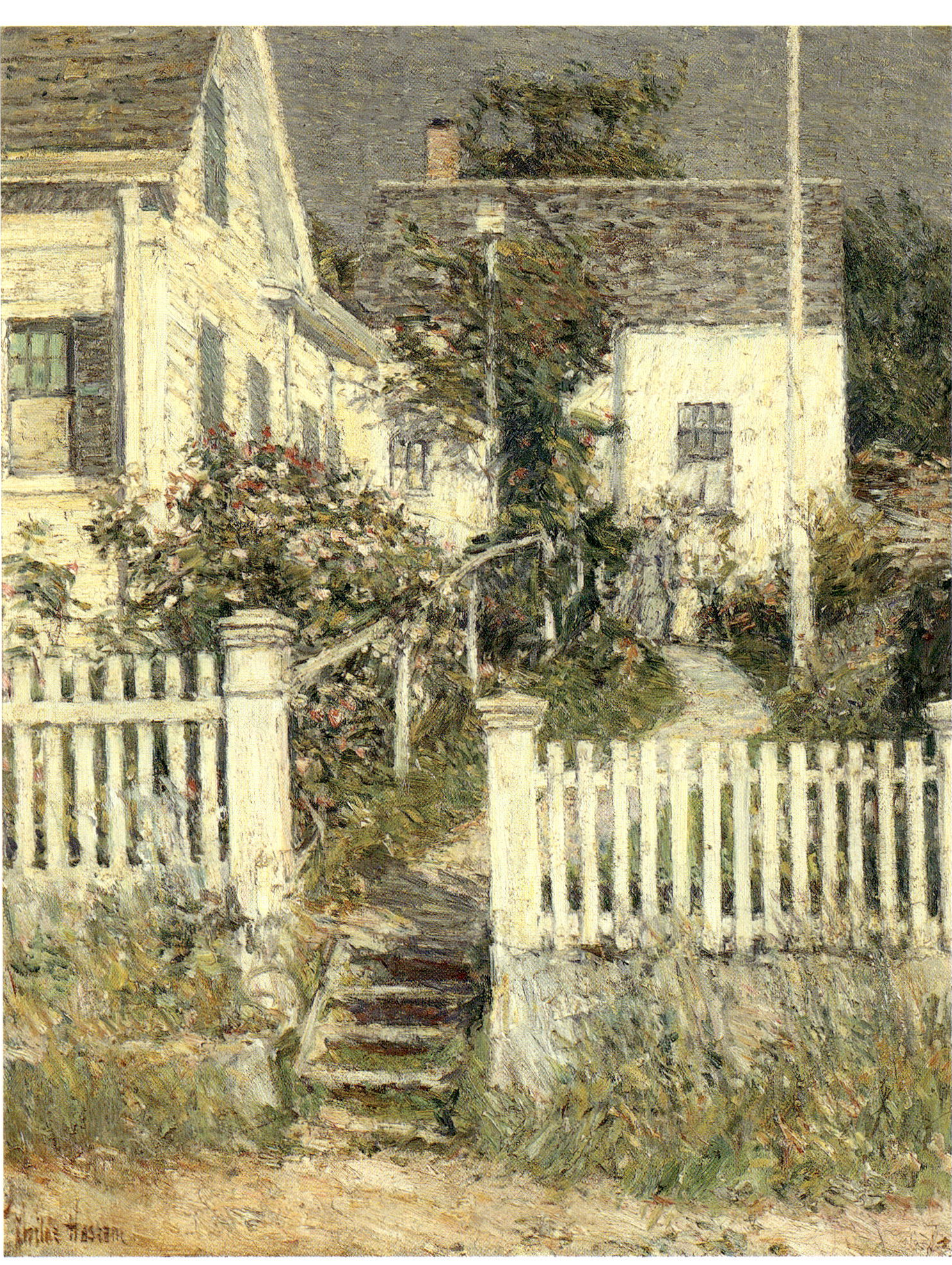

Childe Hassam
The White House, Gloucester, c. 1895
Oil on canvas, 26 x 21 in.
Washington County Museum of Fine Arts, Hagerstown, Maryland
Gift of Mr. & Mrs. William Henry Singer, Jr., Olden, Norway, 1931 (A02)

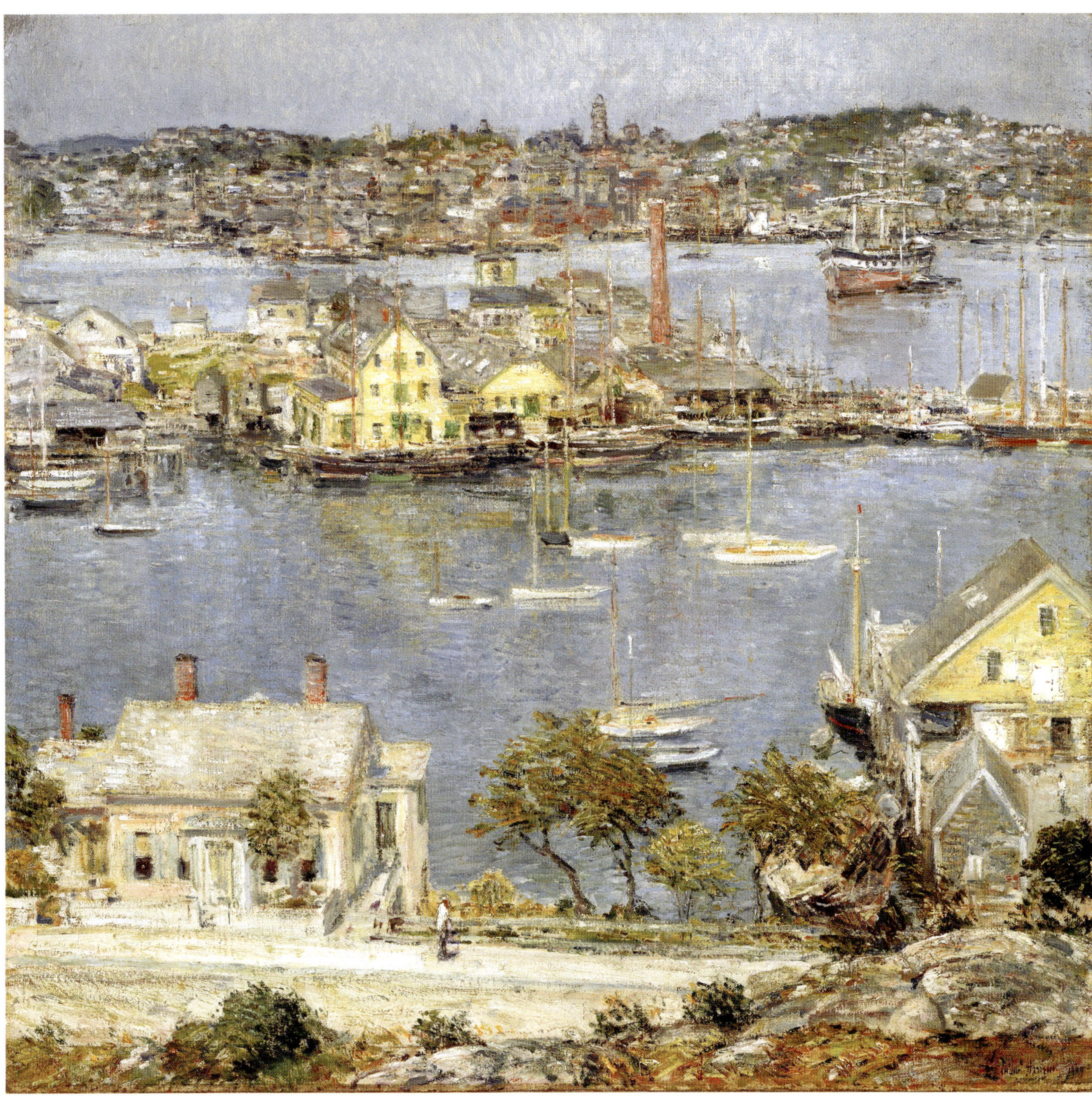

Childe Hassam
Gloucester Harbor, 1899/1909
Oil on canvas, 25 x 26⅛ in.
Norton Museum of Art, West Palm Beach, Florida
Bequest of R. H. Norton (53.77)

Childe Hassam, N.A. (1859-1935)

When one considers the broad scope of Childe Hassam's career—wood engraver, water colorist, oil painter and lithographer—it becomes obvious why Hassam was the linchpin of American Impressionism at the turn of the twentieth century. Dynamic and flamboyant, Hassam began painting in an impressionist manner long before it became fashionable to do so. "The true artist," he said, "should see things frankly, and suffer no trickery or artifice to anywhere distort his vision."[34] Thus, Hassam developed his own tenet regarding impressionism and disavowed the French technique of a spontaneous reaction to nature via the instinctive vision.

Perhaps because Hassam had no formal art school training, and therefore emulated no Master or mentor, he followed his own maxim when it came to expressing himself in paint. As a youth he was forced to drop out of high school in order to bolster the family income. Putting his childhood talent for drawing to good use, Hassam found

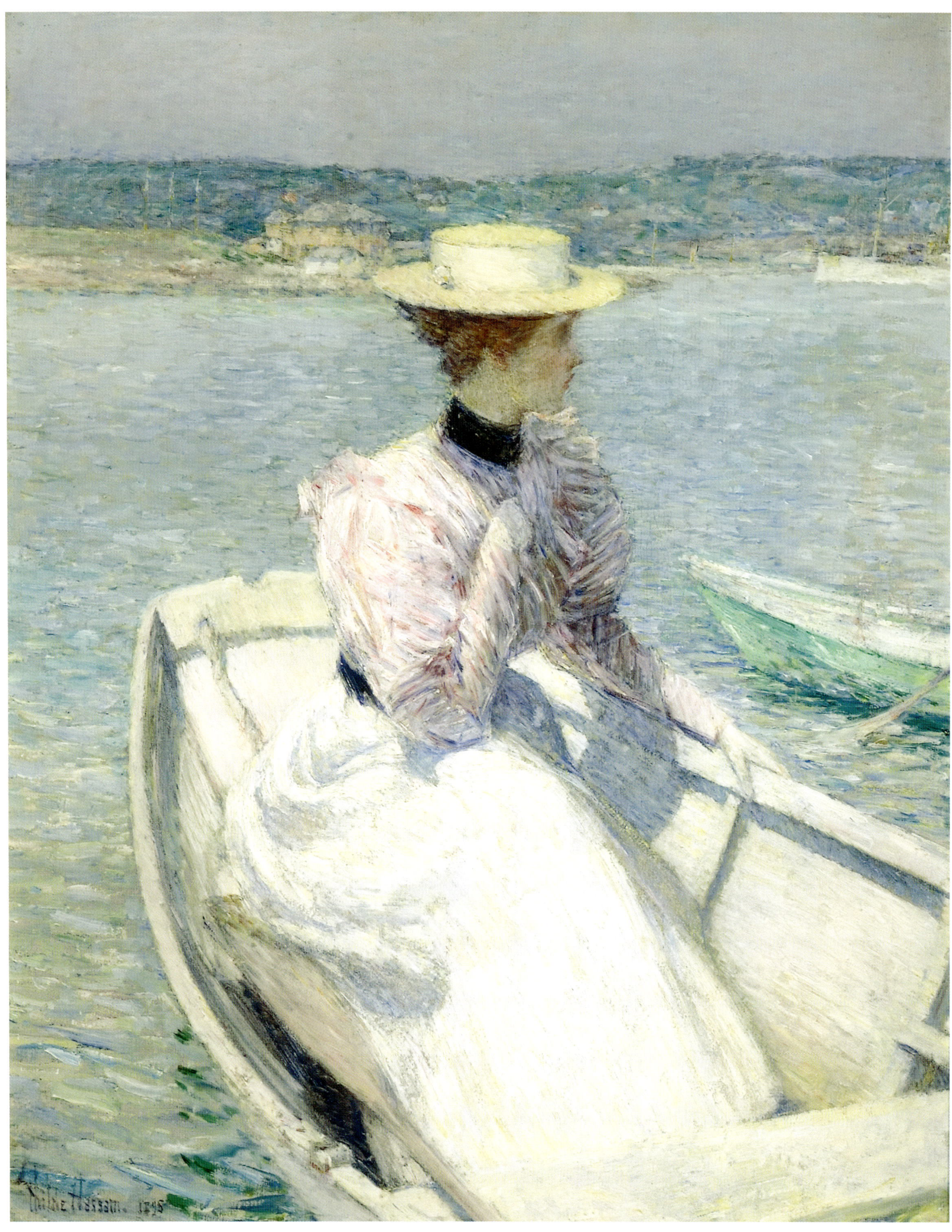

work with a Boston wood engraver, and quickly rose from apprentice to staff artist. He branched out into commercial illustration, selling work to magazines such as *Harper's, Scribner's* and *The Century*, and took evening drawing classes at the Lowell Institute to refine his skills further. Hassam also took instruction from Tommasso Juglaris, an Italian artist who had come to Boston via the Parisian atelier of Jean-Léon Gérôme.

In the spring of 1883, in the company of his friend Edmund Garrett, Hassam set out for Europe visiting Scotland, England and the continent, before returning to America with sixty-seven watercolors, which he exhibited at the Williams & Everett Gallery in Boston in 1884. In 1886, Hassam returned to Paris, studying briefly at the Académie Julian, which he disliked for its lack of vision, and spending the rest of his time painting whatever scenes inspired him, particularly the busy Parisian streets and the racetracks.

Returning to the United States in 1889, Hassam began carving out his own niche in American art. New York became his winter home where he reverted to painting cityscapes, capturing the urbanization of that city at a time when huge changes were being made in both architectural style and aesthetic mannerisms. In the summer, Hassam still traveled to his favorite painting spots in New England, especially Gloucester, which he returned to a dozen times over the next two decades. Some of Hassam's best known works from his Cape Ann sojourns—*The Summer Girl, The White Dory, White House, Gloucester*, and of course, his quintessential views of Gloucester Harbor—emphasize an avant-garde approach to art. He employed vibrant color often laid down with rapid, nervous brushwork as a means of imitating a flickering mosaic of light. The overall effect is a harmony of artistic discipline and painterly expression.

In 1919, after an absence of ten years, Hassam returned to Cape Ann, where he found the bustle of the city at work and leisure a constant source of inspiration. He wrote to his friend, C. E. S. Wood, "It is as fine as ever—they can't ruin Cape Ann."[35] During these later visits to Gloucester, Hassam was often invited to show at the elite Gallery-on-the-Moors in East Gloucester where his work was always singled out for praise, "'Indian Summer - Colonial Days' is a most charming subject in delicate green tones, with the characteristic stroke of genius by Mr. Hassam.... We enjoy viewing Mr. Hassam's work, as we are reminded of his earlier days spent in East Gloucester, his love for the place."[36]

An audacious man with a vigorous and intense personality, Hassam often eclipsed those around him. He was in the forefront, with John Twachtman, in establishing the Ten American Painters group, which included DeCamp and Willard L. Metcalf. Its mission, as Hassam saw it, was to save American art from the stagnation and decay into which it was falling. Arguably the most innovative of the Ten, Hassam was often considered closer to the French Impressionist style than his colleagues.

Hassam did not return to Cape Ann after 1919, but his paintings and etchings of the area served to immortalize Rocky Neck as the premier art colony in the nation. In 1936, a year after Hassam's death, Royal Cortissoz described Hassam as employing "[The] American way of profiting by European example without falling victim to European convention."[37] Hassam, ever the individualist, would have loved the tribute.

Childe Hassam
The White Dory, 1895
Oil on canvas, 26 x 21 in.
Private collection

Willard L. Metcalf (1858-1925)

Of the eminent artists who have painted on Cape Ann since the late 1800s, few captured the essence of Gloucester Harbor better than Willard Metcalf. Born July 1, 1858 in Lowell, Massachusetts, Willard Leroy Metcalf was the only child of cabinet-maker and sometime violinist Greenleaf Metcalf and his wife, Margaret, a loom tender. The Metcalfs were fervent Spiritualists and encouraged their son's creative talents after a séance during which they were told he would become a great painter.[38] From 1874 onwards, Metcalf perfected his natural drawing skills in evening classes at the Massachusetts Normal School and the Lowell Institute, did a brief apprenticeship with George Loring Brown and finally received a scholarship to the School of the Museum of Fine Arts, Boston. However, his early painting style owes more to a personal interest in the Barbizon technique of John Kensett than any formalized art school training, which he found irritating and pedestrian.

By the end of 1883, Metcalf was in Paris, enrolled at the Académie Julian and working under Gustave Boulanger and Jules Lefèbvre. Naturally sociable, Metcalf quickly assimilated himself into the French lifestyle and learned as much from his fellow students as he did from his instructors. It was during this French sojourn that Metcalf became acquainted with John Twachtman, who was to become a lifelong friend and fellow member of the Ten.

Returning to Boston, Metcalf obtained a one-man show at St. Botolph Club in the spring of 1889, but sales did not meet his expectations. With finances dwindling, he set out first for Philadelphia to establish himself as a portrait painter and then to New York where he became a magazine illustrator. He also taught Life and Cast Drawing at the Women's Art School, Cooper Union and the Antiques class at the Art Students League.

In 1895 Metcalf accepted Childe Hassam's invitation to join him on a painting trip to Gloucester. This was not Metcalf's first visit to Cape Ann, however; he was in Gloucester as early as 1876, visiting relatives of his mother and painting at Good Harbor Beach and Bass Rocks.[39] He was also on Cape Ann in 1877 and 1883. By 1895, however, Metcalf's style had evolved from a somewhat self-conscious Barbizon manner to a surer, more mature hand that created the effect of light and atmosphere with an economy of effort and a new strength of artistic vision.

Childe Hassam credits himself with encouraging Metcalf's use of "divisionist brushwork," however, the broken color and prismatic palette we see in Metcalf's prizewinning *Gloucester Harbor*, painted in 1895, are actually the culmination of his experimentation with techniques absorbed during his years in France. Generally considered his first American landscape after returning from Europe, Metcalf's view of Gloucester Harbor remains the premier interpretation of America's oldest seaport. His perspective from high on Banner Hill, looking west, the sun at his back and the morning light splashing across the inner harbor into the distance, creates a composition par excellence through his use of aerial perspective. Metcalf's skillful design and use of dynamic symmetry direct the viewer along the dock, where spots of luminescent white draw the eye from ship to ship to spire, then to the highlight on the headland, where one picks up the sails that bring the eye back to the sunlit foreground. However, it is not only Metcalf's design that brings vitality to the scene. It is also the way he captures the intensity of Cape Ann's unique light through the use of prismatic color, laid in with swift sure brushwork, to create a harmonious finish and tell us the time of day.

Metcalf's work prior to this Cape Ann trip, while created on sound principles, had a piecemeal look lacking the continuity of key that is so important to the plein air painter. However, his canvases from this Gloucester excursion, which he later included

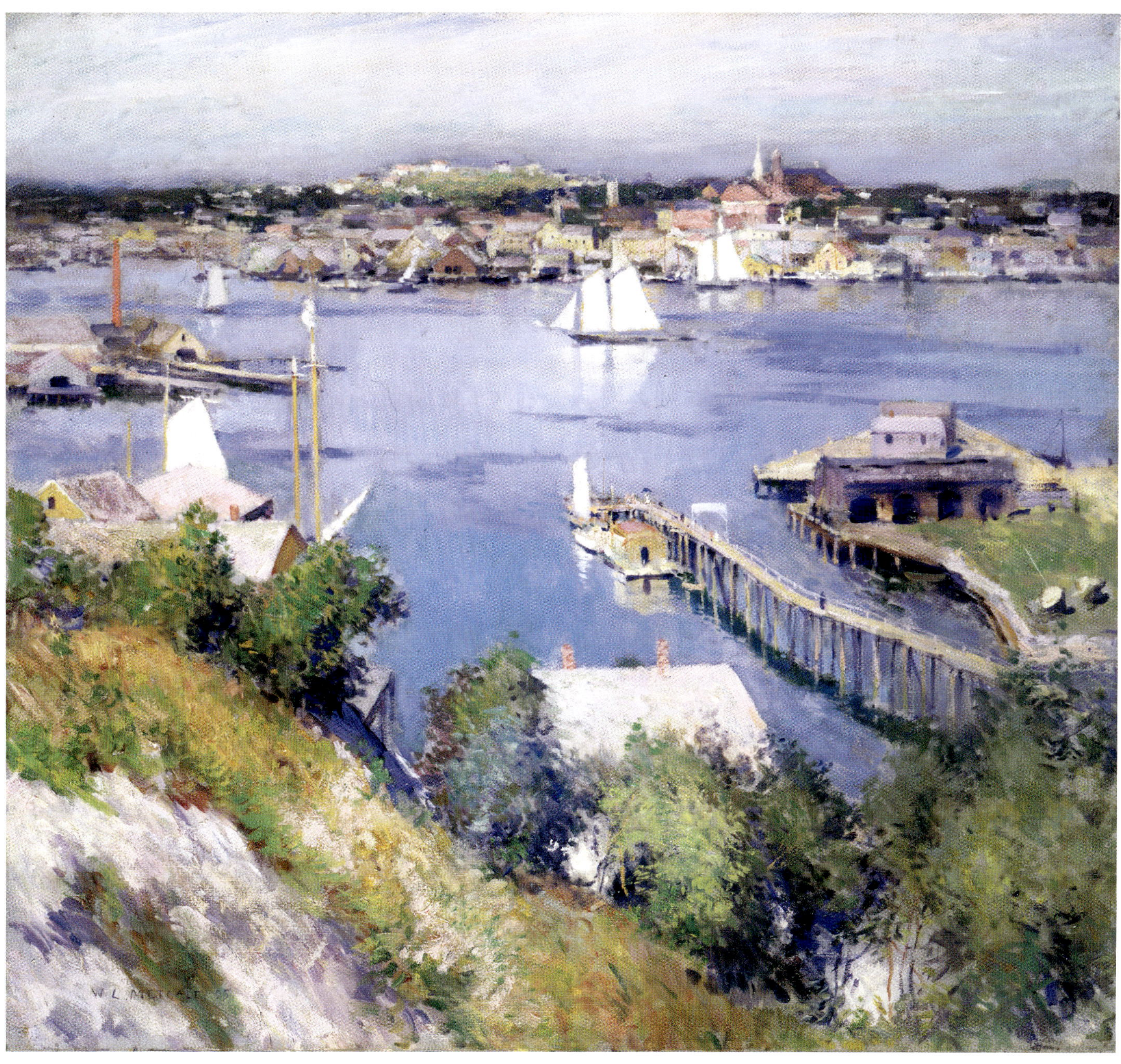

Willard LeRoy Metcalf
Gloucester Harbor, 1895
Oil on canvas, 26⅛ x 29¼ in.
Mead Art Museum, Amherst College, Amherst, Massachusetts
Gift of George D. Pratt, Class of 1893 (ACP.1932.16)

in an exhibition of the Ten, give the impression of being painted on the spot and in one sitting. Although he lost this quality to some extent after leaving Cape Ann, he continued painting landscapes. Encouraged by winning the Webb Prize for *Gloucester Harbor* at the Society of American Artists' 1896 exhibition, he began refining his broken color technique and sumptuous, high-key palette to create other memorable works.

Willard Metcalf's career often suffered from problems in his personal life. He suffered two failed marriages and a string of broken romances, events that both inspired him and took their toll. Metcalf was an incautious drinker, often too ill to work, and in the end his health was a constant concern. Describing his aspirations in a letter to his daughter, Rosalind, he said, "One has thoughts for hardly anything but the making of, the giving everything in one's soul and being over to the endless effort of putting paint on a canvas with a miserable little brush… endeavoring to make it express thoughts and dreams."[40]

Little more than a month later, on March 9, 1925, Willard Metcalf suffered a fatal heart attack.

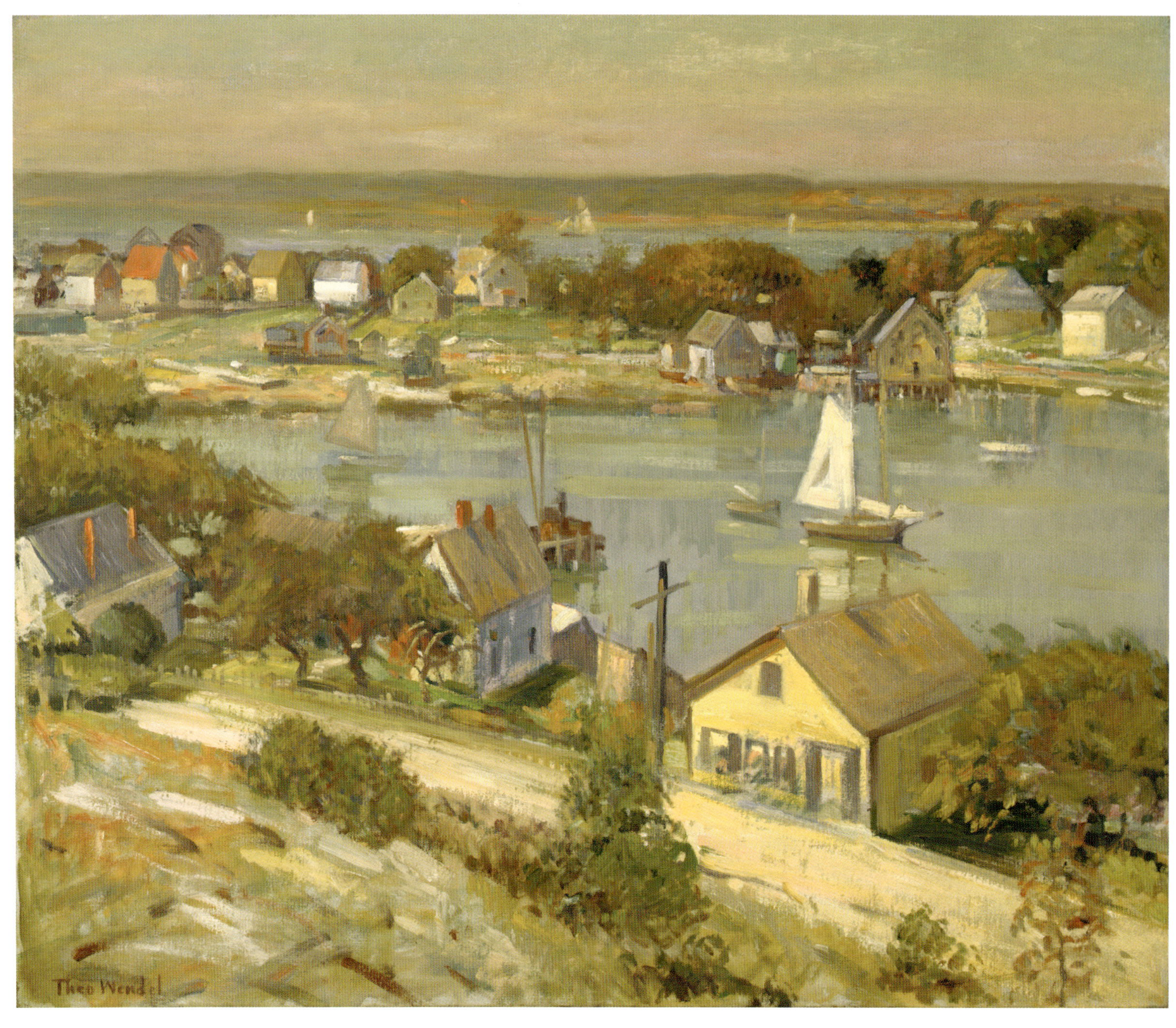

Theodore Wendel (1859-1932)

Like many of his friends and contemporaries, oil painter Theodore Wendel brought sound academic training to his artwork, which he tempered with a touch of impressionism to develop a personal point of view. Wendel, who was born in Midway, Ohio, enjoyed a brief career as a circus acrobat at the age of fifteen[41] and did not begin his formal art studies until 1876 when he enrolled at the University of Cincinnati's School of Design. Later, he continued his studies at the McMicken School of Art where he came under the influence of Frank Duveneck. In 1878, when Duveneck left America to take up a teaching post at the Royal Academy in Munich, Theodore Wendel went with him.

Wendel, and his friend and fellow Cincinnatian, Joseph DeCamp, enrolled in *Naturklass* (life drawing) and hurled themselves into both the curriculum and the bohemian way of life. As fellow student, Julius Rolshoven, described it, "Winter in Munich is severe; top boots and heavy coats are essential to the student while wading

Theodore Wendel
Gloucester Harbor, c. 1900-1915
Oil on canvas, 19½ x 35¼ in.
Daniel J. Terra Collection
Terra Foundation for American Art, Chicago (1999.145)
Photo: Terra Foundation for American Art, Chicago / Art Resource, New York

through snow and ice. I would encounter early mornings Joseph DeCamp, Theodore Wendel… rushing to get the best placing for their easle [sic]…. Wendel was a marksman with snow balls which amused the Bavarians."[42] Wendel received a bronze medal in the Academy's annual exhibition the following year, but was already disillusioned with the rigid aesthetics of the school. Consequently, when Duveneck resigned from the Academy to start his own school in Polling, and later Florence, Wendel and the rest of the 'Duveneck Boys' went along too.

The daily custom of Duveneck's Florence school was rigorous. Wendel's friend, Charles E. Mills, wrote home, "We paint from models every day, the hours being from 8:30 to 10:00 and 1 to 4. Then we draw in the evening from 7 to 9."[43] Later, in the spring and summer of 1880, Duveneck and the boys moved to Venice where Wendel became acquainted with James McNeill Whistler. Whistler cultivated a friendship with the young student because Wendel's room at their pensione overlooked the Grand Canal and he wished to paint from the window. In return, Whistler allowed Wendel to "accompany him with a lantern when he took notes useful for painting a nocturne. Wendel held the light while Whistler penciled notations."[44] Wendel, always open to new ideas, gleaned much from the experience, gaining insight from Whistler's unique style and method.

As a student at the Académie Julian in 1885, he adopted a lighter palette and, the following year, after visiting master impressionist Claude Monet at Giverny, Wendel's style took on the high key color and looser brushwork of French Impressionism. Artist Lilla Cabot Perry, a friend and neighbor of Monet, later reported, "Wendel was the only American painter whose work interested him."[45]

Although adept in various mediums, including etching and pastel, Wendel's first and abiding love was landscape painting in oil, a genre at which he excelled not only because of his ability to render outdoor color with an accurate eye but also because of his solid understanding of compositional balance. When he returned to the United States in 1888, he came to Rocky Neck with Duveneck and found the Cape Ann topography and light inspiring. According to Helen Knowlton, Wendel was delving, "deeply into the mysteries of light upon color. No browns and black enter into his scheme of… pure color, fresh from the tub [sic]"[46] During the early 1890s, Wendel combined painting with teaching, becoming a highly regarded instructor. On April 9, 1891, *The Boston Transcript* reported, "Mr. Theodore Wendel will attract a large class… where he will teach the new gospel of sweetness and light as it may be put on canvas."[47]

In 1897, while teaching at the Cowles Art School, Wendel met and married student Philena Stone, and the two spent a year traveling through Europe before returning to live on the Stone family farm in Ipswich. Wendel continued painting landscapes around Gloucester and Ipswich. He often exhibited with Arthur Wesley Dow, Henry R. Kenyon and Francis H. Richardson—all Ipswich painters—and won medals from the Pennsylvania Academy and the San Francisco Panama-Pacific Exposition in 1915. Beginning with an illness in 1917, Wendel's health gradually declined and he painted less. By the time he died on December 21, 1932, his work had fallen into obscurity and it is only now that we are beginning to see a resurgence of his justly deserved reputation as one of the great American Impressionists.

Herman H. Wessel (1878-1969)

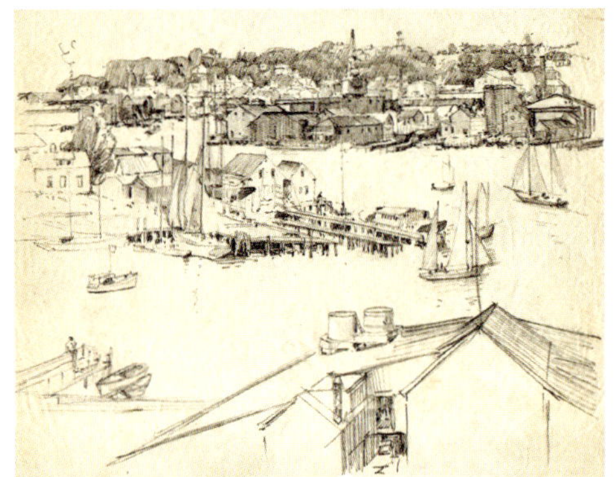

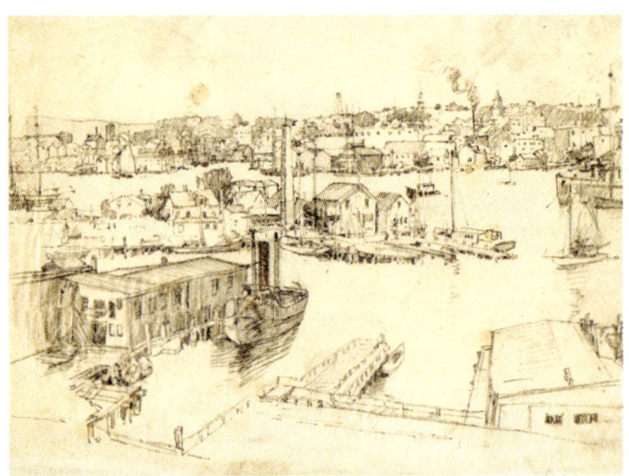

Herman H. Wessel
Drawing A
Pencil on paper, 8½ x 11 in.
Collection of Wessel House Archives, Cincinnati, Ohio

Herman H. Wessel
Drawing B
Pencil on paper, 7 x 8 in.
Collection of Wessel House Archives, Cincinnati, Ohio

Herman Henry Wessel was born January 16, 1878, in Vincennes, Indiana, the second child of Prussian immigrants Charles Frederick Wilhelm Wessel and his wife Caroline Fredricke Henke. As a child Herman attended the exacting German Lutheran school in Vincennes and learned to speak the language fluently but his heart and mind were more interested in the artistic than the academic. Wishing to capitalize on his drawing skills, the young Herman determined to attend art school as soon as it was financially possible, and in 1895, upon the death of his father, Herman sold a parcel of farmland that he had inherited and moved to Cincinnati to pursue a career in art.

At the turn of the nineteenth century, Cincinnati was already noted for its culture as well as its prosperous economy, and vied with Boston and New York for recognition as the major American center for the arts. In addition, the city's Art Academy was considered "the most thorough school in the United States for art education."[48] Frank Duveneck, who played a leading role in creating the Academy's exemplary reputation, was one of Wessel's earliest artistic influences, and the principles that drove Duveneck are readily apparent in Herman Wessel's life and work.

Enrolling at the Art Academy in the fall of 1896, Wessel first had to learn the rudiments of good draughtsmanship in Vincent Nowottny's class. Students would draw for six hours a day—four in the morning and two in the afternoon—first working with casts, and then later progressing to life drawing. Having completed the drawing course, Wessel progressed to Caroline Lord's painting class to learn the essentials, and then advanced to Duveneck's class. There students learned to assimilate the fundamentals of drawing and painting and ultimately transcribe form with color, brush and canvas. In 1902, Wessel was awarded the Laura Ingalls scholarship. Two years later, after taking a day job as a sign painter[49] and studying nights at the Academy, Wessel acquired enough funds to go to Europe where he enrolled first at the Royal Academy in Munich, and later at the Académie Julian in Paris, under Jean-Paul Laurens. He also studied at the Académie Colarossi in Paris, where he not only received a medal for draughtsmanship

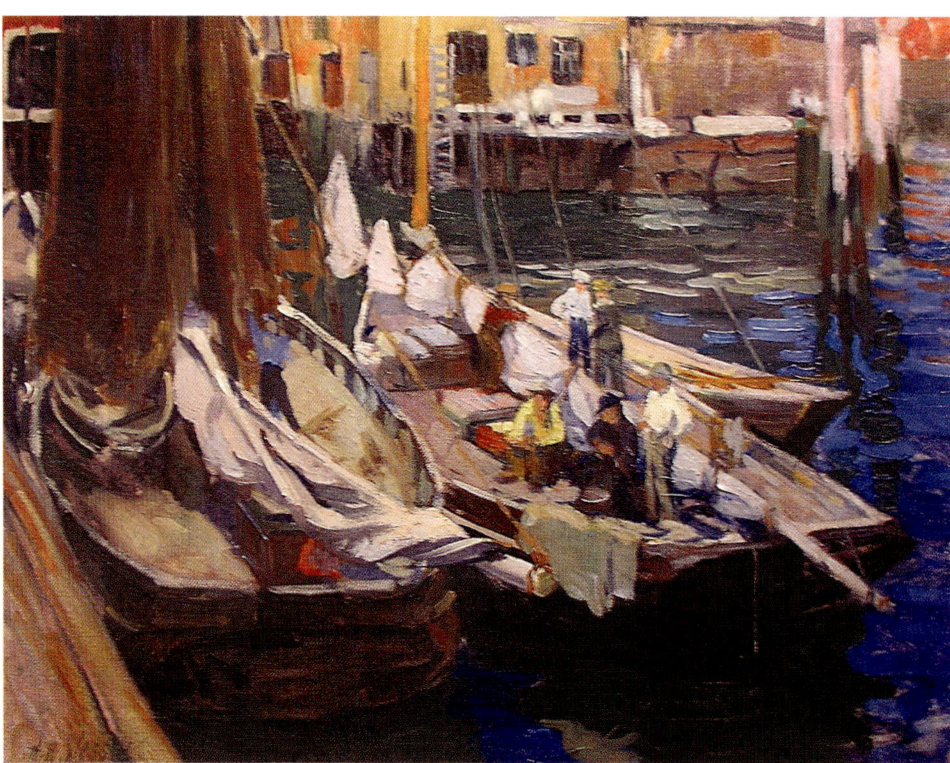

Herman H. Wessel
Gloucester Harbor
Oil on canvas, 20 x 26 in.
Private collection
Photo courtesy of Cincinnati Art Galleries, Cincinnati, Ohio

Herman H. Wessel
Demolition, inscribed "The view from our windows today looking toward Gloucester Aug. 23/60"
Watercolor on paper, 8½ x 11 in.
Collection of Wessel House Archives, Cincinnati, Ohio

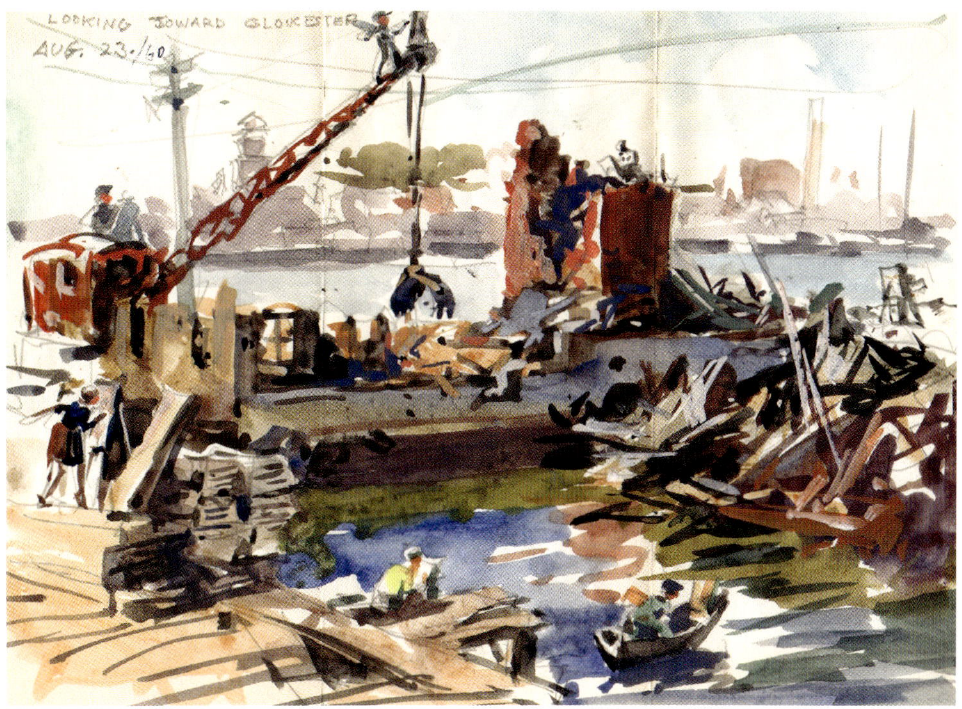

in December 1905 but also taught there part-time.[50] When Wessel returned home in 1908 he became a drawing instructor at the Cincinnati Art Academy, and when Nowottny died later that year, the Academy appointed Wessel to fill the vacant place as anatomy instructor. Wessel held this position for the next four decades.

Over the years, Wessel's style, which initially reflected the somber tones of the Munich school, began to be influenced by the traveling exhibits coming to the Cincinnati Art Museum and by the art Wessel encountered on subsequent trips to Europe. His palette became lighter and more vibrant, and he adopted the spontaneous and broken color brushwork of the Impressionists. Yet Wessel never sacrificed form for effect.

Herman Wessel became a much admired teacher as well as a painter and regularly exhibited with the Society of Western Artists, a group formed in 1896 comprising those artists living west of the Alleghenies to "promote fellowship and the advancement of art."[51] Frank Duveneck was voted in as the Society's first president, although he was not entirely comfortable with public speaking and was relieved when his term ended.[52] "In 1909, the Society was considered the largest and strongest association of artists in the country."[53] Wessel was also a member of the Duveneck Society of Artists and Sculptors, a loosely knit group of Cincinnati artists formed in 1917 for the purpose of mounting annual exhibitions,[54] and the Cincinnati Art Club. In addition, Wessel exhibited work at the San Francisco Panama-Pacific Exposition, the Corcoran Gallery of Art in Washington, D. C., the Pennsylvania Academy of the Fine Arts and the Cincinnati MacDowell Society. Commenting on Wessel's work, which included the gamut of landscape, harbors and figure work, fellow artist and teacher L. H. Meakin wrote that Wessel's work showed "fine, fresh and individual observation, splendid color sense and clear, vigorous expression," as well as generalizing that "the things he painted last summer [1914] on the Isle au Moines [sic] off the Brittany coast are replete with charm and attractiveness and have the song of the place."[55] Wessel was traveling through Europe with fellow artist Jacob Kunz during the summer of 1914, before the pair were forced return home at the outbreak of World War I.

With Europe at war, it was not surprising that many Americans chose to stay home and the art colony at Rocky Neck became even more popular among what the

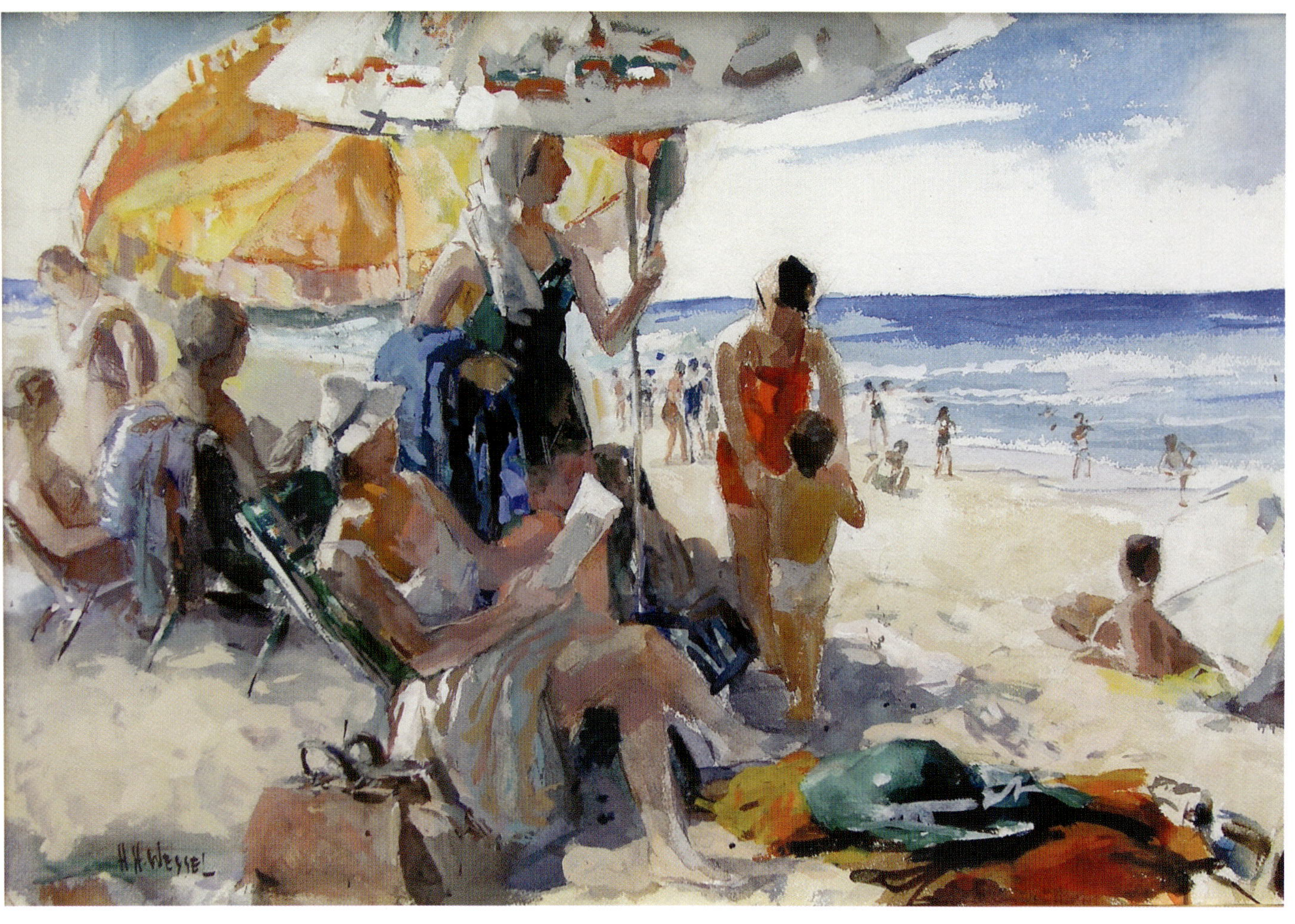

Herman H. Wessel
Good Harbor Beach, Gloucester
Watercolor, 14 x 20 in.
Private collection
Photo courtesy of Cincinnati Art Galleries, Cincinnati, Ohio

Gloucester natives considered the "bohemians." According to a 1916 letter of Herman Wessel's, there were more artists in evidence around Gloucester than bathers[56] and Gloucester was noted for its splendid beaches.

In 1917, Wessel made a life-enriching decision when he proposed to his young Cincinnati Art Academy colleague, Bessie Hoover. The two were married in August of that year in a quiet ceremony held at Frank Duveneck's summer cottage on Bass Rocks, just outside of Rocky Neck. The newlyweds honeymooned briefly in Europe, visiting Italy and Paris, before returning to Cincinnati for the start of the Academy's fall semester. The Wessels returned to Gloucester regularly, even after Duveneck passed away in 1919. Following a conversation with Herman Wessel, *Cincinnati Enquirer* correspondent Mary L. Alexander wrote, "artists have found Gloucester one of the most paintable spots in America and it still continues to be the most popular painting field we have. Several years ago Gloucester claimed to have a thousand artists painting there during the summer.... It is an old field for Mr. and Mrs. Wessel for they spent numerous summer vacations with Duveneck when he occupied his cottage at Bass Rock [sic]. At that time Mrs. Wessel found the hill-side cottages interesting material for her brush...." Herman Wessel preferred the ambiance of the harbor. "On gray days one may see many men around sketching, but when the sun shines the ladies, young and old, with costumes that look as if they were trying to outdo the flowers, are out. They have sweaters and aprons that are either batik, or tied-and-died, or Czecho-Slovaked." Wessel added, no doubt with a twinkle in his eye, "Should a boatman, at 6 a.m., noiselessly raise a sail to dry it after a night's rain it immediately wakes up every artist and they hurry out without any breakfast to get the best place to sketch the sail."[57]

Wessel was a most industrious personality, always painting, teaching or traveling and occasionally combining all three. He was capable of painting small and intimate European views, as well as executing large and complex murals throughout Cincinnati and Ohio. In later life, Wessel had to work through the disadvantages of injuries suffered in an auto accident in 1952, and a decade later, cataracts left him struggling to see through an amorphous veil. Throughout it all, he remained exuberant about life. A critic reviewing a 1965 retrospective wrote, "There is an affirmative character, a ruddy optimism about Wessel's work, and a sensitivity to his rendition of the most commonplace scene or object that marks the hand of the master and the innocence of the child. These are juxtapositions rarely encountered, but irresistible when they are."[58]

Often called "the last of the Duveneck Boys," Herman Wessel died April 13, 1969. Announcing his passing, one newspaper said, "Of the hundreds of successful art students who have passed through Herman H. Wessel's art classes, all of them love and honor him as a great master and teacher, but none of them has surpassed him and few reflect in their art the fine character and spirit that most distinguishes their teacher's art."[59] Wessel was 91 years old.

Bessie Hoover Wessel (1889-1973)

One of four children in the family of Frank M. Hoover and his wife, Minnie Reifel, Bessie Hoover was born January 7, 1889, in Brookville, Indiana. The family later moved to Cincinnati and, after graduating from Woodward High School at the age of seventeen Bessie opted for a career in the arts and enrolled at the city's preeminent Art Academy. In the beginning, she took instruction with Lewis Henry Meakin, and later with Herman Henry Wessel, eleven years her senior, before receiving an invitation in 1909 from Frank Duveneck to join his class. "Mr. Duveneck kept encouraging me. He would say, 'Any reason why you can't come back next year?' There wasn't. Full tuition was $25 and I had a scholarship."[60] Bessie attended the Academy for six years, "and had what would now be considered graduate studies. Those of us who went more than four

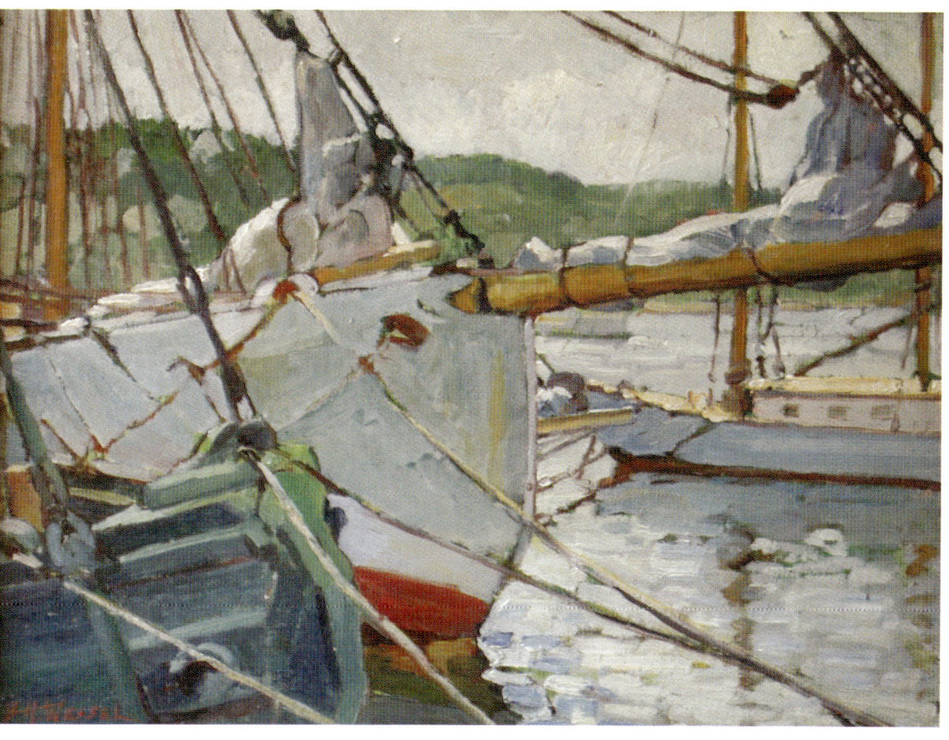

Bessie Hoover Wessel
Boats at Anchor
Oil on canvas board, 15¾ x 11¾ in.
Private Collection

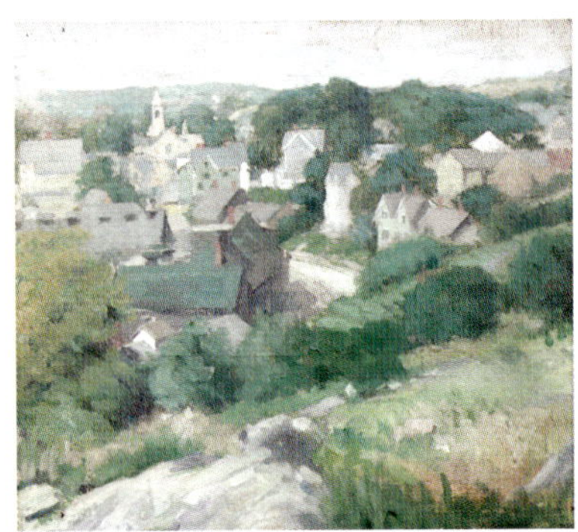

Bessie Hoover Wessel
Banner Hill, c. 1916
Oil on canvas, 18 x 20 in.
Signed B. Hoover on reverse
Collection of Carl and Carol Samson

years were given our own studio and were allowed to have canvases to exhibit."[61] An attentive and dedicated student, Bessie achieved considerable success under Duveneck's tutelage, and often joined in the Academy's annual exhibitions. Specifically an oil painter, she was noted for her landscapes, portraits, still life work, and miniatures executed on ivory.

In 1915, Bessie was offered a teaching post at the Academy. However, unlike Herman Wessel and Frank Duveneck, Bessie Hoover was a more reserved personality and diligent to the point of exhausting herself with concern for her students. "I became so wrapped up in my pupils' work. I couldn't sleep at night for worrying about their problems."[62] Nevertheless, Bessie persevered as a teacher for two years, and a closer relationship blossomed between Bessie and her colleague Herman Wessel. In the summer of 1915, Frank Duveneck's sister, Molly, invited Bessie to spend the summer with them at Rocky Neck. It would be the first of many such summers for Bessie and Herman.

The couple were married quietly in August 1917, and the newspapers thought it very romantic.

> *The wedding took place Friday at the summer home of Mr. Frank Duveneck, at Gloucester, Mass., where Miss Hoover has been painting since early summer. Her especial talent lies in portraiture and miniature painting, in which fields she has already won recognition. The bride is the daughter of Francis M. Hoover of Cincinnati and a sister of Attorney Francis A. Hoover. She was chosen president of the Cincinnati Woman's Art club for the current year.*
>
> *Mr. Wessel's work in landscape painting has long since challenged public attention in art centers of the country. He is recognized as among the ablest of Cincinnati's artists, a success largely due to extensive study here and abroad. Mr. Wessel long since proved what talent, united with technical skill, can accomplish, and his social aptitude*

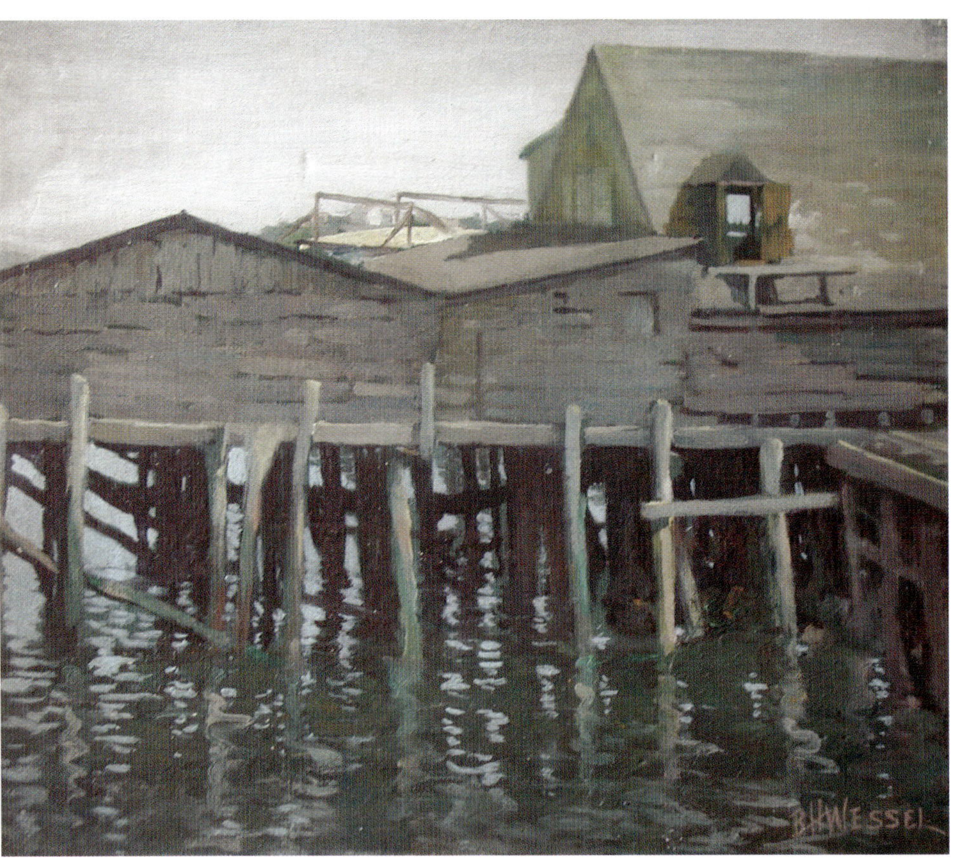

Bessie Hoover Wessel
Dock Buildings
Oil on canvas mounted on board,
11$\frac{3}{4}$ x 13$\frac{3}{4}$
Private collection

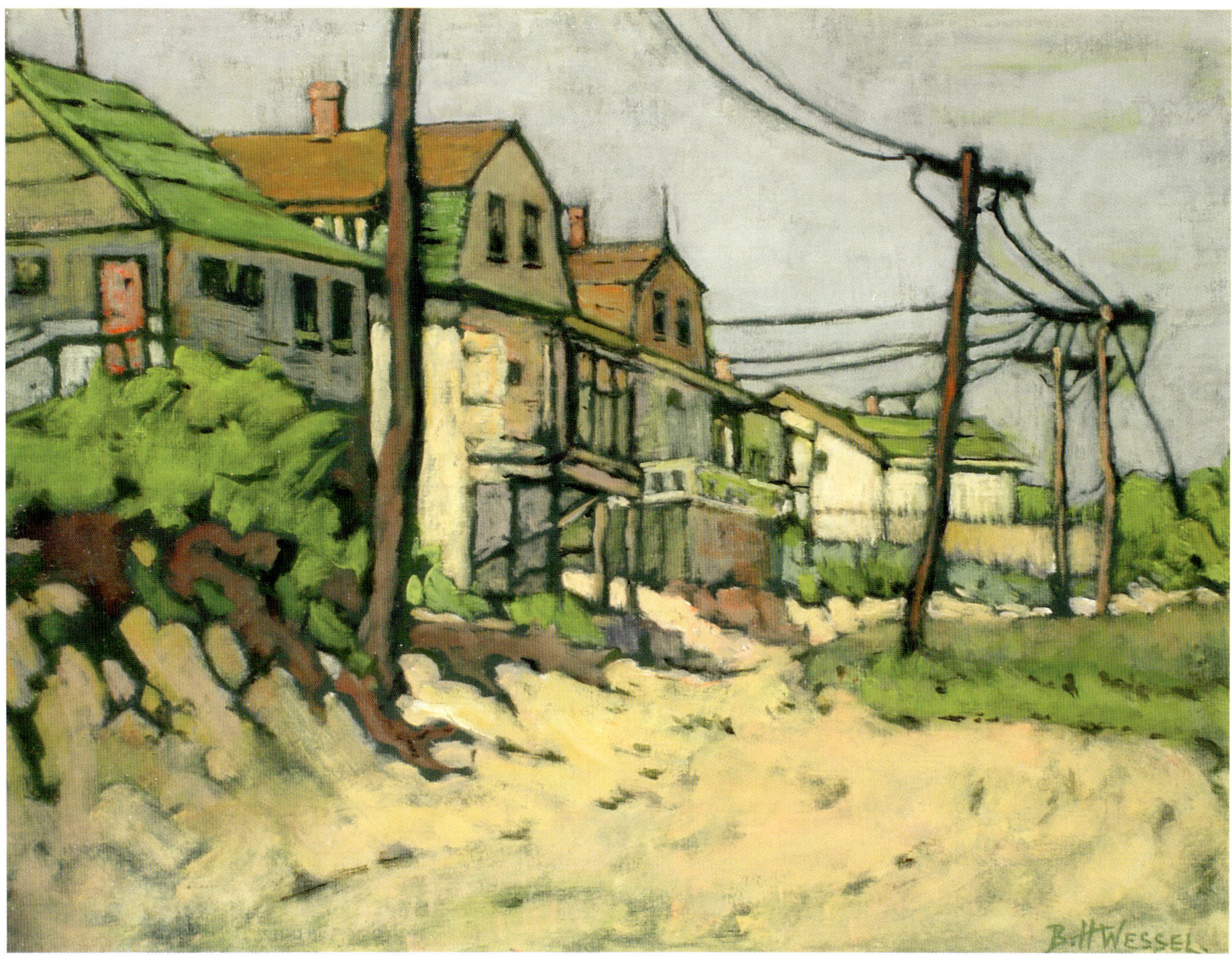

Bessie Hoover Wessel
At the Gloucester Shore
Oil on canvas, 12 x 16 in.
Pierce Galleries, Inc., Hingham, Massachusetts

has rendered him among the most popular of the Cincinnati group of artists.

The sudden death of Mr. L. H. Meakin had a part in the arrangement for a very quiet wedding. Mr. Meakin was at Gloucester before his sudden fatal illness and the shadow of his loss is still upon his friends there. Mr. Wessel and his bride are on a short tour, from which he will return to take up his duties at the Art Academy September 24. Whether Mrs. Wessel will continue her class work there is not yet decided.[63]

Like many women artists, Bessie had to juggle domesticity with her own creative needs, first as a wife, and then as a mother after the birth of their son, Robert, in 1921. Although there were fewer opportunities for her to paint, she made full use of the time available to her and was able to contribute regularly to the annual Woman's Art Club show and the Ohio State Fair. A joint exhibition with her husband at the Traxel Art Galleries, c. 1933, saw her work favorably reviewed by the critics. "Bessie Hoover Wessel has a very individual manner of execution. Her canvases are underpainted in a dark tone. On top of this she places her local colors in short even strokes, following the forms, so that the dark hue shows around each stroke. This gives an unusual effect almost like stained glass and makes a very decorative conception of the whole. The colors are well chosen and pure in tone, the draughtsmanship is sure and distinctive and the values of lights and darks are accentuated with her technique. The compositions are clear and built up with an understanding of the principles of art."[64]

The couple maintained a permanent home and studio near Eden Park, Cincinnati, however, they traveled in Europe as often as they could, and frequently summered in Gloucester. As Robert grew older, Bessie returned to painting full time and continued to build her reputation as a portraitist, painting with bold luscious color to create striking likenesses, making her a favorite with the local populace to paint their loved ones. It is believed she painted over two hundred portraits during a long and distinguished career. She was also well known for painting brilliantly colored landscape and harbor scenes, often on green window shades, which she favored when traveling as they rolled easily and were simple to transport.

As the 1930s progressed, and even the Cincinnati Art Museum changed its curriculum from stressing fundamentals to accentuating personal expression, the Wessels experimented with different styles that relied on flatter masses and more simplified form. Neither of them, however, took technique to the extreme and continued to use painterly representation as the basis of their work. Ultimately, Bessie retained much of her Duveneck training, preferring to build up her portraits through chiaroscuro and sculptured brushwork. Duveneck's method of working up the head in small planes within larger planes is typical of the portraitist who wishes to model the features with paint, with each tone deliberately applied and juxtaposed beside the next correct tone. She later utilized this ability to create a series of Native American portraits shown collectively as "Portraits from the Plains." This 1971 show, a project she undertook after Herman's death in 1969, proved to be Bessie Wessel's last. With her health deteriorating, she painted less and passed away on January 29, 1973.

Notes

1 Judson, Alice, "Putting Scenery First," p. 342, quoted in Love, Richard H., *Carl W. Peters American Scene Painter from Rochester to Rockport* (Rochester, NY: University of Rochester Press, 1999), p. 251.

2 "After all's said, Frank Duveneck is the greatest talent of the brush of this generation," John Singer Sargent said during a London dinner in the early 1890s. Quoted in Heerman, Norbert, *Frank Duveneck* (Boston: Houghton Mifflin, 1918), p. 1.

3 Alexander, Mary L, *Cincinnati Enquirer*, interview with Robert Henri, May 31, 1936, quoted in Neuhaus, Robert, *Unsuspected Genius: The Art and Life of Frank Duveneck* (San Francisco: Bedford Press, 1987), p. 133.

4 Duveneck, Josephine Whitney, *Frank Duveneck Painter-Teacher* (San Francisco: John Howell, 1970), p. 29.

5 Ibid.

6 Ibid., p. 42.

7 Ibid., p. 77.

8 Ibid., p. 79.

9 Ibid., p. 61.

10 Loughmiller, Henry C., "I studied with Duveneck," *American Artist*, March 1965, p. 40, Duveneck Papers, CAHA.

11 Resolution by "the Students of the Duveneck Class," read at a memorial service at the Cincinnati Art Museum, March 30, 1919, Duveneck Papers, CAHA.

12 Biographical Outline Frank Duveneck 1848-1919, p. 7, Duveneck Papers, CAHA.

13 Taylor, Robert, Art Review, "The Gloucester phase of Frank Duveneck," *Boston Globe*, Sunday, August 16, 1987.

14 De Cruz, Adele, *Frank Duveneck, The Gloucester Years, 1892-1917*, exhibition catalog (New York: David J. Findlay, Jr.)

15 Notes from *Gloucester Daily Times*, Duveneck Papers, CAHA.

16 Ashbery, John, *The Indian Summer of Frank Duveneck*, Duveneck Papers, CAHA.

17 Letter to Julia Lyman from Mary Pratt Sears, 1887, Duveneck Papers, CAHA.

18 Weir, J. Alden, quoted in "Twachtman's Gloucester Period: A 'Clarifying Process,'" Hale, John Douglass, *Twachtman in Gloucester: His Last Years, 1900-1902*, exhibition catalogue. (New York: Spanierman Gallery, 1987) p. 14.

19 Dewing, T. W., "John H. Twachtman: An Estimation," *North American Review* 176 (April 1903): 554.

20 Clark, Eliot, "The Art of John Twachtman," *International Studio* 72 (January 1921): 1xxxi, quoted in Gerdts, William H., "John Twachtman and the Artistic Colony in Gloucester at the Turn of the Century," *Twachtman in Gloucester: His Last Years*, p. 40.

21 Clark, Eliot, *John H. Twachtman* (Privately printed, 1924), p. 53.

22 "Art Notes" *New York Times*, April 12, 1891, p. 12, quoted in Hale, John Douglass, "Twachtman's Gloucester Period: A 'Clarifying Process,'" *Twachtman in Gloucester: His Last Years*, p. 12.

23 *Gloucester Daily Times*, June 6, 1900, p. 3, col. 4, Duveneck Papers, CAHA.

24 *Gloucester Daily Times*, September 1, 1900, p. 5, col. 3, Duveneck Papers, CAHA.

25 *Gloucester Daily Times*, September 24, 1900, p. 5, col. 5, Duveneck Papers, CAHA.

26 *Gloucester Daily Times*, August 20, 1901, p. 8, col. 3, Duveneck Papers, CAHA.

27 *Gloucester Daily Times*, June 24, 1902, p. 5, Twachtman Papers, CAHA.

28 *Gloucester Daily Times*, August 8, 1902, p. 7, Twachtman Papers, CAHA.

29 "Edward Potthast, N. A." *The Inspiration of Cape Ann*. Exhibition catalogue, Rockport Art Association, n. d.

30 "Art Exhibit," *Commercial Gazette*, February 6, 1883, p. 8. Quoted in Laurene Buckley, *Joseph DeCamp* (New York: Prestel, 1995).

31 "The Society of Artists," *New York Daily Tribune*, April 24, 1893, p. 4.

32 Buckley, Ibid., p. 142.

33 Resolutions read at a memorial service for Duveneck at the Cincinnati Art Museum, March 30, 1919.

34 Hiesinger, Ulrich W., *Childe Hassam, American Impressionist* (Munich: Prestel, 1999), p. 74.

35 Ibid., p. 165. From Hassam to C. E. S. Wood, Oct. 21, 1919: C. E. S. Wood Papers, Henry E. Huntington Library & Art Gallery, San Marino, CA.

36 *Gloucester Daily Times*, July 26, 1919. Hassam Papers, CAHA.

37 "Cape Ann artist Childe Hassam's work on view," *MassBay Antiques*, February 1990, p. 39.

38 de Veer, Elizabeth and Richard Boyle, *Sunlight & Shadow, The Life & Art of Willard L. Metcalf* (New York: Abbeville Press, 1987), p. 18.

39 Ibid., p. 22.

40 Willard Metcalf to his daughter, Rosalind, 5 February 1925, collection of Rosalind Metcalf Harris, Ibid., p. 154.

41 Gammell, R. H. Ives, *The Boston Painters 1900-1930* (Orleans, MA: Parnassus Imprints, 1986), p. 151.

42 Rolshoven, Julius, "Autobiography," unpublished ms., p. 39, William H. Gerdts Art Reference Library, New York, quoted in Buckley, p.13.

43 Charles E. Mills to his father, December 13, 1879; Frank Duveneck Papers, Archives of American Art, Smithsonian Institution, Washington, D.C., quoted in Buckley, p. 15.

44 Gammell, p. 152.

45 Ibid.

46 Knowlton, Helen M., "A Home-Colony of Artists," *Studio* 5, July 14, 1890, pp 326-327, quoted in Buckley, p. 36.

47 Sellin, David, "Ipswich Figures in A French Background," *The Ipswich Painters at Home and Abroad*, exhibition catalogue (Gloucester: Cape Ann Historical Association, 1993), p. 14.

48 *The Courier*, June 1884, newspaper clipping in Cincinnati Art Museum Annual scrapbook, Record Group 5, series 9, vol. 1, Cincinnati Art Museum Archives, quoted in Cyran, C., *Herman and Bessie Wessel, At Home and Abroad*, exhibition catalogue (Cincinnati, OH: Cincinnati Art Club, 1997), p.11.

49 Wessel, Helen, telephone conversation with Carol Cyran and Carl Samson, Cincinnati, OH, November 15, 1996, quoted in Cyran, p. 12.

50 Cyran, C., ibid.

51 *Commercial Tribune*, December 12, 1909, newspaper clipping in Cincinnati Art Museum Annual scrapbook, Record Group 5, series 9, vol. 4, p. 31, Cincinnati Art Museum Archive, quoted in Cyran, p. 37.

52 Duveneck, Josephine Whitney, *Frank Duveneck Painter-Teacher*, San Francisco: John Howell, 1970, p. 133.

53 Cyran, p. 37.

54 Ibid.

55 "H. H. Wessel," L. H. Meakin (typewritten), Cincinnati Artists file, box 46, Cincinnati Art Museum Archive, quoted in Cyran, p. 38.

56 Ibid., p. 17.

57 Alexander, Mary L., "Cincinnati Artist Writes in Humorous Vein of Gloucester," *Cincinnati Enquirer*, news clipping 1926, H. H. Wessel Papers, CAHA.

58 Darack, Arthur, "A Tripartite Approach to Herman Wessel," *Cincinnati Pictorial Enquirer*, Sunday, December 18, 1966, in Bessie Wessel's scrapbook. Quoted in Cyran, p. 33.

59 "H. H. Wessel, World-Famed Artist, Dies: At Art Academy 40 Years, Also Was Museum Curator," April 14, 1969, unattributed, H. H. Wessel papers, CAHA.

60 Weaver, Margaret, "Bessie Wessel's show evokes great period of Cincinnati artists," *The Post & Times Star*, Cincinnati, Tuesday, April 13, 1971, B. Wessel Papers, CAHA.

61 Ibid.

62 Bell, Eleanor, "Marriage & Painting Mixed Happily," *Cincinnati Post & Times Star.*

63 Unattributed newspaper clipping. B. Wessel Papers, CAHA.

64 Unattributed newspaper clipping. B. Wessel Papers, CAHA.

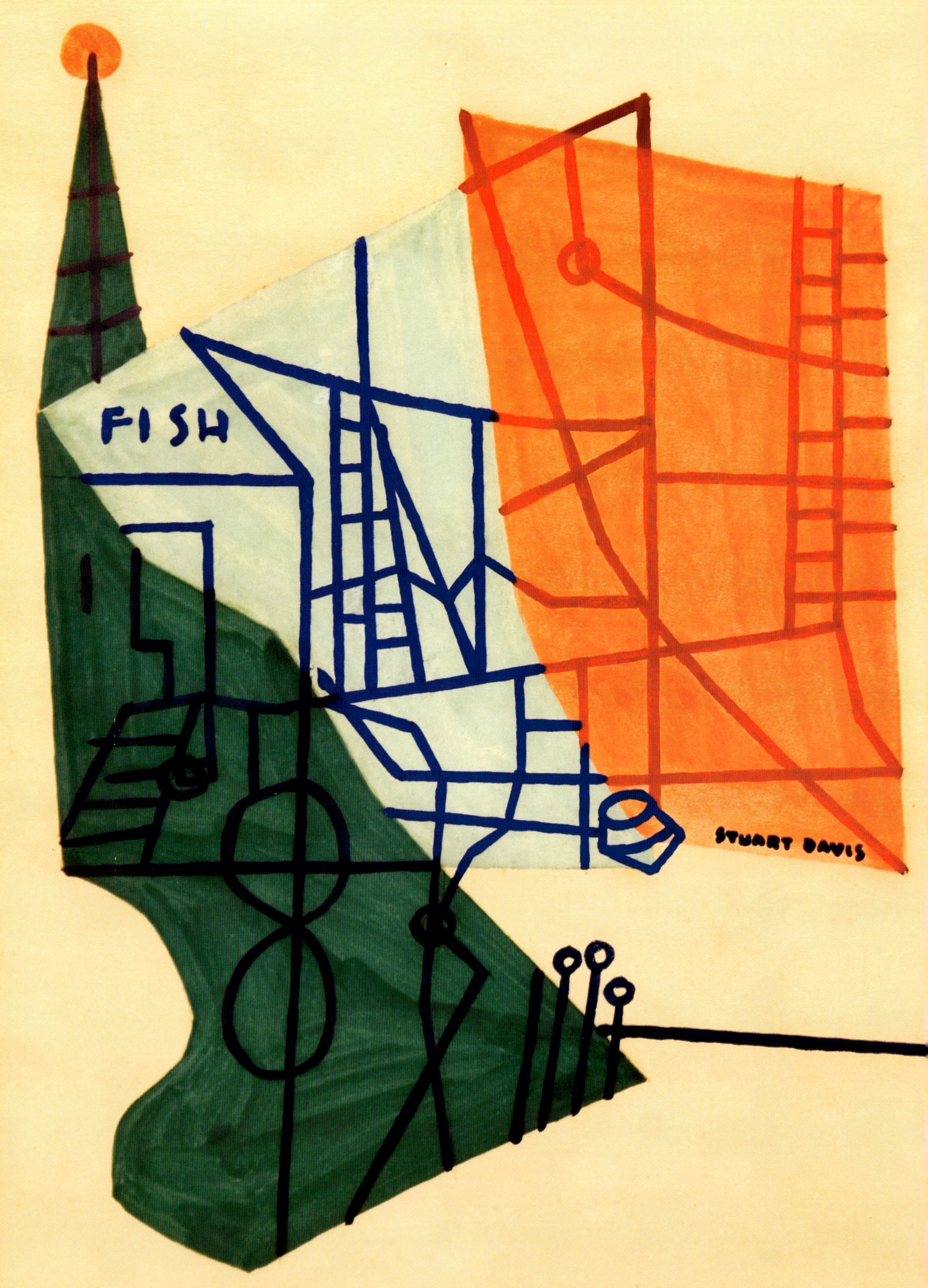
FISH
STUART DAVIS

The Red Cottage Group

"I went to Gloucester, Mass., on the enthusiastic recommendation of John Sloan. That was the place I had been looking for. It had the brilliant light of Provincetown, but with the important additions of topographical severity and the architectural beauties of the Gloucester schooner."

— Stuart Davis[1]

The mystique of the Red Cottage Group lingers still, despite the artists comprising it being together only a few years. The Red Cottage, which still stands on East Main Street, almost opposite the causeway leading to Rocky Neck, was home for several summers to a unique group of New York-based artists. The group came to fruition after Charles and Alice Winter, two of the original editors of a social idealist magazine called *The Masses*—founded to exemplify the spirit of the collaborative movement—called in their friends, John and Dolly Sloan, to help salvage the magazine from financial problems.

[Extract of letter from Stuart Davis to his mother]

Gloucester. Sep. 26, 6pm, 1915 Sunday

Dear Ma,

I could use some money at an early date. Yesterday afternoon Smith and I got Connoyer's [sic] dory. It is the oldest vessel afloat. In these parts anyway. It takes two people to run it. One to row and the other to keep the water from getting any higher than the rower's knees. Smith was a fine bailer. The water never got over my ankles. We went in among the small Portuguese, Italian and Spanish fishing boats.

They are all painted in brilliant colors. Red, blue, green, etc. and the fishermen on them are tremendously interesting. It is just such a scene as you would see in some old fishing village in Europe. I am trying to get a large painting of the scene. Then we rowed further out in the bay and I landed on some rocks that were sticking out of the water.

They were covered with star-fish. The biggest ones I ever saw. We got a couple that were ten inches across.

The other night Cornoyer took the Sloans and Smith down to the Savoy for dinner. The rest of us went to the moving pictures and met them when we came out. The Savoy party was kind of stewed so the women all went home in Paks car and the men decided to walk. We walked a little way and I suggested that we go through a haunted house that I had heard about.

This was eleven o'clock at night. It is an awfully weird looking place and hasn't been inhabited for years. It sets right off Main St. on a big high embankment and has this six story tower commanding a view of the whole city and bay.

Winter and Smith stayed outside and the rest of us went in thro' the cellar. I leading the way and Sloan following on all fours making a noise like a cat. The house has a great many rooms. They were all in a state of the utmost confusion the ornaments

Stuart Davis
Fish, 1939
Gouache and pencil on paper,
$15\frac{1}{2}$ x $12\frac{1}{2}$ in.
Collection of Mr. and Mrs. William H. Trayes

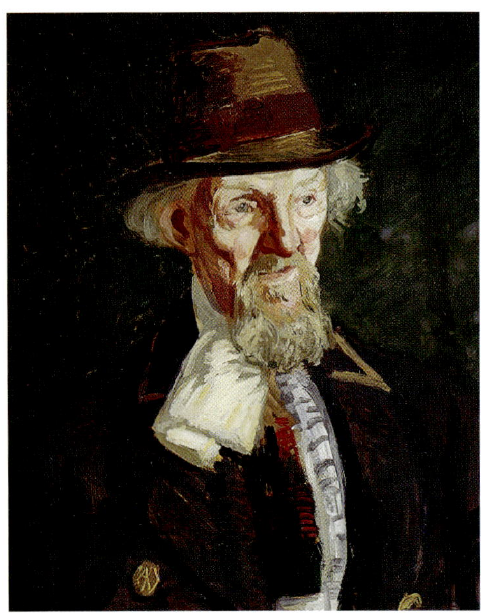

John Sloan
Old Cone (Uncle Sam), 1914
Oil on canvas, 24 x 20 in.
Cape Ann Historical Association, Gloucester, Massachusetts
Gift of Dr. and Mrs. Hollon W. Farr

and plaster being knocked from the walls and the plumbing gone. A regular vacant house. We went all thro' it from top to bottom I Sloan, Cornoyer and Tietjens. The view from the tower in the moonlight was wonderful.

...The rest of the way home was employed in singing, shouting and Sloan chasing cats over the roofs of Gorton-Pews factories in the moonlight. It was really quite funny.

Well that will be enough for this one.

Love,
Stuart [2]

John Sloan (1871-1951)

Sloan hailed from Lock Haven, Pennsylvania, and worked as a staff artist on various Philadelphia newspapers before moving to New York in 1904. There he began exhibiting with the Ashcan School of Robert Henri and Maurice Prendergast, whose painting genre included the realism of everyday backyards and rooftops, and the lifestyle of the common man.

When asked by Winter to help revamp *The Masses*, Sloan came up with "a magazine with a sense of humor and no respect for the respectable; frank; arrogant; impertinent; searching for the true causes... a magazine whose final policy is to do as it pleases and conciliate nobody, not even its readers..."[3] Sloan also brought in new illustrators to work on the magazine, including Stuart Davis, the son of Sloan's old friend, sculptor Helen Stuart Davis, and her husband Edward Wyatt Davis, one-time art editor of the *Philadelphia Press*. Soon the friendships forged at the magazine spilled over into more than just common political ideals. As artists, this group also shared an appreciation for the color theories and compositional ideas of Hardesty Maratta, a paint manufacturer who produced oil paint sets made up of standardized primary colors plus secondary colors, and then the color notes, or values, of those shades in between. These artists

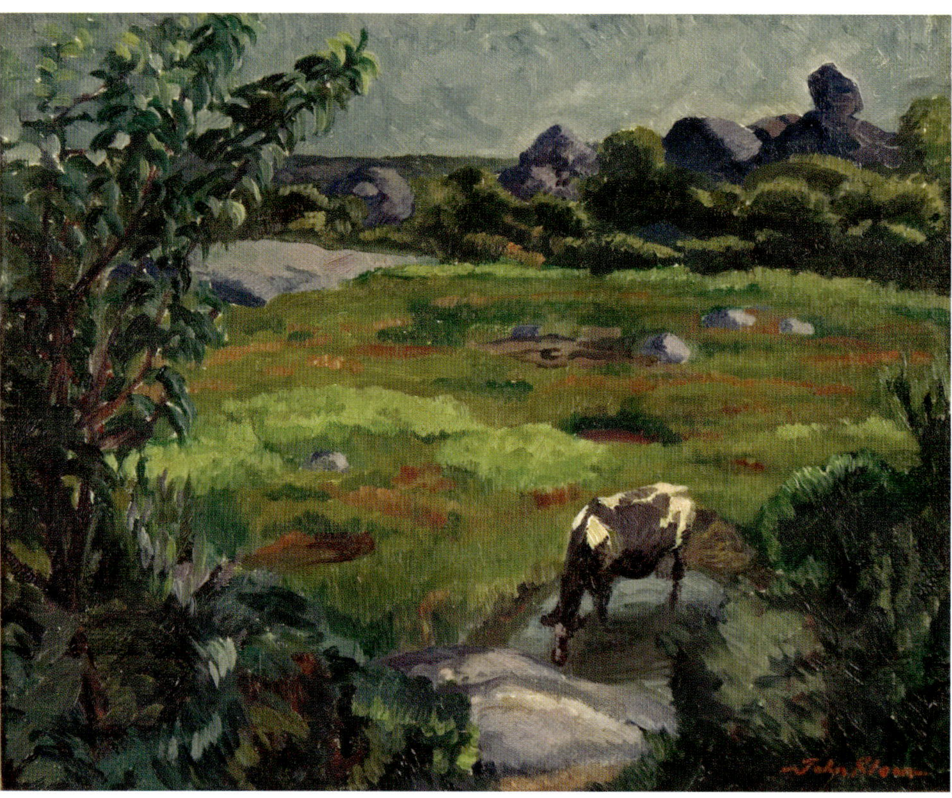

John Sloan
Swamp Cow, Gloucester, 1918
Oil on canvas, 16 x 20 in.
Collection of Mr. and Mrs. William H. Trayes

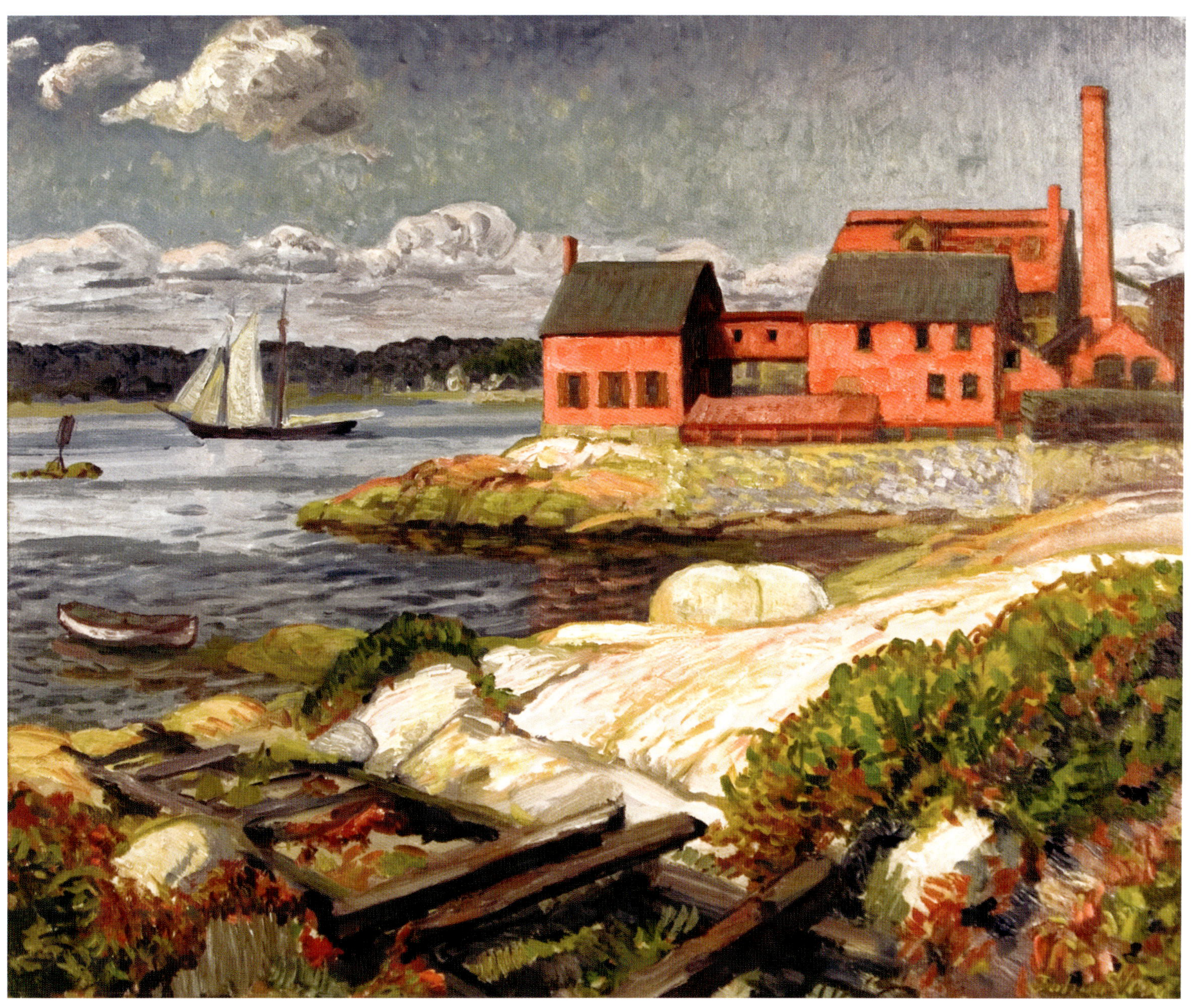

John Sloan
The Paint Factory, 1914
Oil on canvas, 26 x 32 in.
Private collection

were also fervent supporters of New York's avant-garde Armory Show held in 1913, featuring more than 1,500 works typifying the new wave of artistic thought from European post-impressionism to cubism.

Sloan and Davis both exhibited oils, etchings and watercolors in the Armory Show, properly titled the International Exhibition of Modern Art. For Sloan it was, "the beginning of a journey… The blinders fell from my eyes and I could look at religious pictures without seeing the subjects. I was free to enjoy the sculptures of Africa and prehistoric Mexico because verisimilitude was no longer important. I realized that these things were… distorted to emphasize ideas about life, emotional qualities of life."[4] He was especially impressed with the working methods of Van Gogh and Cezanne. A sporadic painter because of his other work, Sloan was astonished at the way the Europeans regularly painted outdoors regardless of subject matter and weather conditions. This was contrary to his own work ethic of waiting for an idea to occur before trying to capture it in paint. "[A]t the age of forty," Sloan recalled, "I realized that I needed some new way to keep at work. I saw that the European artists kept themselves going, with any kind of subject…. This method produces more work, more 'studies';

On the side porch of the Red Cottage, East Gloucester, (left to right)
Seated: *Stuart Davis, Paul Cornoyer, Agnes M. Richmond*
Standing: *Dolly Sloan, F. Carl Smith, Alice Beach Winter, Katherine Groschke, Paul Tietjens and John Sloan*
Photograph by Charles Allan Winter, c. 1915
Cape Ann Historical Association, Gloucester, Massachusetts

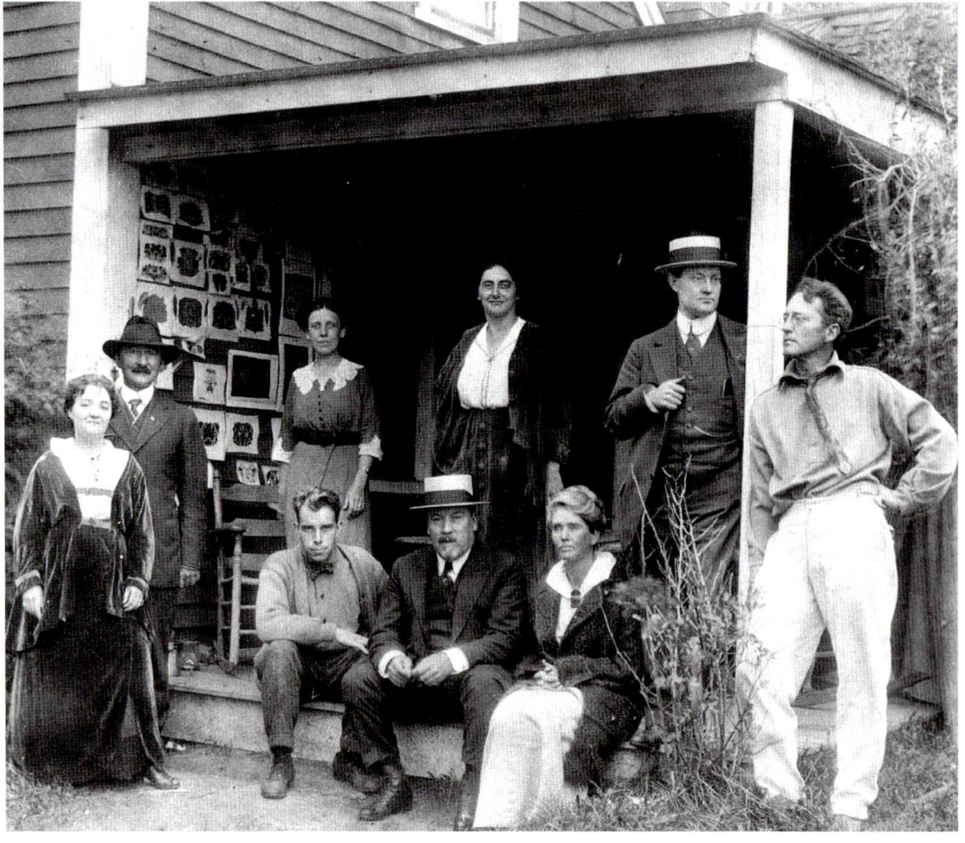

Stuart Davis
Town and Boats, 1932
Gouache, ink and pencil on paper, 11¼ x 15⅜ in.
Collection of Mr. and Mrs. William H. Trayes

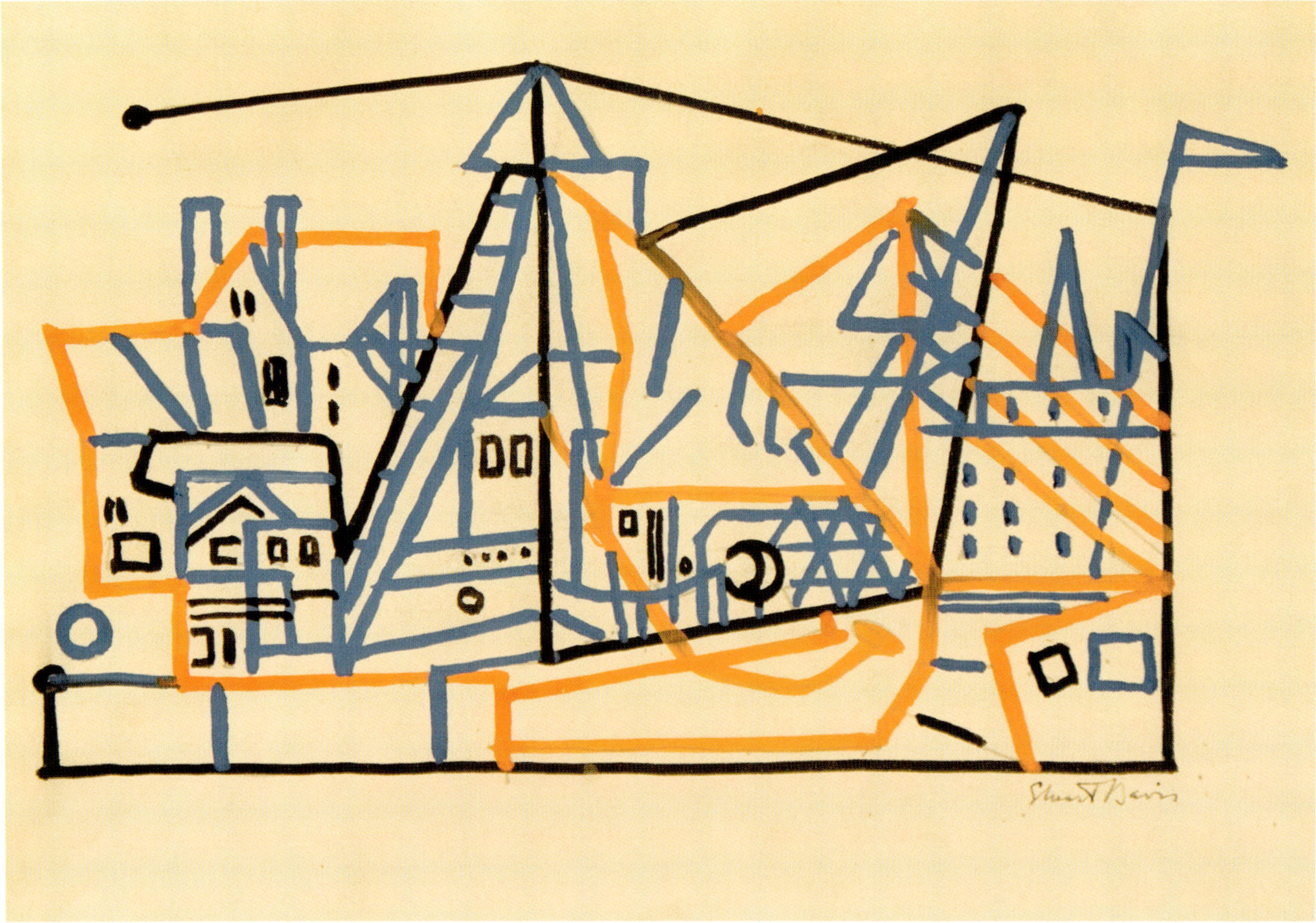

but it also leads to the discovery of new motivations. I made up my mind to take a few months off to paint landscapes in Gloucester."[5]

Sloan chose Gloucester for his first extended painting trip based on the enthusiastic recommendation of Charles and Alice Winter who, after a fleeting visit to Cape Ann in 1911, had spent the summer of 1913 painting outdoors on Rocky Neck. The Sloans found a small red cottage to rent for the summer of 1914, located conveniently close to the Rocky Neck causeway, in the heart of East Gloucester, and shortly after they moved in, Charles and Alice Winter arrived to join them. It was a productive summer for all of them. Sloan, especially, found the light and atmosphere of the old seaport irresistible. The rugged nature of East Gloucester's then undeveloped landscape provided the motivation to paint on a daily basis, and with the benefit of Maratta's color system, Sloan executed more work than he could ever have hoped: 90 paintings on his first visit, and almost 300 over the next five summers that he spent in East Gloucester. Many of these works were landscapes. Although he no longer waited for the muse to strike before going on location, Sloan did spend time searching for just the right spot to inspire an idea, sometimes walking for a mile or more, painting equipment in hand, before finding a subject with what he called "exciting plastic rhythms and color textures that could be the starting point of a theme."[6] By plastic rhythms, one can assume Sloan was looking for subject matter fashioned by nature, with an obvious three-dimensional format and texture that could be translated with paint and modeled on canvas in the best post-Impressionist manner of free and loose brushwork coupled with vivid Maratta hues to portray the intense light and deep shadows of East Gloucester's luminescent atmosphere.

The trip to the red cottage was such a success that the foursome returned the following summer, and were joined by three of the Davis family, artist Stuart, his photographer brother Wyatt, and their mother, Helen, a sculptor. As Stuart Davis said, he came on Sloan's recommendation and found it to be everything he sought as an artist.

Stuart Davis (1894-1964)

Stuart Davis was born in Philadelphia, but in 1910 moved on to New York for a chance to study with Robert Henri. Although he first embraced the ethic of the Ashcan School, Davis, only nineteen when he exhibited five watercolors in the Armory Show, was perhaps more influenced by the burgeoning European movement of modernism than were some of his artistic colleagues. In defense of the new wave of abstractionism, Davis declared a picture to be, "an independent object with a reality of its own."[7] However, when a painter sees the finished object as a separation from the reality of nature and having a veracity of its own then he is, of course, moving away from the essence of the true plein air painter. An artist painting en plein air seeks to represent a fleeting moment of light, executed on site, to convey the chosen scene at a particular time of day. However, the New York contingent had a modern approach to life in general, not only their painting, and were not afraid to challenge traditional mores.

In the early days, the Red Cottage group hosted other visitors such as Agnes Richmond, Paul Cornoyer, Leon Kroll and F. Carl Smith. The whole ensemble would go out on location and paint together, one artist often sketching another at work, such as Smith's rendition of Richmond painting on the rocks of the Back Shore with her husband, Winthrop Turney.

The Red Cottage group also hosted clambakes and croquet games for visiting friends and relatives, such as composer Paul Tietjens and pianist Katherine Groschke.

All were socially minded and as Alice Beach Winter put it, "We all lived together in the little red house; but associated with us were several artists in other lines—old friends, also from New York, but originally from St. Louis, Cincinnati and Philadelphia—who lived near, but could be seen every day at the little red house."[8] They also entertained the neighborhood children. Dolly Sloan and Alice Winter, both childless, encouraged the children to visit and the youngsters would often end up posing for the artists. John Sloan, not noted for his portraiture, executed at least 100 canvases featuring the children, and it was often said of Alice Winter that she painted "every child in Gloucester!" Elizabeth Oakes, who as a young woman posed for Charles Allan Winter's *Portrait of Miss Elizabeth Oakes*, remembered visiting the Red Cottage as a child. "I remember watching Stuart Davis (a real bohemian) painting an ugly gray tenement house on Mt. Pleasant Avenue. John Sloan I remember chiefly as very good natured and full of

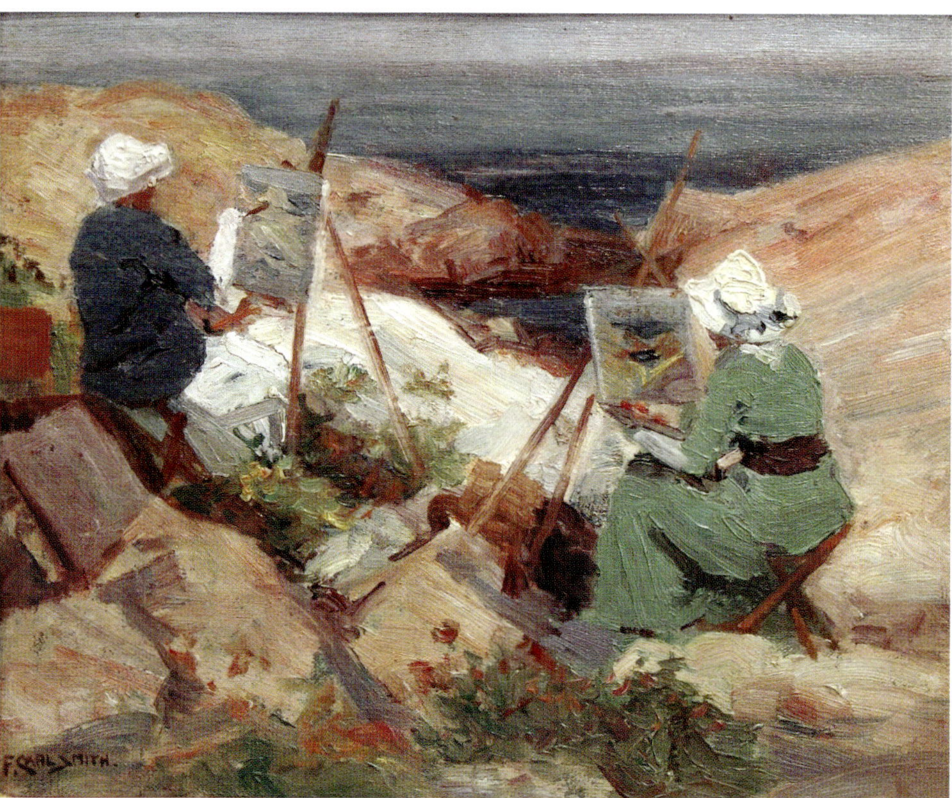

F. Carl Smith
Agnes Richmond and Winthrop Turney Painting
Oil on board, 9 x 12 in.
Boston Art Club, Boston

practical jokes.... My sister and I had outdoor painting lessons with Paul Cornoyer—a very lovable personality... Mrs. Winter retained the artist's wonderful childlike wonder and joy at the life around her. My parents used to wonder how so many people could manage to squeeze into the little red cottage."[9]

The artists enjoyed their close proximity to each other as well as the easy camaraderie, the passionate chess games and the more restrained moments contemplating the day's work with Charles Winter's victrola playing Italian opera in the background.[10] This camaraderie allowed them to explore their approach to painting, extending their theories and techniques by observing each other's methods and assimilating different ideas. "We went out painting," Sloan recalled. "All of us interested in developing different orchestrations of color on the palette. Stuart was just beginning to assimilate ideas from the Nabis and Fauves. It was fascinating to see him re-assemble things he saw in nature sometimes finding a useful house or tree behind him to include in the picture.

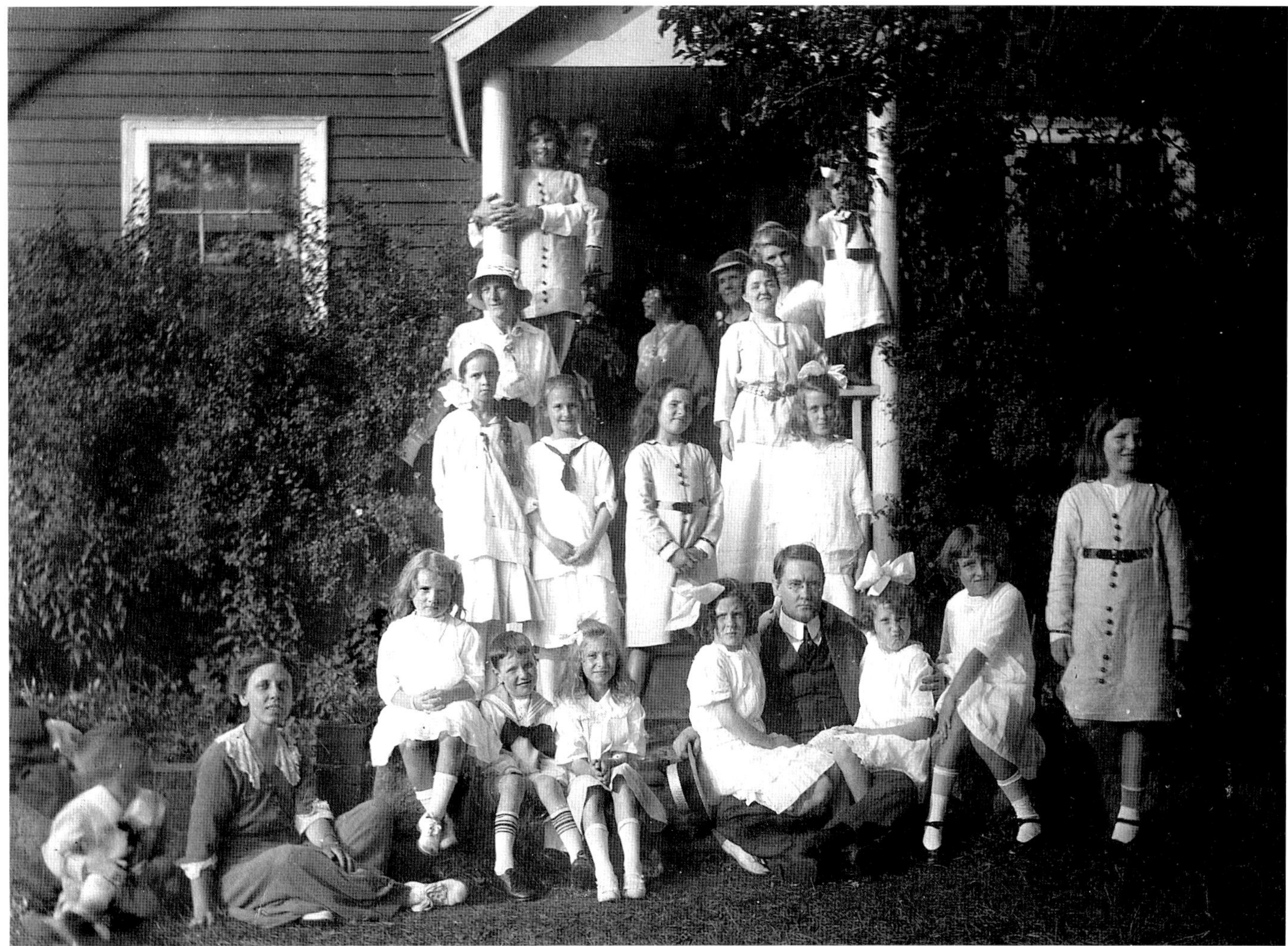

Artists and children in front of the Red Cottage
Photograph by Charles Allan Winter, c. 1915
Cape Ann Historical Association, Gloucester, Massachusetts
Gift of Elizabeth Oakes Colford

Trees and houses were selected to modify the composition seen by the eye. I did this myself sometimes, but in a less original way. Stuart had the finest sense of proportion of any American modern artist.[11]

Eventually, however, Sloan began to feel confined by the increasing popularity of Rocky Neck and East Gloucester. "There was an artist's shadow beside every cow in Gloucester," Sloan grumbled to writer and literary critic Van Wyck Brooks, "and the cows themselves were dying from eating paint rags."[12] The Sloans did not return to Gloucester after the summer of 1919. Within a decade the Red Cottage group broke up, not from lack of affection, but merely a parting of the ways. The artists continued to associate with each other in New York but during the summer, they kept separate and more permanent households. Beginning in 1925, the Davises acquired a home on Mt. Pleasant Avenue, on the way up to Banner Hill, which incorporated a studio for Stuart when he visited; Helen Davis also maintained a sculpture studio on Reed's Wharf, living out her life as a much loved member of the East Gloucester community. The Winters built a home and studio on Mt. Pleasant Avenue and summered there for several years before leaving New York to become year round Gloucester residents.

The Red Cottage group lasted less than a decade, and yet the friendships forged and the work executed in those first fevered years after the Armory Show created a permanent niche in the annals of American art history.

Charles Allan Winter (1869-1942)

Gloucester notable Charles Allan Winter, who found his way to Cape Ann via Cincinnati, Paris and New York, was a true individualist, an academic with a visionary's eye. Born in Cincinnati on October 26, 1869, Winter was the eldest of four children in the family of Alfred and Fannie (Ransley) Winter. The family later moved to Dayton, Kentucky, "a suburb of Cincinnati," according to Winter,[13] "located just across the Ohio river." In 1881, at the age of twelve, he left school and began working for John Ransley, a cousin with a confectionary business in Cincinnati. It was here he first became interested in color science, after realizing one of the boys he worked with could not differentiate between the red and green candies. In 1884, Winter began morning classes at the Cincinnati Art Academy, working at Ransley's in the afternoon, a schedule he followed until 1891 when he finally went to the Academy full time. He studied with Nowottny, Lutz and Thomas S. Noble, and in 1894 was awarded a three-year foreign scholarship. Immediately, he set out for Paris, art capital of the world.

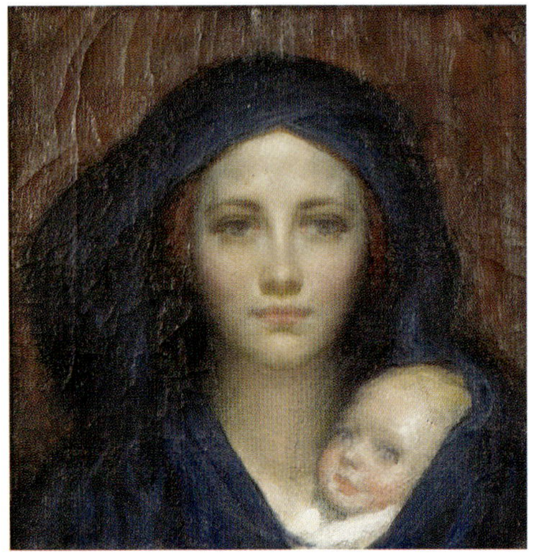

Charles Allan Winter
Mother and Child
Oil on canvas, 17 x 17 in.
Mosher Gallery, Rockport, Massachusetts

Enrolling at the Académie Julian, Winter studied with William Bouguereau and Gabriel Ferrier and at night took classes at Colarossi's. He also spent eight months in Rome studying the Italian masters and copying a portion of Michelangelo's Sistine Chapel ceiling. His copy was later shipped back to Cincinnati to hang in the city art museum. After his scholarship ended Winter stayed on in Europe for an extra year, traveling through Germany, Italy and back to France where he exhibited with the Paris Salon, showing *Antigone* in 1896 and *Fantazie Egyptienne*, two years later. These paintings, particularly the latter, a spectacular work depicting an Egyptian priestess descending from the temple throne with a sacred snake hung around her neck, demonstrate the cerebral side of Winter's nature. When painting large works or murals, Winter often chose to symbolize ideas using objects to signify a state of mind, rather than simply denoting the actual form or aspect of the object. "Everything in my husband's paintings has symbols," his wife once said.[14] "He loved symbolism in good things."

Winter returned from Paris in 1898 after receiving an invitation to teach portraiture at the St. Louis School of Fine Arts. He stayed there three years and then moved to New York in the fall of 1901, acquiring a studio at 53 East 59th Street and becoming a noted illustrator, in demand for his imaginative approach. Many of the popular periodicals of the day used his cover designs, including *Collier's Weekly, Hearst's Century, Scribner's*, and *Cosmopolitan*. Shortly after his move to New York he renewed an acquaintanceship with Miss Alice Beach, a St. Louis School of Fine Arts alum, also carving out a career in New York as an illustrator of books and magazines. The couple announced their engagement at a 1903 Thanksgiving Day dinner for friends and were married on New Year's Day, 1904.

The Winters first came to Gloucester in 1911, returning in 1913, and then sharing the little red cottage adjacent to Rocky Neck with John Sloan and his wife, Dolly, in the summer of 1914. They came again in 1915, this time joined by Helen Davis and her two sons, Stuart and Wyatt. Being like-minded in art theory and politics, they formed an unusually tight knit group within the art colony at Rocky Neck itself. Eventually, John and Dolly Sloan moved on to other locations, but the place and the people so inspired the Winters that they returned to Rocky Neck as regular summer visitors before building their own summer home and studio on Mt. Pleasant Avenue. Their social circle included local artists A.T. Hibbard, and W. Lester Stevens, as well as other summer residents such as Robert Henri, Leon Kroll, Jane Peterson and William Glackens. In 1931, the Winters moved to Gloucester permanently.

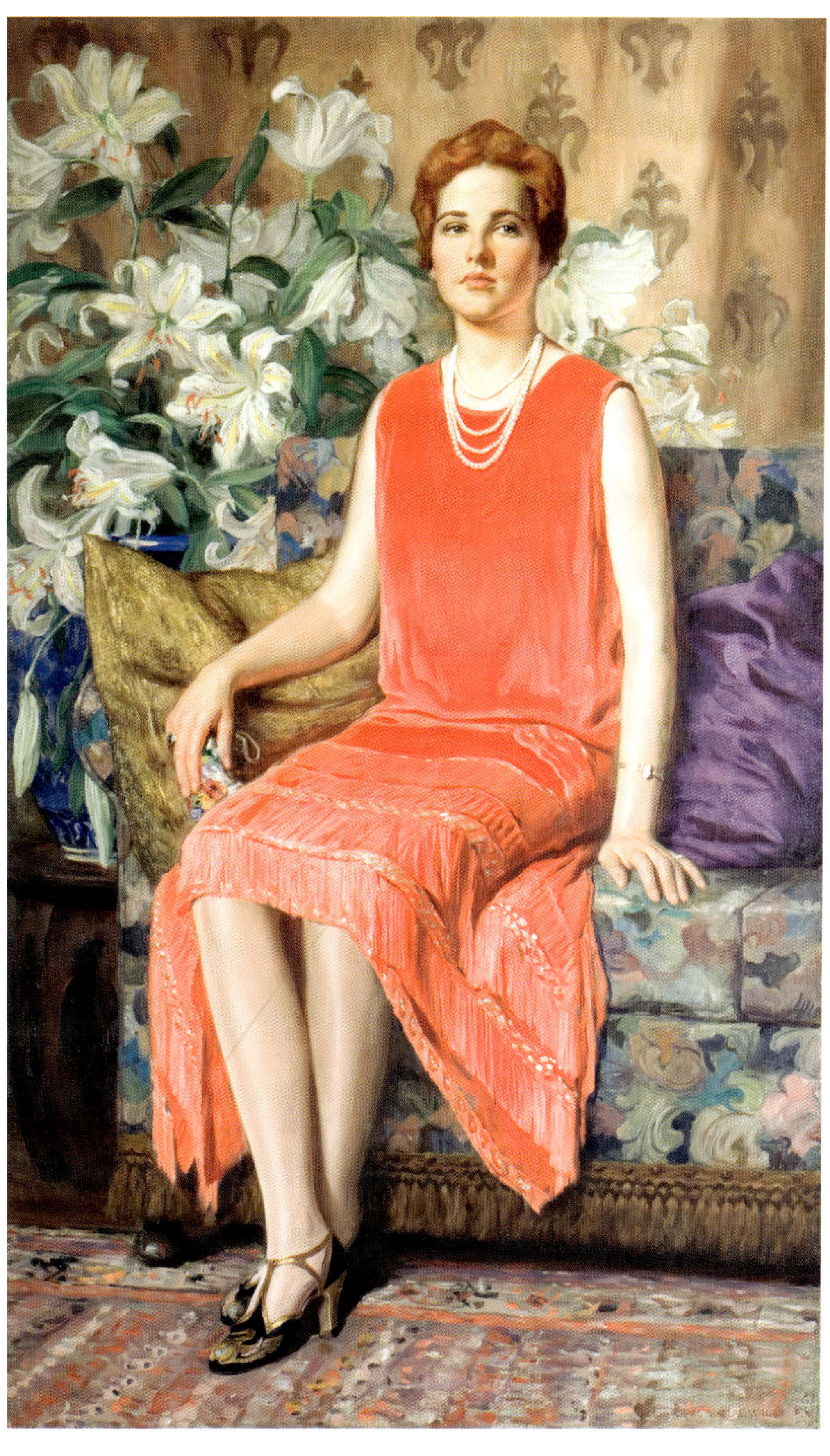

Charles Allan Winter
Portrait of Miss Elizabeth Oakes, c. 1928
Oil on canvas, 60 x 36 in.
Courtesy of Peter Williams
Photo by Joe Greene

In those later years, Charles Winter was a common sight in East Gloucester. "He was an individualist," one reporter wrote, "distinctive in appearance, with his long white hair and a pointed beard, and a keen twinkle in his eyes."[15] He loved nothing more than discussing art and technique, as well as color, on which he was an expert. In a 1933 interview he confided what, for him, was the most disagreeable part of painting. "Finding names for his paintings is an uncongenial task…." wrote Mildred Shute. "He wishes they could be named as music is, Opus 5, or Etude 6."[16] Music played an important part in Winter's life, and he believed it could be interpreted by color. Together with New Yorkers such as Sloan, Davis, Henri, George Bellows and Randall Davey, Winter devised a chart "representing an orchestra," says Shute, "as symbolized in the spectrum." For instance, "The strings, which suggest passion are represented by red prismatic shapes," and so forth. Winter believed that an artist could obtain 11,000 tones from just the three primary colors and white and often lectured on the subject.

Interestingly, Winter could move between different painting styles depending on his subject matter. When executing pure portraiture, such as *Portrait of Miss Elizabeth Oakes* which was exhibited at the Gloucester Society of Artists in 1928, the color is rich, and the finish sophisticated, while *Making Their Own Music* shows a more allegorical

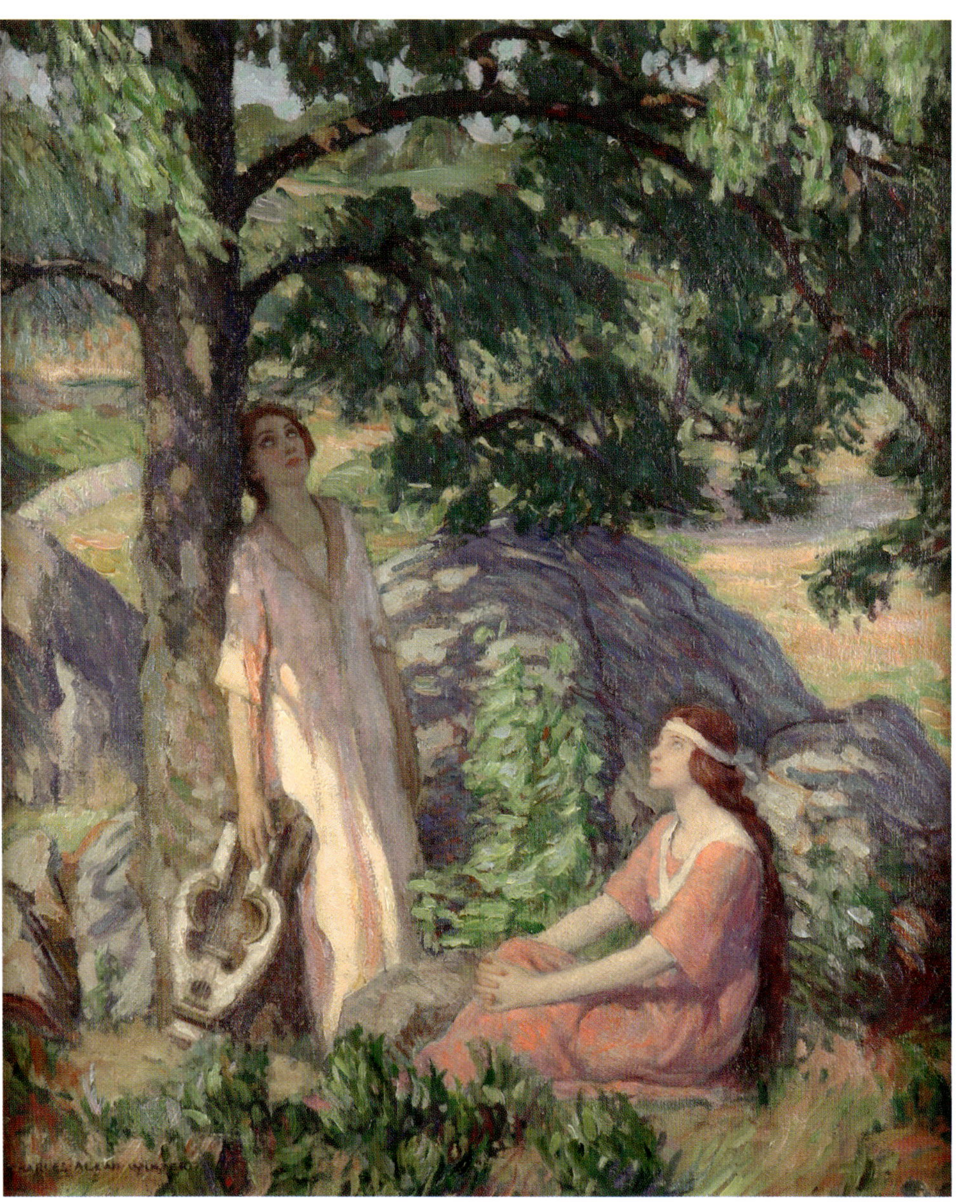

Charles Allan Winter
Making Their Own Music, c. 1918
Oil on canvas, 33 x 28 in.
Charles G. Martignette Collection of American Illustration Art, Hallandale Beach, Florida

approach to both subject matter and technique with the flatter more decorative style of the poet-painter. Charles Allan Winter lived out his life in East Gloucester, passing away at the age of 72 in the Addison Gilbert Hospital after a brief illness. His 1930s murals in the Gloucester City Hall are a permanent testimonial to his skill and acumen.

Alice Beach Winter (1877-1968)

Unlike her husband, Charles Allan Winter, Alice Beach Winter did not have the benefit of a classical European art training. She did, however, have the best that the St. Louis School of Fine Art had to offer, as well as that of the Art Students League in New York, including instruction from Joseph DeCamp and John Twachtman, two of America's finest Impressionists.

Born March 22, 1877 in Green Ridge, Missouri, Alice Mary was one of six children in the family of Edgar and Frances Beach, "a family consisting in the main of talented writers and actors."[17] Alice was only fourteen years old when she was accepted into the St. Louis School of Fine Arts, the youngest pupil in attendance. Here she polished her already impressive skills for developing form and color and often received medals for artistic ability.[18]

Graduating in 1898—the same year Charles Allan Winter joined the faculty as a portrait instructor—Alice moved on to New York and the Art Students' League, where she studied for a season with DeCamp and Twachtman. She then embarked on a career as an illustrator of books and magazines and soon gained recognition for depicting the life of children. At the same time she began receiving portrait commissions. She also renewed her friendship with Charles Winter and the two were married January 1, 1904.

Settling down to life in the studio, the two artists worked side by side: painting, illustrating and entertaining friends, including Henri, Sloan and Bellows, as well as musician Paul Tietjens, composer of the musical score for the original version of the Wizard of Oz, and pianist Katherine Groschke. Although many women struggled for emancipation in the early years of the twentieth century, Alice Winter's talent gained her acceptance in an art world that generally favored men. She was listed in *Who's Who in America* as early as 1907, and her illustrations were well known in every American home that subscribed to the popular periodicals. It is remarkable that, for a woman who loved portraying children and who obviously had an affinity for youth and childhood, Alice never had a family of her own.

Alice enjoyed summering in East Gloucester, where life meandered along at a gentler pace than the frantic deadline-driven routine she experienced in the New York publishing world. Over time her work began to show a greater distinction between the illustrative and the painterly. Art critic F. W. Coburn, writing in the *Boston Herald* (July 13, 1930) said, "Mrs. Winter's 'idea' in art, her interpretation of the wonderful phenomena of the visible world, has gone steadily onward toward vividness and vitality... And what a gain in freedom, in strength, in plangent purity of color!... She will take us past the merely pretty things (if they exist) bringing us to those 'that really matter'... She will show us the harbor itself, below terraced houses among green trees; Gloucester from the moors; East Gloucester village...."[19]

Unlike some women who might be easily overshadowed by the energetic persona of their spouse, Alice Winter was never subordinate to her husband, Charles. Diminutive and unassuming, "yet definitely commanding, quietly fascinating [with a]

Alice Beach Winter
Gloucester, Massachusetts, c. 1917
Oil on canvas, 16 x 20 in.
Vose Galleries, Boston

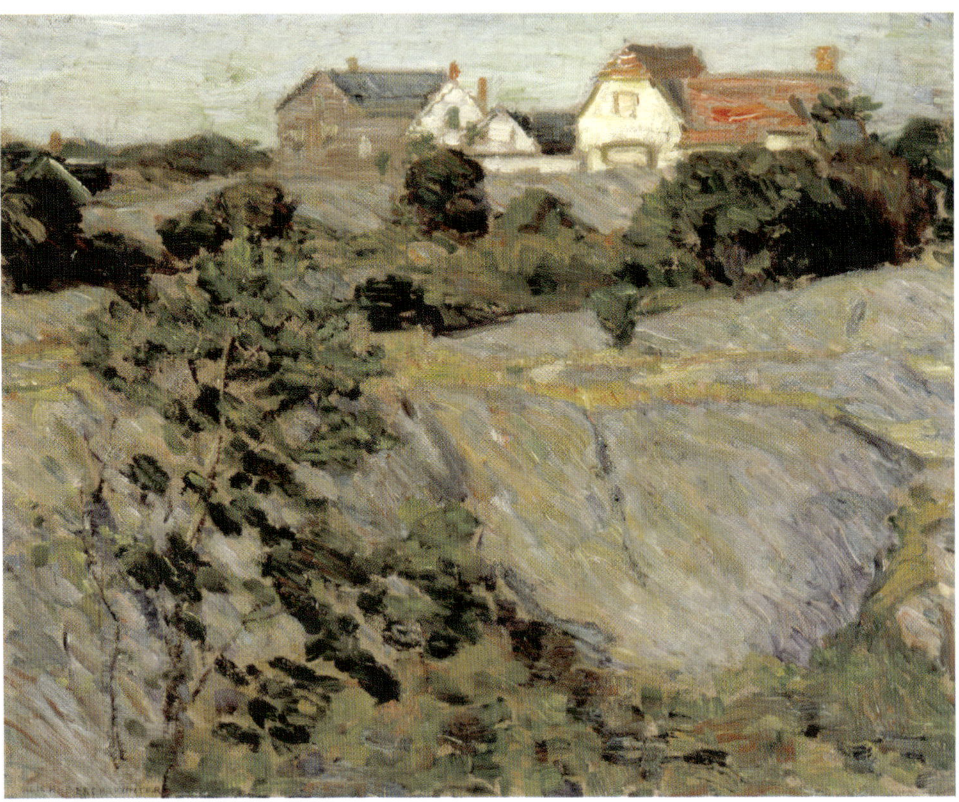

subtly striking personality,"[20] Alice balanced the complex elements of her personality, the socialist provocateur of *The Masses*, with a maternal affection for clear-eyed smiling children, in a way few feminists could equal today. Children's portraiture became her specialty and she practiced her art with sensitivity and acumen for the remainder of her life.

Interviewed on her 90th birthday, the artist said she would spend the day working on a charcoal portrait she had just started because, at her age, it was important to keep busy. Although Alice had always been broadminded in her views on art, supporting non-juried exhibitions at the Gloucester Society of Artists, by age 90 she felt some artists had gone too far and she held strong opinions about what might be termed "new art." "The stuff that's being done now that's called art is an insult. Imagine a doctor practicing medicine without having studied it."[21]

As a well-respected painter, Alice achieved her status in the art world based on sound training and a strong individualistic vision. While her earlier illustrative work was designed to awaken a social conscience in the viewer, her later tender portraits of boys and girls, sitting in gardens and playing at the beach, evoke a nostalgic moment in all of us for those carefree magical days of childhood. And to stir the viewer is the motivation for every artist. Alice Beach Winter passed away in Gloucester only months before her 91st birthday.

Agnes M. Richmond (1870-1964)

Agnes Millen Richmond, noted for her outstanding oil portraits of women, arrived on Cape Ann in the aftermath of the Great War. She first appears in the Gloucester Directory in 1915, listing her occupation as an artist and her address as 1 Eastern Point Road, just beyond the red cottage at the Rocky Neck causeway.

Born circa 1870 to Milnor and Agnes (Millen) Richmond of Alton, Illinois, the young Agnes Richmond grew up to attend the St. Louis School of Fine Arts before moving on to New York City and the Art Students League. Here, in 1901, she was fortunate to receive instruction from John Twachtman. During 1902 and 1903, she studied with Walter Appleton Clark and Kenyon Cox.[22] Later, in 1910, Richmond herself became an instructor at the League and spent four years sharing her knowledge and inspiring a new generation of students. She may have met her husband, New York painter Winthrop Duthie Turney (1884-1965), while at the Art Students League, where he studied with Twachtman.

Richmond and her husband had much in common, sharing a pragmatic view of life, as well as painting subject matter. Turney was particularly interested in the urban themes of the Ashcan School, and the couple moved in circles populated by such realist icons as George Luks and William Glackens, as well as Charles and Alice Winter, and John Sloan. It was possibly at the instigation of the Winters that Richmond and her husband first came to Cape Ann. Certainly it was Charles Winter who first persuaded John Sloan to visit Gloucester in 1914[23] when they shared the red cottage on East Main Street. Richmond is pictured in several well-known photographs of the Red Cottage group where occupants and guests, including Paul Cornoyer, Katherine Groschke and Paul Tietjens are shown on the front stoop in 1915, the year after Richmond finished instructing at the Art Students League. Richmond and Turney were frequent visitors to Cape Ann in the years between the wars, but maintained their primary residence in New York City, first in Manhattan and then in Brooklyn.

During that first visit to East Gloucester, Richmond's work caught the eye of William and Emmeline Atwood, and in 1916, she was invited to show her work at the Gallery-on-the-Moors; an invitation that was repeated the following year. She worked in varying media, including oils, pastels and mixed media and although best known to us today for her strong portrayal of women, she also executed genre subjects, still life, interiors, city views and landscapes. An active member of the National Association of Women Artists, Richmond received the Watrous Figure Prize in 1911 and the Watercolor Prize in 1922. She also exhibited with the National Academy of Design in New York and the Pennsylvania Academy of the Fine Arts.

Richmond's strength as an artist lay in her ability to project both sensitivity and verve onto her subjects. The women she chose to depict now appear to us as a reflection of their time, not only in terms of fashion, but also in their poise and bearing. The faces that look back at us from Richmond's engaging portraits are not only pictorial likenesses, but also representations of women of that era; real women whose composure and resolute demeanor show they have realistic expectations of life and its meaning. Richmond's artistic eye and empathetic nature coupled with her natural artistic skill and training, combined to make her one of the outstanding portraitists of her day. She was frequently asked to serve on painting juries alongside such luminaries and peers as Cecilia Beaux and Bessie Potter Vonnoh.

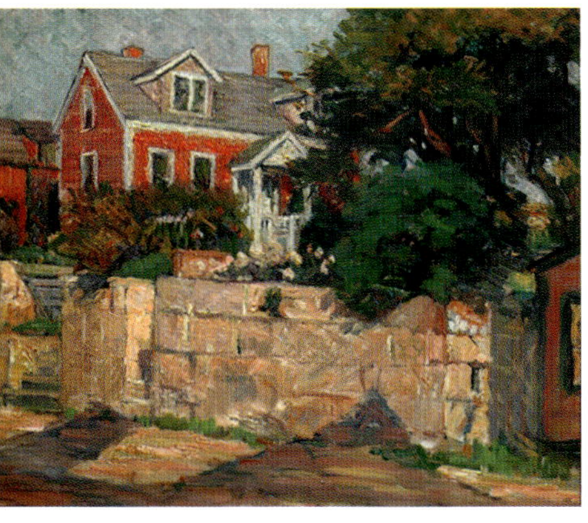

Agnes M. Richmond
The Red Cottage, East Main Street, Gloucester
Oil on canvas, 20 x 24 in.
Knoke Fine Arts, Marietta, Georgia

One can assume from Richmond's choice of subject matter—she often portrayed women of different class and color—as well as her choice of friends, which included the Sloans and the Winters, that she had strong socialist leanings. As early as 1914-1915, Richmond was noted in *Woman's Who's Who in America*, as being "interested in socialism," and "favors woman's suffrage...."[24] Her painting method was compelling and combined flat, tonal brushwork with an academic manner. In this way she emphasized the strength and spirit of her subject, be it a young woman with determined chin, such as *Louise at the Window*, possibly her friend, Louise Upton Brumback—or a sweeter, more sentimental image such as *Fairy Tales*. Richmond's work, whatever the subject matter, regularly drew appreciative reviews.

Inspired by the clear bright light of Cape Ann, Richmond and her husband spent many happy summers painting and socializing with artist friends in both Gloucester and Rockport. Although they did not generally participate in the local art organizations, they did both show with the Gloucester Society of Artists, founded in 1922 by those Rocky Neck artists who preferred the 'No Jury-No Prizes' approach to art. Between them, Richmond and Turney showed a total of eleven paintings in the three exhibitions held in 1926.

In later life, Richmond and her husband divided their time between summering in Mountainville, New York, and their Brooklyn home on Green Avenue. Richmond lived well into her nineties and died in Brooklyn in 1964. Winthrop Turney passed away the following year.

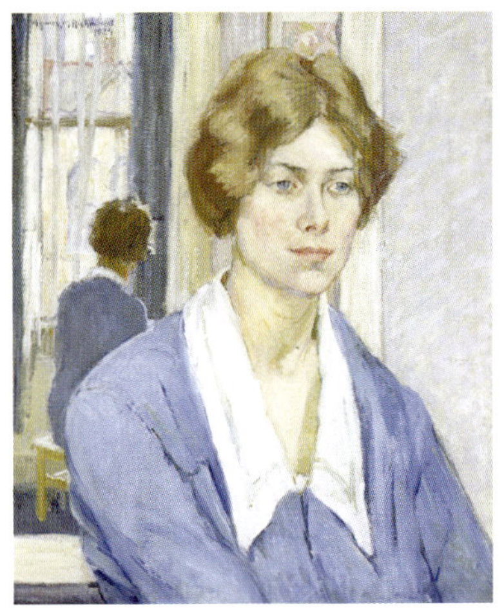

Agnes M. Richmond
Louise at the Window, 1924
Oil on canvas, 24 x 20 in.
Vose Galleries, Boston

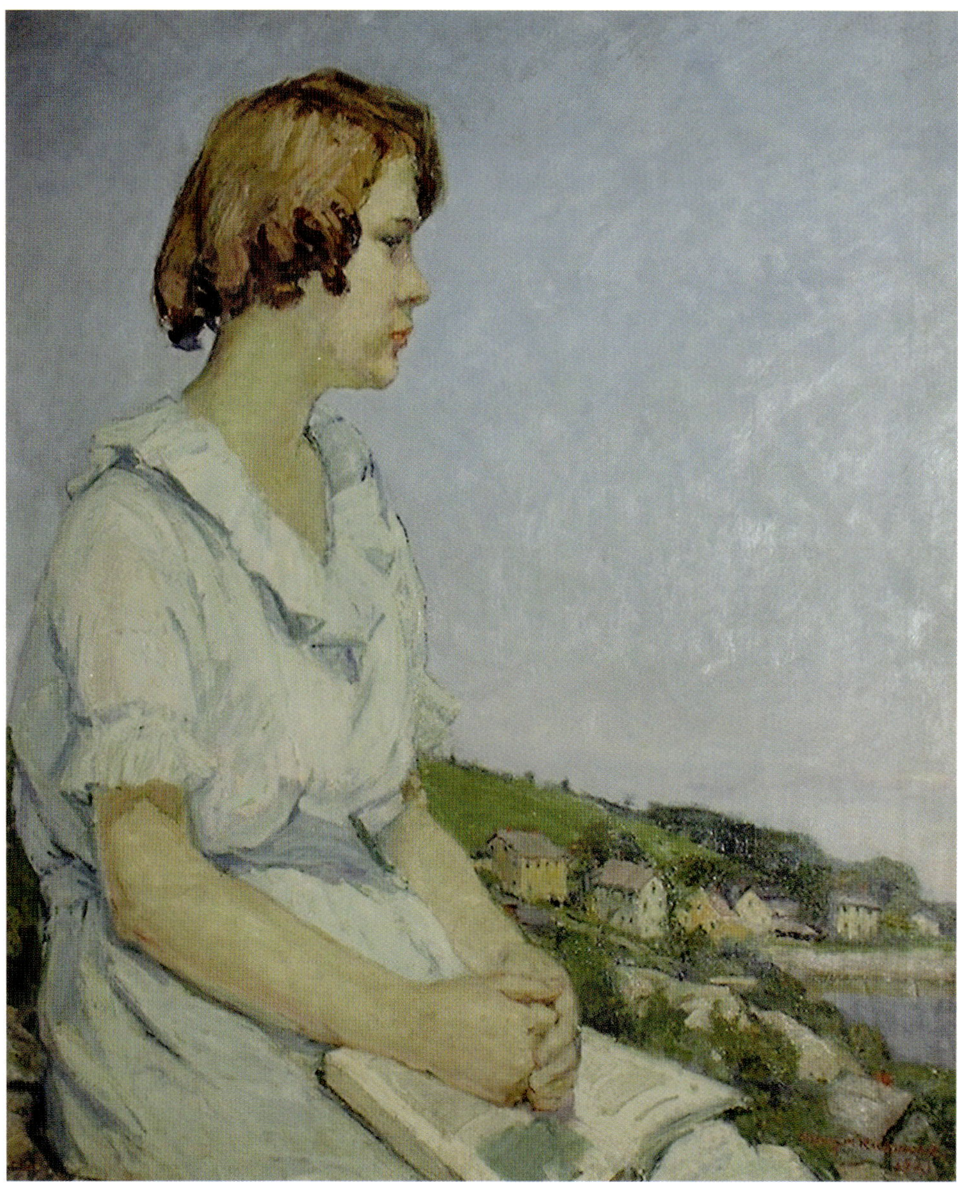

Agnes M. Richmond
Fairy Tales
Oil on canvas, 36 x 32 in.
Boston Art Club, Boston

Notes

1 Davis, Stuart, "Autobiography," in *Stuart Davis*, New York: American Artists' Group, 1945; rpt. in Diane Kelder, ed. (New York: Praeger, 1971), p. 25.

2 Wilken, Karen. *The Place I Had Been Looking For: Selected Writings of Stuart Davis.* Available at: http://www.cultureport.com/cultureport/artists/davis/davis01_ma.html, 11/16/07.

3 *The Masses* 4 (July 1913), p. 2. Quoted in *The Red Cottage*, Britt Crews, Curator, ex. cat. (Gloucester: Cape Ann Historical Association, 1992), p. 9.

4 Sloan, John, unpublished notes, 1950, John Sloan Trust, p. 146a, quoted in Rowland Elzea and Elizabeth Hawkes, *John Sloan: Spectator of Life*, ex. cat. (Wilmington: Delaware Art Museum, 1988), p. 20.

5 Sloan, John, John Sloan Exhibit; p. 5 in Grant Holcomb, *John Sloan: The Gloucester Years*, ex. cat. (Springfield, MA: Springfield Museum of Fine Arts, 1980), pp. 10-11.

6 Sloan, John, John Sloan Exhibit, 5, in Holcomb, p. 13.

7 Kelder, Diane, ed., *Stuart Davis*, New York, 1971, quoted in O'Gorman, James F., *Portrait of a Place: Some American Landscape Painters in Gloucester*, ex. cat. Gloucester 350th Anniversary Celebration, Inc. 1973, p. 82.

8 Winter, Alice Beach, "Looking Backward," Tenth Annual Cape Ann Festival of the Arts (Gloucester, 1961), p. 16.

9 Letter to James F. O'Gorman from Elizabeth Oakes Colford, January 7, 1975, John Sloan papers, CAHA, quoted in *The Red Cottage*, p. 15.

10 Helen Farr, Foreword, *The Red Cottage*, p. 6.

11 Sloan, John Sloan Exhibit, 5, in Holcomb, p. 13.

12 O'Gorman, James F. *This Other Gloucester* (Gloucester: Ten Pound Island, 1990), p. 75.

13 Biographical Sketch of Charles Allan Winter, C.A. Winter Papers, CAHA.

14 Undated news clipping, Winter Papers, op. cit.

15 Undated news clipping, c. September 1942, Winter Papers, CAHA.

16 Shute, Mildred, "Charles Allan Winter and Alice Beach Winter," *Cape Ann (Mass.) Shore*, 19 August 1933, pp 7, 20, 22.

17 "Mr. and Mrs. Charles Allan Winter," *Cape Ann Shore*, August 15, 1931, p. 23, Alice B. Winter Papers, CAHA.

18 Casey, Patricia, "Alice Beach Winter 'keeps busy' painting on her 90th birthday," March 22, 1967, newspaper clipping, A. B. Winter Papers.

19 Newspaper clipping, A. B. Winter Papers.

20 Casey, Patricia.

21 Casey.

22 *American Women of the Twenties: An Exhibition of Paintings by Agnes M. Richmond, 1870-1964.* Introduction, ex. cat. Jeffrey Alan Gallery, NY. November 1981.

23 *The Red Cottage.*

24 American Women of the Twenties.

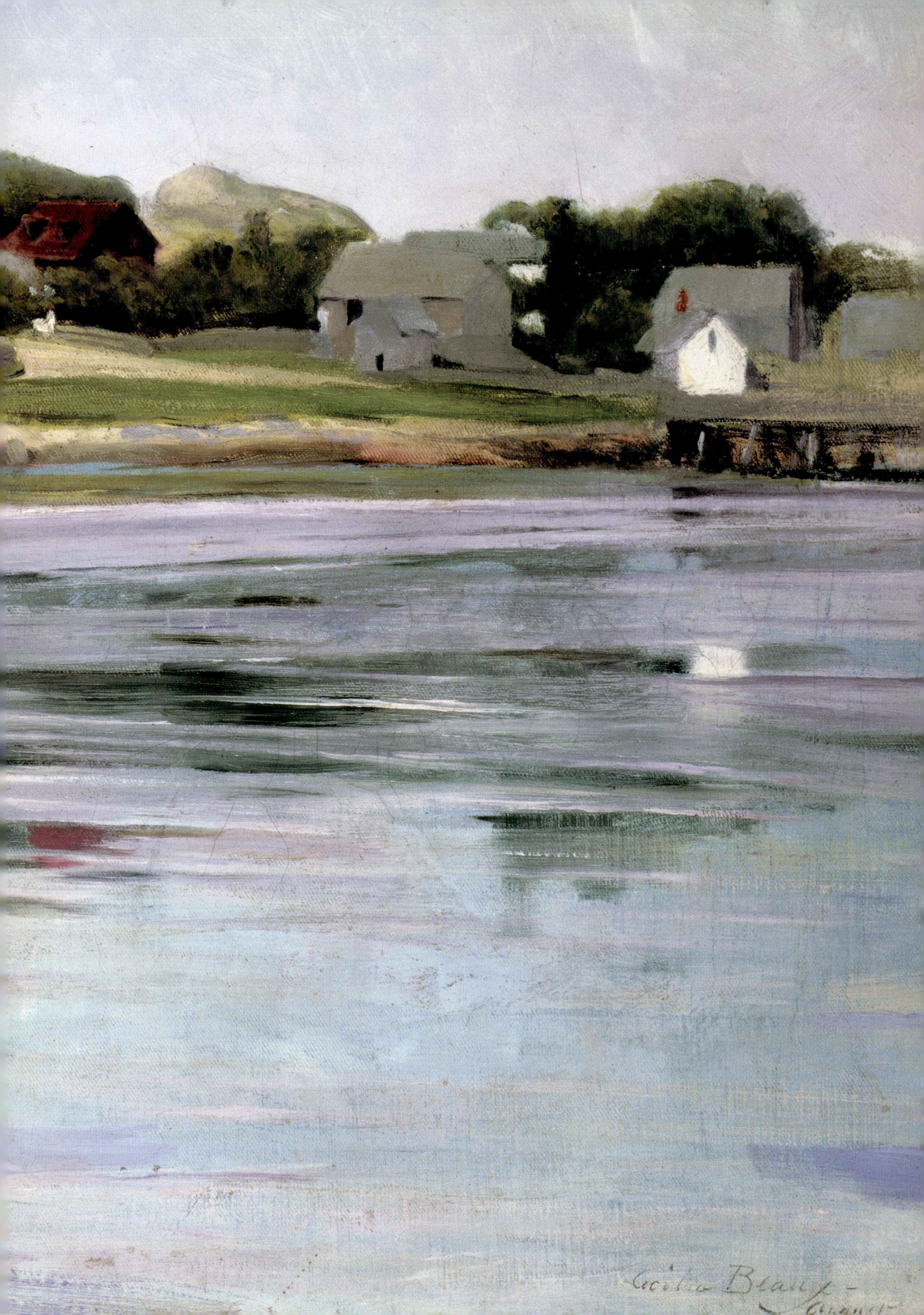

The Rise and Fall of the Gallery-on-the-Moors

"I should like to sing a paean—
A Song that skyward soars
To a blessed little gallery—
The Gallery-on-the-Moors."[1]

So said Adaline D. Piper in a poetic tribute to Emmeline and William Atwood after a celebratory tea marking the end of a second successful season of the Gallery-on-the-Moors in 1917. The Atwoods had opened their gallery on September 2nd the previous year in a generous effort to offer the painters of Gloucester a much needed exhibition space. Yet despite their munificence, the Atwoods were regularly castigated for their selection process, which was by invitation only. Given the hostility from some quarters it is amazing that the gallery lasted as long as it did, a mere seven seasons. Nevertheless, the patronage of the Atwoods bridged the gap between the little that had been available to artists previously, such as a group show hosted by the Hawthorne Inn Casino in 1909 and the "Gallery-on-the-Wharf" instigated by artist Oscar Anderson as a space to show his own work and that of artist friends such as Augustus Buhler, W. Lester Stevens and T. V. C. Valenkamph.

William and Emmeline Atwood came to prominence in Cape Ann society during the first decade of the twentieth century when they decided to extend themselves as patrons of the arts. William, who had studied art both at home and abroad, occasionally showed his work but did not aspire to a professional career as a painter. He came from a cultured and affluent background in a family of fine textile manufacturers from Danielson, Connecticut. Prior to their emergence as Cape Ann's preeminent art lovers, the Atwoods appear to have kept a low profile and little is known of their early lives. Nonetheless, they made their mark when they arrived in East Gloucester in 1916. By that time, East Gloucester was rightly famous for its artistic coterie. As early as August 1909, Cape Ann was called "an ideal section for artists," by the *Boston Post*.[2] Painters arrived daily from Boston and New York, Philadelphia and Cincinnati, to swell the summer population of Rocky Neck to a point where the colony equaled, and then eclipsed, that of Provincetown on the South Shore. Despite the number of well known names—Duveneck, Hassam, Twachtman, Cecilia Beaux and Jane Peterson—Rocky Neck was still better known as an area to paint rather than to sell. As F. W. Coburn, art critic for the *Boston Sunday Herald* observed, "Gloucester bristles with palette knives, flutters with white umbrellas, as never before," and "residents who do a little posing for the painter people are picking up pennies faster… than the same fingers could earn them in blueberry patches."[3]

In order to sell, painters were obliged to open their studios, often little more than chicken coops, or inveigle an exhibition in some hotel lobby. It was not until a fortuitous visit by the Atwoods that a desperate need for central exhibition space was discerned and acted upon. Emmeline Atwood described it thus,

Detail
Cecilia Beaux
Half-Tide, Annisquam River, c. 1905
Oil on canvas, 16 x 20 in.
High Museum of Art, Atlanta
Gift of the Verrill Family in memory of Jean Verrill (2005.294)

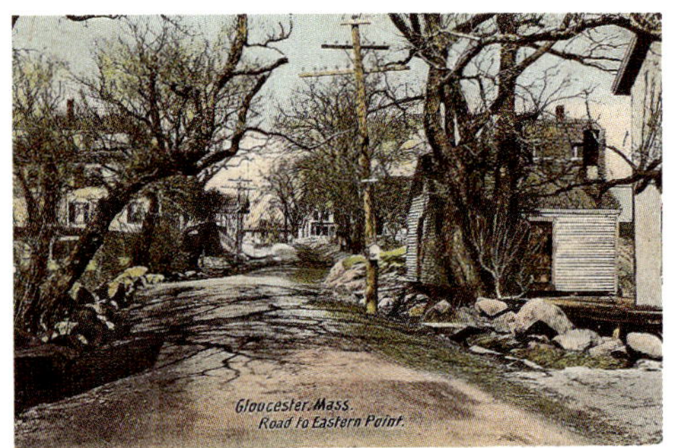

Gloucester, Mass. Road to Eastern Point
Postcard, c. 1910
Private collection

One day we were motoring through Gloucester and, always interested in art, were going from studio to studio to see what the artists were doing and to purchase some pictures for our home on Chebaco Island. We found many of the artists tucked away in dark little lofts, chicken coops, stables, tiny rooms, poorly lighted and unattractive make shift places such as one might find in an old time fishing village, little spaces that had been discarded by fishermen. We were inconvenienced by the difficulty of seeing the pictures and thought others might be. We felt in this active summer colony there might be many like ourselves who would welcome an opportunity to see what the artists were doing. Here was our chance—beautiful pictures, a leisure public anxious to see them. We would provide the place.[4]

Rising to the challenge, the Atwoods asked their friend, Boston architect Ralph Adams Cram, to design a state-of-the-art gallery on Ledge Road, crossing the moorland atop Banner Hill, where they had purchased several acres of land for this very purpose. Cram, who favored revivalist motifs patterned on the cathedral architecture of bygone days, drew up plans for a gallery of suitable gothic stature. When it was finished, Jane Peterson described the gallery as, "rising like a beautiful flower from the wild brush and tangle, built on the weather-beaten old rocks and part and parcel of them, for they themselves were quarried to create it... this little gem of old Gothic... every timber hand hewn, every fixture hand wrought... Reverently should we enter it as a shrine, a pioneer gift to art in America."[5] And a gift the Gallery-on-the-Moors became, both to the artists who exhibited there, and to the suitably well-heeled visitors who could now view the works produced in the art colony in an atmosphere of sophistication and ethos. The Atwoods asked no commission from works sold through the Gallery. They had envisaged a cultural center for the arts where artists could display their talents in a more refined setting than had hitherto been the case, and asked for nothing in return. Indeed, the only concession the Atwoods required was that art works would be accepted on an invitation-only basis, allowing them to oversee the quality of the exhibition as a whole. This one small concession would prove their undoing.

The Gallery-on-the-Moors, situated expediently close to the Rocky Neck causeway and the electric trolley, opened its doors to the public for its first exhibition on September 2, 1916. Among the works on display were 73 canvases and 22 pieces of

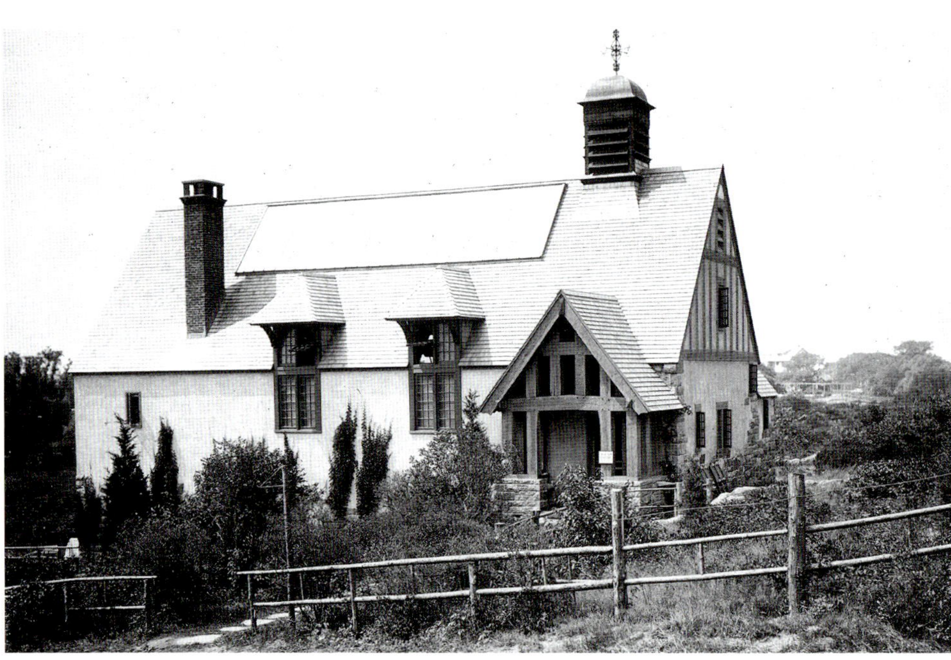

Gallery-on-the-Moors, c. 1917
Cape Ann Historical Association,
Gloucester, Massachusetts
Gift of Myrtle Cameron

sculpture. It was an impressive display by some of the major figures in American art of the day, including Cecilia Beaux, Hayley Lever, Arthur Wesley Dow, Henry B. Snell, and Louise Upton Brumback. Frank Duveneck's painting *Gloucester Wharves* had pride of place in the exhibition. Considered "The Dean" among his peers, Duveneck was then 69 years old, a gold medalist the previous year at the Panama-Pacific Exposition, and had been painting around Rocky Neck for 18 years. Small wonder his work was greeted with accolades by those who appreciated good painting. Stuart Davis was not as fortunate. Still inspired by the Armory Show only three years earlier, Davis sought to introduce a more contemporary view to what he considered a staid approach to art. F. W. Coburn, the *Boston Herald's* art critic, was unable to agree. Viewing Sloan's offering, *A Cove* (later retitled *Rockport Beach*) Coburn complained it was "a panoramic perversion [that] excited much tittering from the uninitiated," leading him to plead for "a commission of artists and scientists to give the public a concise statement of the possibilities and limitations of oil paint as a medium of expression."[6]

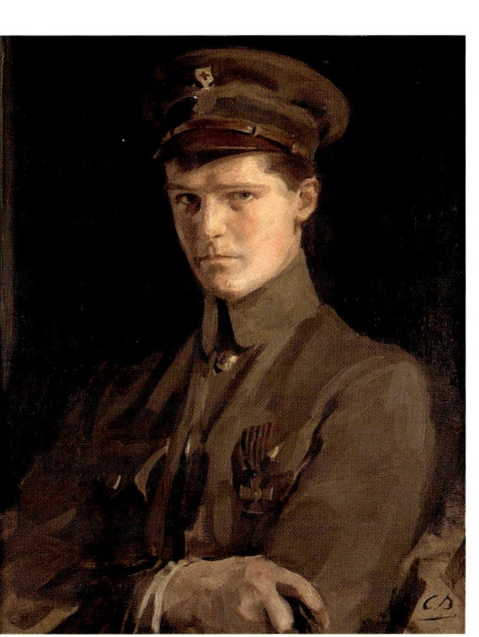

Cecilia Beaux
Portrait of *Leslie Buswell,* 1918
Oil on canvas, 35½ x 30 in. (framed)
Cape Ann Historical Association,
Gloucester, Massachusetts (1999.59)

Coburn, who as an art critic had always been fair minded, was not a lover of the modern trends sweeping in from Europe in the wake of the Armory Show. Nevertheless, Coburn's criticism opened up a totally new line of thought that was to reverberate through the Rocky Neck Art Colony for decades. Who was to be the judge of good art? The gallery owners, who wished to select certain works to hang? A jury of artists sitting in judgment of their peers? The public, which is sometimes, but sometimes not, coincident with the art market? The argument lingers on, almost a century later.

Yet not everyone was critical. On September 5, 1916, the *Boston Transcript* reported, "One of the finest collections of painting and sculpture ever shown on the North Shore is now to be seen by the art-loving public through the generosity of Mr. and Mrs. William Edwin Atwood in the 'Gallery on the Moors,' East Gloucester. Nothing could be more helpful to the artists, more stimulating to the arts, than the founding of a centre for writers, players, musicians, painters, and sculptors; such has been the purpose of Mr. and Mrs. Atwood in erecting their charming Gothic building where exhibitions are to be held, plays given, and literary folk gathered together.... Here no special school is represented, the intention being to present the best work obtainable, the serious endeavor of those who are striving to express their joy and delight in nature as it appears to them."[7]

Ultimately, the Gallery-on-the-Moors enjoyed a successful first season, selling works by Guy Wiggins, Hayley Lever, Henry Snell, Arthur Dow, Mary Weiss, and Louise Brumback. The following year, the gallery hosted two exhibitions instead of one. The first, opening July 26, 1917, was praised by the *Boston Evening Transcript* for what it called "conservatism." "The craze for futurism, cubism, synchronism, might never have existed! Out of the horrors of war have we already garnered some precious things! Lovers of art must rejoice...."[8] This show, however, was quite small, only 28 works by fourteen painters, and two dozen pieces of sculpture, compared with the second exhibition, which encompassed twice as many paintings and a larger selection of contributing artists. John Sloan and Stuart Davis were invited to show, as well as Australian painter Hayley Lever, Charles Hopkinson, George L. Noyes, Frederick J. Mulhaupt, Martha Walter and Theresa Bernstein. One of the most notable paintings in the exhibition was a contemplative portrait of local boy Leslie Buswell in his Field Service uniform, which drew much attention as well as praise for portraitist Cecilia Beaux. The Gallery ended its season with the sale of twenty paintings totaling almost $4,000. Nonetheless, not everyone was happy. Again, there was dissatisfaction in some camps, principally some of the locals who objected to the enormous influx of out of town painters, leading to a

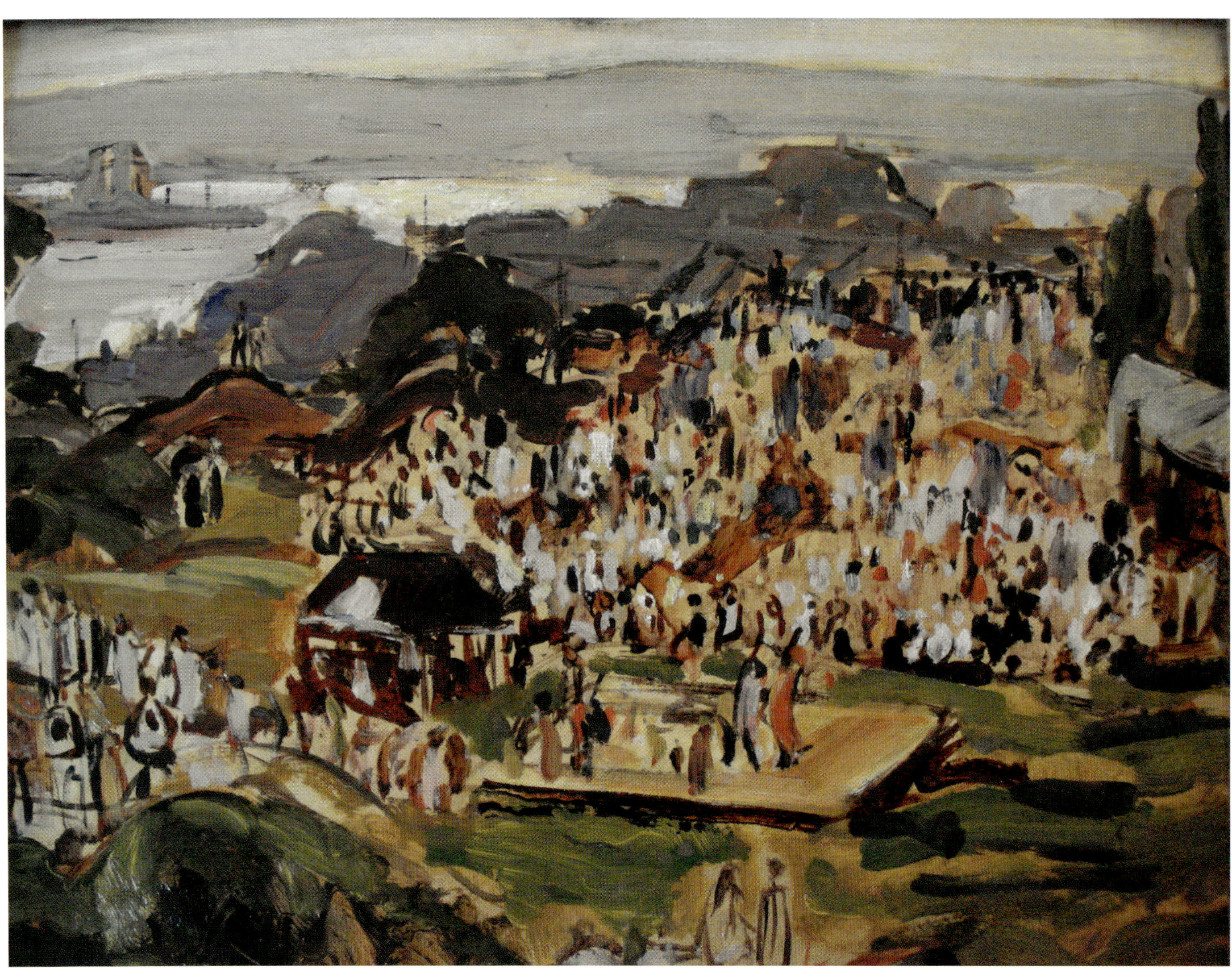

Theresa Bernstein
Grecian Pageant, for the benefit of wounded soldiers, 1918
Oil on board, 20 x 16 in.
Collection of Walter Manninen

healthy rivalry with the "Gallery-on-the-Wharf" on Rocky Neck Avenue, featuring works by the resident artists of Cape Ann, such as Oscar Anderson, Lester Stevens and A.W. Buhler.

By the time the third season of the Gallery-on-the-Moors rolled around in 1918, the size of the exhibition had swelled to an incredible 125 works, mostly paintings, but including some graphics and sculpture. New among the exhibitors was Childe Hassam returning to Rocky Neck after an absence of some years. He had been a regular visitor in the mid to late 1890s, when he had invited Willard Metcalf to join him and the two had painted Gloucester Harbor from the top of Banner Hill. As usual, the exhibition was well received in some quarters, and vilified by others. "The show," a critic writing in the *Philadelphia Inquirer* protested, "was not open to any artist except those invited by the patrons. So… they went far afield to please their painter friends, inviting for mere motives of friendship…. The result is… an exhibition of most uneven merit, hung very badly."[9] As the Atwoods tried to cover the gamut of artistic taste by including works from traditional, impressionist and post-impressionist painters, they received scant appreciation for their philanthropic efforts, and the criticism would only get worse.

During these war years, the Gallery-on-the-Moors also hosted regular patriotic proceedings, including, in 1916, a screening of the film *Our American Boys in the European War*, which described the bravery and dedication of the American Ambulance Field Service founded by Eastern Point resident, A. Piatt Andrew. Leslie Buswell—whose wistful portrait by Cecilia Beaux made such an impression in the first

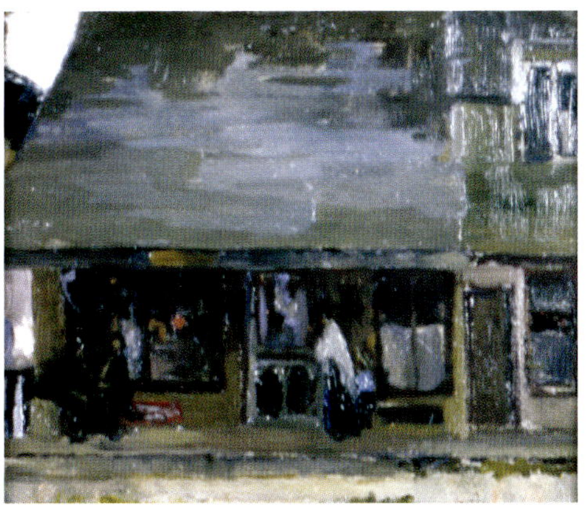

Martha Walter
Rocky Neck Store and My Studio, 1920
Oil on panel, 14½ x 16½ in.
Cape Ann Historical Association,
Gloucester, Massachusetts

exhibition—also spoke on the work of the Field Service and, having participated in that work, was able to confirm how true to life the "realistic scenes from the front," actually were.[10] The war affected everyone, and the art colony was anxious to be supportive. In 1918, sculptress Anna Coleman Ladd was unable to exhibit at the Gallery-on-the-Moors as she was in France, using her artistic skills to help in "restoring the shattered faces of the wounded heroes."[11] Theresa Bernstein also wanted to contribute to the cause and subsequently organized a benefit to aid wounded soldiers. Her painting, *Grecian Pageant*, bears a notation on the back stating "Pageant for the benefit of wounded soldiers given summer 1918, Atwood Estate, Gloucester ~ Theresa Bernstein." This painting clearly shows the view from the moorland estate overlooking the water, and perhaps more than anything summarizes all that the Rocky Neck Art Colony stands for: ambiance, atmosphere and artistic camaraderie.

The following summer was perhaps the turning point in the fortune of the gallery. Although the war was over, the Armistice signed some six months previously, the dynamics of the gallery were beginning to change. The season began with a two-artist show of works by Martha Walter and Felicie Waldo Howell. Walter (1875-1976) was a Philadelphian who had studied first with William Merritt Chase at the Pennsylvania Academy of the Fine Arts and then in Europe at the Grande Chaumière and the Académie Julian. Although originally trained in the academic manner, Walter preferred a personal approach in a style that could be described as unrestrained, jaunty and vibrant. She loved painting the European beach resorts, finding inspiration among the well-to-do at play, juxtaposed against the laboring class of dockworkers and fishermen. When war broke out Walter returned home, after almost a decade of working abroad, and ended up in Gloucester where she found Rocky Neck had everything she could possibly want to paint. Noted for her flair and spontaneity, Walter worked in both oil and watercolor and demonstrated a rare ability to capture the moment in vivid color with judicious use of delineating black paint (not unlike that of Jane Peterson). Peterson herself remarked that Walter's seaside scenes appeared "blown onto the

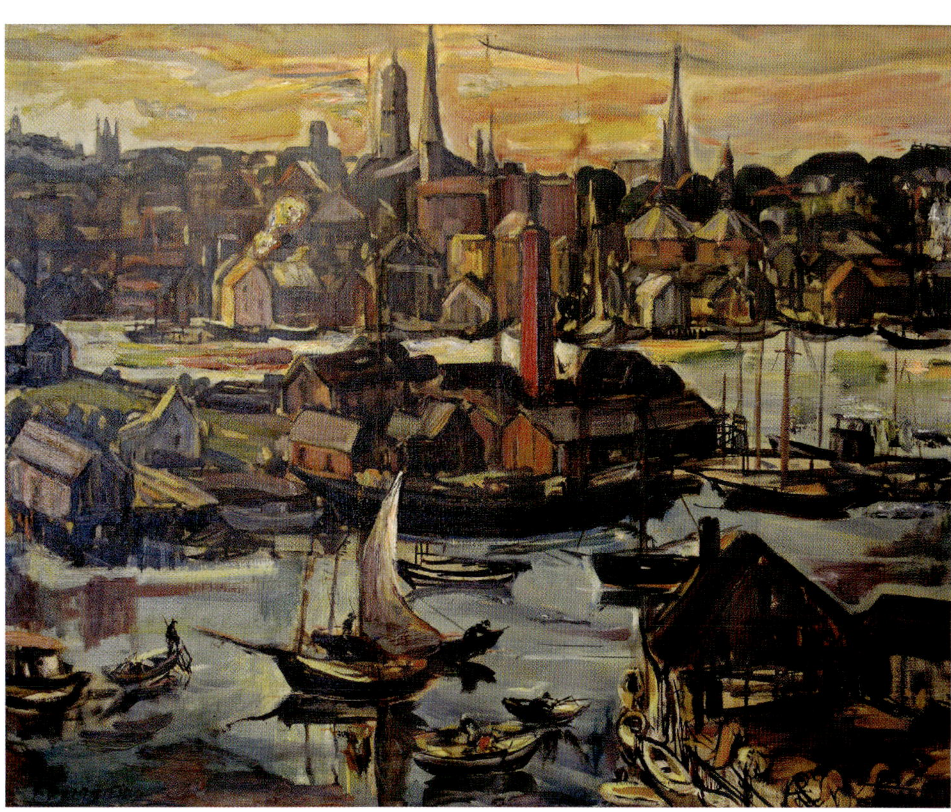

Theresa Bernstein
Gloucester Town with Churches and Steeples, 1916
Oil on canvas, 27 x 34 in.
Collection of E. Bonnie Akerley

canvas."[12] Walter proved a tour de force among the American Impressionist genre and the numerous paintings that make up her Gloucester oeuvre are even more striking than the lively images she captured on her travels through Europe and North Africa.

Coming on the heels of the Walter/Howell exhibition was a group show featuring William Glackens, Hassam, Louis Kronberg, Lever, Jonas Lie, Prendergast, Sloan and Hopkinson. Sloan was not even in Rocky Neck that summer, having opted to visit the Southwest with Randall Davey, but sent some New York work to round out his contribution to the exhibition.

Squabbling was still rife regarding the gallery selection process and in 1920, some of the major names were already missing. Duveneck, mainstay of the original art community, had passed away the year before, and John Sloan and Stuart Davis had headed for less crowded pastures. Conservative critics, such as the *Boston Herald's* F. W. Coburn, were relieved to see that, from their perception, a sense of sanity was returning to art and that for the 73 pieces selected for showing, several hundred more had been rejected. Coburn applauded the decision to finally allow a jury of artists and sculptors, selected by artist ballot, to choose works for the exhibition, rather than the owners of the gallery. This resulted, however, in what others felt was a generic standardization that smacked of the mercantile.

By the time the sixth season came around, the Atwoods had decided to try yet another method of pleasing all parties. Rather than trusting the whims of a ballot, they would select the artist jurors themselves. This second attempt at the jury system appeared to work well, reflecting a conservative approach, a commercial aim and enough major participants to avoid appearing provincial. Repeating the practice the following year, the jury, which included Cecilia Beaux and Charles Hopkinson, found a diminishing pool of talent from which to choose. Possibly the last nail in what was rapidly becoming the Mausoleum-on-the-Moors was a review that appeared in the *Boston Herald*. "The exhibition is so hung that its virtues and weakness appear 'en masse,'… so that the observer is put to some effort to pick out separate works of outstanding merit."[13] The insipid reaction to the seventh season heralded the imminent demise of the Gallery-on-the-Moors. When the Atwoods closed their doors for the last time, the echo could be heard reverberating through the art world, not much of a bang, just a whimper (as local poet T. S. Eliot might have phrased it).

Frederick J. Mulhaupt, A. N. A. (1871-1938)

In an area filled with exemplary painters, it is perhaps difficult to single out one individual over any other and yet Frederick J. Mulhaupt still rises above many of his contemporaries. Born in Rock Port, Missouri, on March 28, 1871, Mulhaupt's early life was probably similar to that of any other boy born to German immigrant parents living on America's western frontier. He was no stranger to hard work, and being an industrious adolescent, had charge of a booth selling newspapers and magazines in Dodge City, Kansas.[14] However, the mayhem of that gateway to the West, filled with gun-slinging cowboys and gamblers, did not sit well with Mulhaupt's sensitive nature, and as a young man he moved to Kansas City, Missouri, where he found a nomadic artist willing to take him on as an apprentice sign painter. Later, he enrolled in more formal art studies at the Kansas City School of Design.[15] Mulhaupt also attended the Art Institute of Chicago while in his early twenties and, in 1895, became a founding member of the Palette and Chisel Club.

Mulhaupt remained in the Windy City for almost a decade. In 1902, he became an

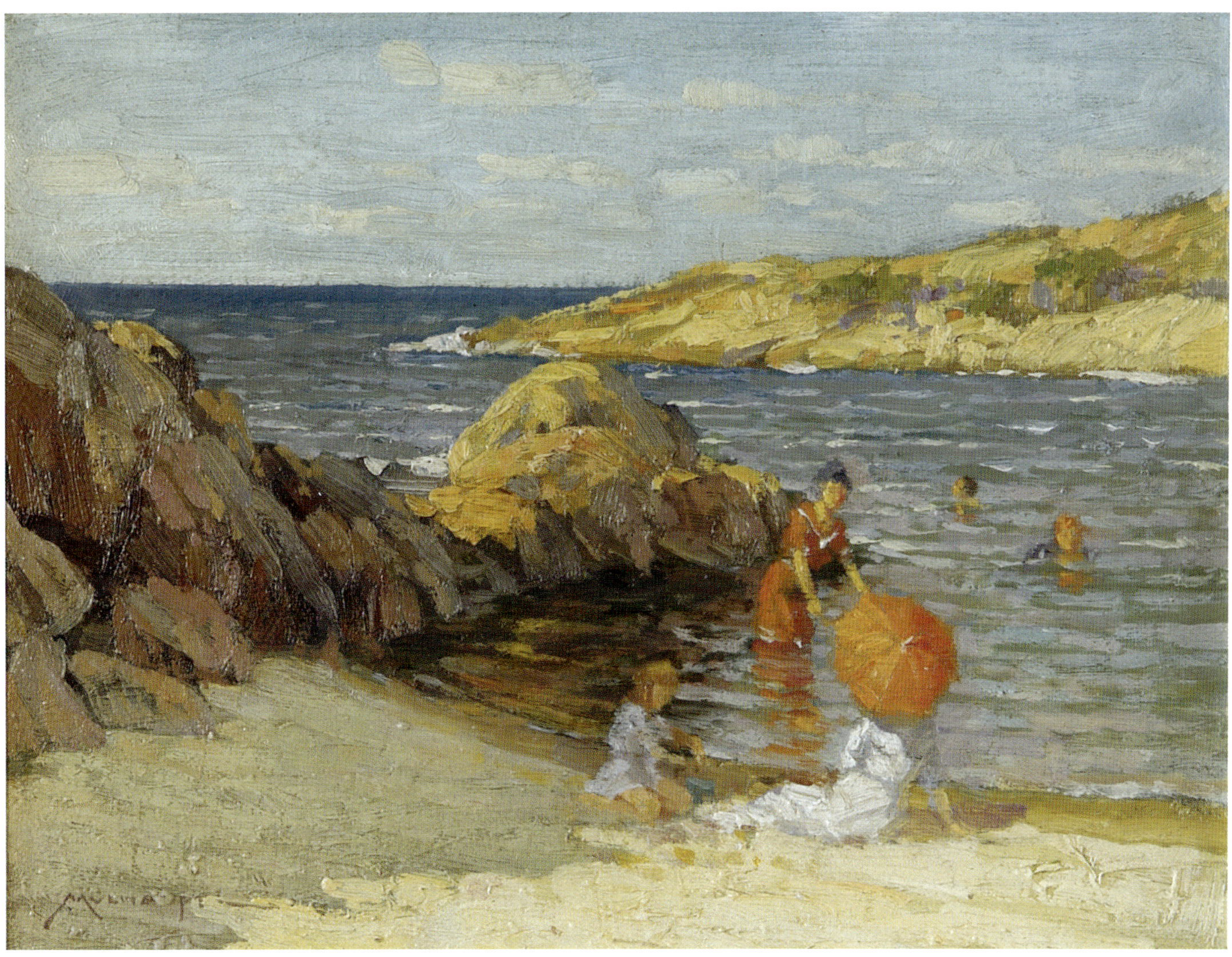

Frederick J. Mulhaupt
Beach at Plum Cove
Oil on board, 11 x 14 in.
Mosher Gallery, Rockport, Massachusetts

instructor for the Art Institute's figure class but stayed only two years before leaving Chicago in favor of New York City. He immersed himself in New York's expansive art scene, but in that first decade of the twentieth century he began taking trips to Europe to develop his education in the artistic milieu of the old world. Unlike his contemporary, Frank Duveneck, who was also a Midwesterner of German descent, Mulhaupt chose to immerse himself in the heady euphoria of Paris, then hub of the art world, rather than the more prosaic atmosphere of Munich. Like many expatriate American painters, Mulhaupt embraced the new aesthetic of impressionism. Yet as his countless paintings show, he never allowed the concept to overpower his sense of composition and draftsmanship. Mulhaupt can be counted among the elite of the American Impressionist movement; those primarily European-trained artists who took the high key palette and broken color style of the French moderniste and combined it with the draftsmanship of the academic and the subtleties of American genre painting.

It is believed Mulhaupt made his first trip to Cape Ann c. 1907, and was impressed enough with the area to return on a regular basis. He began a pattern of summering in East Gloucester and passing the winters in New York until 1922 when he moved to Gloucester permanently with wife, Agnes, and their infant son, Frederick. In the beginning, the Mulhaupts lived at 209 Main Street, Gloucester,[16] before moving out to Rocky Neck ten years later.

Although Mulhaupt could turn his hand to many subjects—pure landscape, nudes and woods interiors—it is the views of Gloucester Harbor for which he gained

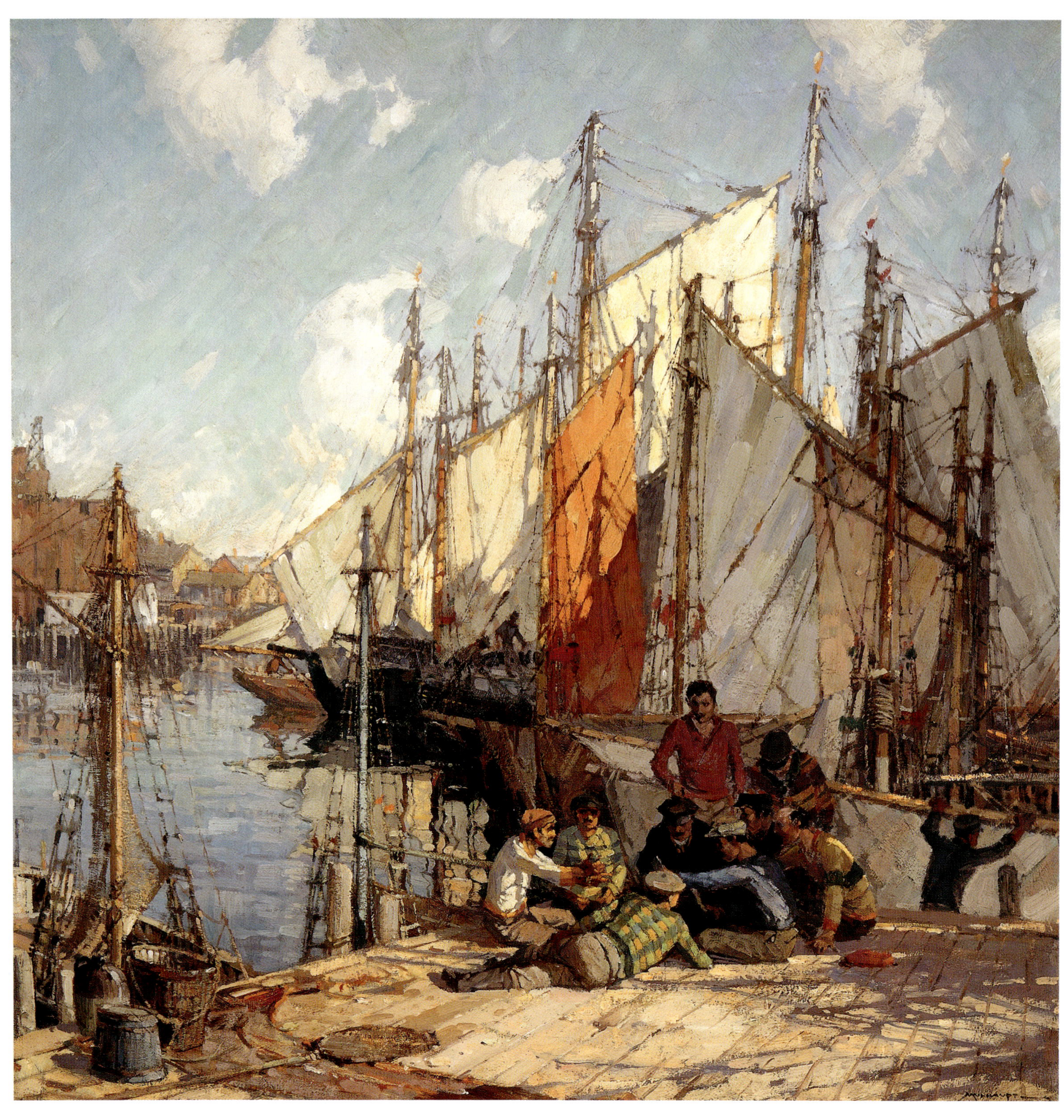

Frederick J. Mulhaupt
On the Dock, Italian Wharf, Gloucester
Oil on canvas, 36 x 36 in.
Collection of Dr. and Mrs. Joel E. Berenson

Frederick J. Mulhaupt
Boats at Gloucester Harbor,
c. 1920-1929
Oil on canvas, 30 x 40 in.
MME Fine Art, LLC, New York

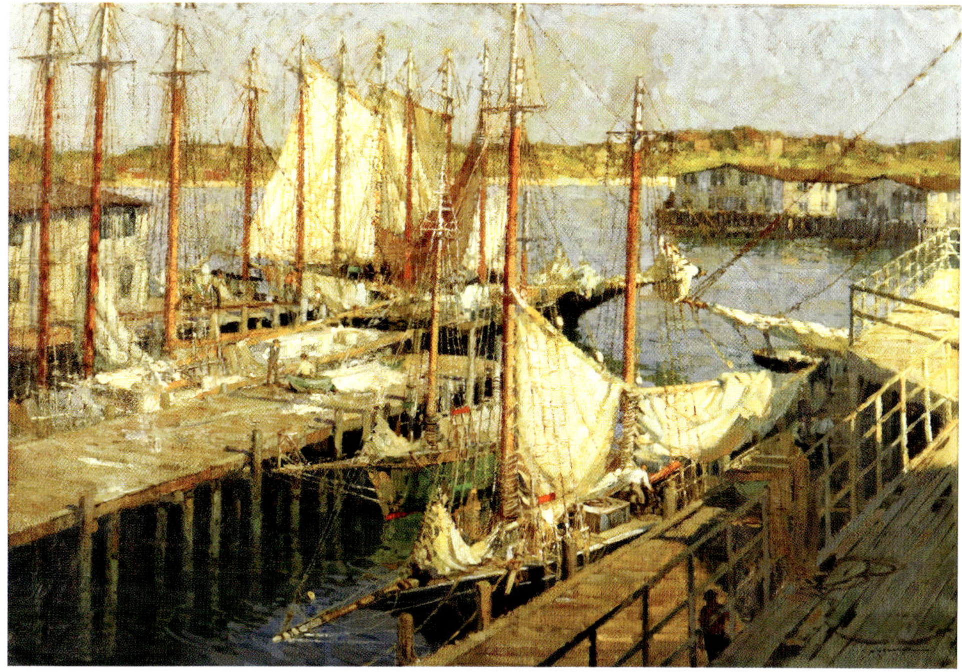

particular renown. He was a fine plein air painter, executing small spontaneous sketches on the spot such as *Beach at Plum Cove*, which captures an ingenuous moment on the beach. In contrast, larger canvases such as *On the Dock, Italian Wharf, Gloucester* and *Boats at Gloucester Harbor* are more likely to be studio paintings, perhaps worked up as composites from several alla prima sketches that he would use as memory aids to capture the momentary detail of atmosphere, light and figure. Mulhaupt was especially adroit at observing the subtleties of winter light, executing tonal atmosphere without sacrificing color. Mulhaupt's ability to keep his tones close together and edges undefined obviously helped in composing his subject matter, allowing him to accomplish symmetry within the design, before refining the edges and values for fundamental contrast, or chiaroscuro (the balance of lights and darks).

As a painter, Mulhaupt was a careful observer of nature, and his ability to explore the spectrum of light and color found in snow, ice and overcast skies made him one of the finest and most popular artists on Rocky Neck. He showed regularly at the Gallery-on-the-Moors and in 1923 joined the newly formed North Shore Arts Association, becoming an artist member of the Board of Trustees.

More introverted than many of his colleagues, Mulhaupt nevertheless endured the teaching process in order to pass on his knowledge to a new generation of painters. Despite his discomfort with instructing, students considered him an indulgent mentor who encouraged them to find their own style rather than copy his.[17] From these same students we also discover Mulhaupt's preferred palette. "He used two reds: alizarin crimson and vermilion," recalled one pupil. "He used a basic yellow, probably a cadmium color. And he used two blues: French ultramarine, mixed with the reds, gave him his basic darks; Prussian blue gave him his tenderer tones. He also used viridian. He avoided black but would use yellow ochre and burnt sienna."[18]

Frederick J. Mulhaupt passed away in 1938, but his memory lives on in the many fine paintings he created of Gloucester Harbor, either set up on a wharf, or from his studio, perched on precarious pilings overhanging the water where he had a fine view of the Gloucester fishing fleet in all its glory.

Cecilia Beaux, N.A. (1855-1942)

In the roll call of Rocky Neck painters, Cecilia Beaux is remembered as an artist of talent and a woman of verve, who lived among the elite summer residents of Eastern Point. A Philadelphian by birth, Beaux was raised by her maternal grandmother and aunts after the death of her mother from complications of childbirth. One could speculate that the subsequent abandonment by her distraught father, Jean Adolphe Beaux, who relinquished his children after the death of his wife, colored Beaux's sensibilities towards men, for she appears to have relished the status of independent woman, and scorned marriage.

Beaux's precocious talent for drawing was encouraged by her family, and at the age of sixteen, she began copy work with a relative, artist Catherine Drinker. A year later, in 1872, she began serious study under Francis Adolf van der Wielen, with whom she studied drawing, particularly the effects of shading, enlarging and perspective. She also studied at the Pennsylvania Academy of the Fine Arts, but refused to work under Thomas Eakins when she discovered his life-class students performed dissection work to study human anatomy. She enrolled in the antiques class instead to study anatomy in a more detached way. In the early 1880s, Beaux also took private critique from William Sartain, and in 1885 received the coveted Mary Smith Prize at the Academy's annual exhibition.

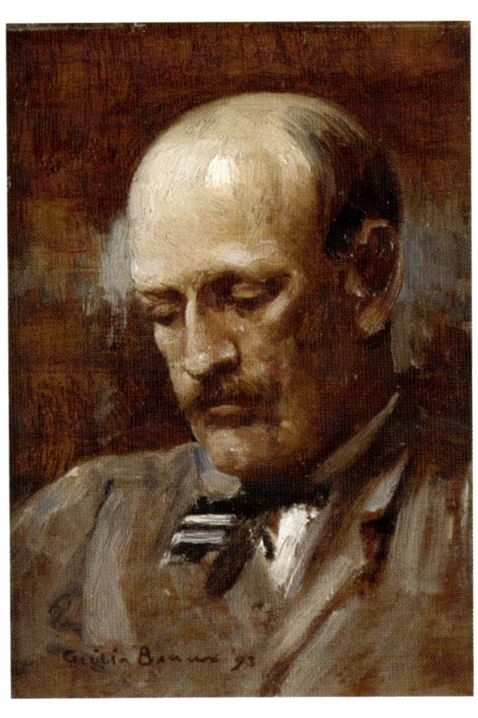

Cecilia Beaux
Portrait of Robert Minor, Sr.
Oil on canvas, 11 x 8 in.
Collection of Mr. and Mrs. William H. Trayes

In spite of her flourishing reputation as a portraitist in Philadelphia, Beaux yearned for more worldly experience and in 1888, after rejecting three different marriage proposals because she felt emotionally unsuited to such a union, she set sail for Paris and the Académie Julian. "Boulanger and Gérôme," Beaux notes in her biography,[19] "had each a great following. Their influence was immense, and deservedly, for their personal view was never imposed. They inspired their students without bending them in any direction..." Nevertheless, she was a little disappointed. The life-class was overcrowded and Beaux found her skills far in advance of her fellow students. She persevered, nonetheless, drawing accolades from her instructors, including Tony Robert-Fleury, and traveling through England and Europe to broaden her horizons.

Returning to America in late 1889, Beaux took a studio in Philadelphia and plunged into a demanding schedule of portrait painting. With her election to associate membership of the National Academy in 1894, Beaux's development into a determined and self-assured young woman was complete. Not only was she fully confident of her own abilities, but she was well aware of the favorable comparison art critics were making between her work and that of the grand manner salon painter, John Singer Sargent. Five years later, when Beaux received the celebrated Gold Medal at the Carnegie Institute's annual exhibition for her double portrait, *Mother and Daughter*, William Merritt Chase declared Beaux "not only the greatest woman painter, but the best that has ever lived."[20]

Elevated to full Academician in 1902, Beaux sought a way to bring a more personal interpretation to her portraiture. Men were shown as authoritarians and generally painted with a dark, tonal palette, whereas women, such as Sarah Elizabeth Doyle, the suffragette and educator, and M. Adelaide Nutting, principal of the nurses training school at Johns Hopkins University, inspired Beaux to reflect the sensitivity and strength of successful, unmarried, professional women.

Beaux appears to have made her first visit to Gloucester as early as 1897 when she stayed at the Fairview Inn. Enchanted with the area, as well as with local aesthetes A. Piatt Andrew and Henry Davis Sleeper, Beaux decided to build her own house on

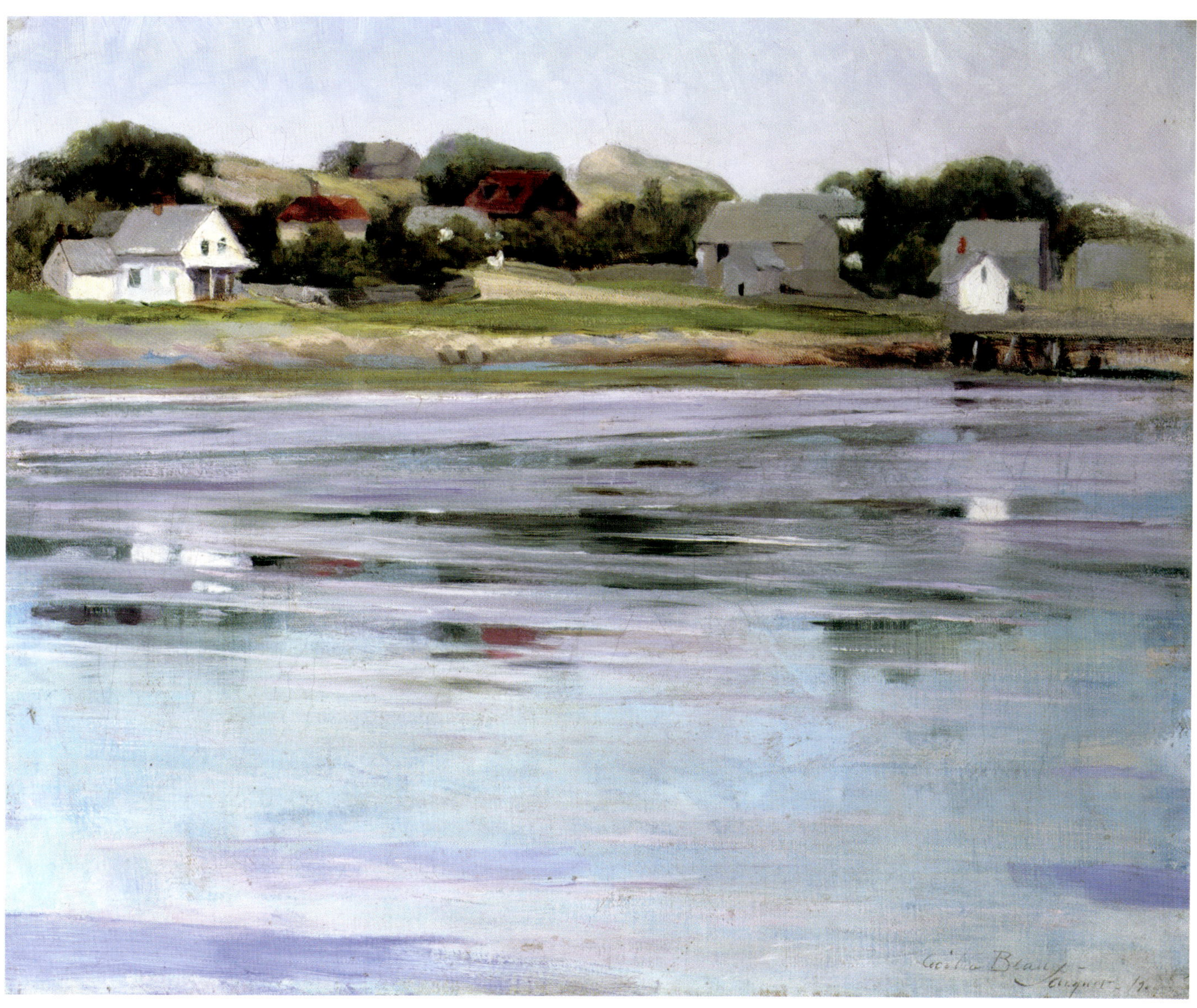

Cecilia Beaux
Half-Tide, Annisquam River, c. 1905
Oil on canvas, 16 x 20 in.
High Museum of Art, Atlanta
Gift of the Verrill Family in memory of Jean Verrill (2005.294)

Eastern Point. She called her new home "Green Alley," and it was completed, together with an adjoining studio, in 1906. Beaux summered in East Gloucester for the rest of her life, surrounded by friends, relatives, portrait-sitters, and staff.

It could be said that Beaux's use of composition and chiaroscuro defined her contribution to the art of portraiture. During her career, she painted presidents and cardinals, world leaders, family and friends. Her *Portrait of Leslie Buswell*, 1918, in his Red Cross Uniform with the Croix de Guerre pinned to his jacket is a poignant reflection of a young man who has endured the horror of war. This painting, when exhibited at the Gallery-on-the-Moors, drew great critical acclaim.

Sadly, Beaux's hip injury, sustained in 1924 after slipping in a Paris street, severely curtailed her career. An early member of the North Shore Arts Association—Beaux served on the first Board of Directors—her name disappears from the roll after 1927. Nevertheless, she was not forgotten. In 1933, First Lady Eleanor Roosevelt presented Cecilia Beaux with the National Achievement Gold Medal of the Chi Omega Fraternity, citing her as the American woman making the greatest contribution to world culture. It was a mark of distinction that Beaux truly appreciated. She died at Green Alley in September 1942.

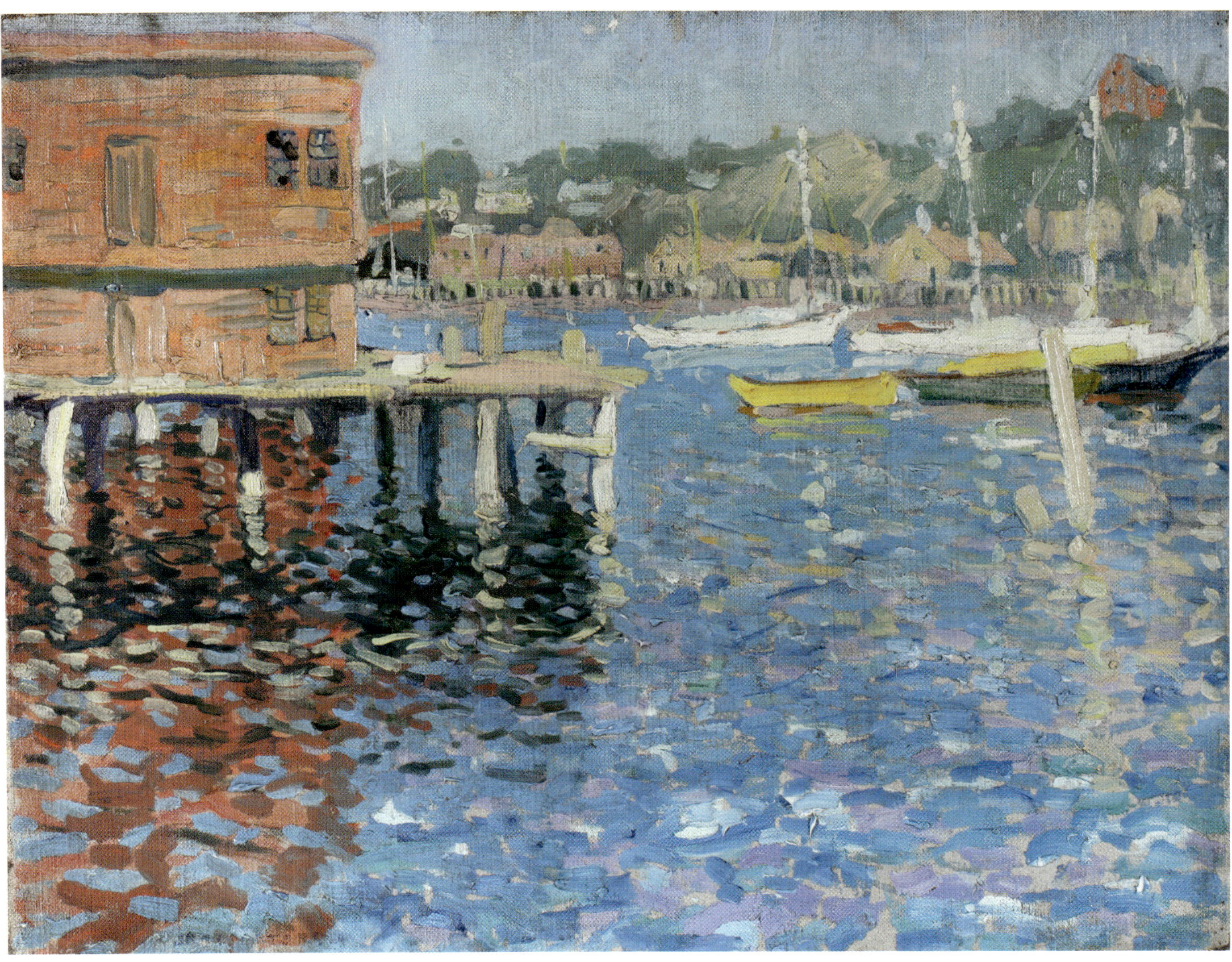

Jane Peterson
Gloucester Harbor
Oil on canvas, 18 x 24 in.
Collection of Matthew W. Panagiotu
Photo: Patrick O'Connor

Jane Peterson, A.W.S. (1876-1965)

Looking back on her accomplishments, the peppery Jane Peterson declared, "The prime requisites for being a fine painter are natural gifts and hard work. Sex has nothing to do with it.... Art is one activity where being a woman is neither a help nor a hindrance."[21] Peterson, a gifted artist with a strong work ethic, was immensely successful in her lifetime, achieving awards and accolades during a career that included more than one hundred exhibitions, over half of them one-woman shows. In 1938 the American Historical Society honored her as the "most outstanding individual of the year" for her achievements in art.[22]

Born Jennie Christine Peterson, in Elgin, Illinois, on November 28, 1876, Peterson enrolled at the Pratt Institute, Brooklyn, New York, at the age of nineteen, determined to become an artist. Here she came under the influence of Arthur Wesley Dow, whom she admired for his technique of uniting line, composition, color and notan, the Oriental method of harmoniously arranging lights and darks. Graduating in 1901, Peterson became Drawing Supervisor of Public Schools in Brooklyn, while continuing her own studies at the Art Students League under Frank Vincent DuMond and Henry B. Snell. In the summer of 1907, after a year on the faculty of the Maryland Institute in Baltimore, Peterson joined Snell and his wife on a painting trip to Europe and was so entranced with the Parisian milieu that she refused to return to America when the tour ended. Instead, she resigned her post at the Maryland Institute, and wired her friend,

Alexander Hudnut, for financial backing to remain in Europe and paint. Hudnut graciously complied, and so began a new era for Jane Peterson.

During the next two years, Peterson sought out the best painters to study their techniques. She spent a short time in England with Frank Brangwyn, whose work she admired for its powerful design and attention to mass rather than detail, and then returned to France. In 1908, as her career began to blossom, Peterson changed her name from Jennie to Jane. American astronomer, Percival Lowell, after meeting Peterson at the Société des Artists Français, returned to America and arranged a one-woman show of her work at Boston's prestigious St. Botolph Club. This was the first of many exhibitions reaping praise and financial success for Peterson. "There is not a dull

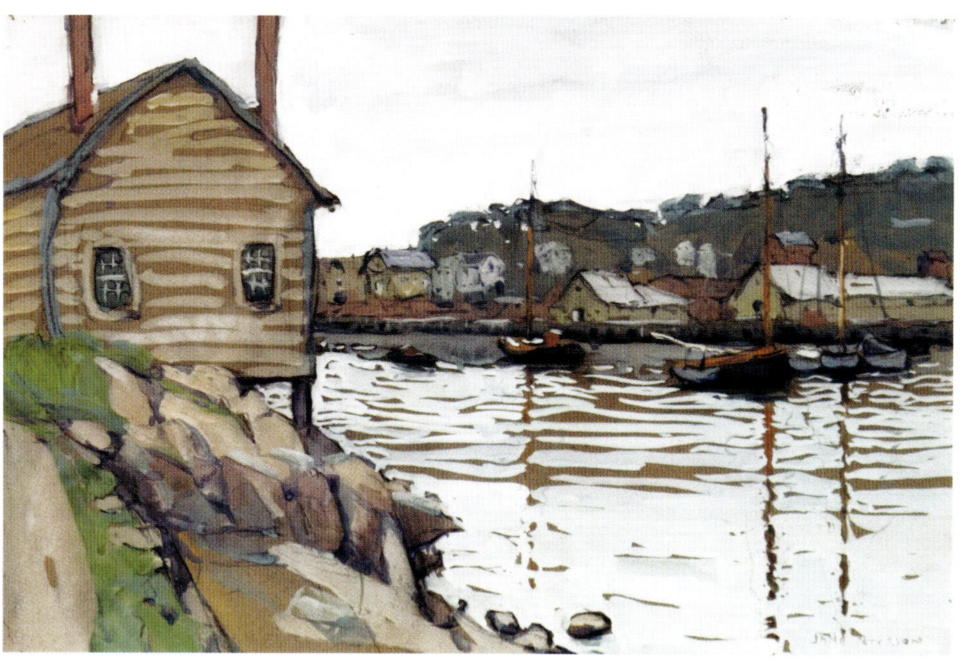

Jane Peterson
Artist's Cottage
Gouache on board, 12 x 18 in.
Private collection

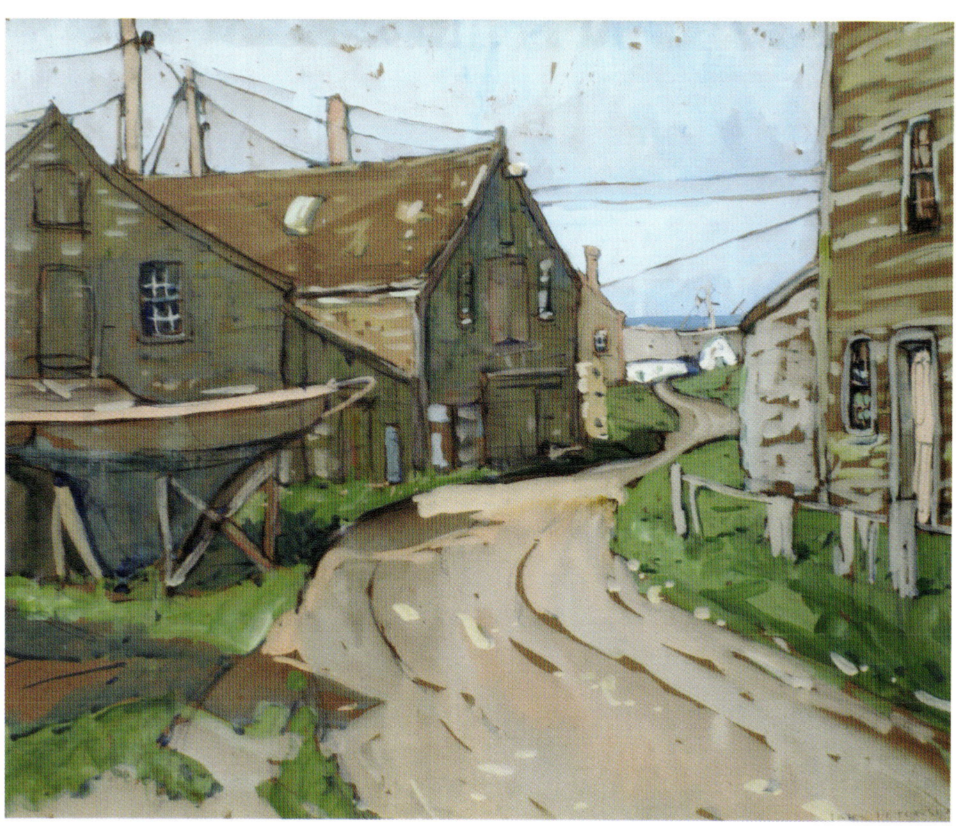

Jane Peterson
Road to the Sea, Gloucester, c. 1924
Oil on canvas, 17½ x 21 in.
Pierce Galleries, Inc., Hingham, Massachusetts

canvas in the entire collection...." raved the review in the January 23, 1909, edition of the *Christian Science Monitor*. "There is an athletic dash and swing to most of the paintings that is stimulating and captivating.... Miss Peterson has ideas, she has talent, has studied here and abroad and then proceeded to do her own work exactly to her individual tastes...."[23]

Beginning in 1909, when she studied with Spanish Impressionist Joaquín Sorolla y Bastida, Peterson's work took a giant leap in a new direction. Sorolla demanded ten sketches a day, forcing her to work faster and more spontaneously, and consequently her work took on a fresher quality, more radiant due to the broad brush application of pure color. Over the next decade, Peterson painted in exotic locations such as Alaska, Egypt, Algiers and Constantinople, undeterred at being a single woman traveling alone. "I always do what I want to do,"[24] was her maxim.

After her marriage in 1925 to M. Bernard Philipp, a wealthy widower twenty-five years her senior, Peterson curtailed her traveling at his request and took up flower painting in the studio that he had built for her in their New York home. She also painted in the flower garden of their summer home in Ipswich, MA. When she was widowed four years later, she resumed painting farther afield.

A prodigious artist, Peterson was a frequent visitor to Rocky Neck for more than fifty years, beginning in the early 1900s, and her work stands out as the creation of an innovative and flamboyant mind, seeing the abstract shapes of the world and defining them through a daring use of color and form. She worked in watercolor, gouache and oil, and found much to inspire her around the wharves and docks of East Gloucester. Her oils and watercolors are executed in bold color notes and loose broken color brushwork, yet when working in gouache and charcoal, she favored a flatter approach with strong outlines to create a linear perspective reminiscent of the Art Nouveau style. At the invitation of the Atwoods, Peterson showed regularly at the Gallery-on-the-Moors and, when that closed, became an early member of the North Shore Arts Association, exhibiting regularly until 1960, and serving as a Board Member from 1953 through 1961.

Throughout her life, Peterson believed that, "The aesthetic nature hungers for beautiful things and the uncultured grow gentle and refined under their subtle charm."[25] Jane Peterson was an expressive, highly individual member of the art world, whose passing in 1969 left a void still to be filled.

Maurice B. Prendergast (1859-1924)

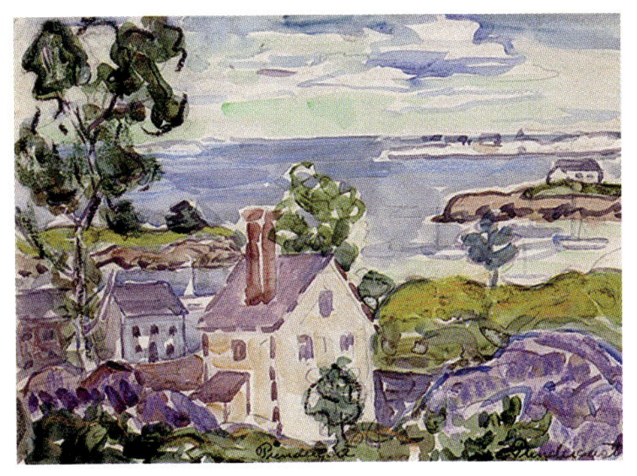

Maurice Brazil Prendergast
The Purple Rock, East Gloucester
Watercolor, pastel and pencil on paper, 14 x 10 in.
Cape Ann Historical Association, Gloucester, Massachusetts

Many critics have endorsed neo-impressionist Maurice Brazil Prendergast as America's first modernist painter, a man of quiet genius, born ahead of his time. No other artist of his era could combine such luscious color and montage of tones to emulate light and movement, or geometric shapes and line to define rhythmic expressionism.

Although experts disagree on the year of his birth (even Prendergast was confused, believing he was born in 1861) the family Bible confirms that Maurice and his twin sister, Lucy, were born October 10, 1859, to Mary (Germaine) and Maurice Prendergast in St. John's, Newfoundland.[26] In those days, Prendergast, Sr., owned and operated a trading post in St. John's, but following the financial failure of the business in 1861, the family moved to Boston, home of their Germaine relatives. The Prendergast children attended local Boston schools but both Maurice and his younger brother, Charles, who would also make his mark on the art world, finished school by the time they were fourteen and found it necessary to obtain jobs to help with the family's finances.

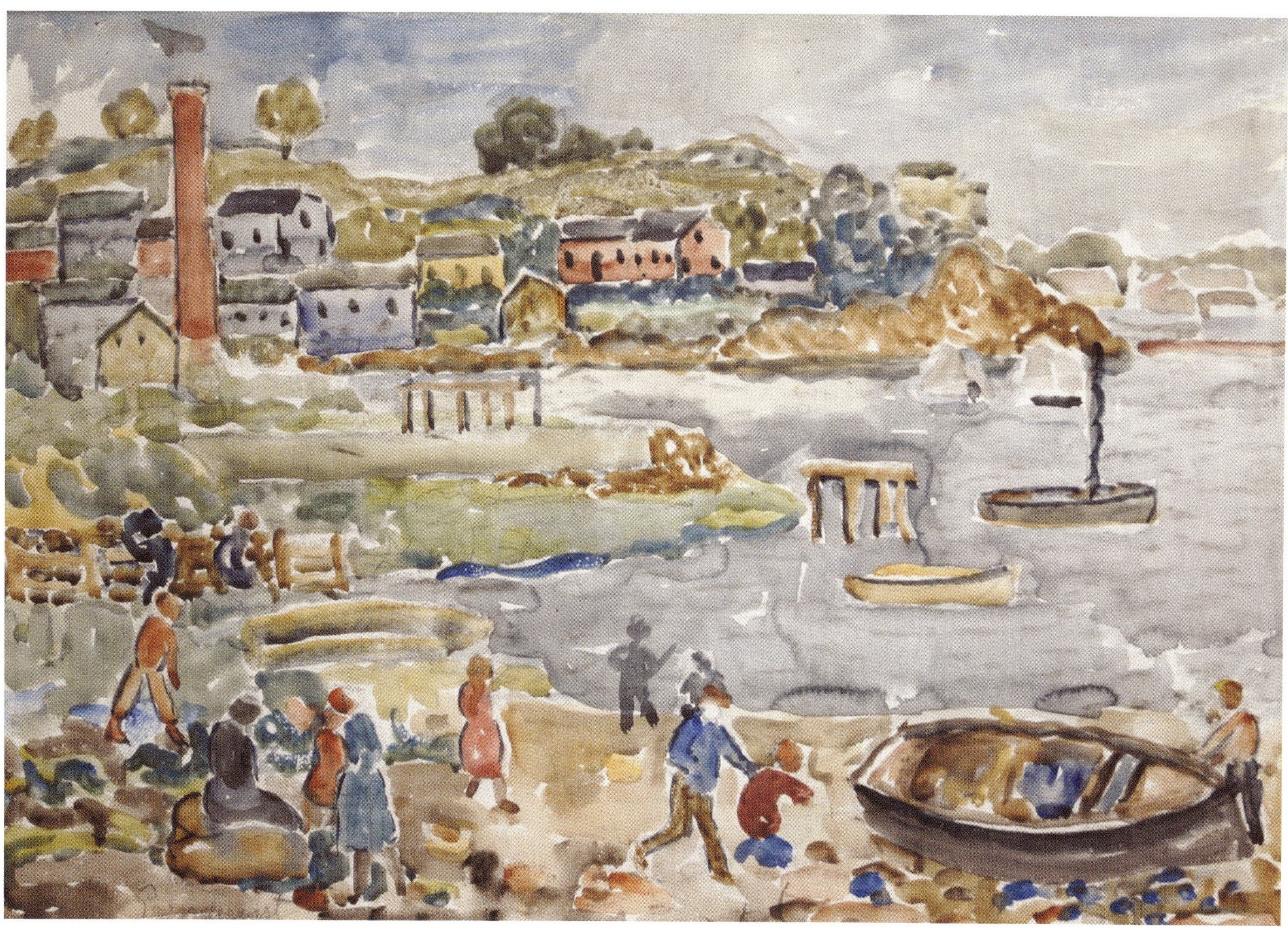

Maurice Brazil Prendergast
Gloucester, 1916
Watercolor on paper, 33.9 x 49.9 cm
The Art Gallery, University of Maryland, College Park, Maryland
Gift of Mrs. Charles B. Prendergast
Courtesy of The Art Gallery

In the beginning, Maurice wrapped packages for a local dry goods store. However, he spent more time filling sketchbooks than attending to his duties and eventually his parents, eager to nurture this creative streak, apprenticed Maurice to a Boston show card painter. A career in lettering and design enabled Prendergast to eke out a living, but his first love was painting outdoors. He would spend his free time in nearby Day's Woods making sketches of the local cattle populace. "In those days Maurice was hell on cows!"[27] his brother, Charles, once joked.

Perhaps because of their mutual interest in art, Maurice and Charles Prendergast enjoyed an unusually close and supportive familial relationship. In the summer of 1886, Maurice, at the instigation of his brother, joined Charles on a painting trip, via cattle boat, to England and Wales, after which the two began planning a sojourn to France. This trip was postponed for almost five years while they garnered enough funds for a lengthy stay, and Maurice was well into his thirties before he finally arrived in Paris. Once there, however, his eclectic Irish-French Huguenot ancestry took over, and he quickly assimilated himself into the milieu of what was then considered the art capital of the world.

Prendergast's early work shows the typical constraint of an unschooled hand both in color and composition, although his composition, being somewhat illustrative, probably owed more to the influence of his lettering and design work than lack of skill. Some experts suggest Maurice studied at Colarossi's under Gustave Courtois, and then at the Académie Julian with Constant, Blanc and Jean-Paul Laurens,[28] but Prendergast himself, when queried about his formal training, merely acknowledged, "I studied in

Paris several years at various schools, Julian's, the Beaux Arts, etc., and was a pupil of Joseph Blanc."[29]

During his three years in Paris, Prendergast developed a talent for rapid sketching, capturing brief moments and memories along the boulevards of the French capital that would serve as remembered images for later use in the studio. The sincerity and freshness of this empirical method proved a valuable foundation on which to build up his new and very personal style. Over the years this style moved away from representational art and toward a feeling of color, light and movement, "whirling arabesques that tax the eye,"[30] according to one 1908 critic.

Despite ill health and difficulties with his hearing, Maurice Prendergast spent the next two decades interspersing a rigorous work schedule at home with half a dozen trips of varying length to Europe. He first came to Cape Ann in 1902, visiting with the Oliver Williams family at their summer home in Annisquam, and completing an oil portrait of Mrs. Williams with her baby son, Oliver, and his nurse. Later, in 1906, Prendergast made a note of his visit, "the country and the seashore, the fine location of the house, the flowers, and the neighbors and the solitary tent on the dunes across the bay — all of which I am not going to forget for a long while."[31]

Although Prendergast was adept in oil, his favorite medium was watercolor, an unusual choice given that watercolor is an unforgiving medium and composition must be designed in advance, an exacting process for a painter practicing such swirling effects of color, mood and light. He made several return visits to Gloucester and exhibited with the Gallery-on-the-Moors. One variegated offering—Prendergast often combined a tapestry and mosaic effect—brought forth the comment, "In sharp contrast to Childe Hassam's style is a jolly, amusing medley of color, called *Entrance to the Harbor*, that looks as if Mr. Maurice B. Prendergast has played joyously with it, as a child with its Noah's Ark animals. He kept his grandmother's sampler in mind, thereby producing an original effect; even to the cross stitch so ably suggested by his technique."[32]

Maurice B. Prendergast, decried by some and enjoyed by many more, was a pioneer in his use of mosaic notes and flourishing brushwork. It was a technique that raised many eyebrows during his career and yet today his works are highly sought after and prized by collectors. Although seen as quiet and unassuming, Prendergast's defining characteristic is best described by his brother: "Monny had the right idea. He knew he wanted to be an artist right from the start, and he didn't let anything stand in his way…."[33]

Alice Schille, A.W. S. (1869-1955)

Alice Schille's sojourn on Cape Ann covered a mere three summers out of a long and distinguished career; nevertheless her Gloucester watercolors are considered by many to be among the finest of her work. A native of Columbus, Ohio, Schille was born in 1869, the daughter of well-to-do soda and bottle manufacturer. She was shy and reserved by nature, resolute when necessary, and little is known of her personal life. Indeed, after Schille's death in 1955, her work was sadly neglected outside her home state, until recently when art historians and scholars created a surge of renewed interest in her work. Schille, who never married, began her training at the Columbus Art School in 1891 and in 1897 continued her studies at the Art Students League in New York. In 1898, Schille began taking instruction from William Merritt Chase at the New York School of Art, which led to her attending his Shinnecock, Long Island, summer school in 1899, where she shared lodgings with artist Martha Walter.[34] Chase greatly admired Schille's skill in watercolor and was a strong influence during his pupil's fledgling years.

At the turn of the century, Schille's work began to attract more attention when she showed with the eminent New York Water Color Club in 1901. It was an auspicious start to what would be four decades of exhibiting with that prestigious group. However, like many before her, Schille felt her artistic experience would benefit from a trip to Europe's celebrated art museums. She left the United States in 1902, stopping briefly in England and then continuing on through Holland, Germany and Spain. Schille's ultimate destination was France, where she spent 1903-1904 studying at the Académie Colarossi under Prinet, Collin, and Courtois. One can clearly see the influence of these years in many of her watercolors, which carry a distinct note of European modernism. In the spring of 1904, Schille was elated to have five paintings, three of them watercolors, accepted into the annual exhibition of the Société Nationale des Beaux Arts, difficult enough for a European artist, let alone an American and a woman.

When Schille came back to the United States in the fall of 1904, her horizons were considerably broader than when she'd left two years earlier. Nevertheless, she chose to return to Ohio and carved out a career in education at her alma mater, the Columbus School of Art, teaching watercolor and portrait painting for the next 44 years. Schille's dedication to teaching was perhaps detrimental to her own painting career in that she had little time available to work on her own oeuvre. Nonetheless, with no family to tie her down Schille was able to spend her summers traveling extensively throughout Europe, the southwest United States and eventually Latin America.

By August 1913, Schille's paintings were attracting critical appraisal, such as Edna Owens' comments in *International Studio*, "the hand of an original and vigorous painter is easily distinguishable.... We can think of no American water-colorist who is more versatile than Alice Schille."[35] In 1914, the war in Europe escalated and, with her intercontinental travels curtailed, Schille looked closer to home for inspiration. Her first visit to Gloucester came in 1916. The previous year, Arthur Wesley Dow—a great admirer of Schille's work—awarded her the Philadelphia Water Color Club Prize while judging the annual exhibition of the Pennsylvania Academy of Fine Arts. Dow had close ties to the artistic communities of Cape Ann and perhaps it was he who suggested Schille experience the unique light and ambiance of Gloucester for herself.

Arriving in Gloucester in the summer of 1916, with a gold medal to her credit from the previous year's Panama-Pacific International Exposition, Schille renounced her typical approach to watercolors and allowed herself to be moved emotionally and spontaneously by the intense light for which Cape Ann is legendary. *Street Scene, Gloucester* combines Schille's strong color sense and eye for rhythmic composition with deliberate and individualized brushwork to create an evocative depiction of Gloucester's Main Street. *Gloucester Harbor, D. H. Lane Fish Company*, on the other hand, takes fluidity one step further with strong draftsmanship to delineate structure coupled with impressionistic color and brushstroke to capture ambiance and light. One can discern a touch of the Fauvist mingled with the spotting of the Pointillist as Schille allowed herself to consider the unplumbed depths of her own talent. During her three visits to Gloucester, Schille was invited to exhibit at the Gallery-on-the-Moors where her work was always well received.

Schille kept copious notebooks, recording her thoughts on the art world of the day, commenting on the "power of mystic penetration," evinced by Cezanne and by Matisse's "return to naked rhythmic expressionism."[36] Perhaps the key to Schille's own work is revealed in her opinion that "the trend of modern art is toward intensification... intensification expresses [the] spirit of our times."[37] Certainly, Alice Schille was never afraid to express intensity in her painting through brilliant color, light and vitality. Although

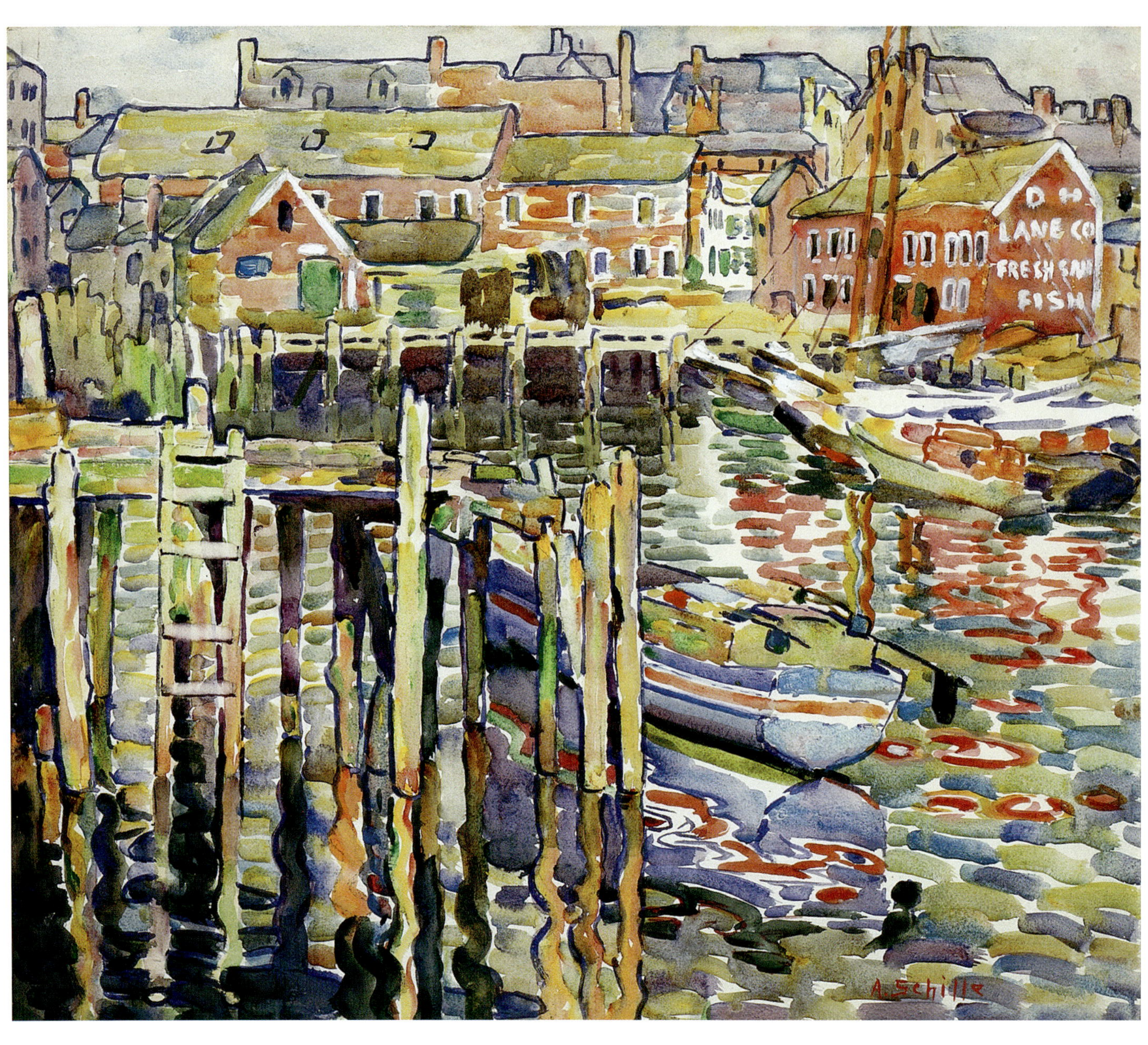

Alice Schille
Gloucester Harbor, D. H. Lane Fish Company, c. 1916-1918
Watercolor, 17½ x 20½ in.
Private Collection
Photo courtesy of Keny Galleries, Columbus, Ohio

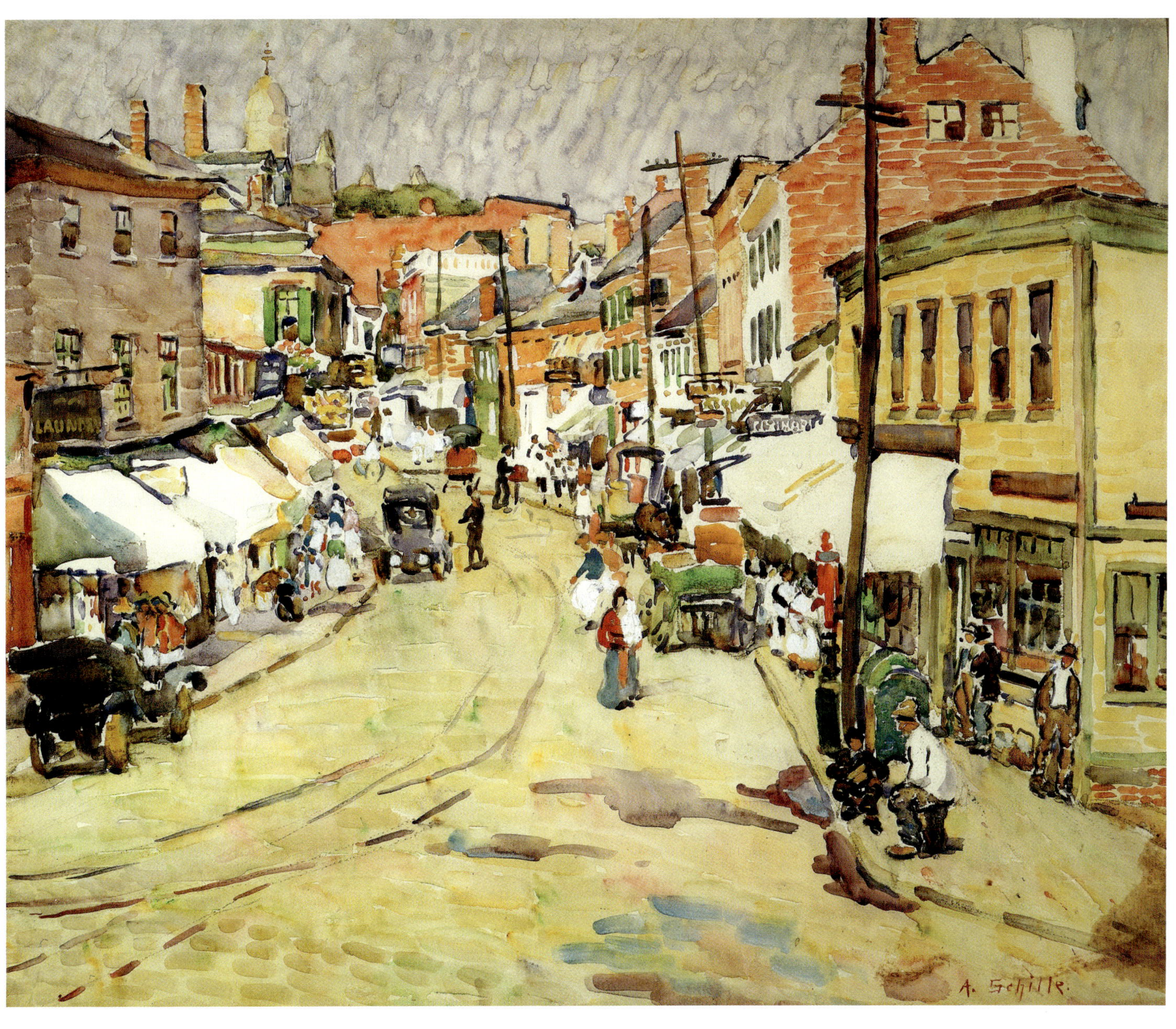

Alice Schille
Street Scene, Gloucester, c. 1916-1918
Watercolor, 20 x 24 in.
Private collection
Photo courtesy of Keny Galleries, Columbus, Ohio

she did not return to Gloucester after 1918, preferring Taos, Santa Fe, and points southward into Guatemala, she continued painting and exploring her own artistic path until 1948 and her retirement from the Columbus School of Art. She died November 6, 1955, in Columbus, Ohio.

Theresa Bernstein (1890-2002)

Theresa Ferber Bernstein, poet, writer, artist and grande dame of East Gloucester—was notable for her longevity almost as much as for her contribution to the school of social realism. Even in the closing years of the twentieth century the forceful Bernstein was an active participant in the North Shore Arts Association and annually demonstrated her talents to an appreciative audience during the Members' Dinner, after which she would not only auction her work as a fundraiser, but join in the bidding in the spirit of the occasion.

Bernstein was born March 1, 1890, in Philadelphia, the only child of European immigrants: Isidore, a textile manufacturer and his wife Anne (Ferber) a talented pianist. The family enjoyed a cultured lifestyle until a reversal of family fortunes left them in reduced circumstances. Bernstein later attended the Philadelphia School of Design for Women, now Moore College of Art, and graduated in 1911. Among her instructors were Daniel Garber and Henry B. Snell, both noted for their plein air painting abilities, and it is possible that Snell, who maintained a studio and summer school in East Gloucester during the early years of the twentieth century, was instrumental in initiating Bernstein's first visit to Gloucester and Rocky Neck around 1915.

Bernstein also worked with American Impressionist painter William Merritt Chase, taking life and portraiture classes at the Art Students' League after her family moved to New York from Philadelphia in 1912. Although her instruction came from academically trained artists, Bernstein herself developed a personal style characterized by vigorous brushwork and robust color. Some of her early painting choices can perhaps be accredited to a trip to Europe she took with her mother c. 1914, when Bernstein adopted the

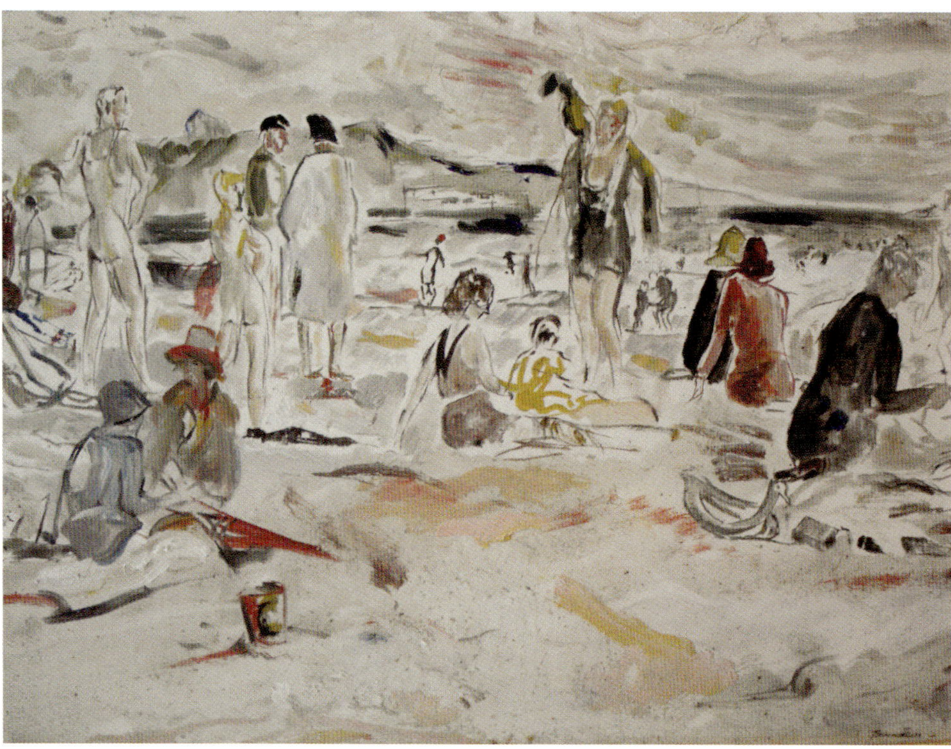

Theresa Bernstein
Good Harbor Beach, c. 1920
Oil on board, 20 x 12 in.
Private collection

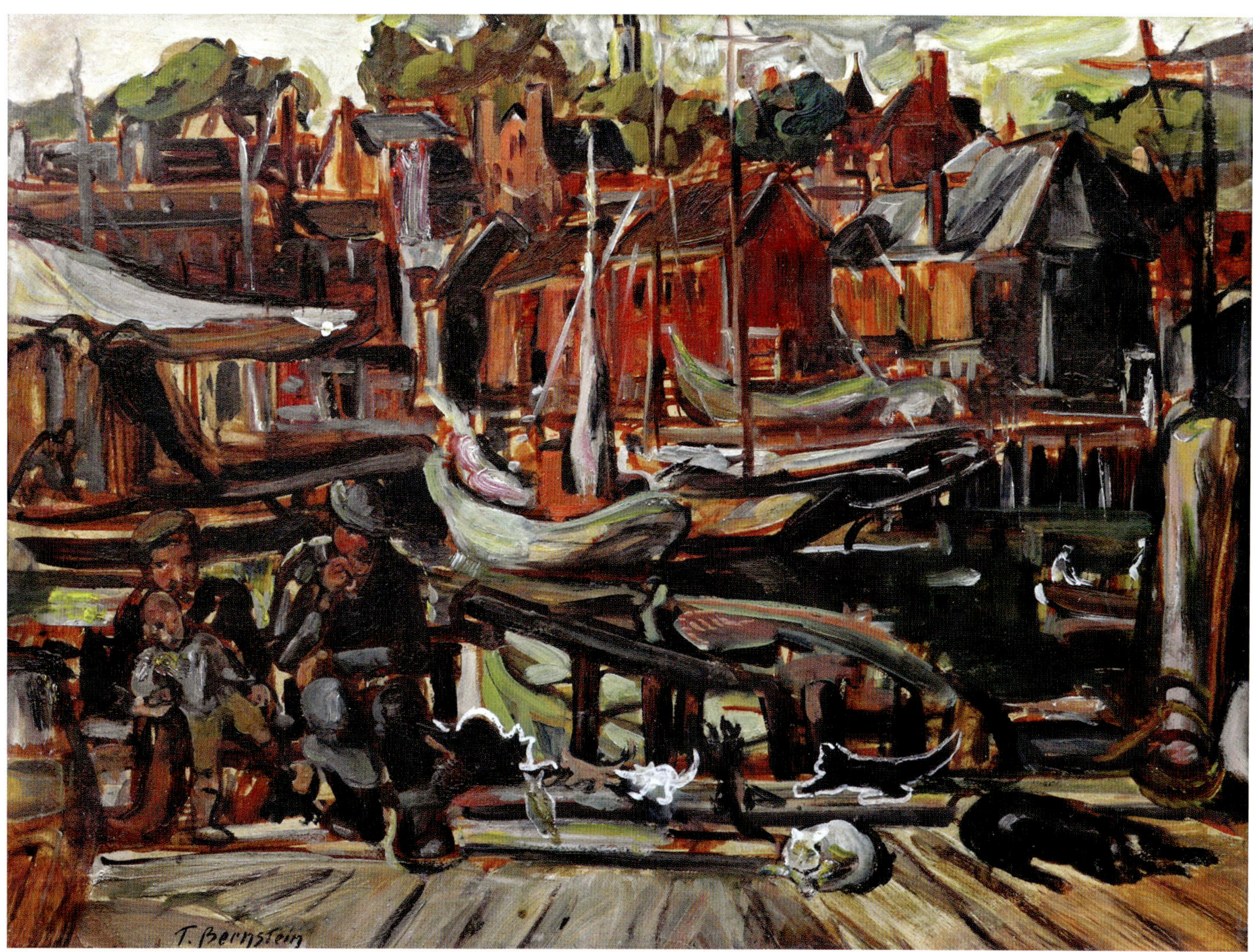

Theresa Bernstein
On The Docks, Gloucester, c. 1916
Oil on board, 14¾ x 19⅞ in.
James B. Hand Fine Art, Gloucester, Massachusetts

somber palette of the Munich School for a while, finding its heavy expressionistic manner more suited to social realism. The Ashcan themes of Henri and The Eight (a New York realist group) that caused such a furor at the 1913 Armory Show were now becoming increasingly popular among those who felt the refinement of the academic painter was superfluous and no longer served the needs of the common man. Whereas painting in the grand manner had once been seen to uplift the spirit, modern thought now suggested painting be brought down to a socially realistic level with which all could identify. Bernstein, in answer to the sudden popularity of urban realism and her own family's changed circumstances, developed an expressionist style to engage this new theme. Her work, always energetic, became more fluid, as she turned to a broad loaded brush and brighter palette to capture New York's citizenry at work and play. From the waterfront to Coney Island, Bernstein's brush immortalized the changing face of America prior to, during, and after the First World War. She also became involved in the Philadelphia Ten, a group of women painters, primarily graduates of the Philadelphia School of Design for Women, who exhibited together beginning in 1917. She broke away from the group in 1931, after a disagreement over where her unconventional work was hung.

In 1919 Bernstein married artist William Meyerowitz, whom she met when he asked for help in organizing an art exhibition to benefit East Side settlement houses. Shortly after their marriage, they began summering on Cape Ann and, like their New York colleagues, John Sloan, Stuart Davis and the Winters, began splitting the year,

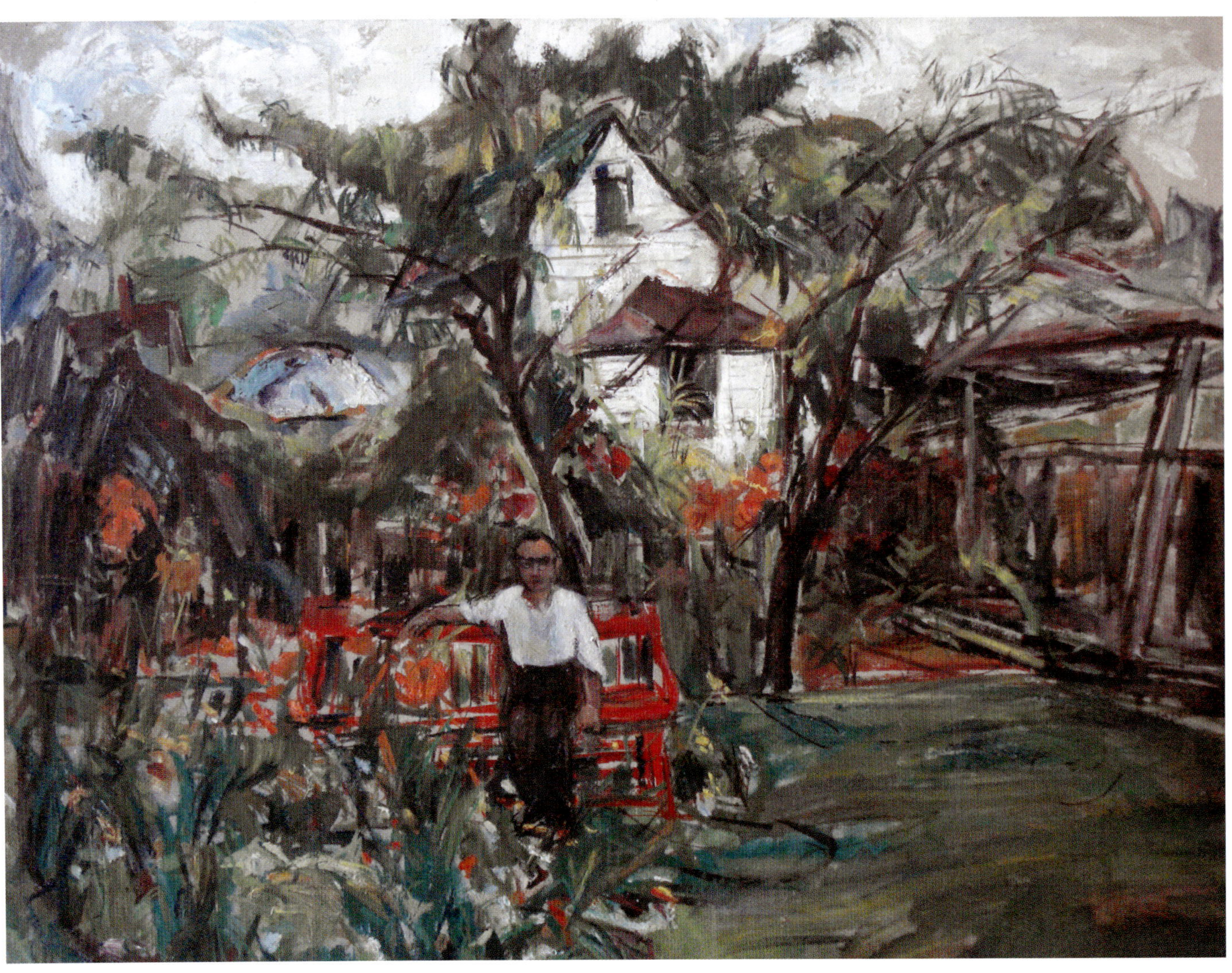

Theresa Bernstein
William in the Garden, c. 1940
Oil on canvas, 32 x 25 in.
Private collection

wintering in the city and spending summer on Cape Ann. To begin with, the couple lodged at the Little House on the corner of Rocky Neck Avenue and Eastern Point Road,[38] close to the heart of the art colony. They rented a cottage at the Hawthorne Inn on occasion and also stayed with friends in Folly Cove. Later they bought a summer home on Mt. Pleasant Avenue in East Gloucester, a stone's throw from the Rocky Neck causeway.

Throughout her career, Theresa Bernstein followed her own inclinations, expressing her thoughts and ideas in singular style. In 1919, F. W. Coburn, art critic for the *Boston Herald*, lamented Bernstein as "a typical seeker after a personal and peculiar manner."[39] However, Bernstein was always true to her own ideals. Her artistic vision missed no important detail and her compositions became a blend of color with form outlined in black. Sincerity was her keynote, simplicity of execution her tour de force. From her early days on Rocky Neck when "we would paint out in the open, near the road of the Hawthorne Casino, which was really a walk with shapely little trees that formed a natural protection against the sun. Strollers-by would be seen, with their parasols flashing in and out of the network of trees,"[40] to depictions of her husband, Bill, sitting on the red bench in the garden of their home on Mt. Pleasant Street. Bernstein's paintings are infused with love of life and love for her work. She deplored stasis and her work constantly evolved as she explored color, intensity and the dignity of her subject.

Bernstein was an active supporter of the art community on Rocky Neck and showed work at both the North Shore Arts Association and the Gloucester Society of Artists. However, although her professional career proved providential, her personal life was not always happy. Her only child, a daughter, Isadora, born in the early years of her marriage, died of pneumonia at only two months of age. In later life, when William Meyerowitz passed away in 1981, loneliness crowded in unrelieved, until Bernstein took up writing to help the grieving process and discovered a new creative outlet. At the age of 91, the artist became a writer, publishing at least six books including children's books and poetry. She passed away February 13, 2002, at the age of 111.

William Meyerowitz, N. A. (1887-1981)

Whenever he was asked, "To what school of painting do you belong?" moderate modernist William Meyerowitz would reply, "What does it matter?"[41] Meyerowitz felt himself to be a free spirit, able to express himself in whatever mood his subject decreed. He pursued many interests, including music, poetry and a love of horses, and often incorporated these themes into his work. "Intuition and common sense are my guidons," Meyerowitz said. "I am independent, bound by the tenets of no narrow academic association and prejudiced against no new discovery or movement."[42]

Meyerowitz was born in Gezelitz, a small village near Kiev in Ukraine, c. 1887. Even as a child, Meyerowitz displayed an interest in the arts and worked for a sign painter when he was barely ten years old. In 1908, he immigrated to New York with his father. The plan was to establish a home and earn enough money to bring the rest of the family to America. Meyerowitz worked in an architect's office, creating model buildings from blueprints. Later, while a student at the National Academy of Design School, Meyerowitz, who had a rich baritone and loved to sing, joined the chorus at the Metropolitan Opera to help supplement his income, much of which went toward supporting the family.

While studying at the National Academy of Design School (1912-1916), Meyerowitz won the Eliot Prize for Painting and Drawing, and in 1916 received First Honorable Mention for *Drama as a Teacher*, a mural that he produced for the prestigious "Prix de Rome" competition. Regrettably, at least from Meyerowitz's point of view, the First Prize went to an artist whom he had recently tutored.[43] Realizing he had

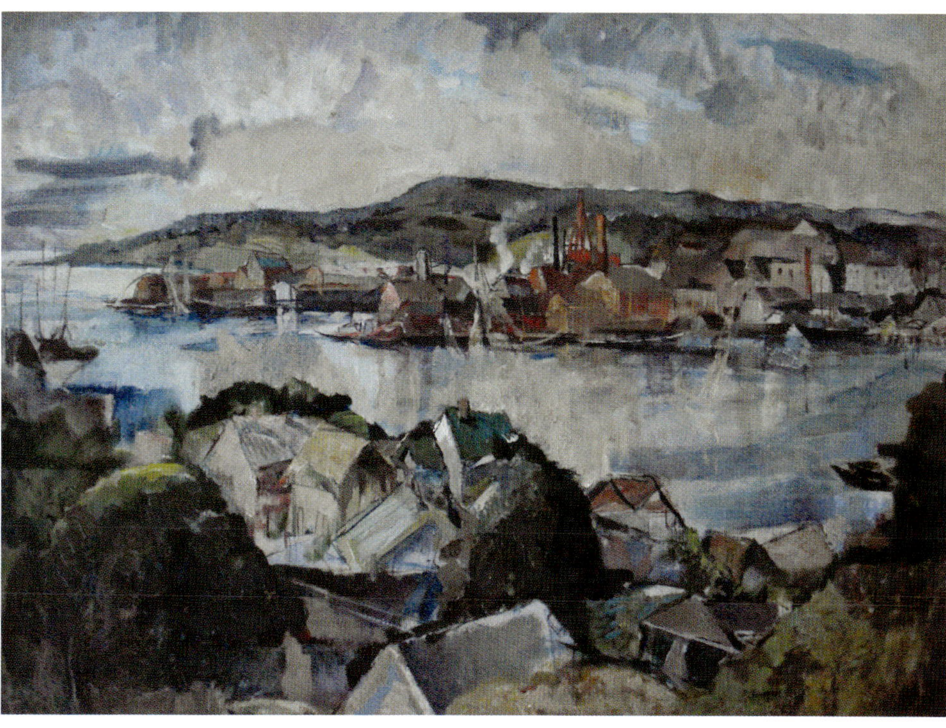

William Meyerowitz
Gloucester Harbor, c. 1920
Oil on canvas, 35 x 27 in.
Private collection

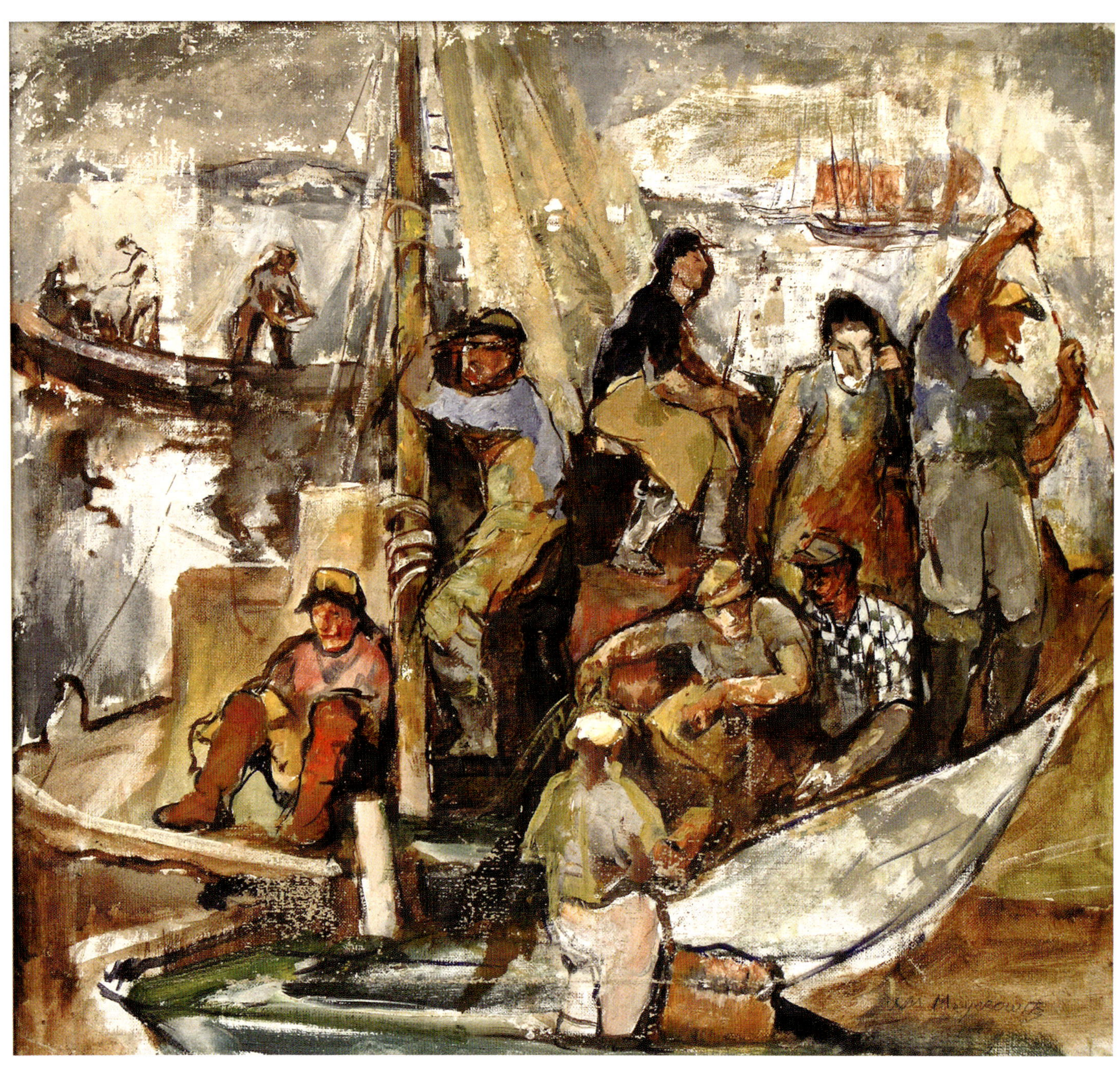

William Meyerowitz
Fisherman's Haven, c. 1925
Oil on canvas, 18 x 20 in.
Collection of E. Bonnie Akerley

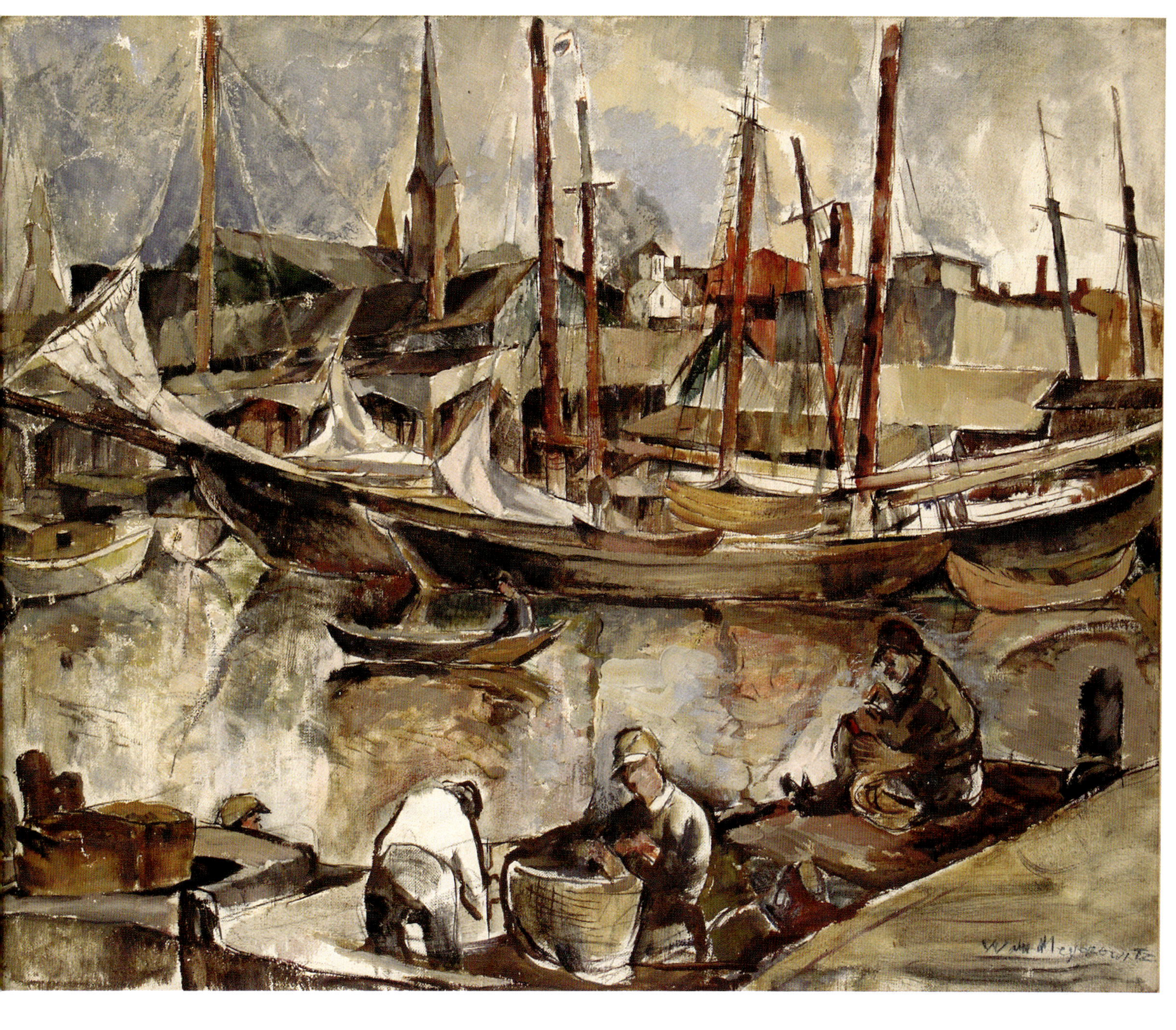

William Meyerowitz
Baiting Up, Gloucester, c. 1925
Oil on canvas, 18 x 22 in.
Collection of E. Bonnie Akerley

learned as much as he could from the school, Meyerowitz decided to leave the Academy and strike out on his own.

A great innovator, Meyerowitz acquired a small printing press and began experimenting with a variety of techniques, such as leaving an inky film on the surface of the plate, creating a tonal effect that, when printed, softened but did not obscure the draftsmanship. This practice became the foundation for his fine-tuning of the color printing process, in which he superimposed different inks in order to use the same plate to print more than one color. Meyerowitz had the distinction of being among the first and foremost color etchers in the country. In 1925, when the Fox Film Company needed an etcher to demonstrate the process in a documentary, Meyerowitz was recommended to them and later appeared in a production called *The Magic Needle*.

Meyerowitz came to Gloucester in 1919 with his wife Theresa Bernstein whom he met in New York while collecting paintings on behalf of the People's Art Guild, a group dedicated to bringing art to the masses in the East Side tenements. The Meyerowitzs enjoyed traveling to new places, hauling painting gear halfway across Europe, and sketching at every opportunity. However, they returned to Cape Ann time and again, sometimes residing at the Hawthorn Inn in East Gloucester, and on one occasion staying at The Thickets in Folly Cove with artists Ellen Day Hale and Gabrielle deVeaux Clements.[44]

During his years on Cape Ann, Meyerowitz actively participated in the local art community, exhibiting at the Gallery-on-the-Moors, the North Shore Arts Association, and even the Gloucester Society of Artists, which prided itself on non-juried shows. Meyerowitz was sympathetic to those artists who struggled to get into juried shows because their work was considered avant-garde, or "non-traditional." He often felt himself pigeonholed as a "gentle modernist," but was never hurt by the label. He received numerous painting commissions, including several U.S. Supreme Court Justices, and was noted for his oil paintings as much as for his etchings. His philosophy was, "It is not possible for any one artist, of any school, to impose arbitrary limitations. A painting may be realistic, abstract, or any other form, yet communicate the truth.... I do not cling to the skeletal facts, their figurative elements are deprived of covering. In my approach I complete the cycle of my emotions by even greater expression of objectivity."[45]

Like many artists of the day, Meyerowitz was inspired by the 1913 Armory show in New York. This show, the first avant-garde art exhibit in America, changed his views about painting and how it could be created, and this new viewpoint allowed him to explore more abstract forms, which we later see reflected in the fractured shapes of his cityscapes during the 1920s and '30s. Although he admired the diligent draftsmanship of Bouguereau and the French academics,[46] Meyerowitz preferred a more spontaneous approach in his own work. "I believe in the à premier coup approach," he said in a 1980 interview, when he was almost 93 years old. "Get the picture done at a stroke."

Throughout his artistic career, William Meyerowitz sought to stimulate human emotion. "We deaden our emotions today.... We're distracted by football, baseball, radio, movies, television. We don't feel things as much—or maybe we don't express what we feel."[47] In an effort to reach those frozen attitudes, Meyerowitz produced work to epitomize the most prevalent characteristics in the cultural attitudes of America. As Alfred Werner so elegantly phrased it, "How many 'little worlds' you have created in the straightforward progression of your intense, dedicated work!... You have never dipped your brush too deeply into the brown sauce of philosophy. I can see reason's diagrams, but it is far more important that you can make me feel living nature that has sparked the productiveness of your creative energy."[48]

William Meyerowitz, National Academician, passed away in New York in May 1981.

Notes

1 Piper, Adaline, D. Quoted in O'Gorman, James F., "Parnassus on Ledge Road," *This Other Gloucester*, (Gloucester: Ten Pound Island, 1990), p. 87.

2 O'Gorman, James F., p. 77.

3 Ibid., p. 78.

4 Ms. Emmeline Atwood, *New York Herald*, September 20, n. d. Quoted in "Gallery-on-the-Moors 1916-1922: An Exhibition of Work from the Museum's Collection by Artists Who Exhibited at Gallery-On-The-Moors," exhibition catalogue (Gloucester: Cape Ann Historical Association, 2006) p. 4.

5 O'Gorman, p. 80.

6 Ibid., p. 83.

7 "Gallery-on-the-Moors 1916-1922," CAHA.

8 O'Gorman, p. 85.

9 Ibid., p. 89.

10 Ibid., p. 81.

11 Ibid., p. 87.

12 Schmoll, Anne W., *Martha Walter (1875-1976): Gloucester Impressions*, exhibition catalogue, Vose Galleries of Boston, July 1992.

13 O'Gorman, p. 92.

14 *Frederick J. Mulhaupt, Dean of the Cape Ann School: A Retrospective*, exhibition catalogue, North Shore Arts Association, 1999, p. ii.

15 Now known as the Kansas City Art Institute and School of Design, quoted in *Frederick J. Mulhaupt*.

16 *Frederick J. Mulhaupt*, p. iv.

17 Movalli, Charles, "Frederick J. Mulhaupt: New England Classic," *American Artist* (January 1977): p. 75.

18 Ibid., p. 76.

19 Beaux, Cecilia, *Background With Figures* (New York: Houghton Mifflin, 1930), p. 120.

20 "Art Jury Awards Miss Cecilia Beaux First Prize." Philadelphia Public Ledger. November 3, 1899. Cecilia Beaux Papers. Archives of American Art. Quoted in Carter Alice A., *Cecilia Beaux: A Modern Painter in the Gilded Age* (New York: Rizzoli, 2005), p. 127.

21 Joseph, J. Jonathan, *Jane Peterson; An American Impressionist* (Boston: Privately printed, 1981), p. 43.

22 Ibid., p. 21.

23 Ibid., p. 27.

24 Ibid., p. 29.

25 Ibid., p. 40.

26 Rhys, Hedley Howell, *Maurice Prendergast 1859-1924,* Museum of Fine Arts (Cambridge, MA: Boston and Harvard University Press, 1960), p. 20.

27 Ibid.

28 Wattenmaker, Richard J., *Maurice Prendergast*, (New York: Harry N. Abrams in association with The National Museum of American Art, Smithsonian Institute, 1994), p. 19.

29 MP to Edgar L. Hewitt, n. d. [fall 1914] Alice Klauber Papers, Archives of American Art, microfilm roll 583, frames 710-711.

30 Rhys, p. 42.

31 Maurice Prendergast Papers, CAHA.

32 *Cape Ann Shore*, August 2, 1919, Prendergast Papers, CAHA.

33 Rhys, p. 17.

34 Wells, Gary, edited by Norma J. Roberts, *Alice Schille, The New England Years 1915-1918.* (Columbus, OH: Keny and Johnson Gallery, 1989), p. 49.

35 Owens, Edna, "The Art of Alice Schille," *International Studio* 50 (August 1913): 31-33.

36 From Alice Schille's notebooks, courtesy of James N. Keny, Keny and Johnson Gallery. Quoted in Wells, p. 10.

37 Ibid.

38 Oakes, Martha, *The Paintings and Etchings of William Meyerowitz and Theresa Bernstein* (Gloucester: Cape Ann Historical Association, 1986), p. 2.

39 O'Gorman, James F., p. 83.

40 "Paintings by Theresa Bernstein," Milch Galleries catalogue, New York, 1919.

41 Meyerowitz, Theresa Bernstein, *William Meyerowitz, The Artist Speaks* (Philadelphia: The Art Alliance Press, 1986), p. 94.

42 Ibid.

43 Ibid., p. 22.

44 Ibid., p. 29.

45 *Meyerowitz, William, N. A.*, The University of Georgia, Georgia Museum of Art, Athens, Georgia, exhibition catalogue June 1-July 15, 1966.

46 Movalli, Charles, "A Conversation with William Meyerowitz and Theresa Bernstein," *American Artist* (January 1980): 64.

47 Ibid., p. 92.

48 Werner, Alfred, *William Meyerowitz N.A.*, New York: Chase Gallery ex. cat. May 16-30, 1959.

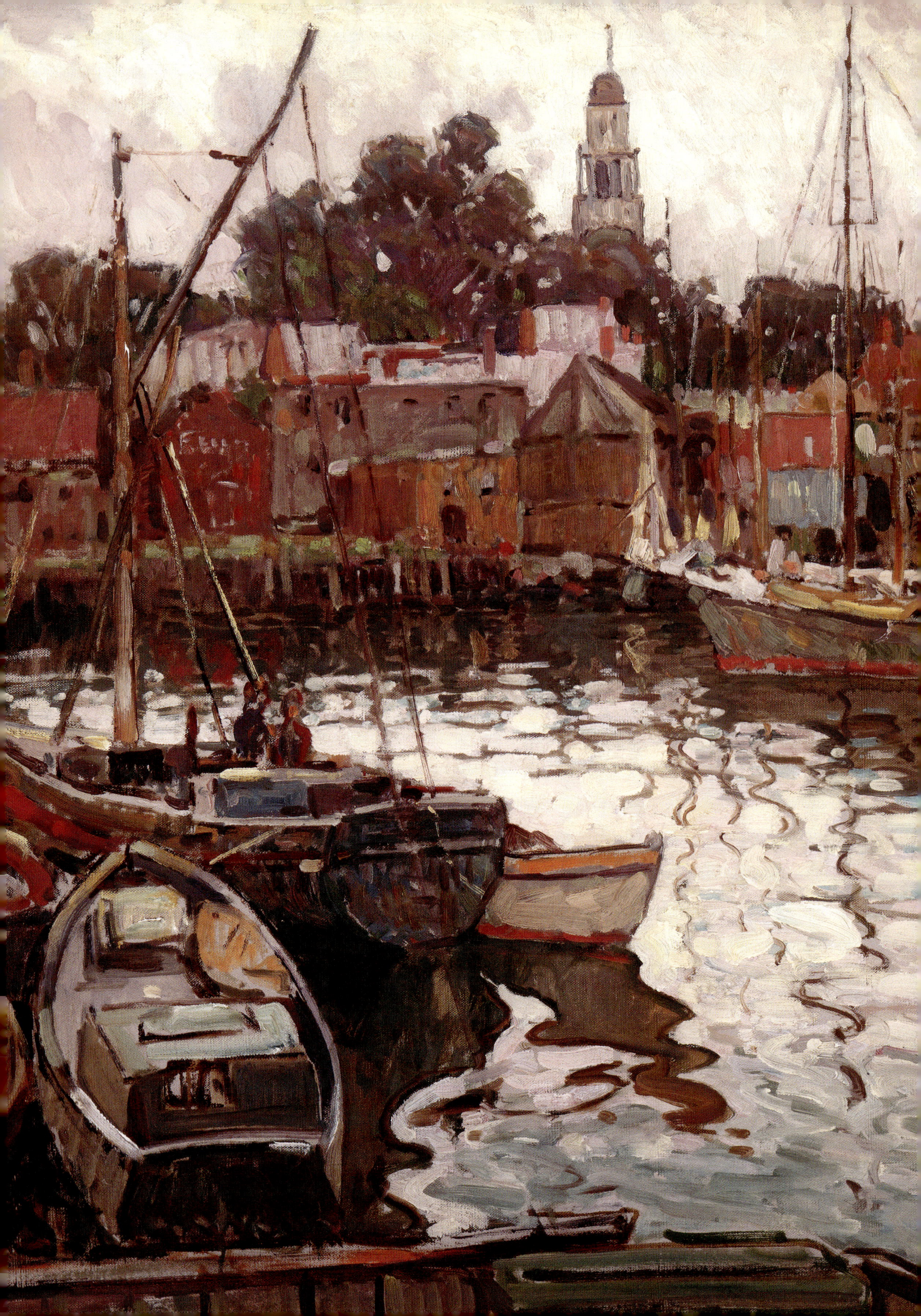

Two Kinds of Thinking

"Open to All and an Equal Chance for All."
— The Gloucester Society of Artists

Before the Gallery-on-the-Moors could embrace its seventh and final season in 1922, the majority of artists in East Gloucester had gathered for an August 5 meeting where they voted to create a new member organization for the benefit of all: painter, sculptor and graphic artist. Some of them, feeling the Gallery-on-the-Moors too far removed from the bustle of Rocky Neck, and up a steep hill at that, advocated a more central location on the waterfront. A small minority felt the gallery was too elitist, pandering only to personal friends of the Atwoods, while yet another faction believed an organization encouraging high standards of artistic thinking and free expression would be just what they needed.

One newspaper correspondent, under the heading "High Jinks in Gloucester," described the imbroglio with relish, "There is a most terrible war going on there in the art world. One bunch—the old standpatters—wants a jury; the new progressives say that art is democratic and that the public is the judge. They have come together over their differences of opinion worse than two steam engines in a movie wreck."[1]

The upshot of this debate was the emergence of the Gloucester Art Association, its president, despite criticism leveled at his running of the vilified Gallery-on-the-Moors, none other than William Atwood. This act alone suggests the majority of artists were grateful to the Atwoods for their attempt to bring a state-of-the-art exhibition space to Rocky Neck, and agreed with the premise that exhibitions should be juried to ensure consistently high quality. In fact, the only alteration of the original format was to house the organization in a larger building in a more accessible location, Thomas E. Reed's spacious warehouse on an East Main Street wharf, just across Smith Cove from Rocky Neck.

However, as in most member organizations, opinions abounded and on August 6, only one day after the naissance of the Gloucester Art Association (the name was changed to the North Shore Arts Association shortly after), a second meeting was held at Grace Horne's Rocky Neck gallery. There a number of disgruntled artists gathered to thrash out a new policy "Open to All and an Equal Chance for All."[2] The whole contretemps behind this clash of ideals, to judge or not judge, stemmed from the international protocol of academia practiced by the major art institutes such as the Paris Salon, the Royal Academy and New York's National Academy of Design. It was their policy to judge all works before they were accepted in order to maintain certain standards. However, in 1863, a number of French artists whose work was considered too radical for the traditional Salon took a stand and created the Salon des Refusés in protest of the Academy's decision to restrict and control what the public was allowed to

Detail
W. Lester Stevens
Gloucester Harbor
Oil on canvas, 36 x 36 in.
Collection of Dr. and Mrs. Joel E. Berenson

see. The Salon des Refusés attracted a lot of freethinking artists who preferred a modern approach to art, and who embraced the opportunity to show their work in public without it being judged by the conservative academicians. The 1913 Armory Show instigated a similar precept in New York, leading to the formation of the Society of Independent Artists in 1917. And now, this freethinking lifestyle had come to Rocky Neck, which, as a microcosm of American art, always reflected the larger concepts affecting the international art world. Although the Rocky Neck rebels tried to induce their comrades at the Gloucester Art Association to join them in their new vision of "democratic welfare in art,"[3] it became clear at a second meeting on August 16 that never the twain would meet. Instead, the 75 artists in attendance voted to form their own group, the Gloucester Society of Artists, whose motto dictated their creed: "Open to All and an Equal Chance for All!"

Charles Allan Winter and Stuart Davis, both vociferous opponents of Academy thinking, disdained anything that limited artistic expression, and insisted on a "No jury —no prize" policy, which was approved by all members. In later years they also instituted a policy of hanging paintings in alphabetical order according to artist, rather than arranging exhibitions around outstanding works in the traditional manner.

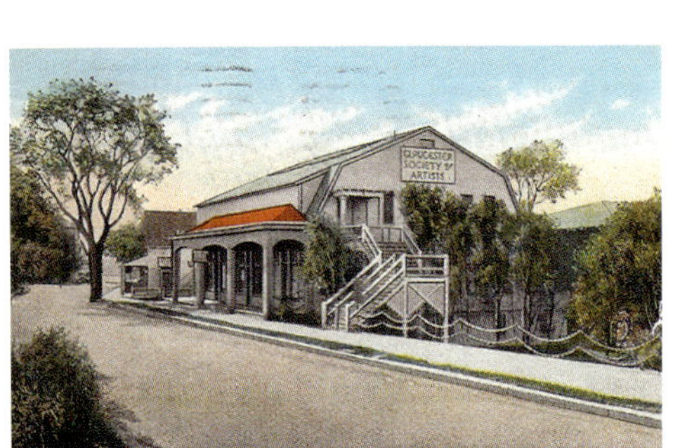

Gloucester Society of Artists Gallery,
Eastern Point Road, Gloucester
Postcard, c. 1927
Private collection

The Gloucester Society of Artists hosted its first exhibition on July 7, 1923, at 59 Eastern Point Road, near the Hawthorne Inn Casino. Some 125 paintings were entered in the exhibition, plus sculpture and graphics, from such artists as Theresa Bernstein, William Meyerowitz, Milton Avery, Charles and Alice Winter and Leonard Craske.

Leonard Craske is best known for his creation of Gloucester's internationally known statue, *Man at the Wheel*, memorializing the hardy Gloucester fishermen; many of whom were lost while bringing the ocean's bounty to the tables of America. The statue was based on an image by A.W. Buhler. Craske, who lived and worked on Rocky Neck for many years, won the commission in the face of strong competition from numerous classically trained sculptors living on Cape Ann when the statue was commissioned for Gloucester's 300th anniversary in 1923. He was born in London, England, in 1882, and came to the United States as a young man seeking his fortune in 1910. In later life, he became well known as a photographer as well as a sculptor, and so entrenched was he at Wonsonhurst, his home on Rocky Neck, that Lawrence Dame, art critic of the *Boston Sunday Herald* called him "a barnacle-firm habitué."[4] Craske was also a proud advocate for his colleagues, promoting their cause with local groups such as the Rotarians, declaring that artists "try to be idealists… certainly they are not commercial." He also suggested that the community had a duty "to help them because they are engaged in a most important work," and asked Gloucester's citizenry to "cooperate with the artists on the Cape, and help bring mutual satisfaction."[5] In the early 1930s, when the Depression was affecting most of America, Craske and the local artists called upon the people of Gloucester to be supportive of the artists in their hour of need, and the city was swift to rally to their cause. "The Chamber of Commerce and the merchants of Gloucester are giving testimonial to the fact that the artist is a very valuable member of the community," the *Gloucester Daily Times* announced. Although Gloucester was famous as "home of the fisherman," it was the artists "attracted to the ancient fishing port" as well as to Cape Ann's "stern and rockbound coast" who had elevated Gloucester to its exalted spot as a cultural center where the arts were not only appreciated but actively encouraged.[6]

Milton Avery
The Nancy B, 1944
Gouache, 21¼ x 30 in.
Cape Ann Historical Association,
Gloucester, Massachusetts
(2510-4)

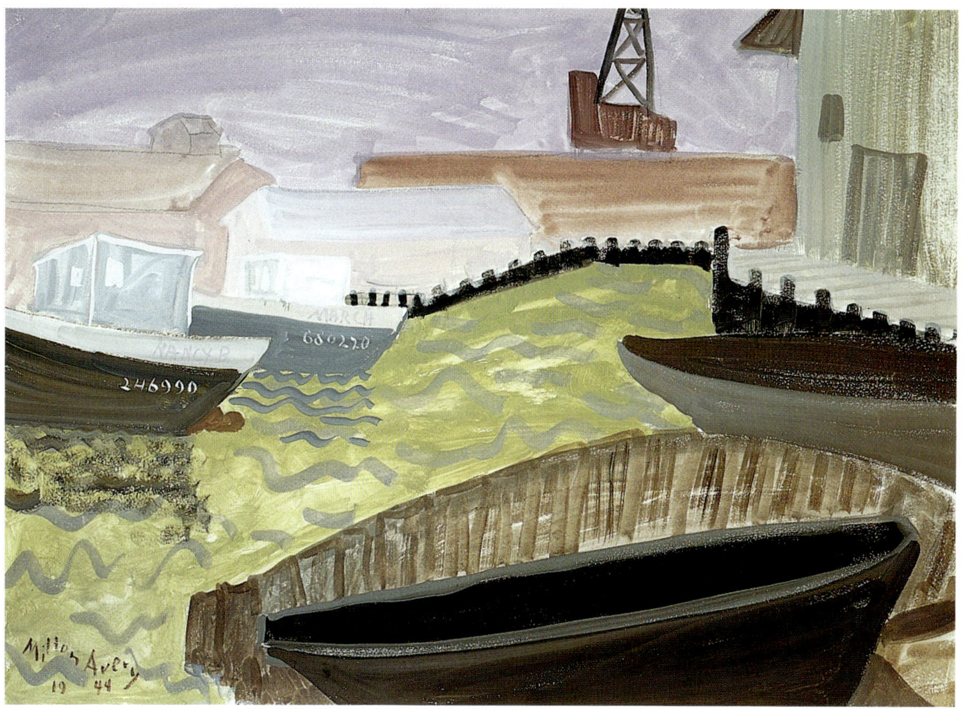

Milton Avery (1885-1965)

Unlike Craske, the transplanted Londoner, Milton Avery enjoyed summering in Gloucester but did not make it a permanent home. A native of Altmar, New York, Avery came to East Gloucester in the summer of 1920. At the time, he was considered more of an American Impressionist than an Abstractionist, influenced as he was by the works of John Twachtman and Ernest Lawson. Avery joined the Gloucester Society of Artists at its inception in 1923, and participated in the first euphoric exhibition. Proficient in charcoal, crayon, gouache, ink, oil and watercolor, Avery built a solid reputation as a painter, printmaker and graphic artist. In 1924, while summering in Gloucester, he met Sally Michel (1902-2003) a young New York art student, and when she returned to New York at the end of summer, Avery followed. They were married two years later, and maintained a New York studio together, painting side by side, critiquing each other's work. Both were graduates of New York's Art Students League and they worked in a similar style. By this time, Avery was moving away from the American Impressionist style of Twachtman and developing more as an Abstractionist with an eye to high key color and semi-figurative form with broad flat areas of color. This approach was less popular with the buying public, however, and for a time it was up to Sally, through her illustrative work, to support the family financially, until Milton's work became the vogue during the 1950s. The Averys had two children, Nancy and March, and Avery named the boats after them in his painting *The Nancy B.* The Averys summered in Gloucester for a number of years, often in the company of artist friends Mark Rothko and Adolph Gottlieb. Avery found the Gloucester environment—particularly painting alongside the ocean—stimulating to his artistic vision, and was fascinated by the intensity and diversity of color and texture found on Cape Ann's coastline. Later, he made pencil drawings on site, and translated them onto canvas in the studio, often using broad palette knife strokes to interpret nature in terms of color, shape and reflected form, rather than simple mass. Ultimately, Avery sought to express nature's fleeting moments in its simplest form: quintessence rather than concept abstraction.

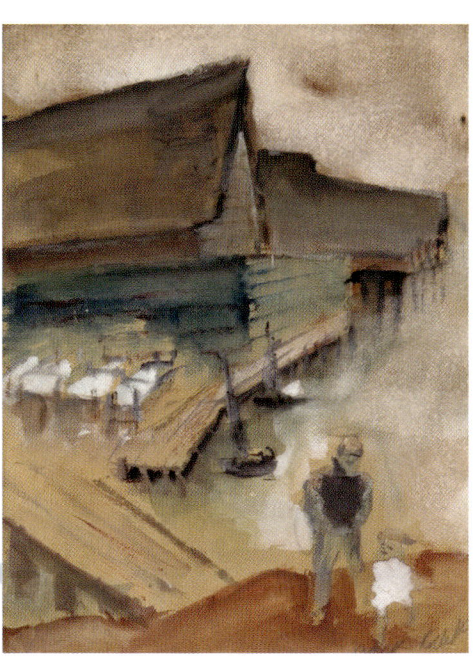

Mark Rothko
Sally and Milton Avery, East Gloucester,
1934
Gouache, 11½ x 9 in.
Collection of Mr. and Mrs. William H. Trayes

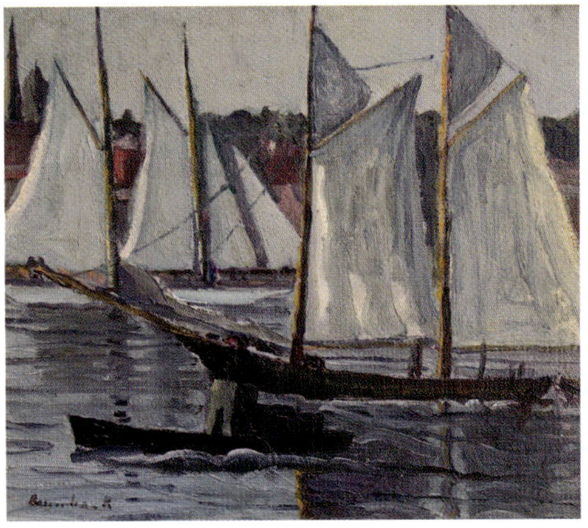

Louise Upton Brumback
Untitled
Oil on wood panel, 13 x 14¾ in.
Collection of Michael Storella

Louise Upton Brumback (1872-1929)

In comparison to Avery, Louise Upton Brumback was much more of a conventional painter, despite modernist leanings toward the non-jury system. Born in Rochester, New York, Brumback trained at the Shinnecock Summer School of Art with William Merritt Chase. Later, she settled in Kansas City, Missouri, with husband Frank Brumback, an insurance attorney, before moving to the East Coast in 1920, and thereafter splitting their time between Gloucester, New York, and Boston. Brumback was well liked and respected among her colleagues and at the inception of the Gloucester Society of Artists was voted in as the first president, a rare accolade in the early 1920s when women had only just received the right to vote in U.S. elections. Brumback was noted for her plein air landscapes, marine themes and floral still life paintings. Her unique style was pictorial, almost decorative in effect, with an interesting color sense coupled with conservative brushwork.

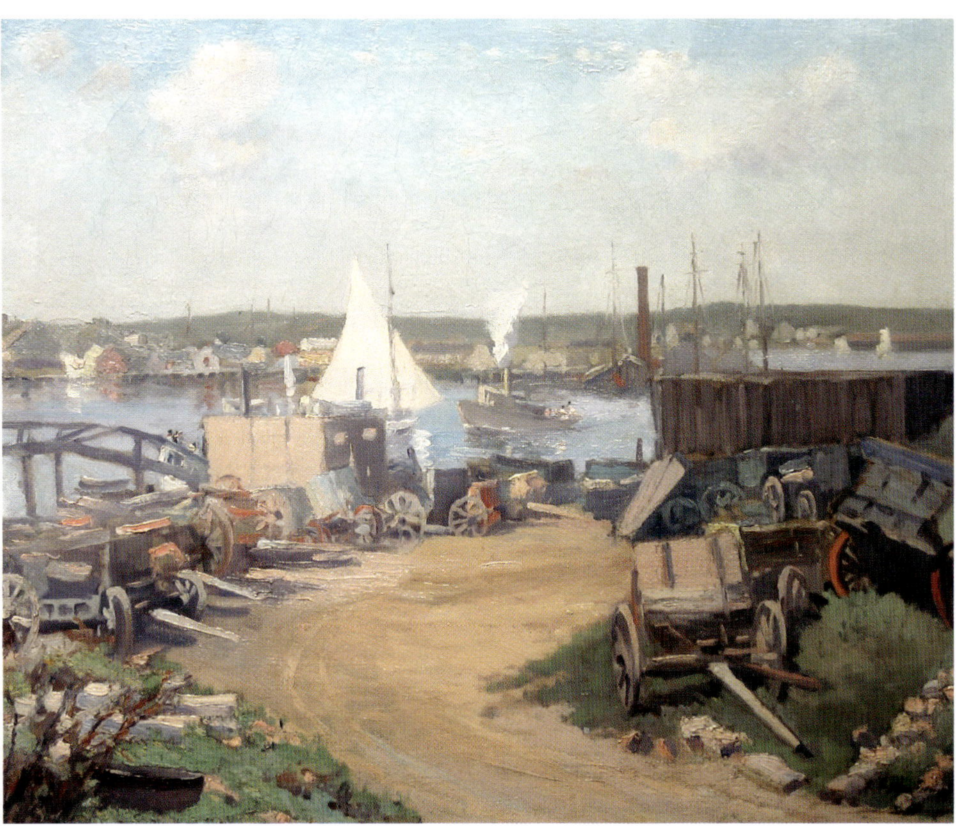

Louise Upton Brumback
Gloucester, Massachusetts
Oil on canvas, 23¾ x 28½ in.
Vose Galleries, Boston

W. Lester Stevens, N.A., A.W.S. (1888-1969)

Unlike many of the Rocky Neck painters, William Lester Stevens, the eldest of several children in a non-artistic family was that rarity, the Cape Ann native. Although Stevens did not live within the purview of Rocky Neck itself, he worked regularly around Gloucester Harbor and was a regular exhibitor at the local art galleries. Capitalizing on a childhood talent for drawing, and perhaps influenced by the artists already working on Cape Ann, Stevens studied first with local marine artist Parker S. Perkins and then spent four years at the School of the Museum of Fine Arts in Boston. There, he was fortunate to work under Edmund Tarbell and William Paxton, two leading practitioners in the newly emerging school of American Impressionism. Stevens admired the artistry of the American Impressionists who, unlike their French counterparts, did not sacrifice line for the fleeting moment. He proved an apt pupil and after only two years

W. Lester Stevens
Gloucester Harbor
Oil on canvas, 36 x 36 in.
Collection of Dr. and Mrs. Joel E. Berenson

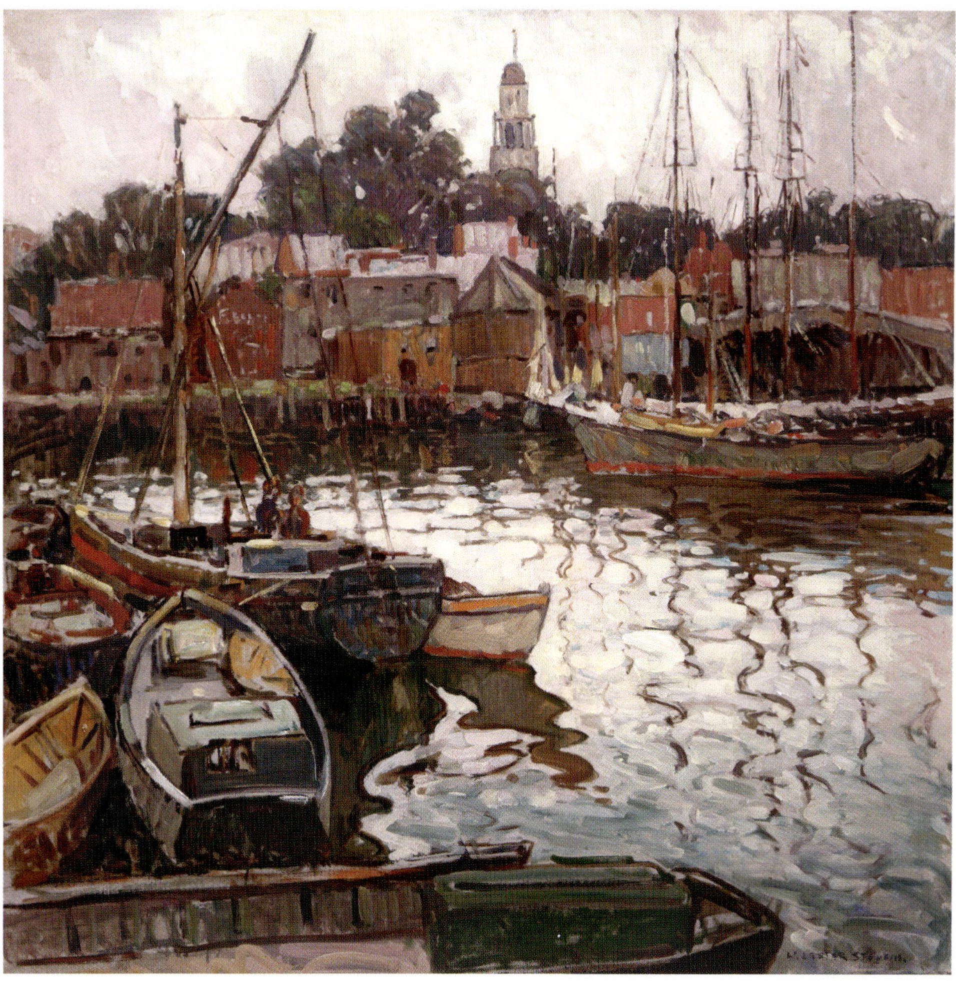

at the Museum School was exhibiting with the Art Institute of Chicago, the Pennsylvania Academy of Fine Arts, and even the prestigious National Academy of Design in their 1912-1913 Winter Exhibition. Upon completion of his studies at the Museum School, Stevens returned to Cape Ann to establish himself as a professional artist. He insisted a painter should be accomplished and also well read, and practiced this as much as possible himself. Although Stevens was a sensitive man, he often repressed his finer feelings in favor of presenting a less vulnerable face to the world. "Great men are isolated and unhappy creatures," he once wrote. "Over sensitive, little understood—lacking all the requirements of the rank and file of humanity. This leads one to the question, is it worthwhile? 'Art is not a pleasure party, it is a fight,' a struggle for self-expression."[7]

Stevens was never afraid to express himself. He believed fine art was the result of a fine mind, and was a strong advocate for establishing a public gallery on Cape Ann. He went so far as to write to a local newspaper in an effort to meet with like-minded people. "I feel," he said, "the fine things of music, art and literature should be the possession of the humblest man who has the mentality to appreciate them."[8] He was invited to show at the Gallery-on-the-Moors, and when that closed its doors in 1922, became a member of the newly formed North Shore Arts Association. When a split formed between those artists supporting the jury system and those looking for a more democratic approach, Stevens—like several other painters in the colony—felt it was appropriate to support both views and became a member of the breakaway Gloucester Society of Artists also. Reviewing Stevens' Cape Ann landscapes, the art critic of the *Boston Evening Tribune* wrote "[Stevens] manifests a sensitive, quick responsive eye for transient effects, which

W. Lester Stevens
Gloucester Docks, c. 1925
Oil on canvas, 24 x 30 in.
Private collection
Photo courtesy of Comenos Fine Arts, Boston

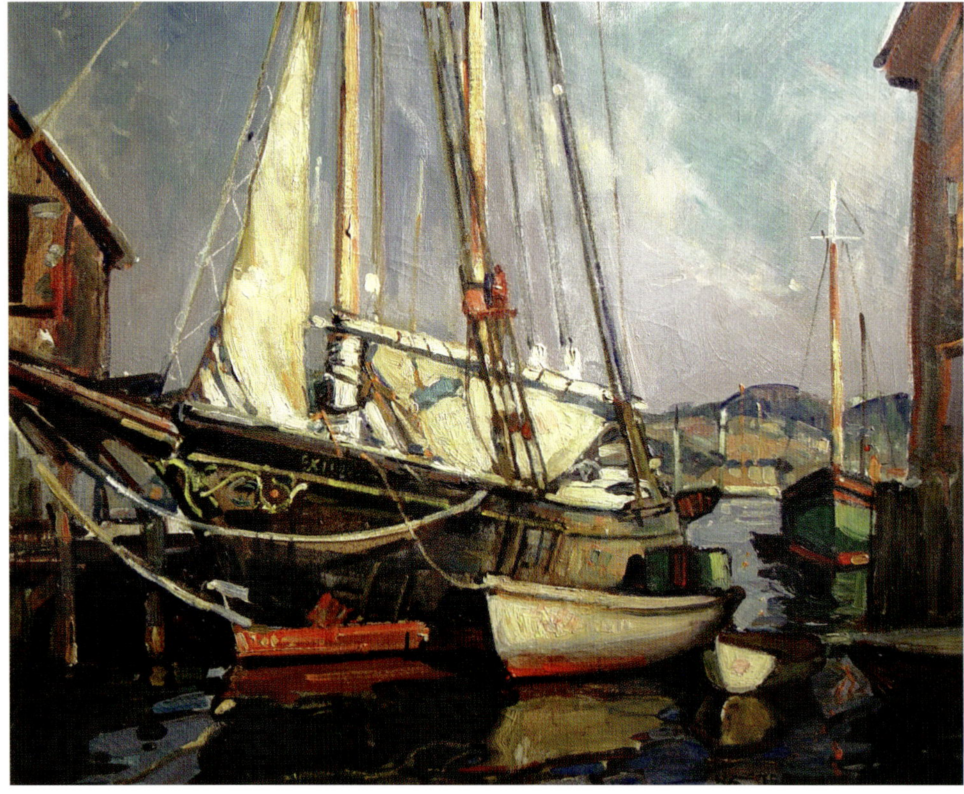

W. Lester Stevens
View from East Gloucester
Oil on canvas, 14 x 18 in.
James B. Hand Fine Art, Gloucester, Massachusetts

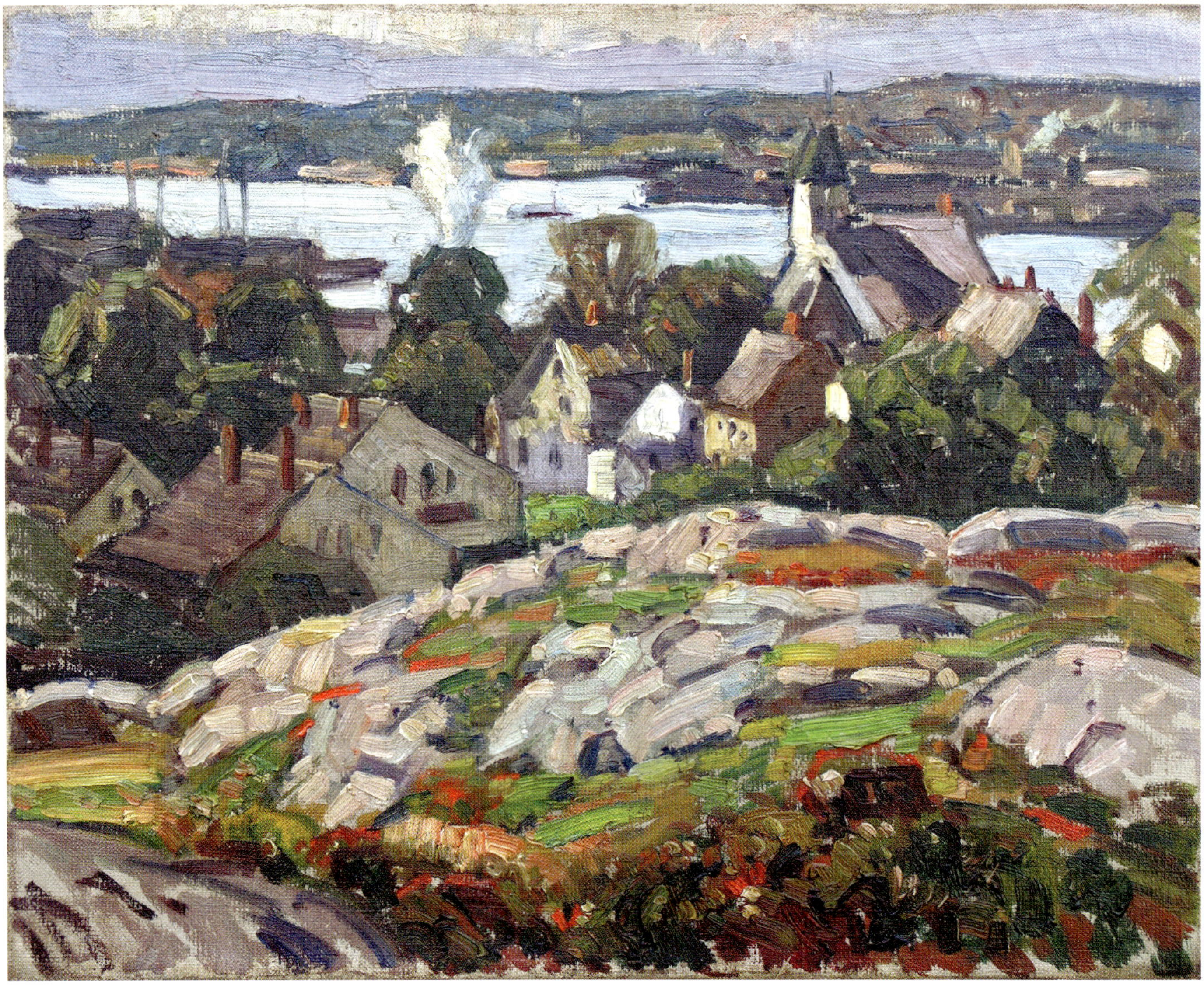

gives great vitality to his impressions."[9] In 1934, discouraged at what he saw as local commercialism, Stevens moved his family to the rural outreaches of the Berkshires where he continued to paint and teach. He died in Greenfield, Massachusetts, June 10, 1969, shortly before his 81st birthday.

Harry A. Vincent, A.N.A. (1862-1931)

Like fellow Rockporter Lester Stevens, Harry A. Vincent did not live on Rocky Neck itself, but he aligned himself with the local galleries preferring the ambiance of East Gloucester to his adopted town on the opposite side of Cape Ann. Vincent was already well established on the progressive American art scene as a plein air landscape and marine painter when he arrived on Cape Ann in 1918. Born in Chicago, Illinois,

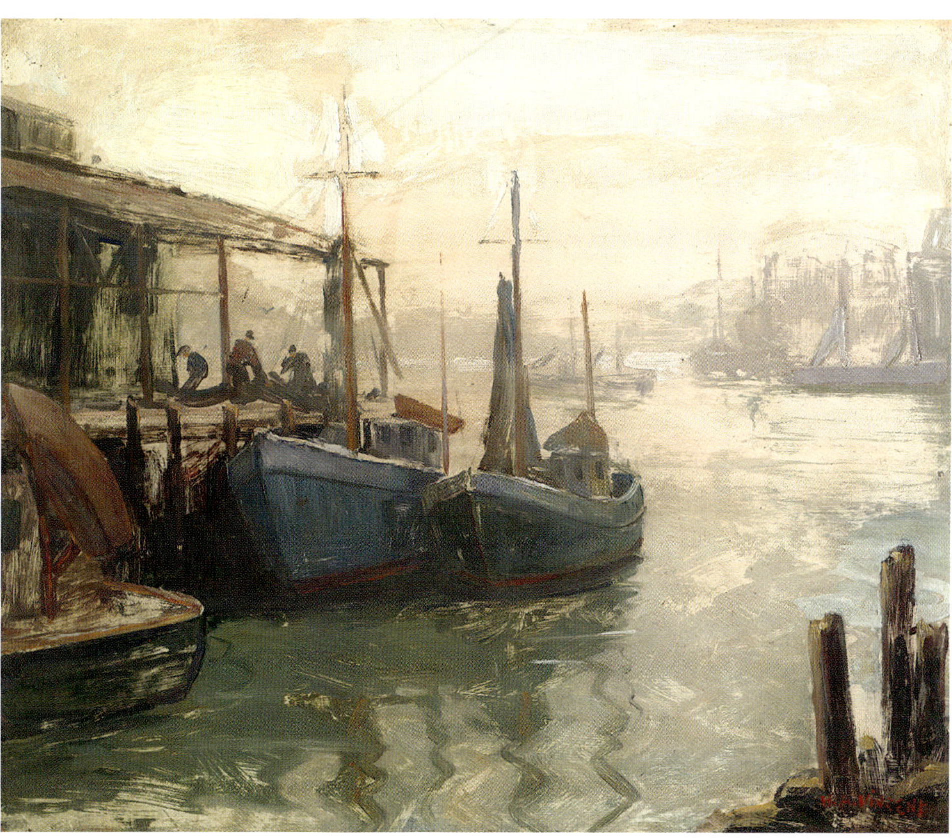

Harry A. Vincent
Gloucester Harbor, c. 1920
Oil on board, 19½ x 23½ in.
Spanierman Gallery, LLC, New York

Vincent claimed to be self-taught and his work displays an intuitive style rather than an academic hand. He left Chicago in the late 1800s and moved to New York, where he lived for 20 years. In the early part of the 1900s he began making regular trips to Cape Cod in search of new material and worked his way northward until he got to Cape Ann, where he found everything he was looking for, including light, atmosphere and the graceful Gloucester schooner. Vincent spent hours painting in East Gloucester, enjoying the character of the harbor and the color and bustle of the wharves, where fishermen were always mending nets and readying their ships for another trip to the Grand Banks. A quiet soul and dedicated to his craft, friends described Vincent as "a man of sound and fair judgment… kind and generous with his fellow men and… always anxious to think the best of everyone."[10] He exhibited at the Gallery-on-the-Moors, and when they closed, joined the fledgling North Shore Arts Association in East Gloucester, serving as a board member as well as a participating artist. He died in 1931.

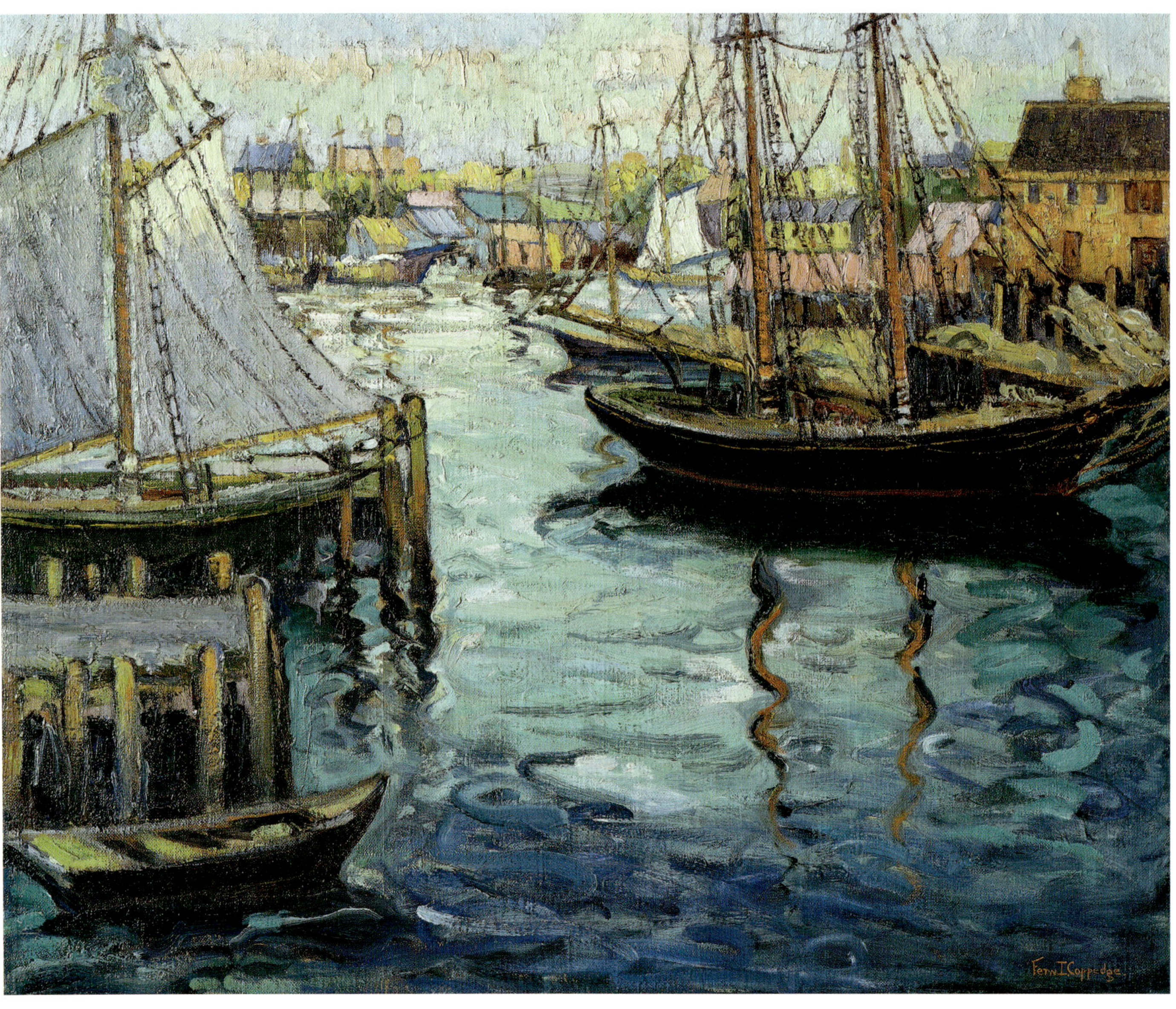

Fern Coppedge
Gloucester Harbor
Oil on canvas, 25 x 30 in.
Collection of Dr. and Mrs. Joel E. Berenson

Fern Coppedge (1883-1951)

While the men certainly outnumbered the women artists in the early twentieth-century art world, the women were no less proficient, and oftentimes showed subtler nuances than their male counterparts. Fern Isabel Coppedge is perhaps better known as a New Hope, Pennsylvania, artist and also as one of the Philadelphia Ten; a group of women artists who banded together to gain greater recognition for their talents through a show of artistic strength. Coppedge showed with them between 1922-1935 yet always maintained an individual style displaying a keen knowledge of radiant color and the fleeting effect of light upon nature. Coppedge was born Fern Isabel Kuns in Decatur, Illinois, but moved regularly while studying at the Art Institute of Chicago (1908-1910), the Art Students League in New York, where she worked with Frank Vincent DuMond and William Merritt Chase and, finally, at the Pennsylvania Academy of the Fine Arts where she came within the sphere of influence of Daniel Garber. While at the Pennsylvania Academy, Coppedge (now married to amateur artist Robert Coppedge) also took private lessons with Henry B. Snell, who had a summer school in Gloucester and may have encouraged Coppedge to visit Rocky Neck. A committed plein air painter, Coppedge's rendition of *Gloucester Harbor* shows strength in both boldness of color and execution. "People used to think me queer when I was a little girl because I saw deep purples and reds and violets in a field of snow," Coppedge once said. "I used to be hurt over it until I gave up trying to understand people and concentrated on my love and understanding of landscapes. Then it didn't make any difference."[11] After 1929, Coppedge stayed closer to home in New Hope and spent the rest of her life painting local scenery. She remained a member of the North Shore Arts Association until 1934, and died in 1951.

Oscar Anderson (1873-1953)

Oscar Anderson, long time president of the Gloucester Society of Artists, was a man of vision who introduced us to not only his unique view of Rocky Neck, but also that well-known artist's friend: the Anderson easel. Elsewhere in the world, this classic piece of equipment is known as the "Gloucester easel," but local vernacular will always put it in terms of its artistic creator.

Born in 1873 on Gotland, a small island in the Baltic Sea a hundred miles off the Swedish coast, Anderson came from a family of farmers who were, at first, nonplussed by Oscar's decision to become a painter rather than follow in his father's footsteps. Eventually, Oscar not only left home to become an artist but also left the country, following his older brother to America. Anderson was seventeen years old when he arrived

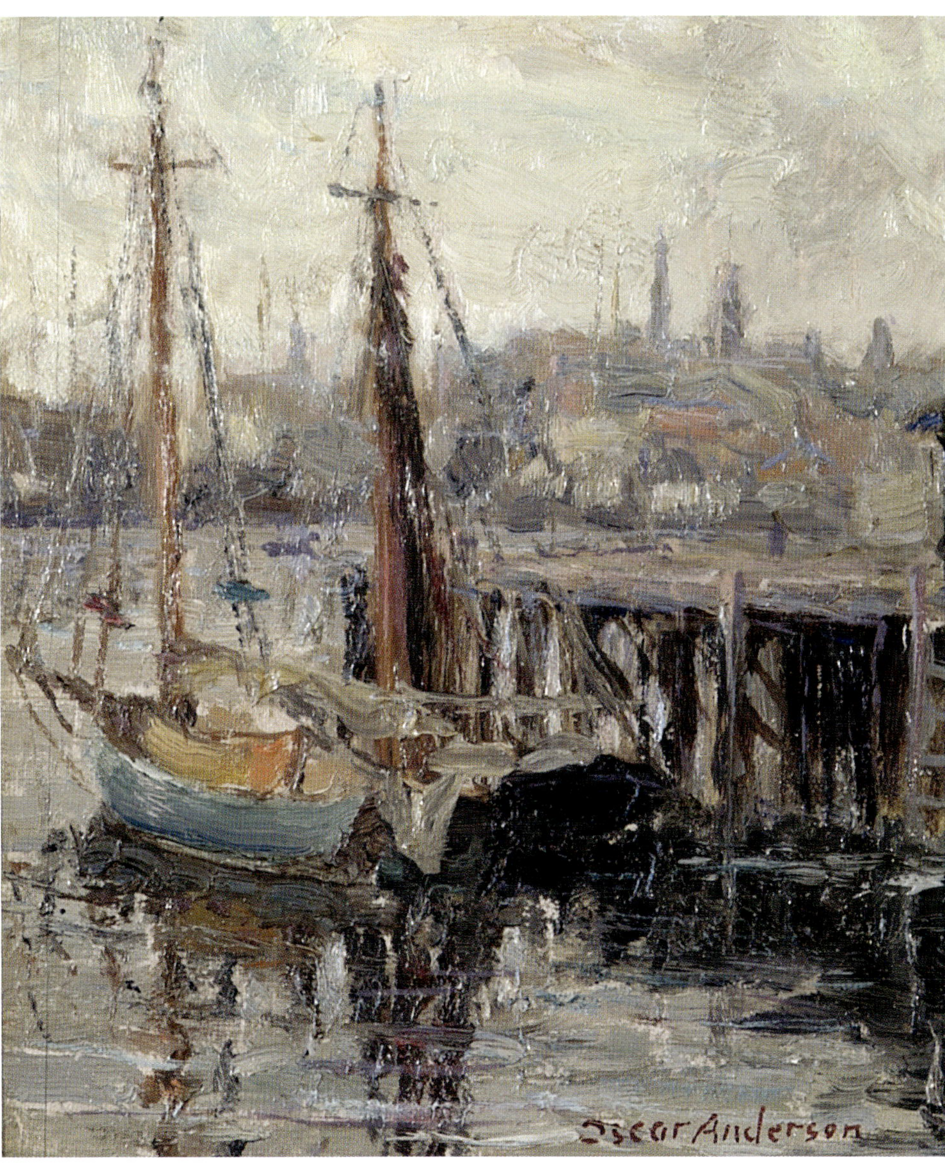

Oscar Anderson
View from East Gloucester
Oil, 10 x 8 in.
Mosher Gallery, Rockport, Massachusetts

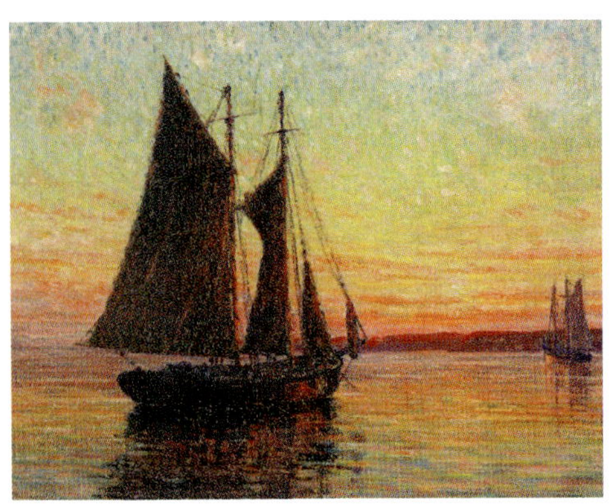

Oscar Anderson
Sunset, Gloucester Harbor
Oil on canvas, 22 x 28 in.
Roger King Fine Art, Newport, Rhode Island

in the United States, and promptly made his way to Connecticut where he worked first as a farmhand, then later as an employee of Lange & Fladd, a German decorating firm, where he stayed for more than eight years. Although Anderson does not appear to have had a formal art education, he did study for a number of years with Charles Noel Flagg, a Hartford-based, Paris-trained artist specializing in portraits. In 1895, Anderson married Alida Charlotte Lindberg and settled in Hartford, becoming closely associated with the Connecticut League of Art Students. In 1908, Anderson made an extended trip to Gloucester. "I fitted myself up a small studio in a little white cottage on East Main Street," he said in "The Lookout," a 1953 column in the *Gloucester Daily Times*. "I stayed on all through the winter, working out of doors, regardless of weather, battling to interpret the moods of nature at dawn and twilight, in calm as well as in the tempestuous fury of the winter storms." An article in the *Cape Ann Shore* of August 8, 1931, reported the same event: "The winter of 1907-08 was continuously severe with the harbor frozen solid for three weeks, and every day… Anderson could be seen tramping across the ice to some point where he would sit and paint the whole day through." Shortly after, the Andersons, together with daughter Edith, settled in Gloucester permanently, building a home and studio on Banner Hill, overlooking Gloucester Harbor where decades earlier Duveneck, Twachtman, Hassam and countless others had also found artistic inspiration.

Early in his Gloucester career, Anderson established a studio gallery in a loft at 73 Rocky Neck Avenue, a building once used by Colonel Charley Fred Wonson's Salt Fish Company, and which later became The Rudder Restaurant. As early as 1914, Anderson instituted an annual "Gallery on the Wharf" exhibition featuring his own paintings as well as works by artist friends such as Augustus Buhler, Lester Stevens, and T. V. C. Valenkamph. Gregarious by nature, Anderson enjoyed the close-knit community atmosphere on Rocky Neck and was an active participant in social activities such as the riotous annual Fakirs' Ball, as well as serving as an officer of the Gloucester Society of Artists, first as vice president and later as president (c. 1928-1935). In 1934, as part of the government-sponsored Works Progress Administration, Anderson and his friend Frederick J. Mulhaupt collaborated to create a series of murals for Gloucester's Central Grammar School. Sadly, these are no longer on view.

Oscar Anderson spent the major part of his life, and certainly his artistic career, on Cape Ann, and his paintings exemplified everything the city is rightly famous for, especially its historic harbor and fishing fleet. Members of the art colony were shocked and saddened when Anderson, a widower for thirteen years, died suddenly, around June 20, 1953, while visiting his daughter in Cincinnati.

Carl H. Nordstrom (1876-1965)

Cape Ann painter Carl Harold Nordstrom, noted for his distinctive style and colorful palette, was born in Chelsea, Massachusetts, on September 18, 1876. He began formal studies with Eric Pape at his School of Art in Boston, and later worked with George L. Noyes in Gloucester and Charles Hawthorne in Provincetown. Adept in both oil and watercolor, Nordstrom specialized in landscape and marine themes although he also enjoyed painting floral subjects, still life studies and murals. His marine paintings, in particular, show an interesting sense of composition coupled with strong draftsmanship and bold color, at a time when the old fishing schooners—plus their "wharf rats" and docks—evoked a sense of character and resilience. He maintained a summer residence and studio at 78 Rocky Neck Avenue from where he directed the popular

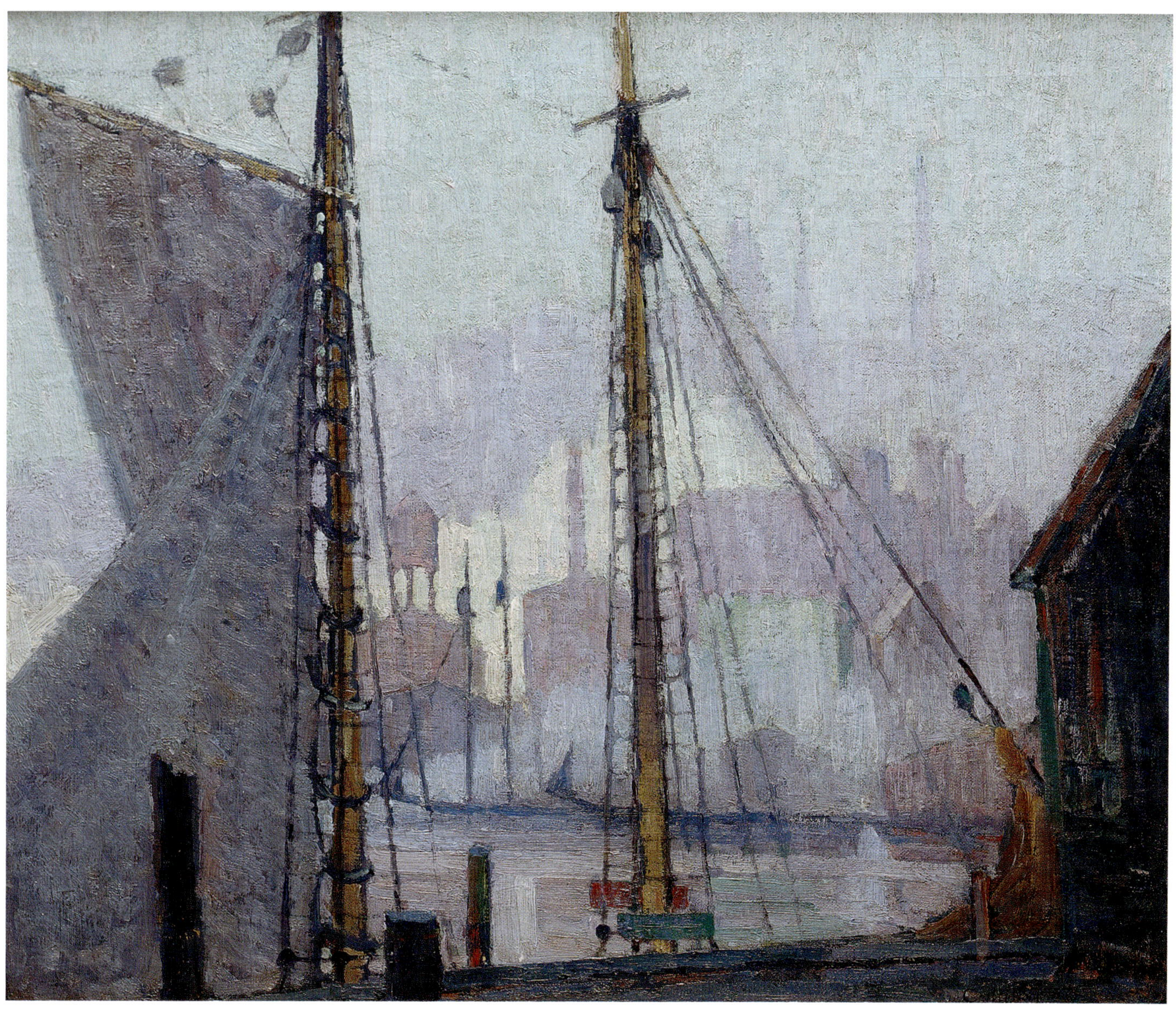

Carl Nordstrom
Gloucester Harbor from Reed's Wharf,
c. 1925
Oil on canvas, 22 x 26 in.
Private collection

Nordstrom Summer School of Art. While living on Rocky Neck, Nordstrom became an active and enthusiastic member of the North Shore Arts Association, beginning in 1932 and lasting for the next twelve years. "Besides being a member," he wrote in his biographical outline, "I was chairman of the Decorating Committee on Grounds decorating. Summer carnivals were held each season for the purpose of raising funds for the Society. I held the Committee Chairmanship on this for 4 seasons (2 carnivals held on Rocky Neck and 2 held on the NSAA grounds). Did similar committee work as an active member in Gloucester Society of Artists doing the ground decorations on two Carnivals for that Society."[12] Nordstrom was also an enthusiastic participant in the local social scene. On August 16, 1930, page 5 of the *Cape Ann Shore* reported, "Carl Harold Nordstrom won Honorable Mention at the Fakirs' Ball for his costume—"Turk."

Nordstrom was particularly active as a Rocky Neck painter during the 1930s and '40s, when his marine paintings were acclaimed by both the public and critics. On August 28, 1937, under the heading "Cape Ann Artists Show Works at Magnolia," the *Cape Ann Shore* declared, "Carl Nordstrom shows finely executed surf paintings." Although Nordstrom was very much a traditionalist, it was his unique sense of composition and design that set him apart from his contemporaries. He was not afraid to take chances with shifting, exaggerating, and even eliminating elements of the scene if it better suited his design, and with the Gloucester fishing fleet still very much in evidence in those days, he had a wealth of material on his Rocky Neck doorstep to contemplate and capture on canvas. One can discern the influence of both Hawthorne and Noyes in these works, in particular the effect of light, and the colorist's palette. Hawthorne was a great advocate of observing the design—the envelope of light and atmosphere on the scene—rather than the scene itself. "Paint things you can almost reach," he told his students, "make a veritable still life out of everything you do. Get up close to whatever you want to paint.... If you are painting a ship get down beside it and look up—the thing you are painting should fill your canvas."[13] Nordstrom certainly took Hawthorne's advice to heart, and loved to portray the towering masts, sails and rigging of the local schooners, frequently designing them to dominate his composition. Interestingly, Nordstrom's watercolors tend to be less highly colored; yet, these too owe much to spontaneous brushwork and a remarkable sense of relationships. In later years, Nordstrom relinquished his summer home and studio in East Gloucester and taught pupils in his studio at Nabby's Point, Ipswich, instead. However, he retained cordial ties with Rocky Neck and was a frequent contributor to the Cape Ann Festival of the Arts during the 1950s. He passed away in 1965.

Nordstrom was not the only artist who enjoyed participating, and frequently creating, the lively and flamboyant Fakirs' Ball of the 1920s and 30s. The *Gloucester Daily Times* covered the first ball in their Thursday, August 23, 1923, edition, reporting,

> *A large gathering completely filled the casino of the Hawthorne Inn and the gallery of the Gloucester Society of Artists at their first annual affair the "Fakirs' Ball," held last evening.*
>
> *The affair presented a rare and unique gathering of folks along the North Shore, prominent country-wide in the arts, writers, artists, sculptors, painters and was a social success of great importance not only for the local art association, but also for all the art clubs along the shore. The ball drew many of the prominent summer residents from along the North Shore as well as the artists.*
>
> *Many people were gathered outside when at 8.30 o'clock, the grand march from the clubhouse to the casino took place. This was a wonderful spectacle and the splendor of the affair may be judged from the fact that the costumes were all designed and made by artists who know how to present colors and designs which will attract.*
>
> *The casino was beautifully arranged, posters in watercolors depicting scenes and characterizations being made for decorative purposes by all the artists. From the girders, balloons... lent to the color of the occasion.*
>
> *The affair was under the direct charge of Mrs. Alice Fischer Harcourt a New York actress, and Leonard Craske, a well-known sculptor. M. Harmer was the master of ceremonies.... These included a performance of two of the artists dressed as trick horses and these animals chose the King and Queen of the Fakirs' ball.*
>
> *It will be remembered that in the first exhibition of the Gloucester Society of Artists, the president of the association had the picture of a "Cow on Dogtown" as one of her hangings. Some of the artists took advantage of the opportunity offered last evening and two dressed in a figure which represented a cow, this costume being labeled, "Mrs. Brumback's Cow."*
>
> *In the brilliantly decorated casino, the balloon dance was a feature, a number of balloons being released on the floor and the couple breaking the last balloon being adjudged the winners. The bursting of the balloons created much fun and the prize was awarded Miss Deike of Cleveland and Rocky Neck, and her partner.*

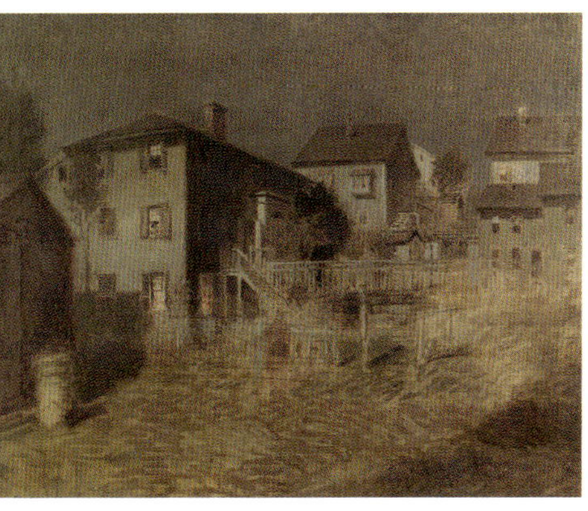

Paul Cornoyer
Old House, Moonlight, Gloucester
c. 1910
Oil and charcoal on paper on canvas, 22 x 27 in.
Spanierman Gallery, LLC, New York

The first prize for the best costume was awarded Eben F. Comins, who wore a costume representing an artist's palette, his head protruding through the opening and he was daubed in all colors even his face receiving liberal treatment....

Music was furnished by Sewall's augmented orchestra. At 11 o'clock refreshments were served in the clubhouse gallery under the direction of Mrs. Louise Upton Brumback, and her assistants. Dancing was then continued until midnight.[14]

Heady days, indeed! Artists, for the most part, are gregarious creatures and in the early part of the twentieth-century, before modern distractions created a more insular lifestyle, they loved nothing more than getting together with kindred spirits for a little relaxation and fun after a hard day at the easel.

Meanwhile, at the same time as the Gloucester Society of Artists was opening with frivolity and flair, its estranged sibling, the North Shore Arts Association, was also drawing its fair share of attention with its opening exhibition. The 230 paintings, graphics and sculpture were juried in by Hugh Breckenridge, George Noyes, William Paxton, and Harry Vincent, and included some of the best painters in American art: A. T. Hibbard, Felicie Waldo Howell, Frederick Mulhaupt, Susette Schultz Keast, and Gertrude Fiske, as well as crossovers from the Gloucester Society of Artists, Theresa Bernstein and William Meyerowitz. The first exhibition was a great success, despite the untimely passing of vice president Paul Cornoyer shortly before the opening.

Paul Cornoyer, A.N.A. (1864-1923)

Paul Cornoyer hailed from St. Louis, and began his art education at the St. Louis School of Art before leaving for Paris in 1889 to study at the Académie Julian under Lefebvre and Constant. After five years, during which he absorbed much of the French Impressionist mannerisms, Cornoyer returned to St. Louis where he practiced a personal style of impressionism based on moderation of tone and brushstroke to evoke

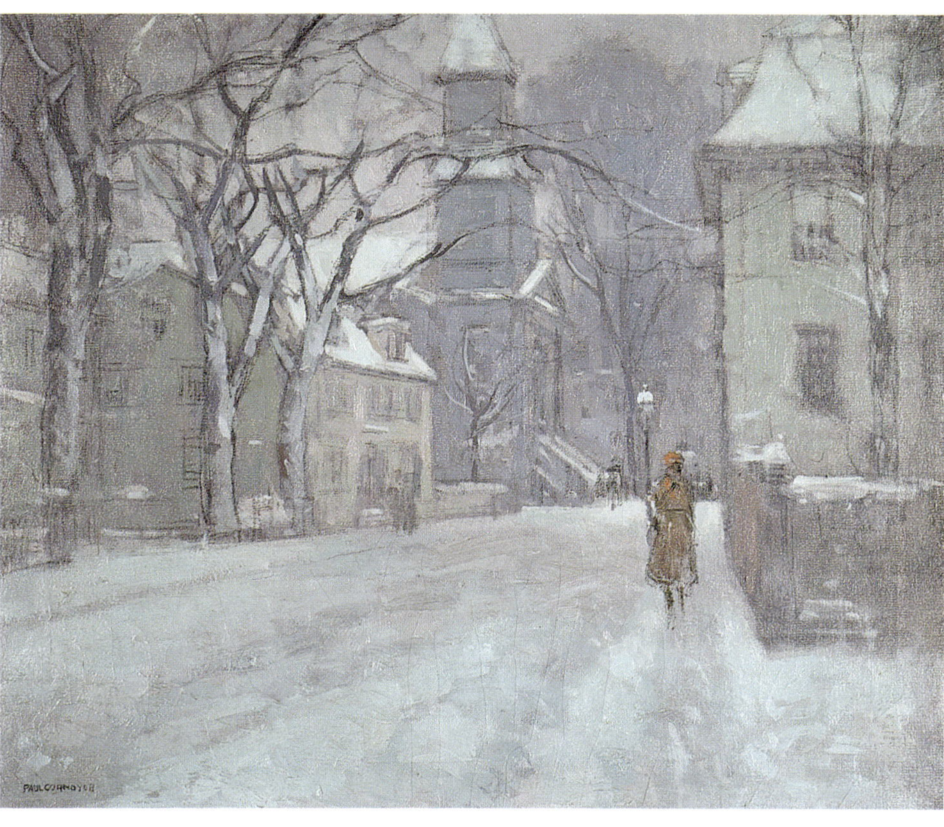

Paul Cornoyer
December
Oil, 22¼ x 27 in.
Cape Ann Historical Association, Gloucester, Massachusetts

lyricism and harmony in his plein air landscapes. Although he was awarded a number of significant commissions over the next few years, Cornoyer especially liked painting atmospheric cityscapes. William Merritt Chase was impressed enough with Cornoyer's work to purchase a painting and subsequently encouraged Cornoyer to leave St. Louis for New York in order to surround himself with dynamic subject matter and like-minded comrades, such as John Twachtman and Childe Hassam. Over the next few years, Cornoyer supplemented his income with teaching at the Mechanics Institute and exhibiting at the major shows, including the National Academy of Design in New York, the Corcoran Gallery in Washington, D. C., and the Art Institute of Chicago. He also became friendly with Charles and Alice Winter as well as John Sloan, and was a regular guest at the Red Cottage in East Gloucester. Eventually, he acquired his own studio in East Gloucester and settled down to teaching and painting around the area. He became a great friend of Frederick J. Mulhaupt who, in a touching eulogy described Cornoyer as a genial and generous soul. "His absolute sincerity in all things," Mulhaupt said, "his honesty of purpose, the capacity for doing things for others without ever a thought of the trouble it took to do it or the thanks to be received for it… sent many a less fortunate one, who came to him, away happy."[15] Cornoyer passed away suddenly in July 1923.

Hugh H. Breckenridge, A. N. A. (1870-1937)

With the untimely demise of Paul Cornoyer shortly before the opening exhibition, it was up to Hugh Henry Breckenridge to step in as vice president of the North Shore Arts Association. Breckenridge, like Charles Allen Winter and William Meyerowitz, was a traditionally trained painter who embraced traditional mores as well as an avant-garde approach to art. Born in Leesburg, Virginia, Breckenridge showed an early interest in the artistic process and moved to Philadelphia around 1887 to attend the Pennsylvania Academy of the Fine Arts. After four years of intensive study, Breckenridge was awarded the PAFA's coveted Cresson Traveling Fellowship and left for Paris where he attended the Académie Julian, working under the great classicist William Adolphe Bouguereau. However, Breckenridge's sojourn in Paris came at a time when the maelstrom of French post-impressionism was causing friction in the halls of academia and, caught up in the excitement, Breckenridge absorbed much of the frenetic energy, freshness and fondness for high key color spots to denote mood and mass that was flooding the French capital. Returning to Philadelphia, Breckenridge supported himself through a teaching post at the Pennsylvania Academy and with commissioned works, including portraits, landscapes and still life subjects, which he executed with impressionistic flair. Interestingly, although Breckenridge explored many styles himself (he has been described as an abstractionist, a neo-impressionist, a modernist and an innovator), throughout his teaching career he advocated the basics of color, composition and drawing as a sound foundation from which students could explore and experiment with the creative process. *The Schooner Seagull*, 1927, dates to an era when Breckenridge was already settled as a summer visitor on Rocky Neck and his summer school was in its eighth year. The school attracted numerous students, particularly women—among them Harriet Randall Lumis and Susette Schultz Keast—who exemplified Breckenridge's complex technique of impressionist seeing with high key broken color brushwork in their own work. Breckenridge loved Gloucester for its wealth of challenging subject matter. Here, he could transpose the traditional view of boats, docks and water into sophisticated planes of jeweled color, light and shadow, creating painterly mosaics of familiar views.

Hugh Breckenridge
The White Schooner, c. 1922
Oil on board, 10½ x 14¼ in.
(This work is two-sided with a painting entitled *Gloucester Harbor,* c. 1934 on reverse)
Collection of Mr. and Mrs. William H. Trayes

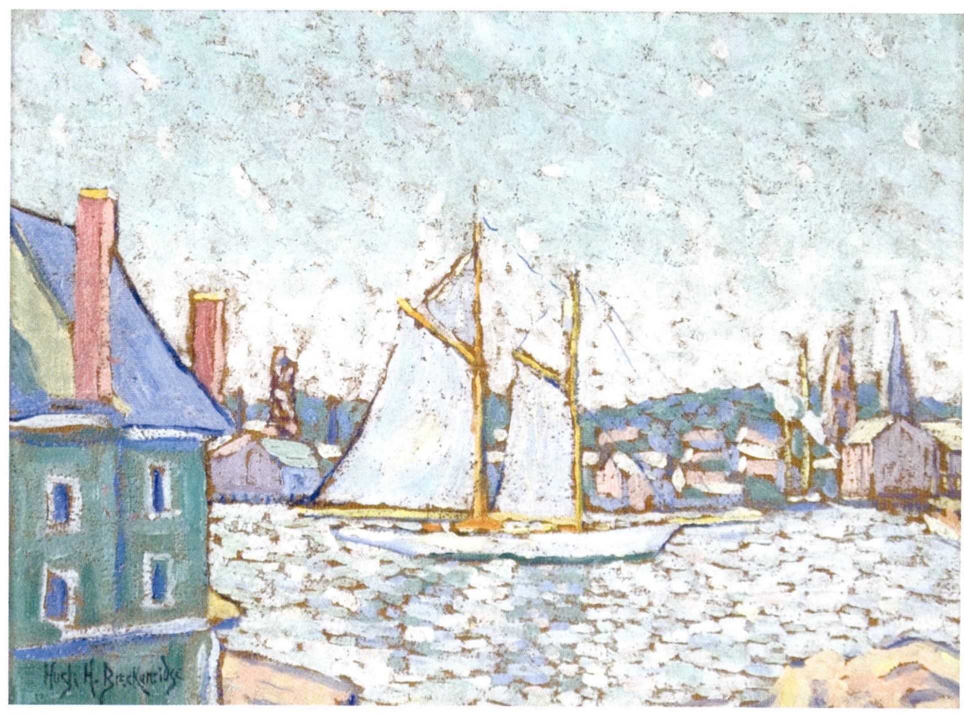

Hugh H. Breckenridge
The Schooner Seagull, 1927
Oil on canvas, 23⅛ x 40⅛ in.
Hollis Taggart Galleries, New York

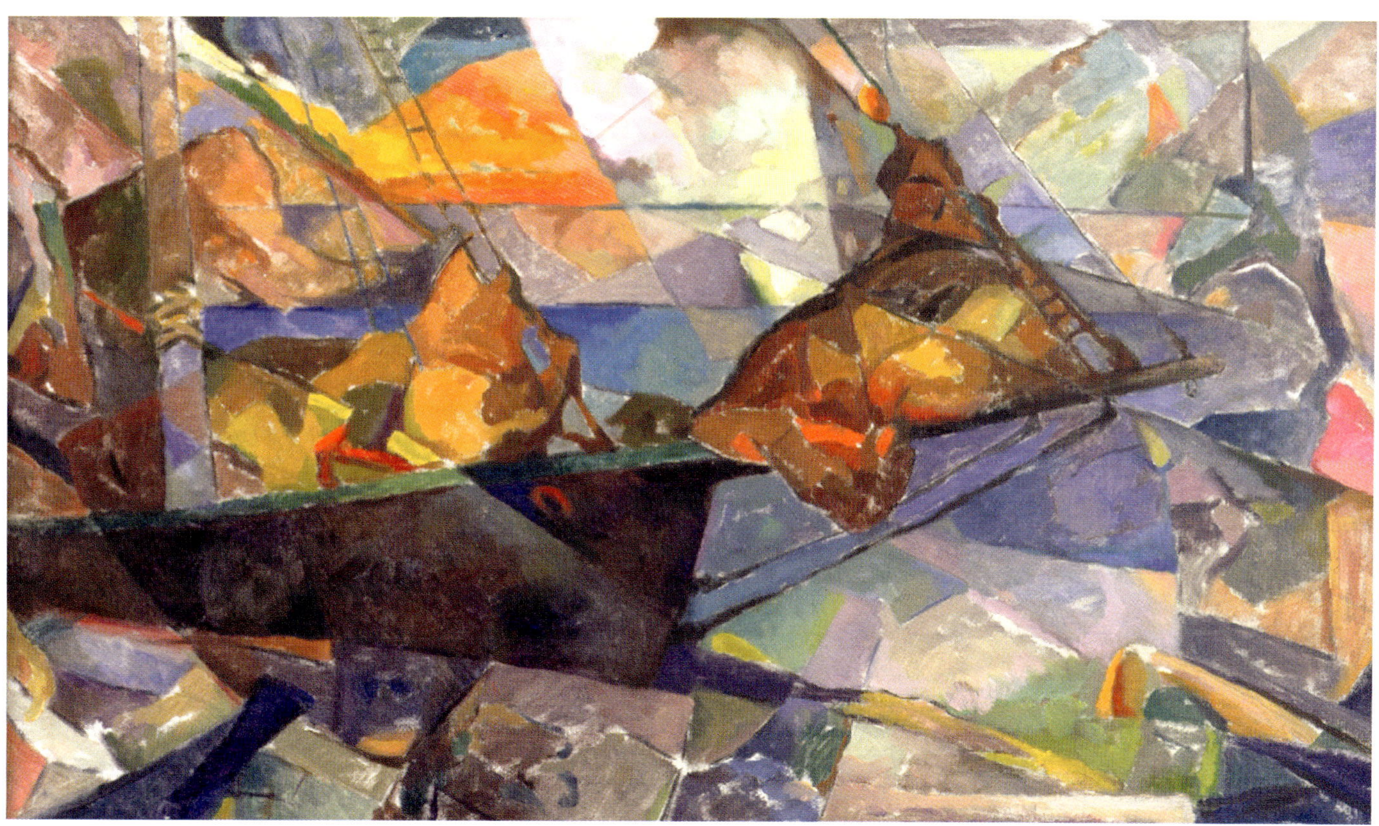

Hugh Breckenridge
Cape Ann Shore, 1924
Oil on canvas, 25 x 30 in.
Cape Ann Historical Association,
Gloucester, Massachusetts

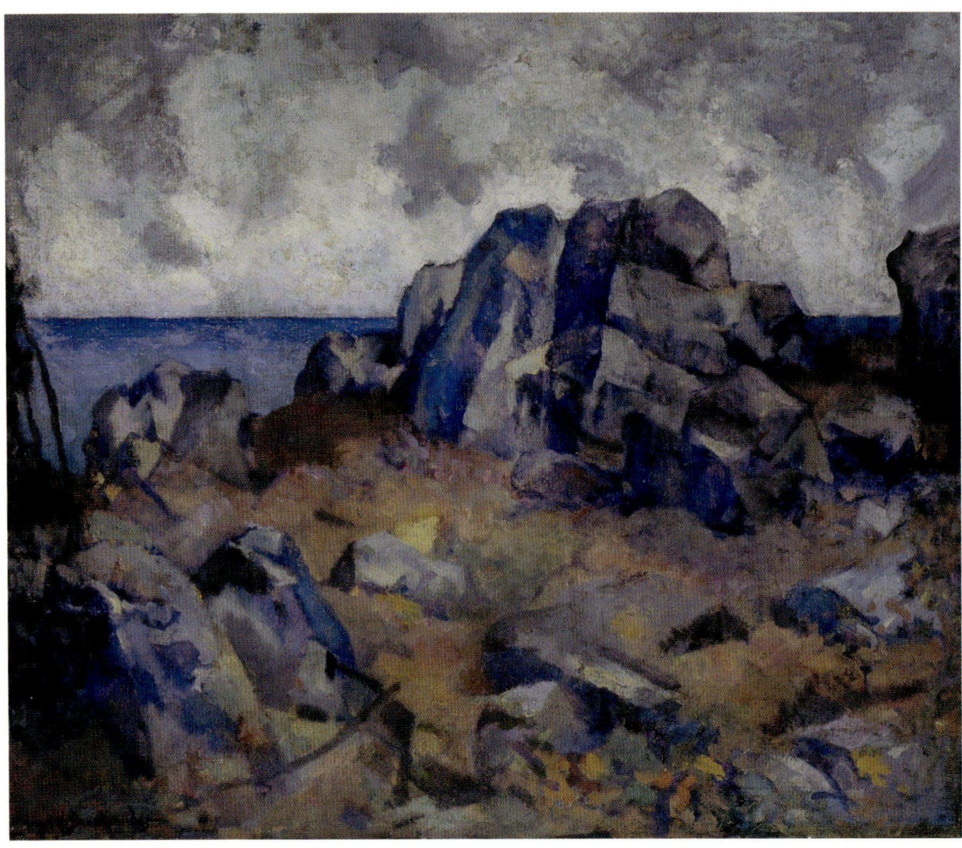

During the first half of the twentieth century, the art colony at Rocky Neck flourished with a regular influx of summer artists, many of whom chose to stay and live in East Gloucester. The area supported two major art associations within a stone's throw of each other, and a friendly rivalry stimulated the competitive spirit. A number of the artists retained membership in both organizations, and the two kinds of thinking—the juried show versus the non-juried—continued to spark lively debate. The progressive thinkers of the Gloucester Society of Artists had high hopes for the continuation of their society. A foreword in the catalogue of their 45th Exhibition, which ran for the month of July 1940, reads:

> *To you who care for the graces and values of life and wish to see them maintained through the present troublous conditions of things and men's mind we wish to offer a word about the pictures you have come to see.*
>
> *As this is an exhibition in which none of the work shown is submitted to the judgment of a jury for acceptance, it presents a cross section of what is being done hereabouts by artists at every level of development up to the mature accomplishments of those of recognized standing.*
>
> *For this reason we believe the exhibition will have a peculiar interest at the present moment in that we expect it will display trends now active in the art of an American community.*
>
> *Left to itself the traditional trend of American art constantly returns to an uncompromising contact with the ordinary realities of our American life and scene.*
>
> *Whenever we have mistrusted our traditions and followed alien trends either good or bad, we have always been the losers. Today a distinction can be made. American art is recognizable and we hope that should you find at least some evidence of it here, it will meet with your friendly appreciation.*

However, it was an appeal made to a populace still set in their ways aesthetically, despite the incongruity of a depression followed by a global war. In 1929 Gwendoline Keene wrote, "A non-jury show is always a tantalizing affair. There's always the possibility that some new genius… may burst into life where doors are open to all…. In Gloucester, it would appear, modernism has pretty well passed out of sight, and it is the Victorians who care enough about painting to paint and to enter their work."[16] A. J. Philpott observed, "Either the eccentrics in painting have died out or they stayed out, and as they were not easily killed it is probable that they went into retirement."[17] Certainly, they were not showing at the Gloucester Society. The two kinds of thinking that were prevalent at this time were not so much traditional versus avant-garde, as whether or not artistic expression would be encouraged by doing away with juried shows. Meyerowitz's painting showing artists streaming into the Gloucester Society on one side, while on the other side artists wait in line at the North Shore Arts Association for their work to be judged, is a humorous poke at academic thinking. Yet, despite its idealistic outlook and the euphoria of its members, the Gloucester Society of Artists was unable to retain its momentum. In the late 1940s, it joined forces with a group of Rockport modernists to become the Cape Ann Society of Modern Artists, but even combining their individual strengths was not enough to save the avant-garde movement on Cape Ann, and the society disappeared in the early 1950s. The North Shore Arts Association, on the other hand, is still a flourishing concern and retains the basic premise of its foundation: the juried show. Once again, Gloucester found itself mirroring current thought in the art world.

William Meyerowitz
Gloucester Humoresque
Oil on canvas, 36 x 52 in.
Cape Ann Historical Association, Gloucester, Massachusetts

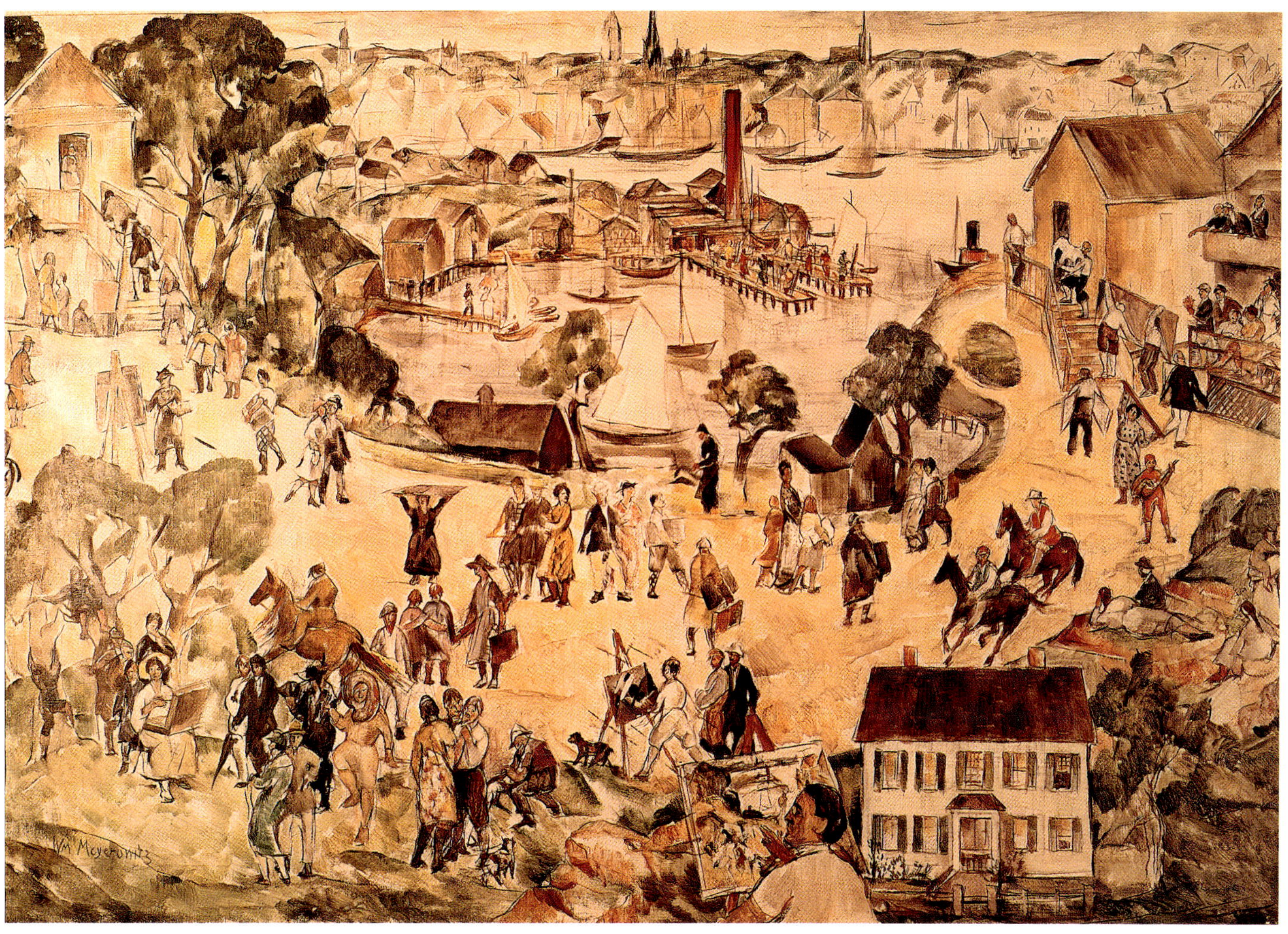

Harriet Randall Lumis (1870-1953)

Harriet Randall Lumis, one of the consummate American Impressionists, came to painting later in life than many, if not all, of her contemporaries. Born in Salem, Connecticut, on May 29, 1870, Lumis did not contemplate the arts, even as a hobby, until after her marriage to Frederick Lumis in 1892. The nuptials took place in Springfield, Massachusetts, and apart from forays throughout New England for artistic study, Harriet Lumis spent the rest of her life in that city.

In 1893, a year after their marriage, Harriet and her husband enrolled in the evening free hand drawing school sponsored by the Springfield school system. Despite her lack of training, Lumis evinced a natural talent, modeling shape and form with enthusiasm and a discerning eye. Mary Hubbard, who trained at the Art Students League in New York and with Benjamin Constant in Paris, was an early inspiration for Lumis, as well as James Hall, whose impressionist leanings influenced Lumis to soften her edges for greater diffusion. Three years later, Lumis began formal art study with Willis Seaver Adams, a tonalist in both doctrine and practice. Then in her thirties, Lumis reached a new plane when she began experimenting with the prismatic color favored by the newly formed Ten American Painters, as well as the effect of fresher, more spontaneous brushwork.

In 1910, after her husband was appointed the City of Springfield Building Commissioner, Harriet Lumis steeped herself deeper in artistic study, seeking instruction and critique from Leonard Ochtman in Mianus, Connecticut. Ochtman, however, leaned toward the tonalism favored by a previous generation and Lumis did not care for the somber palette and opacity of this technique. She subsequently enrolled in the New York Summer School of Art, which encouraged a fresher, more striking impressionist style. By 1912, at the age of 42, Harriet Lumis had three canvases ready for the Buffalo Society of Artists Exhibition at the Albright Gallery in Buffalo, New York. A local art critic commented that Lumis's canvases were "characterized by unusual refinement of color and a poetic, but sure touch."[18] Two years later, after study with Douglas John Connah at the New York Summer School in Bayport, Long Island, Lumis's work was again praised by the critics at the BSA Exhibition who declared, "by an economy of means which seems almost startling to the casual observer… forms are suggested… and her color is laid on in soft tones merging harmoniously into each other."[19] A founder of the Springfield Art League in 1919, and the organization's first treasurer, Lumis brought energy and verve to everything she did. Wishing to continue her personal art studies, Lumis enrolled in the newly opened Breckenridge School of Art in East Gloucester. When she came to Rocky Neck in 1920, she was using a subtle impressionist palette, suitable for capturing the summer warmth of the Berkshires. She found, however, like many before her, that the intense Cape Ann light required a more prismatic approach to allow for broader and more vibrant expression. Lumis's technique of laying in undertones over a charcoal sketch to ensure accuracy of form and key was impressionistic in approach, as was her use of Monet-like divisionist brushwork to dissipate forms in light. Despite being 50 years old when she began studying with Breckenridge, Lumis was not so set in her ways as to cling to a style that no longer served its purpose. Breckenridge was an innovator, encouraging students to experiment with methods and manners that were avant-garde for the day, and three years of study with him saw Lumis creating work worthy of the best American Impressionist, yet with a personal flair that owed credo to none. Her Gloucester paintings are imbued with the impasto quality of a loaded brush

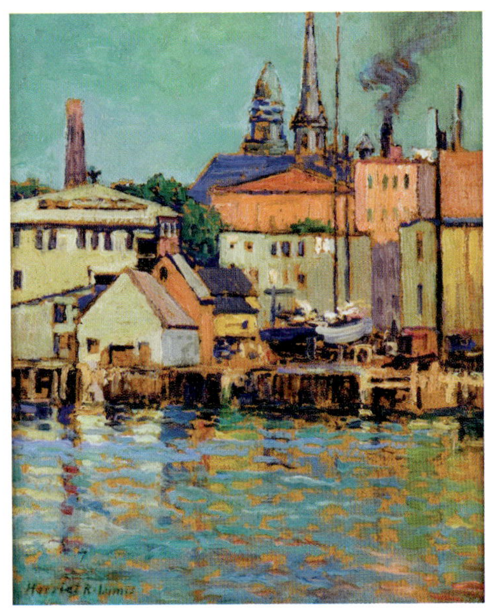

Harriet Randall Lumis
Gloucester Wharf, c. 1920-25
Oil on board, 12 x 9⅞ in.
MME Fine Art, LLC, New York

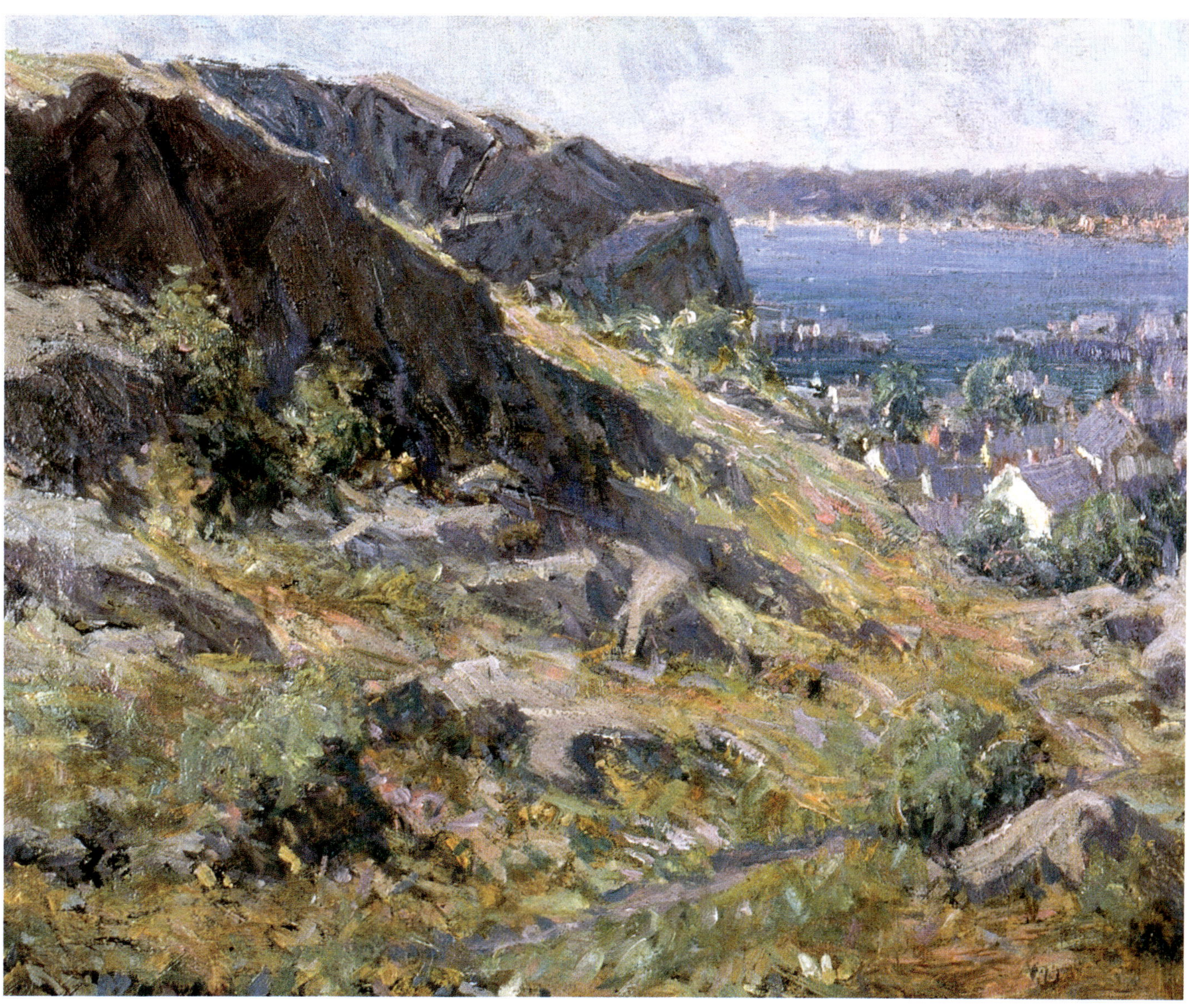

Harriet Randall Lumis
View of Gloucester
Oil on canvas, 17 x 21 in.
Rockport Art Association Museum collection, Rockport, Massachusetts

and pure pigment, and while she allowed herself the freedom to experiment with different effects, she remained true to the basic principles of good composition and draftsmanship. Her work is a prime example of how physical and pictorial elements can be diffused in the mutability of atmosphere and light.

Lumis continued to be active in the art world as both a painter and a teacher for the next 30 years. She showed with many private galleries as well as artist organizations throughout New England and the Midwest, including the Gloucester Society of Artists, and the National Association of Women Painters and Sculptors. She rarely traveled after her Cape Ann sojourn, preferring the security of Springfield and, after her husband's death in 1937, became more rigid in her thinking. She disdained modern art trends and retained a dogmatic signature style of bold color and strong contrast in the manner of traditional impressionism, despite a lack of demand for it in post-war American art. Throughout her career, Harriet Randall Lumis strove to perpetuate excellence in art, and helped found the Academic Artists Association of Springfield in 1949. She passed away five years later, at the age of 82.

Eleanor Parke Custis, A.W.S. (1897-1983)

Eleanor Parke Custis, whose famous "birdcage" home overlooking Rocky Neck is a landmark in East Gloucester, became as well known for her photography as for her painting and illustrative work. Custis spent her formative years in Washington, D. C., and during a genteel childhood, she was encouraged by her parents to try her hand at various creative pursuits. Her earliest art school training was at Washington's eminent Corcoran School of Art in the fall of 1915, where she learned the fundamental skills of drawing and painting with particular emphasis on watercolor. She also took instruction from Henry B. Snell at his Boothbay Harbor, Maine, summer school in 1924 and 1925 and, from this eclectic background, developed a personal style evolving from early exploration of the popular transparent watercolor to the more emphatic gouache, with more than a passing nod to the notan influence of Japanese woodblocks. As Leila Mechlin wrote in her foreword to Custis's 1936 Exhibition of Watercolors hosted by Robert C. Vose Galleries of Boston, "She draws, not merely from having been well taught, but instinctively, and pen, pencil and brush afford her completely natural media of expression. Also she has an excellent color sense."[20] Custis's personal aesthetic developed as a result of her training, her participation in the local Washington art community and a burgeoning worldly outlook, which was the result of three European sojourns between 1926 and 1929. She visited France, Holland, Italy and Switzerland and captured much of their charm and culture in varying media, exploring differing styles, loose and tonal, and tightly drawn with a strong effect of light and shade to give depth of field.

Although we do not know when Custis first came to Cape Ann, she was invited to show her painting, *On the Ways*, at the Gallery-on-the-Moors in August 1921, and was an exhibiting member in the first North Shore Arts Association exhibition in 1923. Custis was obviously much taken with the Gloucester art scene of the 1920s and regularly summered at the Rockaway Hotel with her parents before eventually taking a

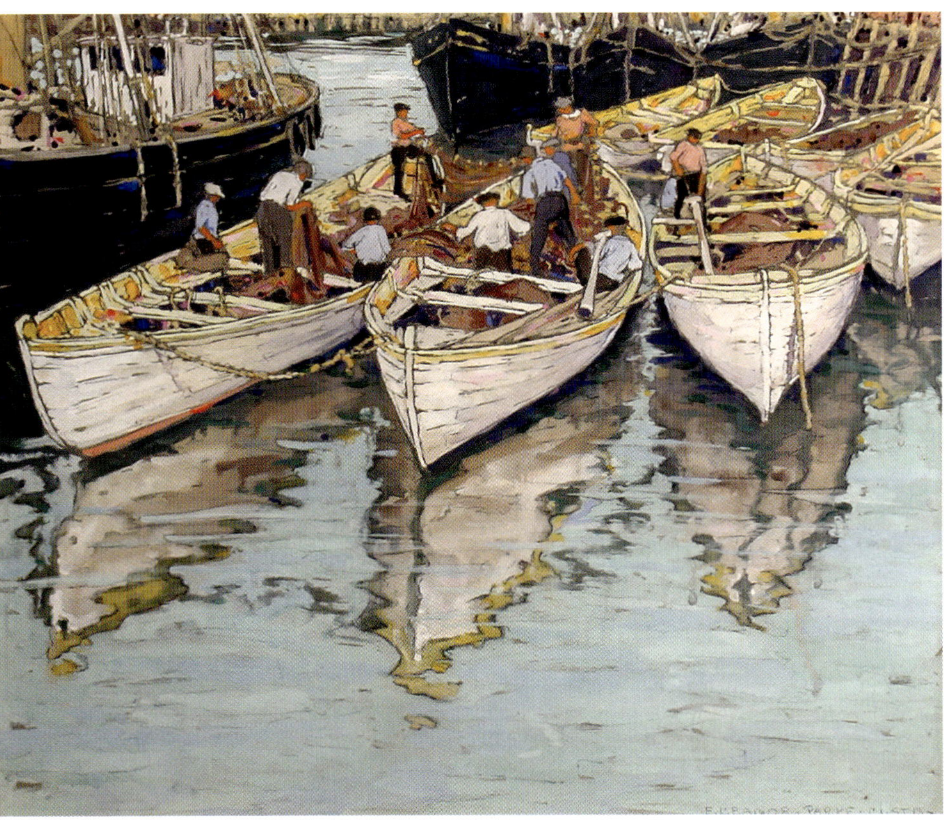

Eleanor Parke Custis
Gloucester Harbor (Men and Boats)
Gouache on paper, 18 x 22 in.
Pierce Galleries, Inc., Hingham, Massachusetts

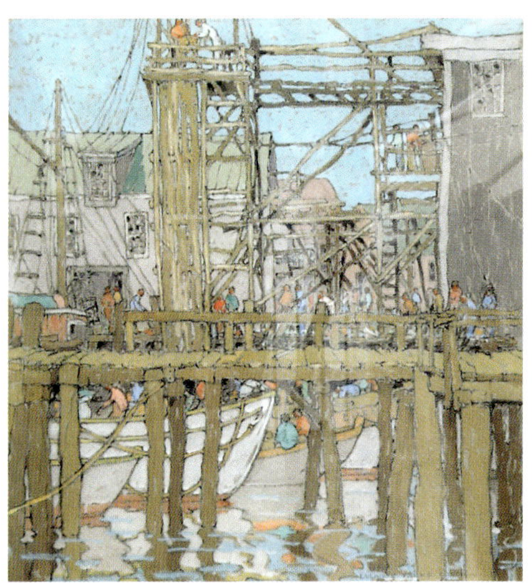

Eleanor Parke Custis
Gloucester Harbor
Mixed media, 16⅛ x 14⅞ in.
Pierce Galleries, Inc., Hingham, Massachusetts

summer studio on Rocky Neck in 1936. Two years later, on June 3, the *Gloucester Daily Times* proclaimed, "E. P. Custis, Rocky Neck Woman, Ranks As One Of America's Great Painters." By the late '30s, however, Custis was dividing her time between painting, illustration and photography. Her childhood interest in photography had been revived during a cruise through the Mediterranean and a visit to North Africa, financed by her wildly successful one-woman show at New York's Grand Central Galleries in 1933. She began to spend more time with photography than with her painting and drawing and eventually published a book on the subject, *Composition and Pictures*, which, according to its advertising, included "Composition simplified and put to work." Custis's training as an artist gave her a sound foundation in the art of dynamic symmetry and composition of the scene. "Do not be afraid to represent the impressions nature gives you," Custis advised. "Remember... the object of making a picture is not to show the map of a certain place, not to show only technical excellence, not to show a diagram of a perfect composition, but to make a picture that will live."[21] She believed the manner of execution in the creation of a painting, etching or photograph, was immaterial compared with elevating the viewer to "a higher plane of being, that inspires living, that stimulates personal activity."[22]

Eleanor Parke Custis was highly regarded in whatever medium she chose to work. She traveled widely, taking in Peru, Chile and Guatemala during winter sojourns away from her summer studio in Gloucester. Numerous awards testify to her creativity and talent and she continued to inspire and move her viewers until she was well into her eighties. As Leila Mechlin wrote in 1936, "Strangely enough, while her paintings are rather detailed, her pictorial photographs are very broadly rendered. In each instance, however, her work is intimate in character, reticent and indicative of her own strong but gentle personality." Custis moved to Gloucester permanently in 1960, making her home on Banner Hill, high above Rocky Neck, where she could enjoy the panorama of the harbor and beyond. She died in 1983.

Emile Gruppé (1896-1978)

Emile Albert Gruppé remains today one of Cape Ann's best known and best loved artist-teachers in an area noted for its painters and educators. His Sorolla-style impressionism, with its bold color notes and expressive brushwork, brought him accolades during his lifetime and has continued to enhance his reputation in the quarter century since his death.

Born November 23, 1896, in Rochester, New York, Emile Gruppé was proud to follow in the artistic footsteps of his father, Charles, but did so using his own intrinsic abilities. Emile was never content to be an imitator, preferring to bring his own unique vision of the world to both his teaching and his canvases. He spent his earliest years in Katwijk Aan Zee, Holland, where Charles Gruppé had relocated his family while immersing himself in the Dutch school of painting. The elder Gruppé—and the artists who came to visit his studio, including Pablo Casals—provided Emile's first formative influence in genre and style, but it was the studying he did on the family's return to New York, at the outbreak of World War I, that proved the catalyst of Emile Gruppé's career.

With encouragement from his father, Emile enrolled at the Art Students League to study the figure with George Bridgman, who taught drawing in terms of expressive contour. Years of guidance by his father had already instilled in the young Gruppé a keen understanding of accuracy, and this training proved its worth when Emile was awarded the Cézanne Medal in his first year at the National Academy School.[23] Gruppé

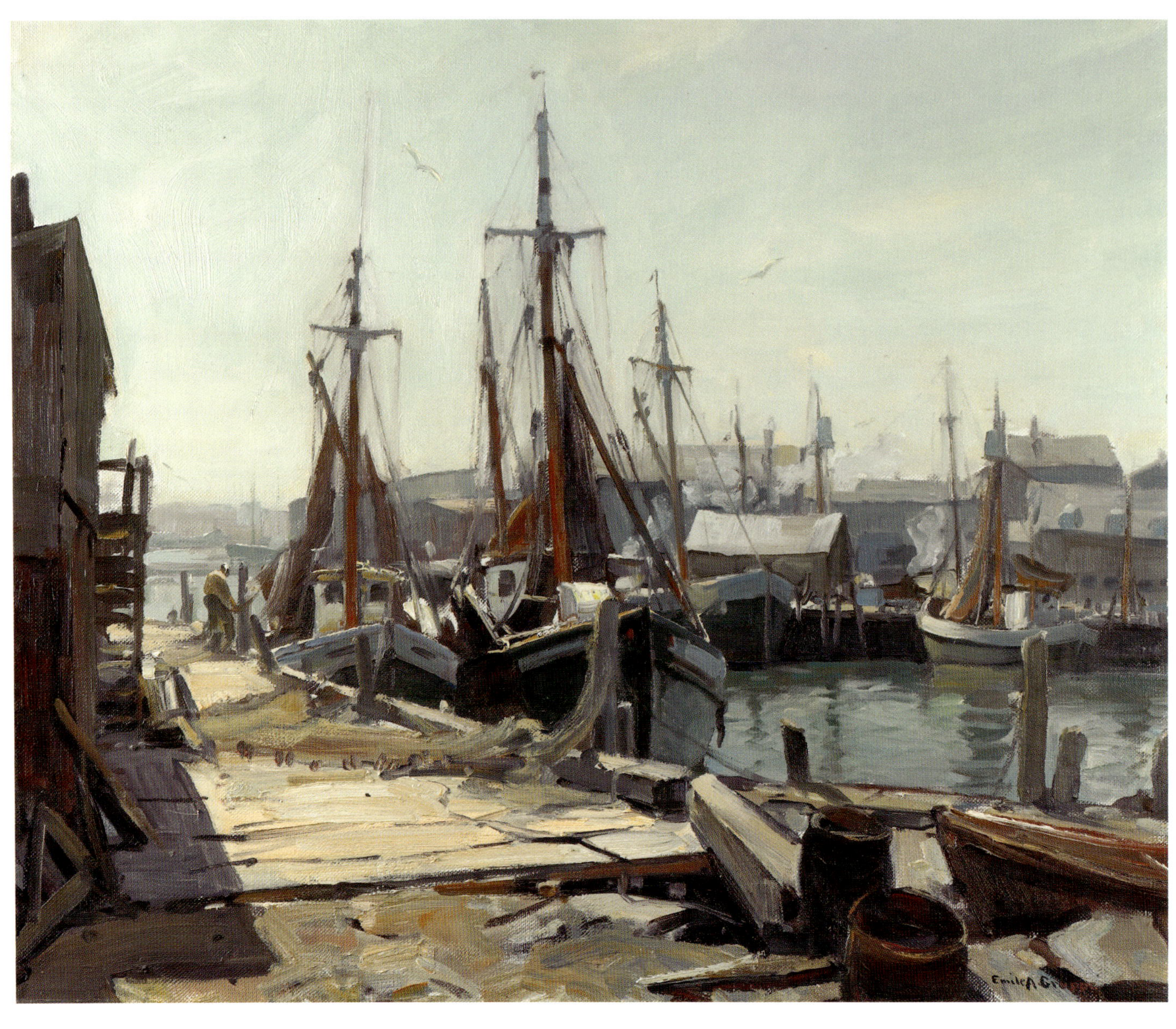

Emile Gruppé
Morning, Gloucester Harbor, c. 1955
Oil on canvas, 30 x 36 in.
Spanierman Gallery, LLC, New York

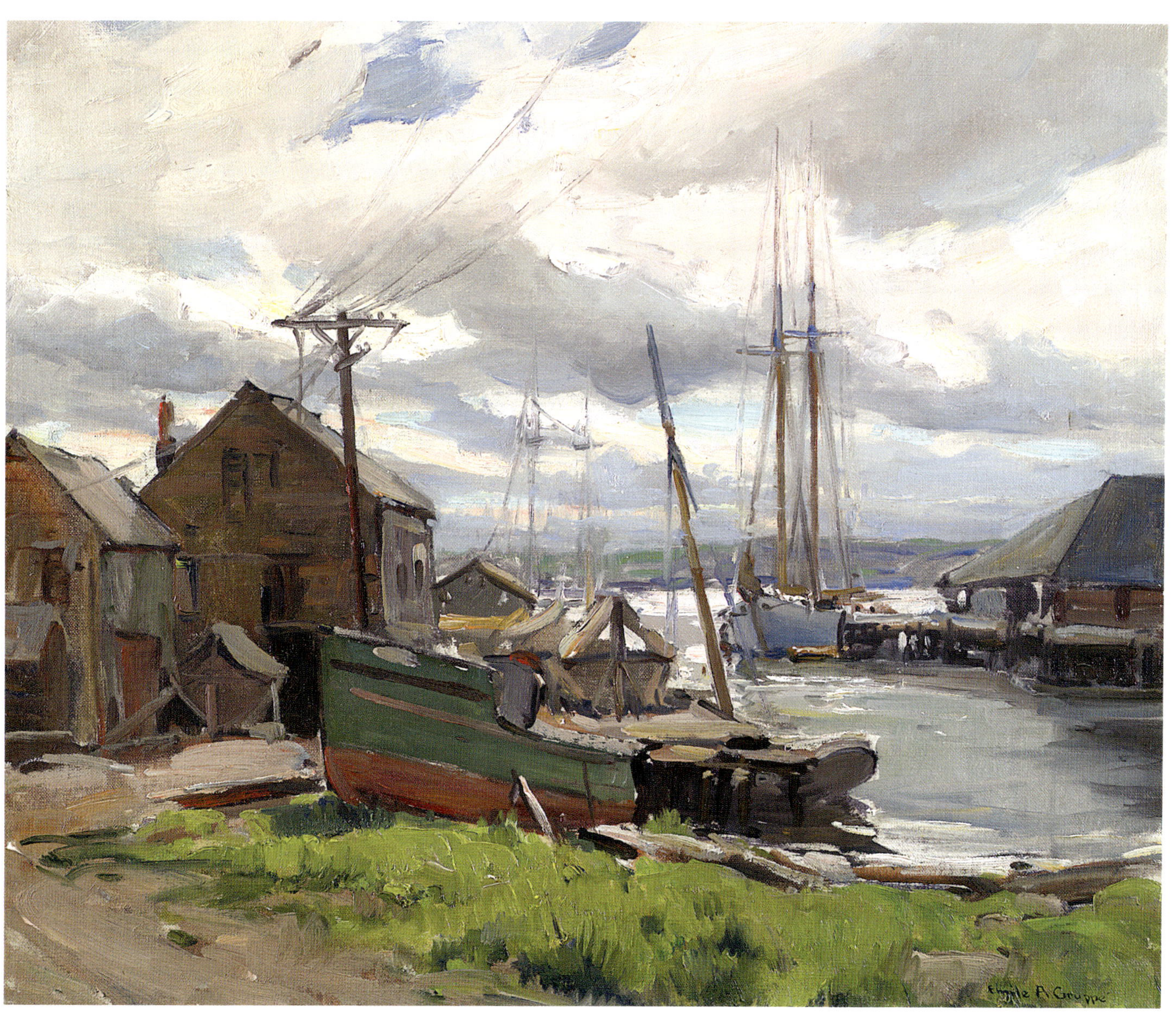

Emile Gruppé
Afternoon Sky over Gloucester, c. 1930s-50s
Oil on canvas, 20 x 24 in.
Private collection
Photo courtesy of Spanierman Gallery, LLC, New York

subsequently enrolled in the Woodstock summer school of the Art Students League where he met landscape master John Fabian Carlson. This encounter was "the best thing that ever happened to me," Gruppé later claimed. "Not only because of [Carlson's] technical advice but also because he proved to me that great painters are always generous and helpful."[24]

Gruppé spent four years studying with Carlson, and much of what he learned became the foundation of his own teaching. "The most important thing to remember is that you should try to draw what you see. Don't think you're doing… a "tree," or a "boat." As soon as you start thinking about the subject, as such, you'll get lost in drawing what you think it looks like. Think of a shape, first…."[25] Carlson also taught Gruppé the subtleties of tonal painting, a method based on restrained color and the sparing use of contrast. Gruppé, in his later years, was certainly not a product of the tonal school; however, without Carlson's emphasis on the importance of value comparisons, Gruppé would not have matured as a master colorist. He knew that the relationship between objects—one color value compared to another—was the real key to good painting. Primarily a plein air painter, he took to heart the concept that nature must always be considered in terms of chroma: the intensity of the foreground compared to the distance, the comparative lightness of the sky to the earth, as well as the subtle veil of atmosphere throughout.

Gruppé also studied with Cape Cod artist Charles Hawthorne who, in contrast to Carlson, played up the effect of color changes due to shifts in sunlight and atmosphere.

Emile Gruppé
Smith Cove
Oil on canvas, 12 x 16 in.
Mosher Gallery, Rockport, Massachusetts

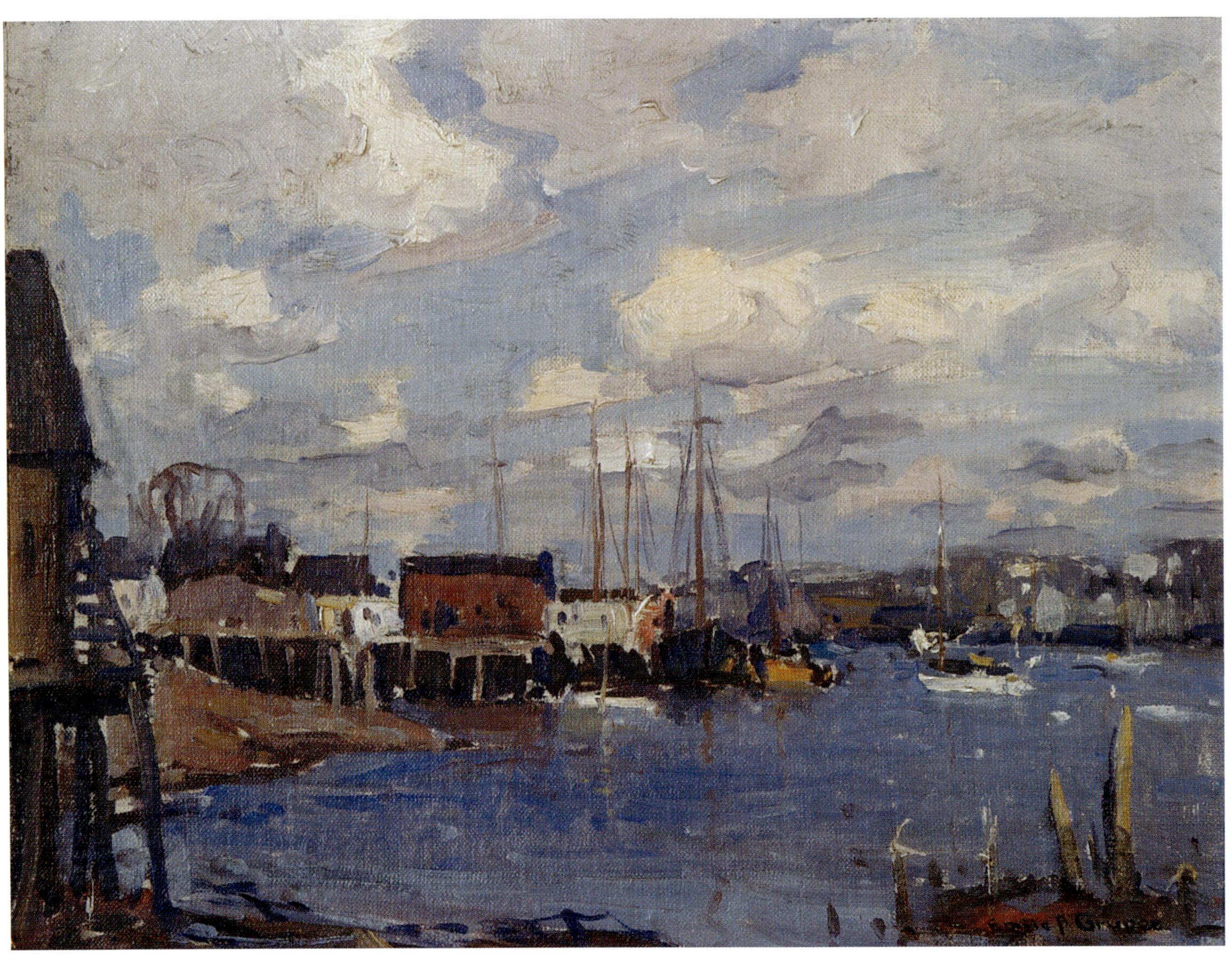

Emile Gruppé
Clam Diggers
Oil on canvas, 30¼ x 32¼ in.
Private collection

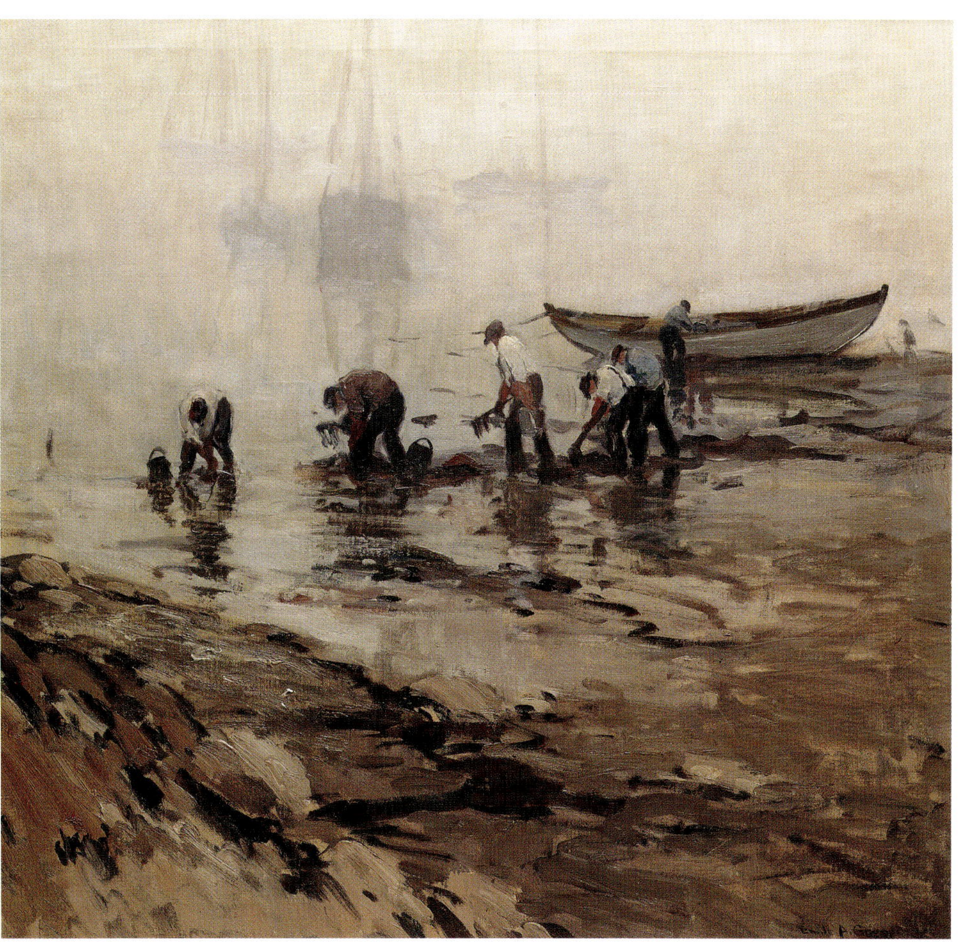

From this, Gruppé learned to analyze his subject as a whole—values and color notes juxtaposed one to the other to find their relationship—and by combining the teachings of both Hawthorne and Carlson he grew to be the vibrant impressionist we know today.

Visiting Cape Ann in the early '20s, Gruppé discovered it to be a haven for the plein air painter. He loved the excitement of the seasons, the mood of the streets and docks. He could find intimate designs in clusters of buildings just as easily as in picturesque cottages, and he spent hours at a time sketching ships and schooners, and generally getting a feel for the character of docks and wharves. Gruppé brought individuality to his work as well as a thorough understanding of color and design. He had an especially fine sense for boundaries, where the effect of lost and found edges give his designs dimension and a sense of atmosphere, and his use of impasto and descriptive brush-strokes emphasize the focal point of his work. He particularly liked striking effects of light, and would often compose his design in terms of front or backlighting depending upon the most vibrant effect.

Gruppé found all he wanted to paint within a stone's throw of East Gloucester and moved to Rocky Neck in 1929 where he remained for the next half century painting his own canvases and, later, from 1940 to 1970, directing the Gloucester School of Painting. He became one of Rocky Neck's best-loved characters, with a fascinating manner and a creative enthusiasm that brought him numerous students. His demonstrations and classes were always filled to overflowing, while many others patiently waited for their turn. A prodigious painter, Emile Gruppé worked almost until the day he died, September 28, 1978, and his memory remains alive in the many and eclectic genre paintings he created during a long and successful career.

Max Kuehne (1880-1968)

Max Kuehne built a long and productive career in the arts upon an eclectic mixture of painting, etching and furniture design. However, for the most part, it is his genre paintings of Gloucester—its streets, harbor and environs—for which he is known and admired.

Kuehne, born in Halle, Germany, on November 7, 1880, immigrated to the United States with his family as a young teen and grew to maturity in Flushing, New York. He came to an artistic career in his late twenties after trying his hand as a dental laboratory assistant, patent law clerk and journeyman printer. After finally deciding on an artistic career, Kuehne began his training at the age of 27, working under Kenneth Hayes Miller and William Merritt Chase at the latter's school in New York. Chase, of course, ranked as a distinguished member of the Ten American Painters—advocates of prismatic color and divisionist brushwork—and this early influence is readily apparent in Kuehne's work, particularly his scenes of Gloucester Harbor. Interestingly, in 1909-10 after leaving Chase, Kuehne took the radical step of studying the opposite artistic view with Robert Henri, leader of The Eight, or Ashcan school, who encouraged innovation and experimentation as a means of expressing social conscience and a progressive view.

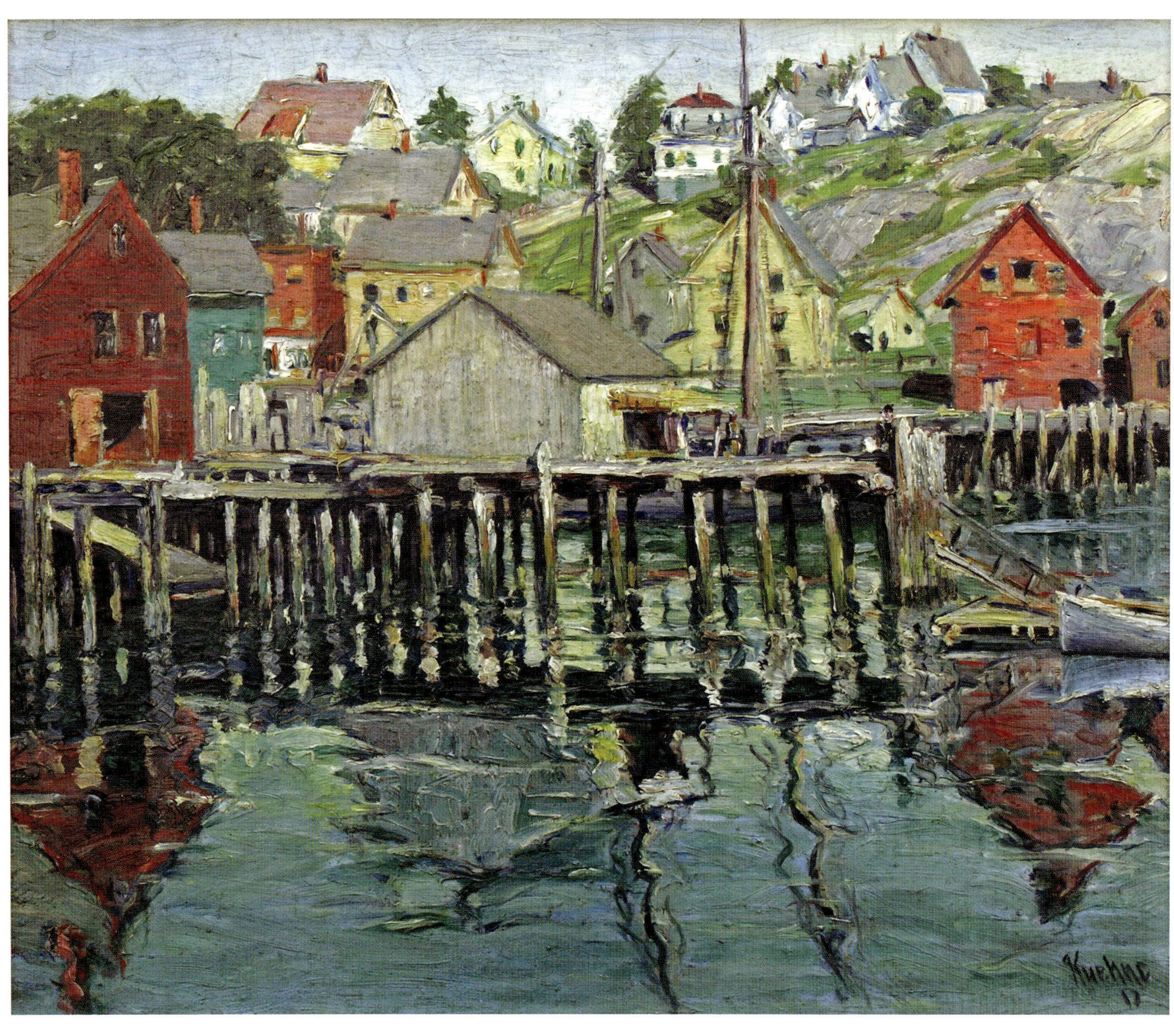

Max Kuehne
Wharves at Cripple Cove, East Gloucester, 1912
Oil on canvas, 20 x 24 in.
James B. Hand Fine Art, Gloucester, Massachusetts

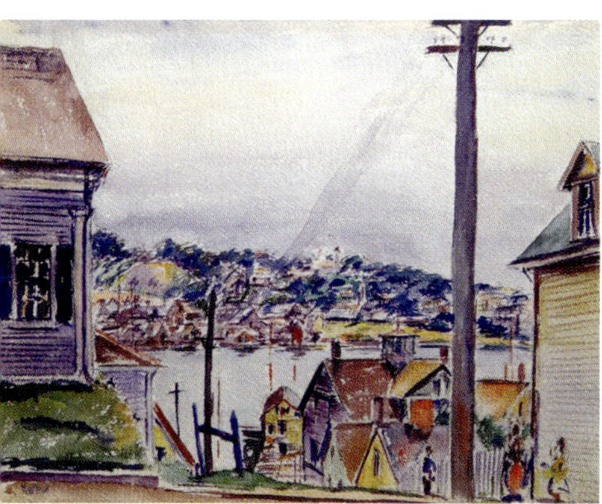

Max Kuehne
Gloucester Harbor Scene, c. 1935
Watercolor on paper, 16 x 20 in.
Private collection
Photo courtesy of Comenos Fine Arts, Boston

Unlike many artists who train in a particular manner and then build a signature style upon that foundation, Max Kuehne took the preeminent ideas of the two diametrically opposed styles of Impressionism and Realism and combined them into a personal and unique statement. Kuehne was well acquainted with the various members of Henri's school and social circle and, while in New York, often socialized and exhibited with Henri and The Eight, as well as classmate George Bellows. Yet despite his alignment with the progressive movement, Kuehne never went to the extremes of either school and preferred to adapt both points of view to his own personal interpretation.

Kuehne spent a year traveling through Europe, visiting the major galleries and sketching his way through England, Holland, Belgium, France and Germany. Although he was impressed with the Old Masters such as Rembrandt and Vermeer, and the new schools of Barbizon painting and French Impressionism, he was wary of the progressive movements of Cubism and Fauvism. He wrote in his diary, "I think I shall stick to a more reserved palette and not go off on the tangent these followers are on."[26]

The artist first came to Gloucester in the summer of 1912, after visiting a New York exhibition entitled "Paintings of Gloucester Harbor and Its Environs," which attracted him as a sailor as much as an artist.[27] Kuehne's plein air work from this era shows great confidence in color, tone and brushwork, as well as a discerning eye for design and aerial perspective. His Gloucester Harbor paintings were well received when shown at the National Academy of Design's exhibition the same year, as well as at the Carnegie Institute's annual exhibition in 1913. Critics, perhaps weary of the pedestrian, admired the way Kuehne followed no set precept but blazed his own path. "[H]e attacks his subject with an unconscious absorption that gives his pictures a quality of alluring naiveté and unpretentiousness..."[28] said the *New York Tribune.*

Kuehne, in company with his German wife, Margaret, spent the next three years painting in Spain, subsequently selling 32 canvases to Archer M. Huntington of the Hispanic Society of America. He did not return to the United States until 1917. The couple settled in Greenwich Village, New York, where the artist renewed his camaraderie with Glackens, Hopper, the Prendergast brothers and other members of The Eight.

In 1918, Kuehne returned to Cape Ann, where he painted around the streets and working piers of Gloucester Harbor. These canvases, when shown at the Whitney Studio Club in New York the following December, drew praise from the critics for their faithful rendering of nature suffused with atmosphere and luscious color. Kuehne returned to Cape Ann regularly over the next decade and in 1926 was awarded an Honorable Mention at the 25th Carnegie International Exhibition for his portrayal of Rocky Neck.

Although best known as a landscapist and oil painter, Kuehne was adept in watercolors and was noted for his etchings. He was also admired for his yachting paintings, designed with a sailor's eye, and his floral still life arrangements. During the Depression years, he turned to woodcarving to support his family, creating ornamental screens, panels and furniture, and decorating them with gesso and silver leaf.

During the last ten years of his life, Kuehne sought a change of painting style, adopting an almost pointillist effect in the manner of Seurat and Pierre Bonnard, "whom he greatly admired for his color."[29] But regardless of the inspiration, the singular Max Kuehne continued to paint his own vision of the world through a unique perspective that gave his work a bejeweled mosaic finish. He died in 1968.

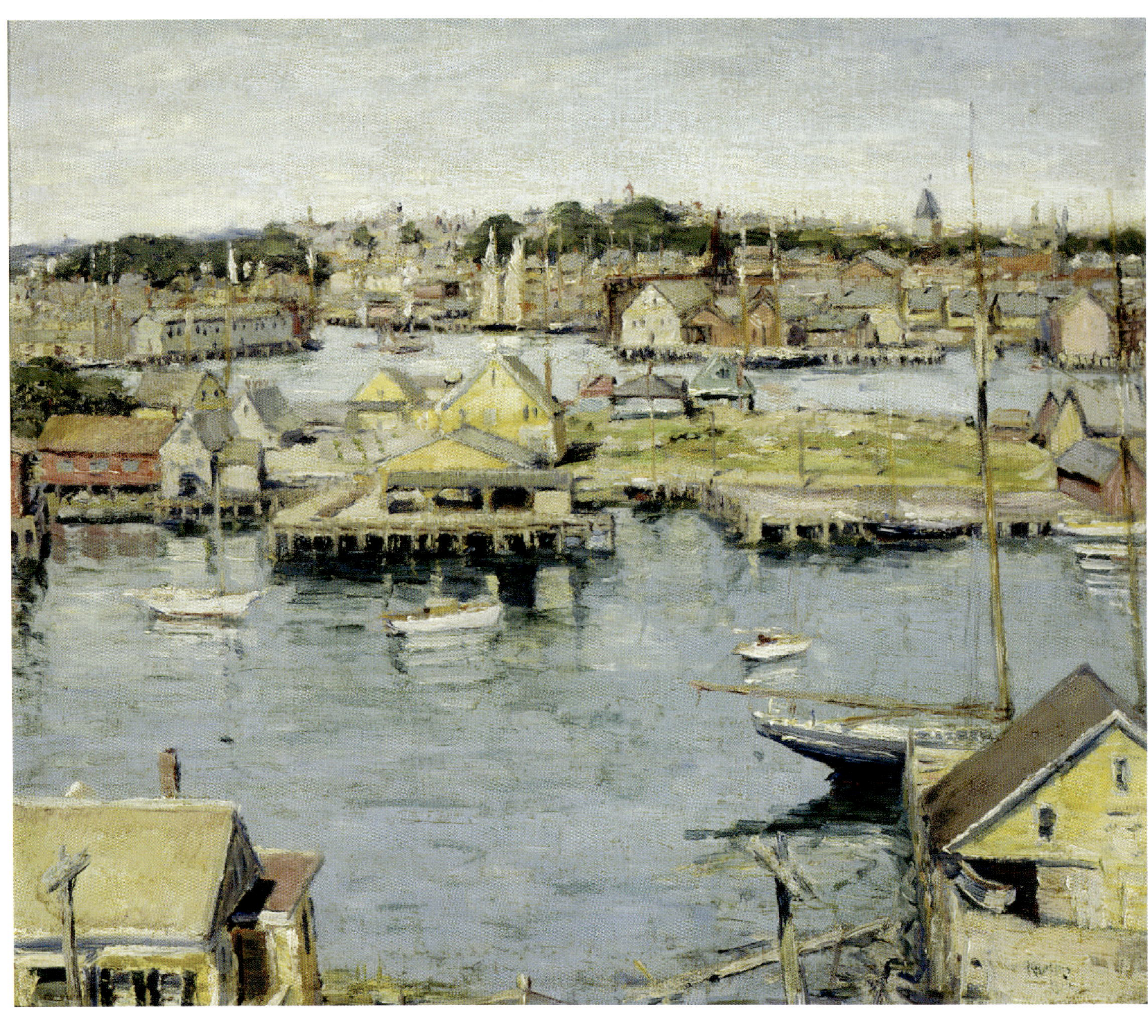

Max Kuehne
Gloucester Harbor, 1912
Oil on canvas, $20\frac{1}{2}$ x 24 in.
Cape Ann Historical Association, Gloucester, Massachusetts

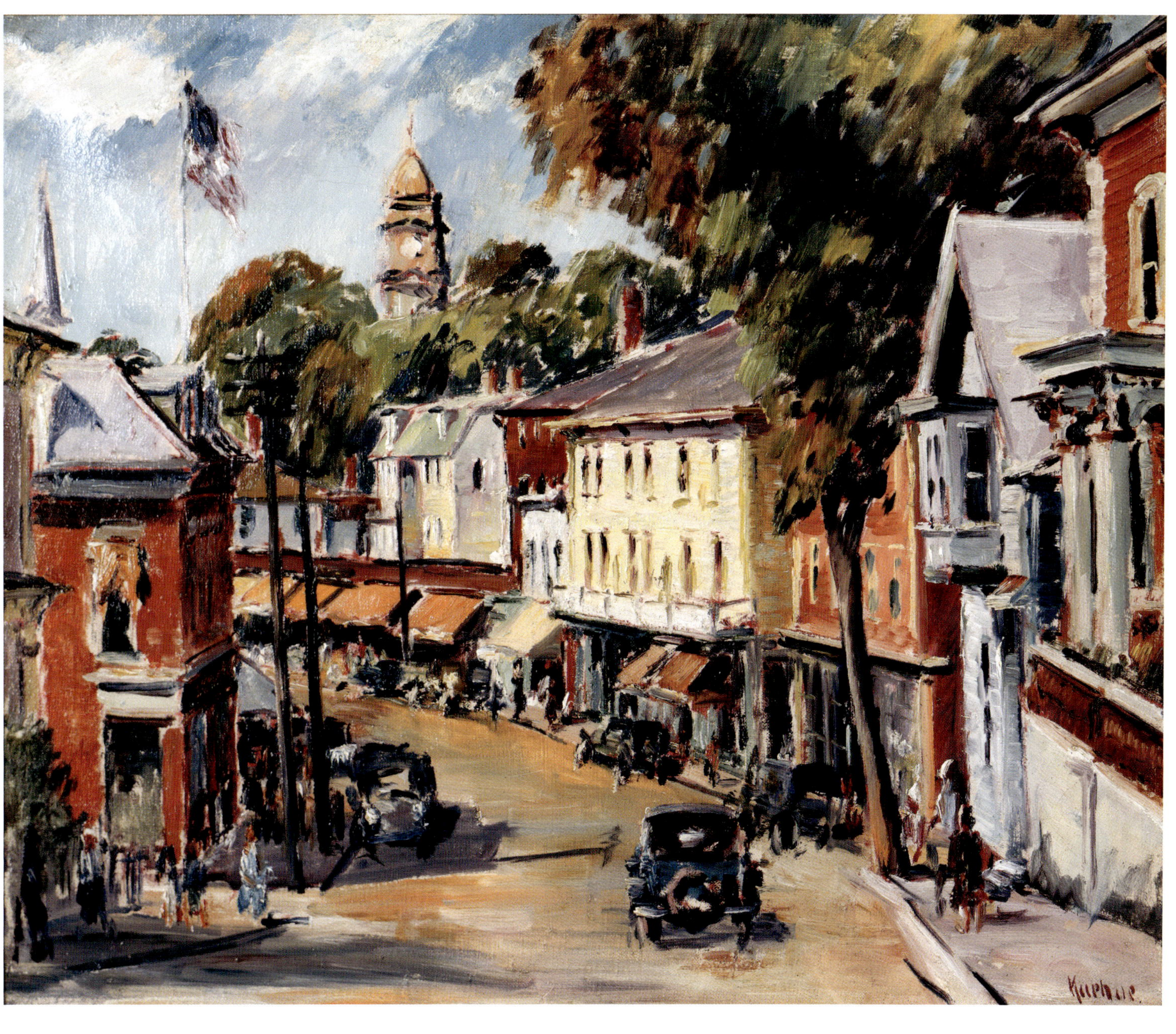

Max Kuehne
Main Street, Gloucester, 1932
Oil on canvas, 20¼ x 24 in.
Private collection

Alden Bryan, A.W.S. (1913-2001)

Alden Bryan first sailed into Gloucester Harbor with his bride, sculpture student Mary Taylor Lewis Bryan, in the latter part of the 1930s, and what he found on his arrival changed his life forever. Born in Carthage, Missouri, Bryan was a keen sailor and tennis player, and in his youth attended various summer tennis camps in Vermont. As a young man, he played on the Harvard tennis team while majoring in economics, and this university education and eclectic background set him a little apart from his contemporaries, most of whom had an art school background on which to build their careers. While Bryan became skilled as a painter, he also spent much of his time juggling numerous entrepreneurial concerns. These included ownership of The Rudder, an ancient fish house adjacent to the Bryan Gallery on Rocky Neck Avenue, which he bought and converted into a much-loved local restaurant, as well as running tennis camps, a farm, an inn, and several others business ventures in Jeffersonville, Vermont.

Arriving in 1930s Gloucester, the Bryans were surprised to find Rocky Neck filled with outdoor landscape artists, and were impressed with the concept and allure of plein air painting. Although his wife had an artistic background in sculpting, Bryan himself appears to have had no creative impulses prior to his arrival in East Gloucester. However, within a very short time he was studying with Emile Gruppé, Rocky Neck's most prominent artist and teacher at the time. Like everything he undertook, Alden Bryan immersed himself in his new passion and in 1939 traveled to Vermont to extend his studies under Charles Curtis Allen, N. A. That trip was the start of the Bryans' love affair with Jeffersonville, Vermont, and they returned often to paint the rugged winter scenery.

Alden Bryan also studied with A. T. Hibbard, one of America's finest snow painters, who spent his summers on Cape Ann and his winters in Vermont. Bryan studied at Hibbard's Summer School of Painting and Drawing for a short time and later, in the '40s, assisted as an instructor at the school. One can easily discern the influence of both Hibbard and Gruppé in Bryan's use of broken color and broad impressionistic brushwork, as well as his choice of subject matter. A focused and authoritative man, Bryan quickly developed a good eye for composition and a painterly style that garnered him numerous prizes from the various art organizations to which he belonged, including

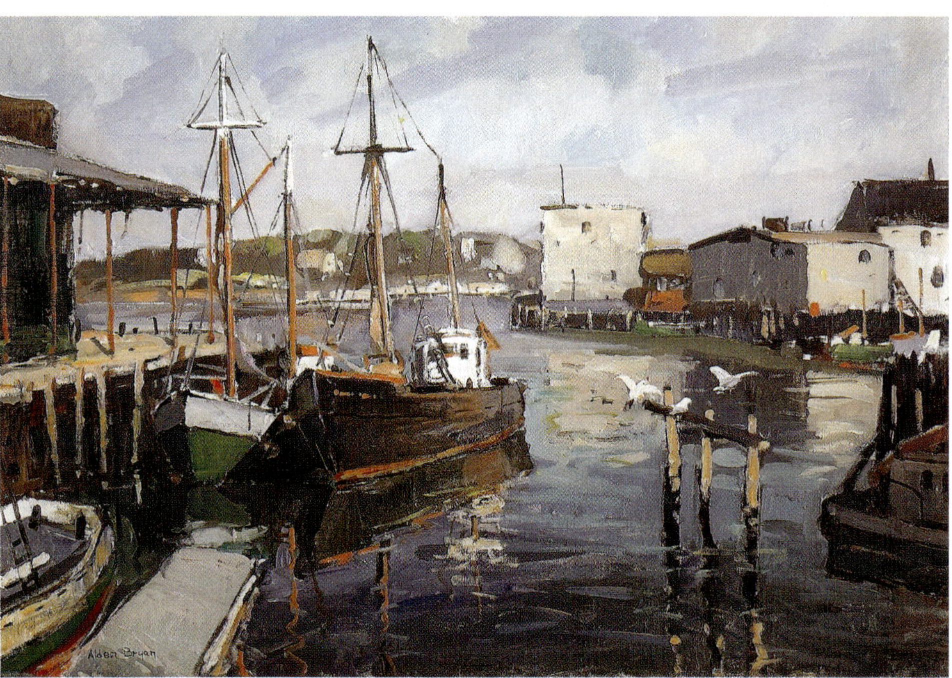

Alden Bryan
Gloucester Boats
Oil on canvas, 20 x 30 in.
Bryan Memorial Gallery,
Jeffersonville, Vermont

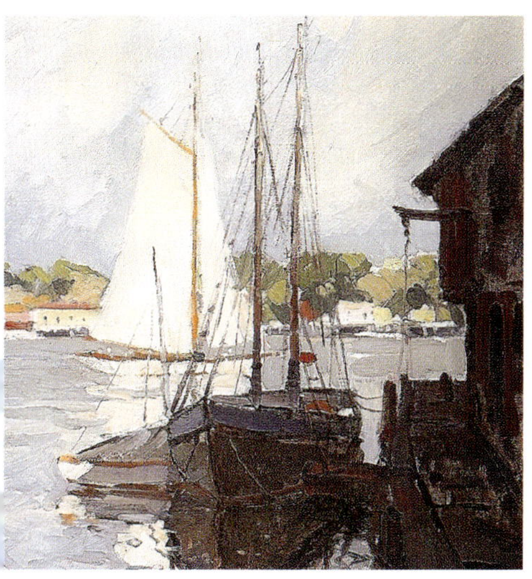

Alden Bryan
Smith Cove, Gloucester
Oil on canvas, 18 x 20 in.
Bryan Memorial Gallery,
Jeffersonville, Vermont

the North Shore Arts Association, the American Watercolor Society and the Guild of Boston Artists. His choice of subject matter embraced the pastoral as well as the pictorial genre of Rocky Neck's docks and wharves, which were literally on his doorstep. His Gloucester boats were always executed in fine style, with a sailor's eye for detail and strong broken color notes defining reflections in the water.

Throughout their married life, the Bryans enjoyed sailing and traveling, and painted in many exotic locations around the world including Hong Kong, Katmandu, Indonesia, Cape Horn, Africa, the Antarctic, and Quebec. Bryan especially liked recording the changes in some of his favorite locations, noting, in many instances, the unfortunate evolution from picturesque to progressive. Throughout his career, Alden Bryan displayed both an appreciation and an understanding of the color and texture of oil paint. His robust nature and vitality are apparent in the handling of light and shadow, and his vigorous brushwork shows a confidence that many never achieve. He passed away peacefully at his home in Jeffersonville in 2001.

Mary Bryan, A.W.S. (1907-1978)

In contrast her husband, Alden, Mary Bryan had a background in the arts before arriving in East Gloucester. She was born Mary Taylor Lewis in Carlsbad, New Mexico, and moved east to Connecticut with her parents while still quite young. The family later moved west again, settling in California. Like many with creative inclinations, Mary was an average student when it came to academics, but showed impressive ability in art-related subjects. She was particularly interested in three-dimensional art and her first serious artistic studies were with Laura Gardin Fraser, the noted sculptor and an Associate member of the National Academy of Design, and with Carl Illiver. By 1938, however, after her marriage to Alden Bryan and their subsequent visit to Gloucester, Mary became enthralled with the painting process, and gave up sculpture in favor of painting. When the Bryans first moved to Rocky Neck, Mary studied oil painting with her neighbor, artist and teacher Emile Gruppé. In 1946 and 1947, she studied watercolor with Eliot O'Hara at his school in Goose Rocks Beach, Maine.

An accomplished artist, Mary Bryan was far more retiring and unassuming than her flamboyant husband, and much preferred creation to commerce. She became adept in oil and watercolor as well as gouache and acrylic, and expressed her versatility in varying media according to her mood. She excelled in watercolor, acrylics and "plastic tempera, a method by which she combined opaque watercolor with plastic spray giving a varnished, quick drying effect…."[30] She had a studio built to accommodate a potter's wheel and kilns of every size. She was always creating, and tried endless different media: enamel, decoupage, and lacquer, as well as weaving and spinning her own wool.

Mary Bryan's painting technique was quite different than her husband's despite having studied with the same teacher initially. Her work shows little influence from Gruppé, evincing a very personal style. She often utilized a palette knife rather than a brush, and rarely began painting with any kind of lay-in or lines of symmetry. "Lines," she explained, "tend to distract me, and disturb the mental image. I start to paint directly with the palette knife, working from the center of interest and establishing the basic forms of the composition as rapidly as possible. These forms are painted as areas, not indicated in drawing, and are related to each other in size, volume and tension."[31] Although originally impressed with the plein air artists of Rocky Neck, Mary Bryan rarely executed finished pieces outdoors, being ill at ease with the difficulties and hardships of painting in varying weather conditions and dealing with onlookers. However, she trained herself to be observant and often created brief sketches to capture the moment for use in later studio work. Her palette frequently veered into monochromatic with neutral color tones, although she was not afraid to use broad color washes or swathes of broken color applied with a palette knife if called for by the subject. She worked for effect, considering form and space and unity to create a pleasing design, not restricted to the pictorial. She died in Waterville, Vermont, in September 1978, and six years later, Alden Bryan dedicated a gallery in her name—the Mary Bryan Memorial Gallery in Jeffersonville, Vermont—to celebrate her lifetime's accomplishments and to promote excellence in the arts.

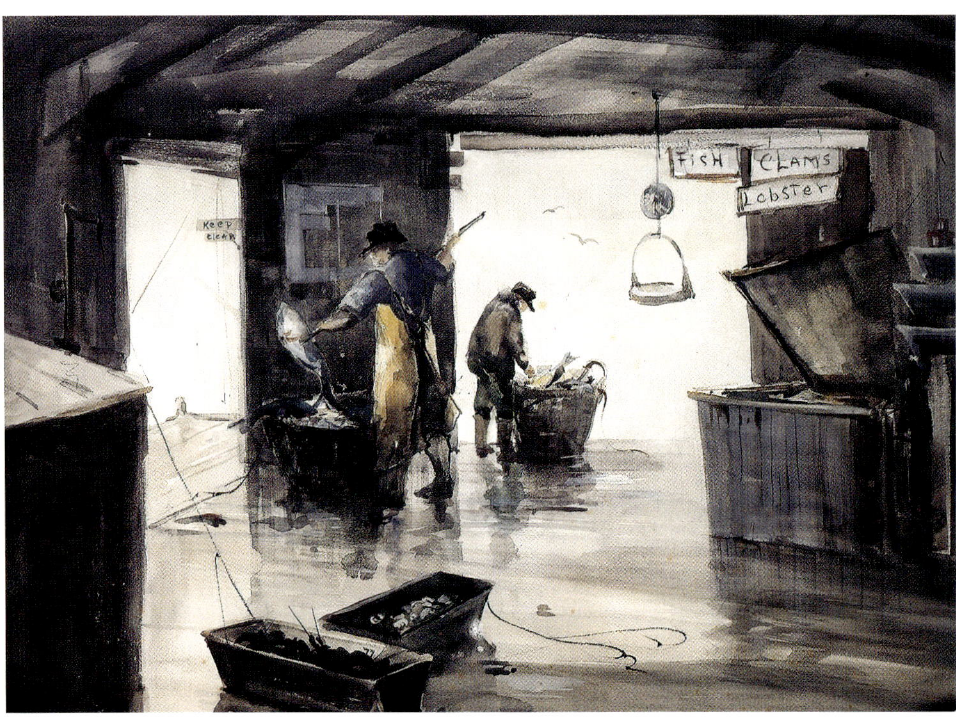

Mary Bryan
Gloucester Fish Market
Watercolor, 22 x 30 in.
Bryan Memorial Gallery,
Jeffersonville, Vermont

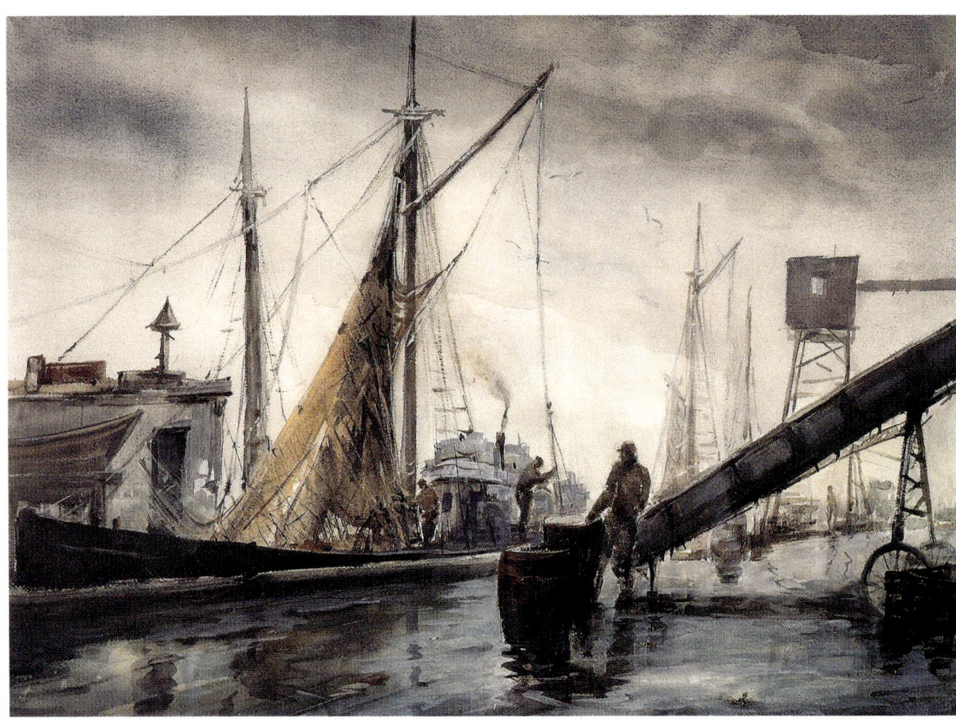

Mary Bryan
Unloading the Fish
Watercolor, 22 x 30 in.
Bryan Memorial Gallery,
Jeffersonville, Vermont

Notes

1 Unidentified and undated newspaper clipping in Gallery-on-the-Moors Scrapbook #3, CAHA, quoted in O'Gorman, James F., *This Other Gloucester*, p. 92.

2 Handwritten note, Alice Beach Winter File, CAHA.

3 Ibid.

4 Dame, Lawrence, *Boston Sunday Herald*, August 11, 1946, quoted in Babson, Roger W., and Foster Saville, *Cape Ann Tourist's Guide with Comments on Business Cycles* (Gloucester, MA: Cape Ann Community League, 1954), p. 86.

5 "Told of Artists' Feeling toward Rest of World," *Gloucester Daily Times*, August 1, 1933, p. 6.

6 "Gloucester and Art," *Gloucester Daily Times*, 12 August 1933, p. 1. Quoted in Love, Richard H., *Carl Peters, American Scene Painter from Rochester to Rockport* (Rochester, NY: University of Rochester Press, 1999), p. 251.

7 Handwritten note from the Stevens family scrapbook; on microfilm at the Greenfield Community College Library, Greenfield, MA.

8 Undated newspaper clipping. Stevens family Scrapbook, ibid.

9 'Paintings By Mr. Stevens,' *Boston Evening Tribune*, October 20, 1921.

10 "Harry Aiken Vincent—An Appreciation," K. P. R., *Gloucester Daily Times*, 'Rockport Daily News,' p. 2.

11 "Fern I. Coppedge," available at <http://artists of the commonwealth.org/artists/coppedge. html> March 27, 2007.

12 Nordstrom Papers, CAHA.

13 Hawthorne, Mrs. Charles W., *Hawthorne on Painting* (New York: Dover Publications, 1938), p. 23.

14 "Fakirs Costume Ball Drew Many Summer Folks," *Gloucester Daily Times*, August 23, 1923, p. 4, Alice Beach Winter File, CAHA.

15 Mulhaupt, Frederick J., "Paul Cornoyer, Painter—An Appreciation," *Cape Ann Shore*, July 14, 1923.

16 Keene, Gwendoline, *Boston Evening Transcript*, July 13, 1929, quoted in O'Gorman, p. 96.

17 Philpott, A. J. *Boston Globe*, quoted in O'Gorman.

18 Love, Richard H., *Harriet Randall Lumis: 1870-1953 American Impressionist* (Chicago: R. H. Love Galleries, 1977), p. 14.

19 Ibid.

20 Custis Papers, CAHA.

21 Quoted from *Composition and Pictures* in Introduction by Feay Shellman, 1986 Bakker exhibition catalog, Custis Papers.

22 Ibid.

23 Gruppé, Emile A., edited by Movalli Charles, *Gruppé on Color: Using Expressive Color to Paint Nature* (New York: Watson-Guptill, 1979), p. 9.

24 Ibid., p. 10.

25 Gruppé, Emile A., edited by Charles Movalli and John Lavin, *Gruppé on Painting* (New York: Watson-Guptill, 1976), p. 25.

26 From Max Kuehne's travel diary, 1910, in the collection of Richard Kuehne. Quoted in Worley, Sharon, "Max Kuehne," *American Art Review*, Vol. IX, No. 5, October 1997, p. 125.

27 Kuehne, Richard E., "A Reminiscence," *The Early Paintings of Max Kuehne* (New York: Hirschl & Adler Galleries, 1972).

28 Exhibition review of Kuehne paintings at Charles Daniel Gallery, newspaper clippings, Kuehne archives. Quoted in Worley, Sharon, p. 126.

29 Kuehne, Richard E., Ibid.

30 'Mary Bryan' catalog, Bryan Memorial Gallery, Jeffersonville, VT, p. 21.

31 Ibid., "In Her Own Words", inside cover.

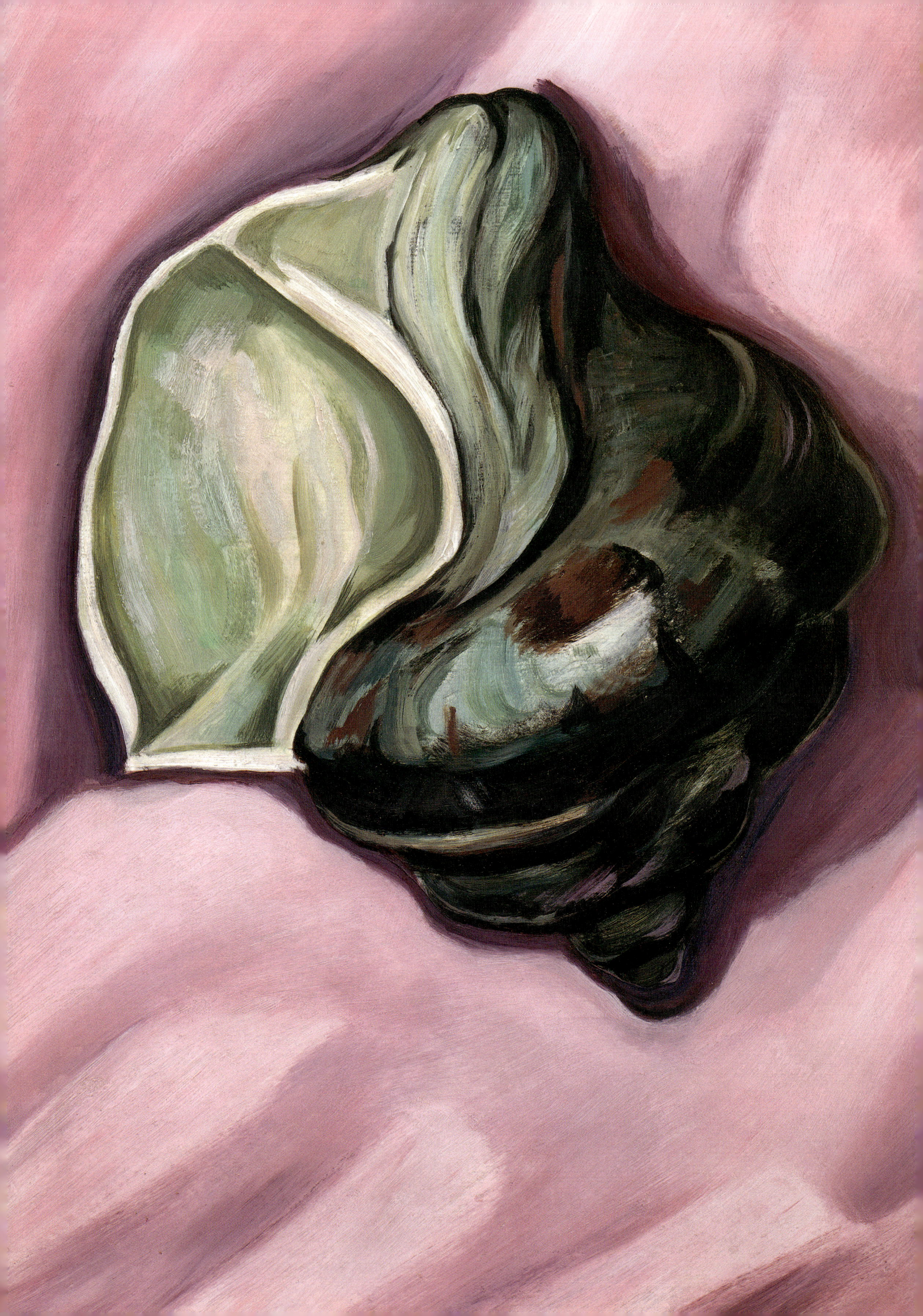

The Independent Muse

"Art is magic... But how is it magic? In its metaphysical development? Or does some final transformation culminate in a magic reality? In truth, the latter is impossible without the former. If creation is not magic, the outcome cannot be magic."

—Hans Hoffman[1]

While the art colony at Rocky Neck is best known for its traditional painters, it has also hosted some of the great independent thinkers of the art world, including Hans Hoffman, DeHirsch Margules and Helen Stein as well as Nell Blaine, Marsden Hartley and Edward Hopper.

Hans Hoffman (1880-1966) summered in Gloucester in the early 1930s and also instructed at Ernest Thurn's School of Art at 197 East Main Street. Thurn specialized in still life subjects and abstract compositions based on shape, color and texture. Hoffman also was noted for his abstract paintings, which he based on imagination and nature, bringing together the natural elements and interpreting them in terms of mass and geometric shape defined by both positive and negative space. "Creation," he told his students, "is dominated by three absolutely different factors: First, nature, which works upon us by its laws; second, the artist, who creates a spiritual contact with nature and his materials; third, the medium of expression through which the artist translates his inner world."[2] He was well respected among the avant-garde as a teacher and as a painter of powerful works that combine a hint of the Cubist, a splash of the Fauvist and more than a touch of Abstract Expressionism. And yet he claimed that regardless of whether a painting was a naturalistic work or an abstract, "visual expression must still follow the same fundamental laws. ...In nature," he said, "light creates the color. In the picture, color creates the light."[3]

In 1934, Hoffman opted to leave Gloucester to open his own art school in Provincetown where he attracted a number of progressive thinking students, including Nell Blaine.

Detail
Marsden Hartley
The Seashell, 1929
Oil on board, 17½ x 14½ in.
Courtesy of Alexandre Gallery, New York

Nell Blaine, N.A. (1922-1996)

In the mid-1950s, Nell Blaine, an "academic realist"[4] who evolved into an Abstractionist, stands out as the leading practitioner of the avant-garde among the painters of the Rocky Neck Art Colony. Raised in Richmond, Virginia, Blaine left the School of Art of the Richmond Professional Institute (now known as Virginia Commonwealth University) after only two years of instruction and headed for New York to study with Hans Hofmann, master of the abstract. Of Hofmann she said, "[He] helped you see what was false, to know the difference between organic and static.... the work is an extension of your blood and body; it has the rhythm of nature."[5] She was also heavily influenced by Piet Mondrian's balance and interaction of vertical and horizontal shapes. While in New York, Blaine developed a deep love of jazz, which in turn influenced her artistic development, "Like each improvisation in jazz, each color in abstract painting was to have a life of its own in the picture."[6] Blaine married musician Robert Bass in 1943, and during the summer the couple made what, for Blaine at least, would be the first of many visits to Gloucester. Sadly, the marriage did not last and was annulled in 1948.

Blaine's work matured over the years, evolving from exploring the abstract to embracing it with a sure hand, a vibrant palette, and a fluidity of line and brushwork. She returned to Gloucester in 1954 and again in 1958, renting a large studio overlooking the Rocky Neck wharves and creating numerous watercolors and pastels in her own inimitable style. Blaine was always a daring painter, her whole personality a bold synthesis of originality and energy, and even a devastating bout with bulbar-spinal polio in 1959 only slowed her down temporarily. After months of recuperation, an operation to regain the use of her right hand, and then rehabilitation, Blaine was able to begin painting again. She taught herself to be ambidextrous, using her right hand for watercolors, which required less physical effort, and her left hand for painting in oil. Her months of illness and recovery taught her to work with even greater spontaneity, catching the vitality of her subject, be it a loosely observed figure or a bouquet of

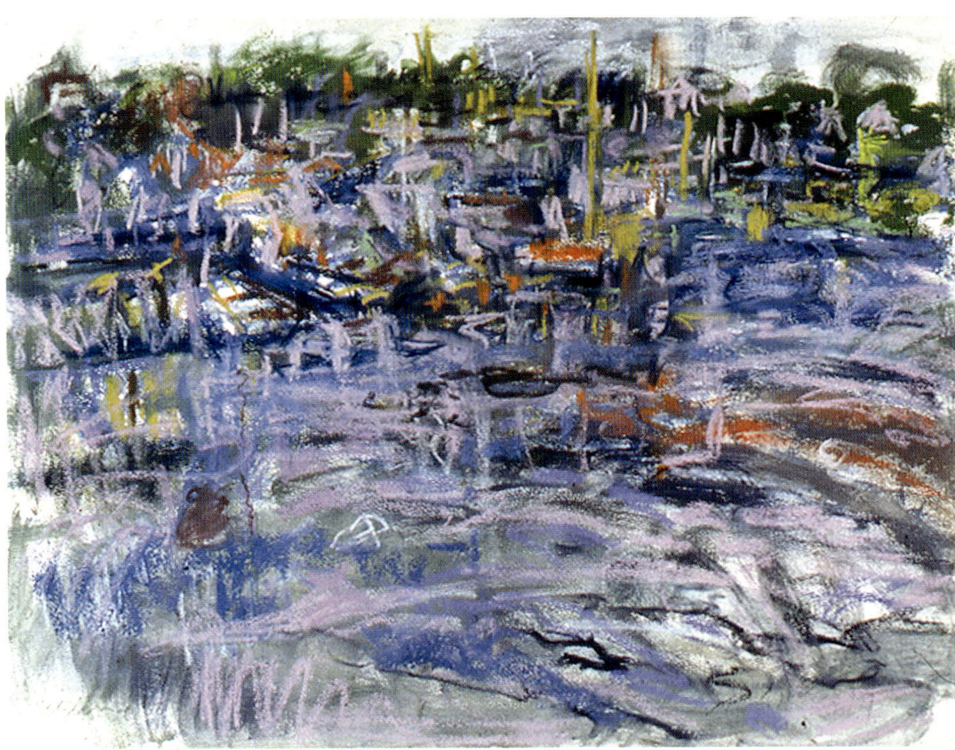

Nell Blaine
Gloucester Harbor, Dusk
Pastel on paper, 22 x 30 in.
Courtesy of Tibor de Nagy Gallery, New York

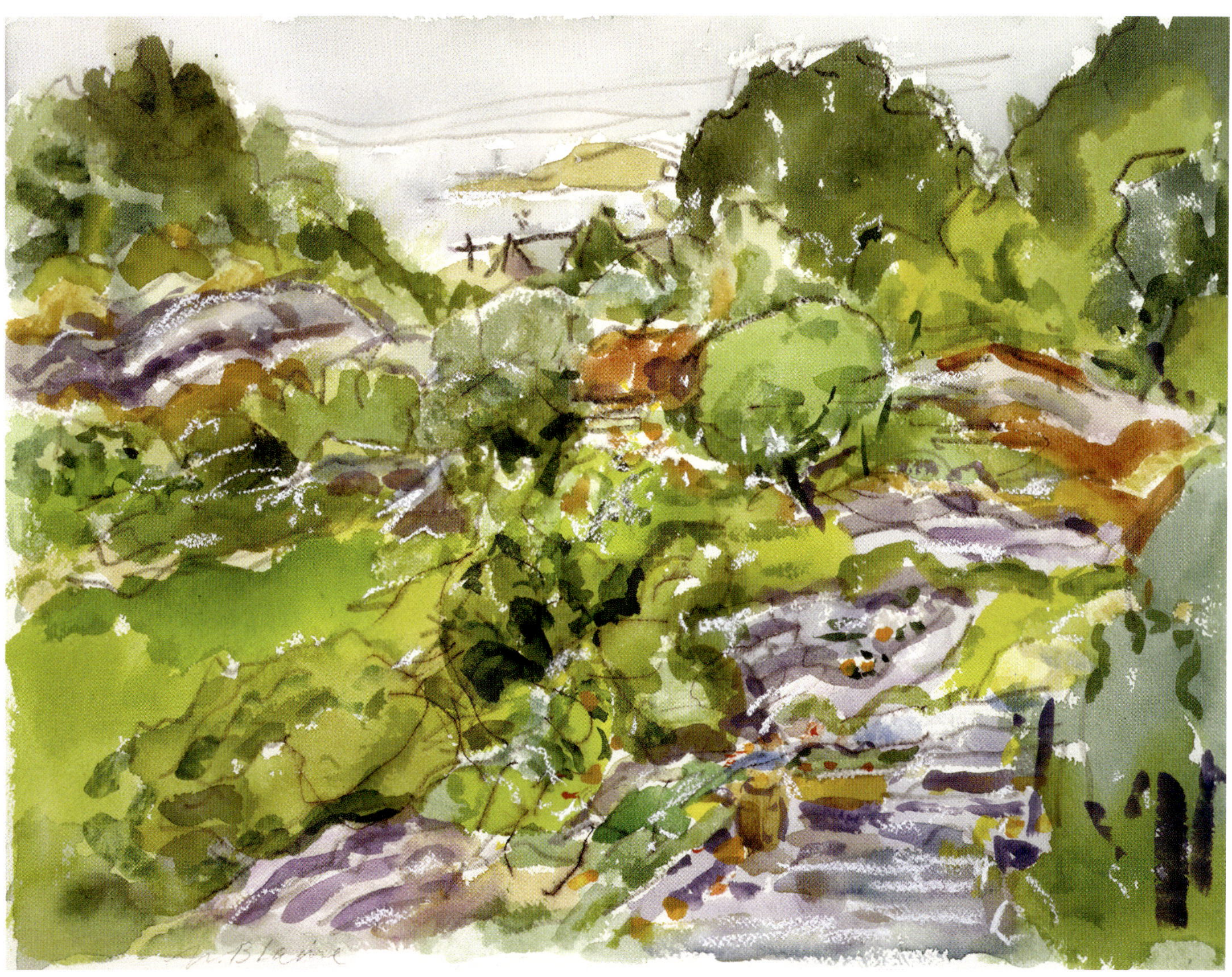

Nell Blaine
A Light Fog
Watercolor on paper, 12 x 16 in.
Courtesy of Tibor de Nagy Gallery,
New York

nature's vivacious blooms, in simplified forms and pulsating color. When Blaine returned to Gloucester in 1963, she brought with her a new way of seeing: a way of executing her work with veracity whether painting tonal mud tones at low tide, or a high key interior on a hot summer day. In painting, and interpreting the juxtaposition of wharf and water, Blaine was able to lose herself in her work and forget her afflictions for a short while. With the help of friends and aides, Blaine continued to be an enthusiastic traveler, yet she was always happy to return to Rocky Neck where, in 1974, she purchased her own home, "a weathered clapboard building, earlier a truck garage, and before that a barn… overlooking Gloucester's Outer Harbor."[7] Blaine raised the roof and added an elevator and second floor studio to her new home, as well as pocket gardens and a painting deck among the granite outcroppings overlooking the harbor. Blaine named her home "Eudora Cottage," and it became a pleasant refuge from the summer heat and dust of New York. She continued to paint, even in the closing years of her life when the effort was the greatest, and when she died in 1996, the modern art world lost one of its most flamboyant practitioners. A decade after her passing, Nell Blaine is still revered by many for her impressionistic brushwork and adrenaline-rush of color that is the singular trademark of her finest work. Eulogized by her peers, Blaine summed up her painting philosophy in simple terms, "Realism in painting consists of order, rhythms, growth and shapes, rather than the actual appearance of things."[8] Nobody said it better.

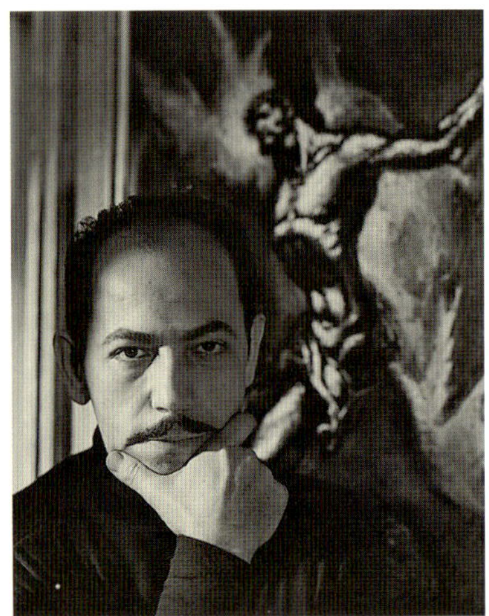

Umberto Romano
Photo courtesy of the Rockport Art Association, Rockport, Massachusetts

Umberto Romano, N.A. (1905-1981)

Of the many independent thinkers who painted on Rocky Neck in the first half of the twentieth century, none were more passionate than the flamboyant Umberto Romano. During a long and distinguished career, Umberto Romano was considered to be a poignant yet provocative artist whose probing mind sought expression in unconventional terms. The breadth of his creativity spanned traditional works such as his portrait of Sara Delano Roosevelt, through heroic size murals, the war-ravaged canvases of the 1940s, his illustrations for Dante's *Divine Comedy* and, finally, to his *Great Men* series.

Romano, born February 26, 1905, in Bracigliano, Italy, came to this country as a child and settled with his family in Springfield, Massachusetts. Nurturing an early love of drawing, he graduated from high school with enough prizes and scholarships to allow him four years of study at New York's prestigious National Academy of Design. When he began his studies at the N. A. D., the modern art movement, which gained momentum in the aftermath of World War I, was firmly entrenched in the hallowed halls of the Academy. Nevertheless, aspiring art students still received a solid training in the essentials of their craft, and Romano wasted no time in building upon that foundation. Later, with a Pulitzer Traveling Scholarship under his belt, as well as a Tiffany Foundation Fellowship, Romano left for Italy, where he spent 1926-27 studying at the American Academy in Rome, with emphasis on the art of the Renaissance and the style of Italian primitives.

On his return to the United States, Romano obtained a 1928 show at the Frank K. M. Rehn Galleries in New York. The show won him widespread attention and invitations to join major art exhibitions across the nation. For the next five years, Romano's work reflected the lingering influence of the Italian primitives, although he never allowed it to overwhelm his own creative vision. In 1933, he opened an art school in East Gloucester, where he instructed students in painting, drawing, and sculpture. While it is not clear what brought Romano to Cape Ann in the first place, it is certain that he enjoyed the ambiance of the area enough to stay for the next 30 years. In fact, four years later, in 1937, while working as head of the Worcester Art Museum School, Romano purchased the Gallery-on-the-Moors in East Gloucester, and made it into a home, studio and gallery.

In 1935, his work drew accolades from the *Boston Sunday Advertiser's* art critic. "Again it seems Umberto Romano has stolen the show. At the North Shore Arts Association his two canvases, *Him* and *Diana* stand out brilliantly. *Him*, being of recent date, is the more mature, the more strikingly forceful work, while in *Diana* are evidenced the romanticism of the painter's earlier years. While essentially of his day, Romano has been influenced strongly by the Italian Renaissance painters. He is a fastidious and thoughtful workman. His canvases are architecturally designed, and one is conscious of the preconceived idea having been brought surely to realization.... one finds the originality of conception, the unity of form, the firmly molded contours, the sureness of the rhythmical line that have won Romano recognition at an early age as one of the foremost Classical Modernists."[9]

Not everyone cared for his work, however, and in 1935 William Germain Dooley, reviewing the 36th Exhibition of the Gloucester Society of Artists wrote, "Umberto Romano is off on a new color treatment in *Venus Resurrected*.... With all the technical skill at form and color which this artist commands, the present painting lacks movement and ease."[10] In 1938 the same critic admonished Romano for showing a lack of development and direction in his work. Romano was unmoved. "No matter under what

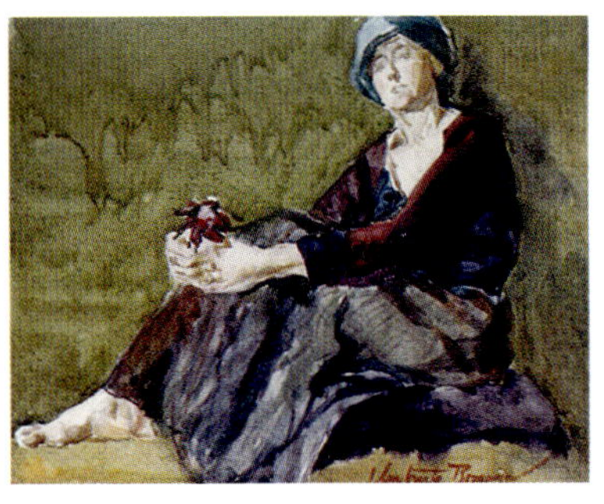

Umberto Romano
Seated Woman
Watercolor over pencil sketch on heavy wove, 9 15/16 x 12 5/16 in.
Marilyn Pink / Fine Art, Los Angeles

Umberto Romano
The Jazz Singer
Oil on plywood, 30 x 22 in.
Collection of Mr. and Mrs. William H. Trayes

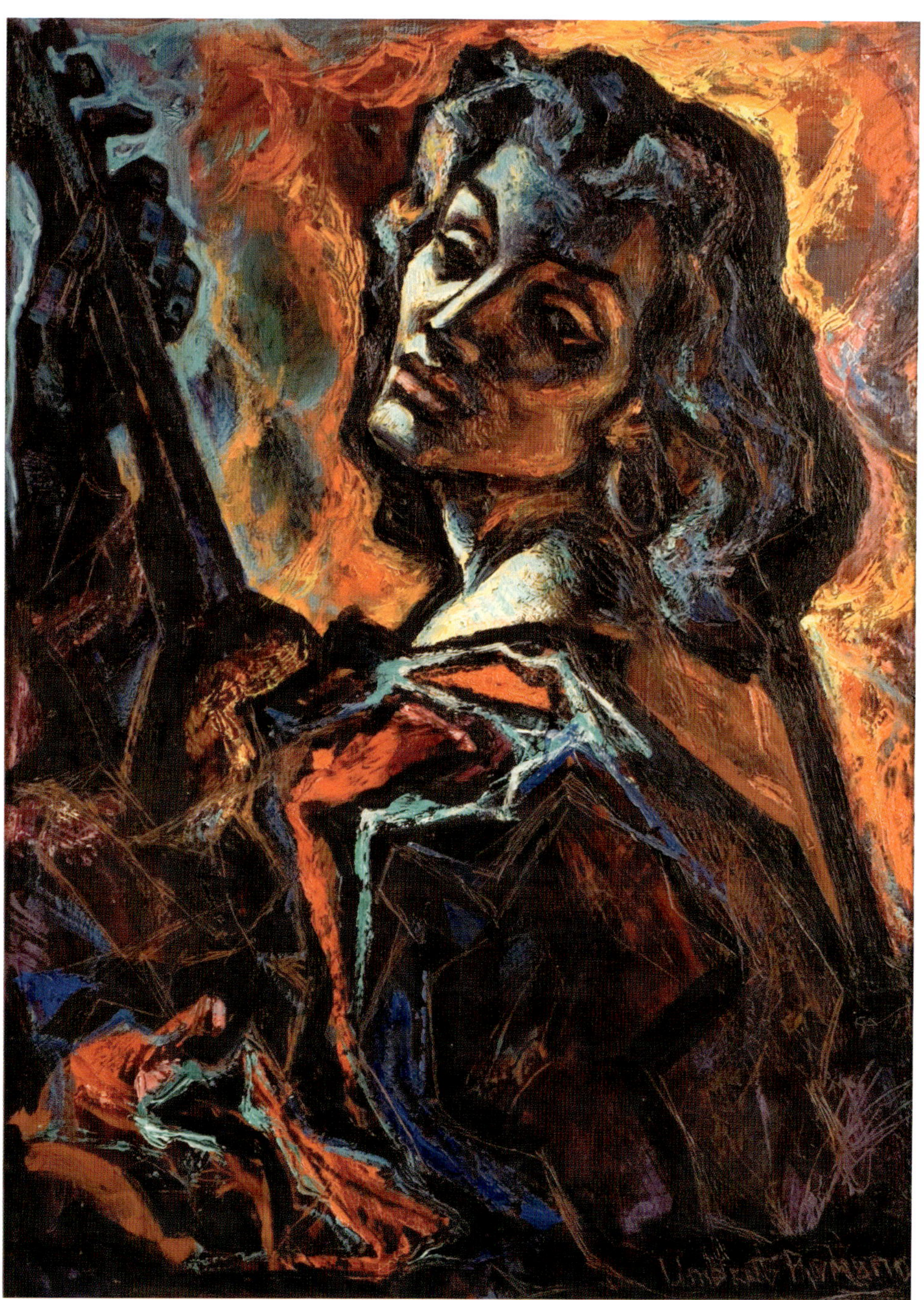

title my work is classified," he announced, "it will always remain a sincere personal experience, emotionally felt and intellectually controlled.... I have a conception of what I want to do in my lifetime sufficiently intense to keep me independent of the fads of the prevailing French influence or of erotic surrealism or of the Red Barn School."[11]

Romano's artistic conception took a new turn in the early 1940s when, in the words of his friend, art critic Edward Alden Jewell, Romano's work became "dramatizations of the artist's emotional response to what is afoot in a bloody and reeling world.... painted from within, it is the inner flame of anguish and wrath and pity that attains externalization in paint."[12] Romano agreed. "Can one go on painting serene, calm, undisturbed, unemotional paintings in such turbulent, chaotic times?" he demanded. "The air... vibrates with destruction of people, nations, races; destruction of culture... destruction of the tortured soul of man."[13]

Romano's tormented psyche was apparent in his work for the remainder of his career. Turning away from the romanticized portraiture of his early years, he concentrated on making a personal artistic statement through the grotesque and contorted exaggerations of human form. "Even when the mood is of a gentler, more patiently brooding sort, as in the picturing of clowns," said one reviewer, "tragic implications are stressed with the same unremitting zeal that marks the socially pointed religious subjects and those that have more simply to do with aspects of war and peace."[14]

In 1965, discouraged by the lack of appreciation from his peers for what he called "expressionist work," Romano sold the Gallery-on-the-Moors, and moved to Provincetown. "Cape Ann," he complained, "has ceased to be an art center. It caters to mundane pictures on the wall. It is not fertile ground for a creative artist, it is dead artistically and esthetically. I had to go."[15] He split the rest of his life between Provincetown and New York, and remained a potent force on the forefront of modern art.

Marsden Hartley (1877-1943)

Marsden Hartley
The Seashell, 1929
Oil on board, 17½ x 14½ in.
Courtesy of Alexandre Gallery, New York

Marsden Hartley was born Edmund Hartley in Lewiston, Maine. He trained at the Cleveland School of Art, but left there in 1899 to attend art school in New York with the help of a five-year stipend offered by school trustee Anne Walworth, who was impressed enough with his art to encourage Hartley in his aspirations. He studied for a year with William Merritt Chase and then moved on to the National Academy of Design where he studied four more years. While at the National Academy, Hartley received the Suydam Silver Medal awarded for still life drawing.[16] In 1906, Hartley adopted his stepmother's maiden name to become Edmund Marsden Hartley, and then two years later, he dropped his given name to become Marsden Hartley, a name that would resonate with the aficionados of avant-garde American art.

In these early years of his career, Hartley often spent time at retreats in Maine, where he not only painted the mountains in a formal academic style, but also experimented with imagery and realism after a stay at one mystic and intellectual retreat in Eliot, Maine, where he learned to appreciate the subtleties of Eastern religion.[17]

In the beginning, Hartley was influenced by the impressionist works of John Henry Twachtman with their ethereal atmosphere and muted tones, and then later he was inspired by the Neo-impressionist work of Maurice Prendergast who was at the opposite end of the spectrum to Twachtman in his use of vibrant color and nervous brushwork. Prendergast showed some of Hartley's work to William Glackens and other artist members of The Eight, the noted Ashcan school realists. In 1909, Hartley became acquainted with Alfred Stieglitz, one of New York's most influential dealers of modern American art and a celebrated photographer in his own right. It was the beginning of a long and successful relationship for both men. Over the next three decades, Hartley showed regularly at Stieglitz's Gallery 291, in the company of John Marin and Georgia O'Keeffe as well as in several solo shows.

At the age of 35, Hartley made his first trip to Europe. He settled in Paris for a time but disdaining French aesthetics moved on to Berlin, which he found much more to his liking. Hartley's stay in Berlin lasted well into the First World War. During that time he worked on a series of paintings celebrating male comradeship, which later became known as the German Officer paintings. Hartley's life became a nomadic journey, painting and writing poetry, while restlessly moving between France, Germany, Bermuda and Mexico, as well as the American Southwest and California. His muse was an elusive, or perhaps metaphysical, goal. In 1931, when Hartley came to Gloucester, he discovered Dogtown, a stark and lonely common rising between Rockport and Gloucester, noted for its natural monuments such as the huge granite formation known as "Whale's Jaw."

Hartley found considerable inspiration among nature's chthonic sculpture and returned again in 1934 and 1936. While most artists visiting Cape Ann preferred the camaraderie of Rocky Neck, Hartley preferred the loneliness and austerity of Dogtown, which he rendered with cubist sympathies reflecting the ice-age topography and capturing something of the divine spirit that he constantly sought. He called it a region "of rock, juniper and weeds," and said that "nature had at last formed one spot where she can live for herself alone."[18] Hartley did not return to Gloucester after 1936. He suffered from ill health in his declining years and died of heart failure in 1943. Although his style did not appeal to all art lovers, Hartley knew he was true to his own ideals and that his name would live on. He wrote to his sister towards the end of his life saying, "I am not a "book of the month" artist, and I do not paint pretty pictures; but when I am no longer here my name will register forever in the history of American art."[19]

Edward Hopper (1882-1967)

Edward Hopper is one of America's best-known painters, and yet, as an artist, he was somewhat reclusive. He regularly painted urban settings with sunlight and shadow as his focal points rather than people. Hopper neither joined the local art associations that Gloucester offered, nor entered into the festivities such as Rocky Neck's Beaux Arts Ball. He was much more of an introvert than his artist wife Jo Nivisen, but occasionally he socialized with one or two of the summer artists, especially if he knew them from New York.

Hopper was born in Nyack, New York in 1882 and began his formal art training at the New York School of Art where he worked under Robert Henri and Kenneth Hayes Miller. He also made three trips to Europe in the early part of the century although it seems to have had little influence on his work. At the beginning of his career Hopper supported himself through commercial artwork and illustration, and in the years between 1915 and 1923 did very little fine art work other than etching.[20] He made the first of several visits to Gloucester in 1912, and the oil paintings from this era show strong brushwork and a profound understanding of chiaroscuro, the balance of light and dark. These paintings were also "firmer in construction," Lloyd Goodrich says, in his landmark account of the artist's life and work, "firmer… and already marked by his characteristic angularity."[21] Hopper himself remembered artist Leon Kroll commenting, that "the modernists would like the angles of the houses and rocks"[22] in East Gloucester. At the time Hopper was unfamiliar with cubism and its philosophy and could only consider the subject from his own point of view. "The angularity was just natural to me," he said. "I liked those angles."[23] His early Gloucester scenes were simple, direct compositions with light and shadow creating the focal points and a dearth of humanity to clutter the composition. The austerity of these paintings is balanced by the richness and vibrancy of color that Hopper always achieved in his work.

Hopper returned to Rocky Neck in the summer of 1923 and once again the ornate Victorian architecture of the area appealed to his sense of design. He was particularly struck by the way the intense Gloucester light created strong shadows accentuating the mansard roofs with their towers and turrets, and how it lit up the gingerbread ornamentation on shady porches. He especially liked the old house on Clarendon Street with its brilliant white paintwork and provocative shadows. Jo Nivison—then his neighbor in Greenwich Village, as well as an old friend from art school—saw the finished painting when Hopper returned to New York and persuaded him to enter it in the Brooklyn Museum's upcoming watercolor show. Although he had received neither success nor

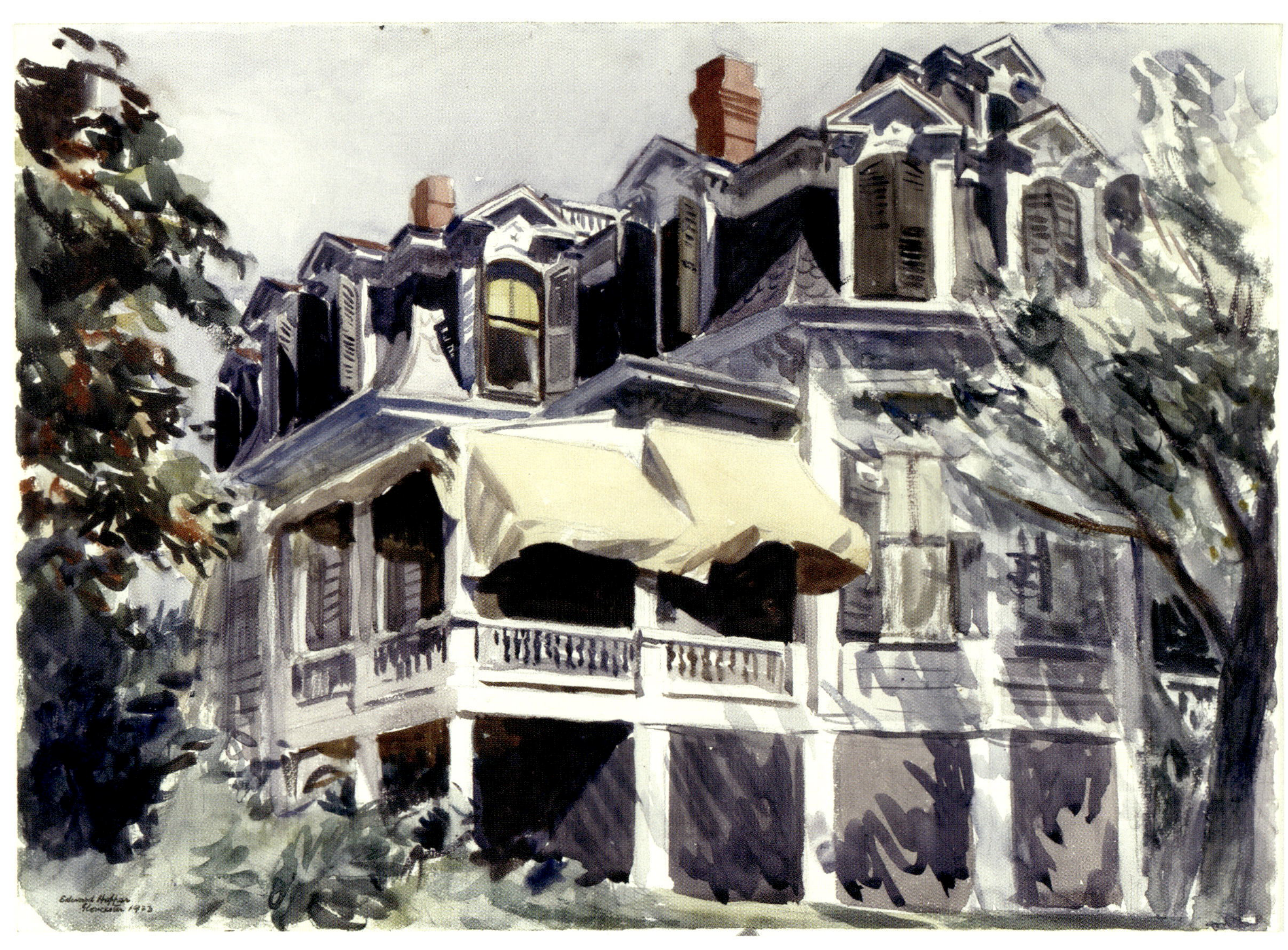

Edward Hopper
The Mansard Roof, 1923
Watercolor over graphite on off-white, moderately thick, moderately textured wove paper, 13⅞ x 20 in.
Brooklyn Museum, Brooklyn, New York
Museum Collection Fund (23.100)

encouragement in the past, Hopper followed Jo's advice and sent the painting to the Brooklyn Museum. To his surprise, the painting was not only accepted, but was purchased by the museum for their permanent collection. He received only $100 for the painting, but the boost to Hopper's confidence was priceless. From then onwards, Hopper was considered to be one of America's definitive artists, producing urban genre works such as *Nighthawks, Chop Suey,* and dramatic skyline images, which he painted from his Washington Square apartment where he and Jo lived in New York. Although Hopper painted many houses in Gloucester during his visits in 1923, 1924, 1926 and 1928, *The Mansard Roof* remains a particular favorite with audiences. When interviewed by Ruth Gurin Bowman for her WNYC radio program, *Views on Art*, the introspective, not to say taciturn, Hopper recalled, "It was painted in Gloucester, I think in the residential district where the old sea captains had their houses—and they're very fine, some of them. It interested me because of the variety of roofs and the windows—the mansard roof, which has always interested me and I don't know why. It was a very windy day, as I remember it, and I sat out in the street, I think, and I don't think it was done at one sitting, but I don't remember really. It might have been one or two."[24] Apart from his first trip to Gloucester in 1912, Hopper primarily used watercolor when painting on Cape Ann because he had no car of his own and it was easier to walk to a location with watercolor equipment than to carry a heavy easel with tubes of paint, brushes and a stretched canvas. However, he did execute a number of oils during his visits when the subject matter permitted, or perhaps decreed, a different medium.

In later life, the Hoppers—when not traveling or wintering in New York—preferred to spend their summers in Maine or on the South Shore of Massachusetts, around South Truro, where they finally built a house. They did not return to Gloucester after 1928.

Hopper's art does not fit neatly into any particular school of thought. He was always independent, seeking to portray the scene with sophisticated simplicity using large geometric shapes rather than abstractionism. His philosophy was simple. "To me, form, color and design are merely a means to an end, the tools I work with, and they do not interest me greatly for their own sake.... My aim in painting is always, using nature as the medium, to try to project upon canvas my most intimate reaction to the subject as it appears when I like it most; when the facts are given unity by my interest and prejudices. Why I select certain subjects rather than others, I do not exactly know, unless it is that I believe them to be the best mediums for a synthesis of my inner experience."[25] Edward Hopper, still something of a recluse, died in 1967. His wife, Jo, died ten months later.

Conclusion

The art colony at Rocky Neck has progressed from being a gathering of artists convening for a summer of sketching and socializing, to a loose coalition of painters that became incorporated in 1973, to its present status as a not-for-profit organization dedicated to nurturing excellence in all manner of visual arts and celebrating the artistic history and cultural heritage of Rocky Neck. Currently the Rocky Neck Art Colony includes in its membership various galleries and restaurants, in addition to the numerous oil painters, watercolorists, and those working in other media, such as batik, photography, jewelry, sculpture and ceramics. Rocky Neck Avenue is as lively today as it ever was, filled with brilliant color and the bustle of creative energy. Tantalizing aromas emanate from inviting eateries where patrons can rest and revive themselves at waterfront tables set on shady patios overlooking Smith Cove. The Avenue abounds with art lovers—both patrons and painters—lured to the area by the promise of sailing ships and the romance of the sea. As far as the eye can see, the land and the buildings, the ships and the sea, are bathed in brilliance as sunlight rebounds from the granite coastline into the dense sea air producing the rosy glow beloved by the plein air painters.

Crossing the causeway—once Peter Mud's Neck—one can imagine an earlier age, when the artists arrived on Rocky Neck with bundles of painting gear and a joyful summer ahead of them. They filled local hostelries with their art and their laughter, and encouraged new generations of artisans to enjoy the ambiance of that gregarious entity: the art colony.

Notes

1 Hans Hoffman: Master of Abstract Expressionism," available at http://www.hanshofmann.net/quotes.html. July 26, 2007.

2 Ibid.

3 Ibid.

4 Sawin, Martica. *Nell Blaine, Her Life and Art,* (New York: Hudson Hills Press, 1998), p. 17.

5 Ibid., p. 21.

6 Ibid., p. 25.

7 Ibid., p. 100.

8 Arb, Renée, "They're Painting Their Way," *Harper's Jr. Bazaar,* 1947, p. 81. Quoted in Sawin, ibid. p. 30.

9 Marsters, Ruth, "Noticeable Displays in Summer Art Galleries," *Boston Sunday Advertiser,* July 7, 1935.

10 Dooley, William Germain, "Promises and Performances on Cape Ann—Waves of Contemporary Art Pound Aimlessly on its Rockbound Coast," *Boston Evening Transcript* Magazine Section, August 17, 1935.

11 *Art Digest,* Nov. 15, 1938, Romano Papers, CAHA.

12 Jewell, Edward Alden, 'Romano Portrays Horrors of War,' *New York Times,* undated news clipping, CAHA.

13 Ibid.

14 *Who's News and Why,* Vol. 15, No. 3, March 1954 (New York: H. W. Wilson, 1954), CAHA.

15 Crotty, Frank, *Around These Parts,* Romano Papers, Rockport Art Association Archives.

16 "Marsden Hartley," available at http://www.hollistaggart.com/artists/hartley.htm. July 28, 2007.

17 Ibid.

18 O'Gorman, James F., p. 58.

19 Phelan, Joseph, "The Return of the Native," *Marsden Hartley: American Modernist.* Available at http://www.artcyclopedia.com/feature-2003-07.html, July 28, 2007.

20 "Edward Hopper," available at http://www.museum.cornell.edu/HFJ/handbook/hb181.html, July 28, 2007.

21 Goodrich, Lloyd, *Edward Hopper* (New York: Harry N. Abrams, 1971), p. 27.

22 Ibid.

23 Ibid.

24 Audio clip from Ruth Gurin Bowman's WNYC radio program, *Views on Art,* 1967–1973, Archives of American Art, Smithsonian Institution. Available at http://nmaa-ryder.si.edu/hopper/p05-hear.html. July 26, 2007.

25 Goodrich, Lloyd, p. 163.

Selected Bibliography

Books

American Women of the Twenties: An Exhibition of Paintings by Agnes M. Richmond, 1870-1964. Introduction, exhibition catalogue. New York: Jeffrey Alan Gallery, November 1981.

Atkinson, D. Scott and Jochen Wierich. *Winslow Homer in Gloucester.* Exhibition catalogue. Chicago: Terra Museum of American Art, 1990.

Babson, Roger W. and Foster H. Saville, *Cape Ann Tourist's Guide with Comments on Business Cycles.* Gloucester, MA: Cape Ann Community League, 1954.

Beaux, Cecilia, *Background with Figures.* New York: Houghton Mifflin, 1930.

Buckley, Laurene, *Joseph DeCamp.* New York: Prestel, 1995.

Clark, Eliot, *John H. Twachtman.* Privately printed, 1924.

Connolly, J. B., *The Port of Gloucester.* New York: Doubleday, 1940.

Cooper, Anice Page, *About Artists.* New York: Doubleday, 1926.

Cox, Kenyon, *What is Painting? "Winslow Homer" & Other Essays.* New York: W. W. Norton, 1988.

Craig, James A., *Fitz H. Lane, An Artist's Voyage through Nineteenth-Century America.* Charleston, SC: History Press, 2006.

Crotty, Frank, *Around These Parts,* Romano Papers, Rockport Art Association Archive.

Cyran, C., *Herman and Bessie Wessel, At Home and Abroad.* Exhibition catalogue. Cincinnati, OH: Cincinnati Art Club, 1997.

Davis, Stuart, "Autobiography," *Stuart Davis,* New York: American Artists' Group, 1945.

De Cruz, Adele, *Frank Duveneck, The Gloucester Years, 1892-1917.* Exhibition catalogue. New York: David J. Findlay, Jr.

De Fontaine-Wade, H. and Norman Kent, *Gordon Grant Sketchbook.* New York: Watson-Guptill Publications, 1960.

De Veer, Elizabeth and Richard J. Boyle, *Sunlight & Shadow, The Life & Art of Willard L. Metcalf.* New York: Abbeville Press, 1987.

Duveneck, Josephine Whitney, *Frank Duveneck: Painter-Teacher.* San Francisco: John Howell, 1970.

Frederick J. Mulhaupt, Dean of the Cape Ann School: A Retrospective. Exhibition catalogue. Gloucester, MA: North Shore Arts Association, 1999.

Gammell, R. H. Ives, *The Boston Painters 1900-1930.* Orleans, MA: Parnassus Imprints, 1986.

Gerdts, William H., "John Twachtman and the Artistic Colony in Gloucester at the Turn of the Century," *Twachtman in Gloucester: His Last Years.* Exhibition catalogue. New York: Universe/Ira Spanierman Gallery, 1987.

Goodrich, Lloyd, *Edward Hopper.* New York: Harry N. Abrams, 1971.

Grant, Gordon, *Sail Ho! Windjammer Sketches Alow and Aloft.* New York: William Farquhar Payson, n. d.

Gruppé, Emile A., edited by Charles Movalli. *Gruppé on Color: Using Expressive Color to Paint Nature.* New York: Watson-Guptill Publications, 1979.

Hale, John Douglass, "Twachtman's Gloucester Period: A 'Clarifying Process'," *Twachtman in Gloucester: His Last Years.* Exhibition catalogue. New York: Universe/Ira Spanierman Gallery, 1987.

Havens, George R., *Frederick J. Waugh: American Marine Painter.* Orono, ME: University of Maine Press, 1969.

Hawthorne, Mrs. Charles W., *Hawthorne on Painting.* New York: Dover Publications, 1938.

Heerman, Norbert, *Frank Duveneck.* Boston: Houghton Mifflin, 1918.

Hiesinger, Ulrich W., *Childe Hassam, American Impressionist.* Munich: Prestel, 1999.

Holcomb, Grant, *John Sloan: The Gloucester Years,* Exhibition catalogue. Springfield, MA: Springfield Museum of Fine Arts, 1980.

Joseph, J. Jonathan, *Jane Peterson; An American Impressionist.* Boston: Privately printed, 1981.

Kelder, Diane, editor. *Stuart Davis.* New York: Praeger, 1971.

Kenney, Herbert A., *Cape Ann, Cape America.* Philadelphia: J. B. Lippincott, 1971.

Kristiansen, Rolf H. and John J. Leahy. *Rediscovering Some New England Artists 1875-1900.* Dedham, MA: Gardner-O'Brien, 1987.

Kuehne, Richard E., "A Reminiscence," *The Early Paintings of Max Kuehne.* Exhibition catalogue. New York: Hirschl & Adler Galleries, 1972.

Love, Richard H., *Carl Peters: American Scene Painter from Rochester to Rockport.* New York: University of Rochester Press, 1999.

————. *Harriet Randall Lumis: An American Impressionist.* Exhibition catalogue. Chicago: R. H. Love Galleries, 1977.

Mary Bryan. "In Her Own Words." Exhibition catalogue. Jeffersonville, VT: Bryan Memorial Gallery.

McAveeney, David C., *Kipling in Gloucester, The Writing of Captains Courageous.* Gloucester, MA: The Curious Traveller Press, 1996.

Meyerowitz, Theresa Bernstein, *William Meyerowitz, The Artist Speaks.* Philadelphia: The Art Alliance Press, 1986.

Meyerowitz, William, N. A. Exhibition catalogue. Athens, GA: The University of Georgia, Georgia Museum of Art, June 1–July 15, 1966.

Neuhaus, Robert, *Unsuspected Genius: The Art and Life of Frank Duveneck.* San Francisco: Bedford Press, 1987.

Oaks, Martha, *The Paintings and Etchings of William Meyerowitz and Theresa Bernstein.* Exhibition catalogue. Gloucester, MA: Cape Ann Historical Association, 1986.

O'Gorman, James F., *Portrait of a Place: Some American Landscape Painters in Gloucester.* Exhibition catalogue. Gloucester, MA: Gloucester 350th Anniversary Celebration, 1973.

————. *This Other Gloucester,* Gloucester, MA: Ten Pound Island Book Co., 1990.

Parrish Jr., Maxfield, *Stephen Parrish (1846-1938).* Exhibition catalogue. Boston: Vose Galleries, 1982.

The Red Cottage, Britt Crews, Curator. Exhibition catalogue. Gloucester, MA: Cape Ann Historical Association, May 29–September 26, 1992.

Rowland, Elzea and Elizabeth Hawkes, *John Sloan: Spectator of Life.* Exhibition catalogue. Wilmington, DE: Delaware Art Museum, 1988.

Rhys, Hedley Howell, *Maurice Prendergast, 1859-1924.* Cambridge, MA: Museum of Fine Arts, Boston, and Harvard University Press, 1960.

Sawin, Martica, *Nell Blaine Her Life and Art.* New York: Hudson Hills Press, 1998.

Schmoll, Anne W., *Martha Walter (1875-1976): Gloucester Impressions.* Exhibition catalogue. Boston: Vose Galleries of Boston, July 1992.

Sellin, David, "Ipswich Figures in A French Background," *The Ipswich Painters at Home and Abroad.* Exhibition catalogue. Gloucester, MA: Cape Ann Historical Association, 1993.

Wattenmaker, Richard J., *Maurice Prendergast.* New York: Harry N. Abrams, in association with The National Museum of American Art, Smithsonian Institution, 1994.

Wells, Gary. *Alice Schille, The New England Years 1915-1918,* ed. Norma J. Roberts. Columbus, OH: Keny and Johnson Gallery, 1989.

Wilmerding, John, *Fitz Hugh Lane: 1803-1865, American Marine Painter.* Salem, MA: Essex Institute, 1964.

Wyeth, Betsy James, ed., *The Wyeths, the Letters of N. C. Wyeth, 1905-1945.* Boston: Gambit, 1971.

Articles

Alexander, Mary L., "Cincinnati Artist Writes in Humorous Vein of Gloucester," *Cincinnati Enquirer,* 1926.

"Allied Artists Compare Favorably with Academy," *The Brooklyn Daily Eagle,* Sunday, December 6, 1925.

Anonymous. "Buhler Painted Fishermen," *Gloucester (MA) Daily Times,* August 27, 1969.

————. "Cape Ann Artist Childe Hassam's Work on View," *MassBay Antiques,* Feb. 1990, p. 39.

————. *Gloucester Daily Times,* June 6, 1900.

————. *Gloucester Daily Times,* September 1, 1900.

————. *Gloucester Daily Times,* September 24, 1900.

————. *Gloucester Daily Times,* August 20, 1901.

————. *Gloucester Daily Times,* June 24, 1902.

————. *Gloucester Daily Times,* August 8, 1902.

————. *Gloucester Daily Times,* July 26, 1919.

————. "H. H. Wessel, World-Famed Artist, Dies: At Art Academy 40 Years, Also Was Museum Curator," April 14, 1969.

Arb, Renée, "They're Painting Their Way," *Harper's Jr. Bazaar,* 1947.

"Art Exhibit," *Commercial Gazette,* Feb. 6, 1883.

"Art Notes" *New York Times.* April 12 1891.

Ashbery, John, "The Indian Summer of Frank Duveneck," Duveneck Papers, Cape Ann Historical Association.

Bell, Eleanor, "Marriage & Painting Mixed Happily," *Cincinnati Post & Times Star,* 1964.

Cape Ann Shore, July 12, 1930. Quoted in Usher, Donald K., *Gloucester's Own George and Martha,* Annisquam Historical Society, March 28, 1981.

Casey, Patricia, *"Alice Beach Winter 'Keeps Busy' Painting on her 90th Birthday,"* March 22, 1967.

Clark, Eliot, "The Art of John Twachtman," *International Studio 72,* January 1921.

Commercial Tribune, December 12, 1909, newspaper clipping in Cincinnati Art Museum Annual scrapbook, Record Group 5, series 9, vol. 4, p. 31, Cincinnati Art Museum Archive.

Composition and Pictures in Introduction by Feay Shellman, 1986 Bakker exhibition catalogue. Custis Papers, Cape Ann Historical Association.

The Courier, June 1884, newspaper clipping in Cincinnati Art Museum Annual scrapbook, Record Group 5, series 9, vol. 1, Cincinnati Art Museum Archives.

Dame, Lawrence, *Boston Sunday Herald,* August 11, 1946.

Darack, Arthur, "A Tripartite Approach to Herman Wessel," *Cincinnati Pictorial Enquirer,* Sunday, December 18, 1966.

Dewing, T. W., "John H. Twachtman: An Estimation," *North American Review* 176, April 1903: 554.

Dooley, William Germain, "Promises and Performances on Cape Ann—Waves of Contemporary Art Pound Aimlessly on its Rockbound Coast," *Boston Evening Transcript Magazine Section,* August 17, 1935.

"Edward Potthast, N. A.," *The Inspiration of Cape Ann.* Exhibition catalogue. Rockport Art Association, n. d.

"Fakirs Costume Ball Drew Many Summer Folks," *Gloucester Daily Times,* Thursday August 23, 1923.

"Fifty Fine Art Works," *Boston Sunday Post,* December 15, 1901: 3.

"Gallery-on-the-Moors 1916-1922," An Exhibition of Work from the Museum's Collection by Artists Who Exhibited at Gallery-On-The-Moors. Exhibition catalogue. Cape Ann Historical Association, August 19, 2006–January 31, 2007.

"Harry Aiken Vincent–An Appreciation," K. P. R., *Gloucester Daily Times,* Rockport Daily News, Tuesday, September 29, 1931: 2.

James Jr., Henry, "On Some Pictures Lately Exhibited," *The Galaxy,* 20:1, July 1875: 90.

Jarzombek, Nancy Allyn, "Paintings of George L. Noyes," *American Art Review,* April 2001: 119.

Jewell, Edward Alden, "Romano Portrays Horrors of War," *New York Times,* n. d.

Judson, Alice, "Putting Scenery First," *American Magazine of Art,* June 21, 1930: 340-343.

Keene, Gwendoline, *Boston Evening Transcript.* July 13, 1929.

Knowlton, Helen M., "A Home-Colony of Artists," *Studio 5,* July 14, 1890: 326-327.

Kraeft, June and Norman, "Down To The Sea In Prints," Exhibition catalogue. Bethlehem, CT: June 1 Gallery, September 1987.

Loughmiller, Henry C., "I Studied with Duveneck," *American Artist,* March 1965: 40.

Marsters, Ruth, "Noticeable Displays in Summer Art Galleries," *Boston Sunday Advertiser,* July 7, 1935.

Movalli, Charles, "Frederick J. Mulhaupt: New England Classic," *American Artist,* January 1977: 75.

———. "A Conversation with William Meyerowitz and Theresa Bernstein," *American Artist,* January 1980: 64.

"Mr. and Mrs. Charles Allan Winter," *Cape Ann Shore,* August 15, 1931.

Mulhaupt, Frederick J., "Paul Cornoyer, Painter—An Appreciation," *Cape Ann Shore,* July 14, 1923.

Owens, Edna, "The Art of Alice Schille," *International Studio 50,* August 1913: 31-33.

"Paintings By Mr. Stevens," *Boston Evening Tribune,* October 20, 1921.

"Paintings by Theresa Bernstein." Exhibition catalogue. New York: Milch Galleries, 1919.

Shute, Mildred, "Charles Allan Winter and Alice Beach Winter," *Cape Ann (MA) Shore,* August 19, 1933: 7, 20, 22.

Taylor, Robert, Art Review, "The Gloucester Phase of Frank Duveneck," *Boston Globe,* Sunday, August 16, 1987.

"The Society of Artists," *New-York Daily Tribune,* April 24, 1893: 4.

"Told of Artists' Feeling toward Rest of World," *Gloucester Daily Times,* August 1, 1933: 6.

Van Rensselaer, M. G., "American Etchers," *Century Magazine,* vol. 3, (n. s.), no. 4, February 1883.

Weaver, Margaret, "Bessie Wessel's show evokes great period of Cincinnati artists," *The Post & Times Star,* Cincinnati, Tuesday, April 13, 1971.

Werner, Alfred, *William Meyerowitz, N. A.* Exhibition catalogue. New York: Chase Gallery, 1959.

Who's News and Why, Vol. 15, No. 3. New York: H. W. Wilson, 1954.

Winter, Alice Beach, "Looking Backward," *Tenth Annual Cape Ann Festival of the Arts,* 1961: 16.

Worley, Sharon, "Max Kuehne," *American Art Review, Vol. IX, No. 5,* October 1997: 125.

Other Media

Archives of American Art, Smithsonian Institute, Washington, D.C., Sylvester Rosa Koehler papers, Microfilm reel D189, frames 274-275, letter from Parrish to Koehler, March 4 1887.

Audio clip from Ruth Gurin Bowman's WNYC radio program, *Views on Art,* 1967-1973, Archives of American Art, Smithsonian Institution. Available at http://nmaa-ryder.si.edu/hopper/p05-hear.html. July 26, 2007.

"Augustus Waldeck Buhler," *Maine in America,* Farnsworth Art Museum. Available www.farnsworthmuseum.org/collections/downloads/Maine_in_America6.pdf, February 8, 2007.

Biographical Outline Frank Duveneck, 1848-1919, p. 7, Duveneck Papers, CAHA.

Biographical Sketch of Charles Allan Winter, C.A. Winter Papers, CAHA.

Boer Notes: Harbor View Hotel, Roster Notes (TT).

Custis Papers, CAHA.

"Edward Hopper," available at http://www.museum.cornell.edu/HFJ/handbook/hb181.html. July 28, 2007.

"Fern I. Coppedge," available at http://artists of the commonwealth.org/artists/coppedge.html. March 27, 2007.

"Hans Hoffman: Master of Abstract Expressionism," available at http://www.hanshofmann.net/quotes.html. July 26, 2007.

"H. H. Wessel," L. H. Meakin (typewritten), Cincinnati Artists file, box 46, Cincinnati Art Museum Archive.

Letter to Julia Lyman from Mary Pratt Sears, 1887, Duveneck Papers, CAHA.

"Marsden Hartley," available at http://www.hollistaggart.com/artists/hartley.htm. July 28, 2007.

MP to Edgar L. Hewitt, n. d. [fall 1914] Alice Klauber Papers, Archives of American Art, microfilm roll 583, frames 710-711.

Phelan, Joseph, "The Return of the Native," *Marsden Hartley: American Modernist.* Available at http://www.artcyclopedia.com/feature-2003-07.html. July 28, 2007.

Resolution by the "Students of the Duveneck Class," read at a memorial service at the Cincinnati Art Museum, March 30, 1919, Duveneck Papers, CAHA.

W. Lester Stevens family scrapbook; on microfilm at the Greenfield Community College Library, Greenfield, MA.

Special thanks to the Cape Ann Historical Association and the Rockport Art Association for making their artist files available for research.

Index